Terrorist Organisations and their Modus Operandi

2 Volume Set

Volume 1

Terrorist Organisations and their Modus Operandi

2 Volume Set

Volume 1

Vijay Kumar Verma

MD Publications Pvt Ltd
New Delhi
www.mdppl.com

Published by :

MD Publications Pvt Ltd
"MD House", 11, Darya Ganj,
New Delhi - 110 002
Phone : +91-11-41563325 (Customer Service)
+91-11-41562846 (Editorial)
E-mail (orders): order@mdppl.com
Website: www.mdppl.com

ISBN: 978-81-7533-223-2 (Set of 2 Vols.)
978-81-7533-224-9 (Vol. 1)

Published and Printed by Mr. Pranav Gupta on behalf of **MD Publications Pvt Ltd at Times Press, New Delhi.**

PREFACE

There exist many different definitions of terrorism, but terrorism most commonly includes these elements: Use of unlawful violence or the threat of unlawful violence; Targeting civilians; Non-state actor; Absence of a state of war (specifically conventional warfare), thus excluding war crimes; Designed to coerce, frighten, or "send a message" to the public or a government (thus excluding organized crime performed for personal gain). The organizations have verifiably used or attempted to use terrorist tactics and their description here made purely for study and research purposes.

The new modus operandi was to attack soft targets, including major landmarks and also kill foreign nationals. Soft targets are those that are not subject to special protection that are frequented by the public, which could be local nationals or foreigners and compared to a classical car bomb or suicide attack, this tactic has the advantage for the terrorists of remaining in the news for a much longer time. It has also a much higher psychological value on the population it kills the feeling of security since terrorists can hit anywhere.

There are hundreds of thousands of potential soft targets of terrorists all over the country. It would be just impossible for the government to provide them with physical security. There are various reasons for which terrorists periodically attack soft targets in widely dispersed areas. Firstly, they want to demonstrate their reach. Secondly, they want to discredit the intelligence agencies, the police and other security agencies in the eyes of the people by demonstrating their capability to strike despite the vigilance of these agencies. Thirdly, they want to make the police and the security agencies over-react in response to their successful strikes. Fourthly, attacks on soft targets are also undertaken in reprisal for perceived wrongs allegedly committed by the government or the police towards the members of the community from which the terrorists have arisen or even towards the terrorists themselves. One cannot totally eliminate attacks on soft targets, but one can reduce them by effective intelligence capability and policing in order to detect and neutralise them.

I am very grateful to Mr. Pranav Gupta, Director of MD Publications Pvt Ltd, New Delhi, for his kind cooperation and support for this book.

Vijay Kumar Verma

Contents

Vol. 1

Vol. 2

1

Definition and Forms of Terrorism

Few words have so insidiously worked their way into our everyday vocabulary. Like 'Internet'—another grossly over-used term that has similarly become an indispensable part of the argot of the late twentieth century – most people have a vague idea or impression of what terrorism is, but lacks a more precise, concrete and truly explanatory definition of the word. This imprecision has been abetted partly by the modern media, whose efforts to communicate an often complex and convoluted message in the briefest amount of airtime or print space possible have led to the promiscuous labelling of a range of violent acts as 'terrorism'. Pick up a newspaper or turn on the television and – even within the same broadcast or on the same page – one can find such disparate acts as the bombing of a building, the assassination of a head of state, the massacre of civilians by a military unit, the poisoning of produce on supermarket shelves or the deliberate contamination of over-the-counter medication in a chemist's shop all described as incidents of terrorism. Indeed, virtually any especially abhorrent act of violence that is perceived as directed against society – whether it involves the activities of anti-government dissidents or governments themselves, organized crime syndicates or common criminals, rioting mobs or persons engaged in militant protest, individual psychotics or lone extortionists is often labelled 'terrorism'.

Dictionary definitions are of little help. The pre-eminent authority on the English language, the much-venerated Oxford English Dictionary, is disappointingly unobliging when it comes to providing edification on this subject, its interpretation at once too literal and too historical to be of much contemporary use.

TERRORISM: A SYSTEM OF TERROR

a. Government by intimidation as directed and carried out by the party in power in France during the revolution of 1789-94; the system of 'Terror'.
b. A policy intended to strike with terror those against whom it is adopted; the employment of methods of intimidation; the fact of terrorising or condition of being terrorised.

These definitions are wholly unsatisfying. Rather than learning what terrorism is, one instead finds, in the first instance, a somewhat potted historical – and, in respect of the modern accepted usage of the term, a uselessly anachronistic – description. The second definition offered is only slightly more helpful. While accurately communicating the fear-inducing quality of terrorism, the definition is still so broad as to apply to almost any action that scares ('terrorises') us. Though, an integral part of 'terrorism', this definition is still insufficient for the purpose of accurately defining the phenomenon that is today called 'terrorism'.

A slightly more satisfying elucidation may be found in the OED's definition of the perpetrator of the act than in its efforts to come to grips with the act itself. In this respect, a 'terrorist' is defined thus:

TERRORISM: AS A POLTICAL TERM

a. Applied to the Jacobins and their agents and partisans in the French Revolution, especially to those connected with the Revolutionary tribunals during the 'Reign of Terror'.
b. Any one who attempts to further his views by a system of coercive intimidation; specially applied to members of one of the extreme revolutionary societies in Russia.

This is appreciably more helpful. First, it immediately introduces the reader to the notion of terrorism as a political concept. As will be seen, this key characteristic of terrorism is absolutely paramount to understanding its aims, motivations and purposes and critical in distinguishing it from other types of violence.

Terrorism, in the most widely accepted contemporary usage of the term, is fundamentally and inherently political. It is also ineluctably about power: the pursuit of power, the acquisition of power, and the use of power to achieve political change. Terrorism is thus violence – or, equally important, the threat of violence – used and directed in pursuit of, or in service of, a political aim. With this vital point clearly illuminated, one can appreciate the significance of the additional definition of 'terrorist' provided by the OED: 'Any one who attempts to further his views by a system of coercive intimidation'. This definition underscores clearly the other fundamental characteristic of terrorism: that it is a planned, calculated, and indeed systematic act.

Given this relatively straightforward elucidation, why, then, is terrorism so difficult to define? The most compelling reason perhaps is because the meaning of the term has changed so frequently over the past two hundred years.

DIFFERENT FORMS OF TERRORISM

Given the number of definitions of terrorism available in academic resources, it is almost inconceivable that there should be a lack of any unified definition of terrorism. The following discussion will focus on the different dimensions of terrorism, in order to establish a framework of understanding. Considering the basic elements of terrorism, Schmid and Jongman's definition of terrorism seems to be the most comprehensive.

They write:

"Terrorism is an anxiety-inspiring method of repeated violent action, employed by (semi)

> clandestine individual, group, or state actors, for idiosyncratic, criminal, or political response, whereby – in contrast to assassinations – the direct targets of violence are not the main targets. The immediate human victims of violence are generally chosen randomly (targets of opportunity) or selectively (representative or symbolic targets) from a target population, and serve as message generators. Threat and violence-based communication processes between terrorists (organisations), (imperilled) victims, and main targets are used to manipulate the main target (audience), turning it into a target of terror, a target of demands, or a target of attention, depending on whether intimidation, coercion, or propaganda is primarily sought."

Apart from Schmid and Jongman's definition, numerous other definitions of terrorism are useful. In terms of the present analysis, the following definition is particularly relevant:

> "Terrorism is the deliberate employment of violence or the threat to use violence by sub-national groups and sovereign states to attain strategic and political objectives. Terrorists seek to create overwhelming fear in a target population larger than the civilian or military victims attacked or threatened. Acts of individual and collective terrorism committed in modern times have introduced a new breed of extralegal 'warfare' in terms of threats, technology, targets and impact."

South Africa has, since 1994, adopted internationally acknowledged definitions and categories of terrorism. According to Schönteich, the South African government's official policy on terrorism defines terrorism as:

> "An incident of violence, or the threat thereof, against a person, a group of persons or property not necessarily related to the aim of the incident, to coerce a government or civil population to act or not to act according to certain principles."

The draft anti-terrorism bill of 2000 defines terrorism as:

"Any act which does or may endanger the life, physical integrity or freedom of any person or persons, or causes or may cause damage to property and is calculated or intended to intimidate, coerce or induce any government or persons, the general public or any section thereof; or disrupt any public service, the delivery of any essential service to the public or to create a public emergency; or create unrest or general insurrection in any state."

ELEMENTS OF TERRORISM

Despite the numerous definitions of terrorism, the international community and academics have, to date, been unable to provide one definition of terrorism. Instead of deciding on a single definition, the following elements of terrorism are presented in the existing definitions:

- Nature of the act

This usually takes the form of violence or the threat of violence; other criminal, unlawful, politically subversive, or anarchic acts; piracy; hijacking of aircraft; and taking of hostages. According to Crenshaw, terrorism is an attractive method to use because it is relatively inexpensive. This point is also discussed under modus operandi, below.

- Perpetrators

Terrorism is a form of warfare and can be perpetrated either by individuals or by governments. Hanle differentiates between state terrorists (state terror to control the domestic population) and revolutionary terrorists (who seek nothing less than the total destruction of the targeted regime). These two groups may demand different levels of response to achieve their goals. Issue-motivated groups and criminal syndicates also use terrorism as their modus operandi, driven by the success of revolutionary terrorist groups.

MOTIVATION

The best known motivational factors of terrorists include:

- Rational motivation

The rational terrorist thinks through his goals and options, making a cost-benefit analysis. He seeks to determine whether there are less costly and more effective ways to achieve his objective than terrorism. To assess the risk, he weighs the target's defensive capabilities against his own capabilities to attack. He measures his group's capabilities to sustain the effort. The essential question is whether terrorism will work for the desired purpose, given societal conditions at the time.

- Psychological motivation

Psychological motivation for terrorism derives from the terrorist's personal dissatisfaction with his life and accomplishments. Terrorists tend to project their own antisocial motivations onto others, creating a polarised "we versus they" outlook. According to Mazrui, the "us versus them" confrontation is the most persistent theme in world-order perceptions. "There is a tendency in monotheism to divide the human race between believers and unbelievers, between the virtuous and the sinful, between good and evil, between 'us' and 'them'."

- Culture and religion

Cultural differences create a feeling of belonging even across borders. Muslims all over the world, for example, belong to a universal ummah (Islamic community). "The ummah is not founded on race, nationality, locality, occupation, kinship or special interest. It does not take its name after the name of a leader or a founder or an event. It transcends national borders and political boundaries. The foundation of the community in Islam is the principle, which designates submission to the will of Allah, obedience to His law and commitment to His cause. What is required of the community at large is likewise required of every individual member."

Terrorism in the name of religion can be especially violent. Like all terrorists, those who are religiously motivated view their acts with moral certainty, and religiously motivated terrorists even consider their acts to have divine sanction. What would otherwise be extraordinary acts of desperation, become a religious duty in the mind of the religiously motivated terrorist. This helps explain the high level of commitment and willingness to risk death among religious extremists. Acts of religious terrorism are primarily committed in the belief that complete knowledge can be achieved (in the human world). Religiously motivated terrorist groups believe that they know which the 'good' is (or what is sanctioned by God or by their beliefs) and that this knowledge obligates them to destroy the evil and the unjust, according to their own perceptions of good and evil.

Religion has re-emerged as a major component in the understanding of contemporary political development, especially in the Middle East, Asia and Africa. The return to religious roots and the mobilisation of religious faith to reform societies is far from being limited to Third World countries. The manifestation of this phenomenon and its symbolism varies from religion to religion and culture to culture but there are some parallels in the organisation of religious groups and in the methods used by activists to arouse a popular response.

OBJECTIVES

Most often fear, extortion and radical change are the objectives of terrorist acts. Terrorism is a process that has three elements:

- The act or threat of violence;
- The emotional reaction or extreme fear on the part of the potential or future victim; and
- The social effects that follow the violence.

The desired effect of terrorism is not the physical hurt to the victim, but the psychological impact on the target. As a consequence, the terrorist's victims must be carefully selected to assure the maximum possible psychological impact on the target. The subjects of terrorist attacks generally have little intrinsic value to the terrorist group but represent a larger human audience whose reaction the terrorists seek. The objectives that terrorists have in mind may be classified as long-term objectives (that differentiate terrorist groups) and short-term or proximate objectives (that unite all terrorist groups over the whole spectrum of ideologies).

The latter are defined in terms of the reactions that terrorists want to achieve in their different audiences. The most basic reason for terrorism is to gain recognition or attention. Violence and bloodshed always excite human curiosity, and the theatricality, suspense and threat of danger inherent in terrorism enhance its attention-drawing qualities. In fact, publicity may be the highest goal of some groups; international recognition encourages transnational terrorist activities in escalation, and destructive power. The larger the audience grows, the greater the extremes to which terrorists will go. Terrorism is also used to disrupt and discredit the processes of government: terrorism as a direct attack on a regime aims to promote the insecurity and demoralisation of government officials, independent of any impact on public opinion.

HIDDEN OR CONCEALED AGENDAS

Certain states sponsor terrorism as part of a campaign of geographic expansion of political control at the expense of existing state structures. According to Crenshaw, terrorism also serves as an internal organisational function of control, discipline and morale building within the terrorist group, and may even become an instrument of rivalry among factions within a resistance movement. Through counter-reaction against specific individuals from the targeted government, terrorists increase publicity and demonstrate to the people that their charges against the regime are well founded. Through these martyrs, recruitment follows and more funds are collected, especially under state-sponsored terrorism. For example, Hizbollah make use of video recordings of their attacks. These recordings are then sent to Iran, from where they receive their financial backing and instructions.

TARGETS

Terrorists often direct their violence and threats at a target group that is not directly involved in the political decision-making process that the terrorists seek to influence. Hanle distinguishes between direct terrorism (where the target of influence and the target of terror are one and the same) and indirect terrorism (where the entity targeted to receive the terror and the entity targeted to be influenced is separate). According to Crenshaw, different forms of terrorism involve various degrees of selectivity in the choice of victims. Some acts of terrorism discriminate precisely, while others are broadly indiscriminate. Schbley, after interviewing 26 Lebanese Shi'a Muslims, listed the most likely targets of Shi'a religious terrorist groups. Topping the list of preferred hostages are diplomats, and civilian and military intelligence officers. Other targets include national symbols of state, namely heads of state, public officials, airlines and national security key points.

Terrorism against key economic targets is another trend. In Turkey, Egypt and Spain, terrorist groups have systematically targeted the tourist sector in order to inflict economic damage. In Latin America, South Asia and the former Soviet Union, terrorism has become increasingly interwoven with organised crime and drug trafficking, undermining the viability of the fragile and corrupt governments in those areas. In Colombia, for example, 43% of the targets of terrorism represent the commercial sector. Here, attacks are directed against oil pipelines and mines owned by multinational corporations. In a single Revolutionary Armed Forces of Colombia (FARC) attack in September 1997, Exxon suffered an estimated US$3 million in losses. With reference to the situation in South Africa, especially in the Western Cape, it could be argued that the alleged target selection of People Against Gangsterism and Drugs (Pagad) changed from drug and gang leaders to restaurants associated with the United States (for example, Planet Hollywood, Kentucky Fried Chicken and McDonalds).

According to Laqueur: "the terrorist of the future will be less ideological, more likely to harbour ethnic grievances, harder to distinguish from other criminals, and a particular threat to technologically advanced societies". Ethnic terrorism draws on greater public support than ideologically motivated terrorism does. Organizations that adhere to a nationalist or separatist ideology – such as Muslim extremists, the Provisional Irish Republican Army (PIRA) and the Basque Fatherland and Liberty (ETA) – have a larger constituency of potential recruits, supporters and more political clout and resources than the extreme ideological groups (for example, the Red Brigades in Italy) whose activities are on the decline.

MODUS OPERANDI

The most common weapons of terrorists are threats, as well as sabotage, assassination, hostage taking, murder, kidnapping and bombing. According to Crenshaw, terrorists use whatever means are available to further their objectives – the technological advances of the modern era have made this possible and have created opportunities and vulnerabilities. Professional terrorists have become increasingly ruthless, sophisticated and operationally competent. Although most terrorist groups remain technologically conservative, using off-the-shelf weaponry, some groups adapt or improvise their weaponry. For example, terrorists used readily available fertilizer as the main component of their device to bomb the World Trade Centre in New York in February 1993.

Although the modus operandi of international terrorist groups is to a large extent static, the first use of chemical weapons by terrorists occurred in March 1995 when members of the Japanese cult, Aum Shinrikyo, placed sarin gas on five trains in Tokyo. Bombings still characterize most international terrorist incidents. Between 1968 and 1999, more than 7000 terrorist bombings were recorded. Bombing, armed assault, fire-bombing, sabotage, kidnapping and hijacking are the main methods used in order of prevalence. Business facilities were first on the hit list, followed by diplomatic representatives, government facilities and armed forces. The trend is a shift away from attacking specific targets towards indiscriminate killings. The dividing line between urban terrorism and other forms of terrorism has become less distinct, while it is often impossible to draw a line between politically motivated terrorism and the operation of national and international crime syndicates. The most serious concern is that terrorists are seeking to kill and injure more and more people.

BOMBING

This has been the most common tactic used by terrorists since the manifestation of international terrorism in the 1960s. The objectives have changed from symbolic bombings, not intended to produce casualties (especially in the 1970s), to incidents where the ultimate objective is to cause as many casualties as possible. The latter objective emerged in the 1980s, especially with the suicide bombings used by religious extremists in the Middle East and North Africa. The most obvious reason for the popularity of bombing as a *modus operandi* is that explosives can be easily purchased, stolen or manufactured from commercially available materials. Knowledge of how to build a bomb and explosives can be obtained from books and the Internet.

Individuals have access to conventional as well as unconventional bomb-building material through mail order catalogues. Iranian President Ali Akbar Hashemi Rafsanjani refers to this access as "the poor man's nuclear bomb". The Internet is also being used by terrorist groups to gather information on weaponry and techniques, and to spread propaganda.

Terrorists are further exploring advanced technologies and are utilising more imaginative ways of operating explosives, detonators, communications, and concealed devices. Bombings require little organisation and can easily be one-man operations. As diplomatic and military targets have become better protected, terrorists have focused their attacks on soft targets. Terrorists are also exhibiting a lack of discrimination in target selection with the trend towards huge truck bombs in urban centres such as, for example, Buenos Aires and Moscow. In December 1988, a bomb exploded on flight Pan Am 103. Pieces of the plane fell onto the Scottish town of Lockerbie, killing 259 people on the plane and 11 people on the ground. This incident is regarded as the worst air-disaster of the 20th century.

The Popular Front for the Liberation of Palestine-General Command (PFLP-GC) was suspected of being responsible for planting the bomb. Despite the threat of economic sanctions Libya initially refused to deliver two of its nationals, who were the main suspects of the bombing – Abdel Basset al-Megrahi and Al-Amin Khalifa Fhimah – after they were charged with murder, conspiracy to murder and contravention of airline security. In April 1999, with the contribution of former South African president Nelson Mandela, Libya extradited the two suspects to stand trial in the Netherlands according to Scottish law. The trial commenced in May 2000. Al-Amin Khalifa Fhimah was alleged to belong to Libyan intelligence and to have been the station officer of Libyan Arab Airlines in Malta at the time of the bombing. In January 2001 Fhimah was acquitted of the charges against him.

Abdel Basset al-Megrahi was alleged to have been a senior officer of the Libyan Intelligence Services and head of Libyan Arab Airlines security in Malta in December 1988. Al-Megrahi bought clothes from a Maltese store that were contained in the suitcase bomb on board flight Pan Am 103. Al-Megrahi was convicted and sentenced to life imprisonment. Terrorists use computers, cellular phones and encryption software to evade detection. These methods of evading detection, as well as the forging of documents and passports, were used extensively by Ramzi Ahmed Yousef and his gang, who were convicted of a plot to blow up 12 US airliners over the Pacific in 1995. Yousef was arrested in Islamabad, Pakistan, in February 1995, after fleeing from the United States and was sentenced to 240 years imprisonment in November 1997. Yousef was convicted of the explosion at the World Trade Centre in New York in which six people died and more than 1 000 were injured, and of planting a bomb that killed one person on a Philippines Airlines flight to Tokyo in 1994.

Another example of the use of technology in the planning of terrorism is illustrated by Osama Bin Laden, who uses computers and cellular phones to coordinate the activities of his international network of operatives. (Bin Laden is also linked to Yousef. Three years before Yousef was charged for the World Trade Centre bombing, he lived in a Pakistan guest house paid for by Bin Laden.) After the Afghan war, Osama Bin Laden emerged as one of the primary role-players in exporting transnational terrorism.

During the Afghan war, close cooperation was established with Muslims from different nationalities that form part of the current network of Islamic extremist elements. Bin Laden heads the large Islamic organisation Al-Qaeda. Most of the groups that participate in his front remain independent, although the organisational barriers between them are fluid. In the centre of Al-Qaeda is Bin Laden's own inner group, which conducts missions on its own. The best-known terrorist act with which Osama Bin Laden is connected is the bombing of the US embassy in Nairobi, Kenya, in August 1998, which killed more than 200 people. Ten minutes after the Nairobi blast, a bomb placed in a refrigerator truck exploded outside the US embassy in suburban Dar es Salaam, Tanzania, killing 11 people.

HOSTAGE TAKING

Hostage taking, whether by kidnapping individuals, hijacking airlines or storming buildings, has always been a popular tactic due to its demonstrated effectiveness. Although Jenkins argued in 1987 that the seizing of embassies would decrease because of an increase in their security measures, the left-wing Tupac Amaru Revolutionary Movement seized the Japanese embassy in Peru in 1997. Hostage situations are on the increase among desperate groups in many Third World countries. In fact, there was a 33% rise in the kidnapping of foreigners in the 1990s.

ASSASSINATION

In modern times, types of assassination have included:

- Diplomatic assassination (group or state);
- Murder involving religious issues (individual, group or state);
- Murder where the driving motive is nationalism (individual, group or state);

- Murder where the driving motive is class struggle (individual or group); and
- Murder committed for reasons of state (state).

A recent example of this type of international terrorism took place in June 1995, when gunmen attempted to assassinate Egyptian president Hosni Mubarak during a visit to Ethiopia. Ethiopian counter-terrorist forces and Egyptian security forces foiled the attempt. Al-Gama'a al-Islamiyya (Islamic Group or IG), masterminded by Egyptian citizen Mustafa Hamza, claimed its responsibility for the assassination.

According to Egypt's security forces, Khartoum's Islamist junta was involved in the attack. Hamza took refuge in Khartoum and holds a Sudanese diplomatic passport. With reference to the situation in South Africa, the most prominent examples were the assassinations of Captain Bennie Lategan, a member of the SAPS' Pagad Investigation Team, in January 1999. Captain Lategan was investigating cases of urban terrorism in the Western Cape. He was shot 10 times at point blank range.

Ismail Edwards and Ebrahim Jeneker, both members of Pagad's G-Force, have been implicated in this assassination. Ismail Edwards was convicted in May 2000 for his part in a pipe bomb attack on Lansdowne police station in January 1998 and for the attempted murder of Nazeem Smith, an alleged drug dealer. Ebrahim Jeneker is facing 124 charges including, nine for murder, 12 for attempted murder, ten for armed robbery, eight for the possession of unlicensed firearms and one for the possession of explosives. Jeneker is also implicated in attacks on the police and businessmen.

Magistrate Piet Theron, in September 2000. Theron, who was presiding over urban terrorism cases, was assassinated in front of his house. He was shot five times in the head and chest.

Support

Oots identifies the following types of support given to the whole spectrum of terrorist organisations:

- Financial support;

- Training & weapons
- Organisational support: groups and friendly regimes supply terrorists with passports, documents or propaganda support (the recognition of their cause and sympathy); and
- Operational support: terrorist organisations may support other terrorist organisations because of ideological compatibility, or a shared ideology of revolution.

Zones of Public Action

The first level of the zones of public action reflects the constitutional order, with a basic level of stability within a democratic society. The second level is the comfort zone of usual activity, involving legitimate dissent and protest, both within and outside parliament. Legitimate protest is regarded as a valuable mode of political communication, criticism and democratic consultation. In a liberal democratic society, peaceful protest and agitation should be regarded as legitimate and vital aspects of social reform. Political and moral pressure includes the mass campaign of marches, processions, demonstrations and mass meetings, inevitably coupled with massive media publicity and pressure on the government and political parties.

The third level encompasses the zone of ambiguity. This could be defined as a 'grey' area where contentious issues in society and the behaviour of individuals and groups result in disorderly conduct and acts of civil disobedience and conscientious objection, although the initial objective leading to these acts does not involve a comprehensive rejection of the state's legal authority. Although it is a non-violent means of individual resistance to authority, it may, on occasion, provoke a repressive response by the authorities or by members of the community hostile to the objector's position. Peaceful acts of civil disobedience may on occasion be infiltrated or may even be taken over by those who have no inhibitions about the use of violence, or who have an ulterior motive. In other cases, the demonstration, however peaceful in intent, may provoke a violent counter-demonstration of response.

Therefore, a peaceful campaign of civil disobedience can

result in violent confrontation, especially if 'protesters' are swept up into more dangerous and destructive emotions and actions. There is a tendency for such demonstrations to become more aggressive, partly because of the rising threshold of shock needed to attract media attention, and partly because, when peaceful demonstrations fail to achieve results, frustration usually leads to more violence. The fourth level of the zones of public action is the security zone, a level of disorder where the potential or actual occurrence of crime, conflict, violence and subversion poses a threat to society or the state. An escalation of the problem could lead to conditions of anarchy, militarisation and social collapse. Internal violence can be divided into two groups based upon the prime objectives.

The first directly endangers the survival and stability of the constitution itself; the second indirectly and cumulatively undermines the state's authority and support by major defiance of law and order and by endangering the lives of citizens to the point where confidence in the state's authority is eroded. Legitimate public dissent may lead to violence associated with terrorism, inter-communal violence and crime for a number of reasons. According to Leventhal and Chellaney, the longer terrorists are involved in underground campaigns, the more brutal and hardened they tend to become, and the greater is their desperation to attract national and international attention to their cause. It is also possible to detect a shift inside terrorist organisations, away from the more pragmatic 'politically-minded' terrorist leaders to individuals obsessed with vengeance and violence. In order to keep the public's attention and to recover coercive power lost as governments become more resistant to their demands, terrorist groups are 'forced' to use more coercive tactics.

The longer individuals and groups are involved in illegitimate dissent, the more resources and technical knowhow needed to operate at a higher, more lethal level become available. Terrorist movements have political as well as military wings. Through this dual strategy the political arm is able to conduct overt operations, while the military or covert structure is engaged in ambushes and assassinations.

The strategy enables the political leadership to dissociate itself publicly from the operations of the military wing. In some cases this strategy has become flawed as armed wings have begun to operate independently, rather than remain under the control of their political wings. In fact, individuals have begun to lose sight of the aims and objectives of the larger movement.

The above-mentioned factors listed as contributing to the potential escalation from legitimate dissent to violence and terrorism does not imply that all protest actions develop into violence. Instead, the possibility of violence is presented. For example, when discussing the activities of Pagad, it is useful to bear in mind that although the initial objectives of Pagad were to rid the community of drugs and gangs and to let the government know that something would be done about its lack of response to crime, Pagad as a pressure group has developed into a vigilante group that seems to be associated with acts of terrorism.

CATEGORIES OF TERRORISM

Table 1.0 given below distinguishes between the four main categories of terrorism based on the level of government and individual involvement in terrorism.

Table 1.0: Government and Individual Involvement in Terrorism

	Government controlled	Nationals of more then one state
Domestic terrorism	Yes	No
International terrorism	Yes	Yes
State-sponsored terrorism	Yes	No
Transnational terrorism	No	Yes

Since the 1960s, the threat posed by terrorism has changed. The changing nature of this threat and changes in the primary character of terrorism are represented schematically in Table

1.1 given below. The different forms of terrorism may, however, occur in different periods and are not necessarily exclusive to one period.

Table 1.1: Eras of Terrorism

Period	**1960 – 1979**	**1980 – 1989**	**1990s**
Type	Revolutionary terrorism	State-sponsored terrorism	Transnationa terrorism
Threat	National stability	Regional stability	International stability
Character	Instrument to combat colonial rule	Cold War instrument used by the former super-powers and their allies	Instrument in the hands of individuals in an international network

Domestic Terrorism

Domestic terrorism occurs when the violence and terror associated with it are confined to national territories and do not involve targets abroad. In practice, it is, however, very difficult to find any intensive terrorist campaign that remains purely internal as the terrorists eventually look across their national borders for support, weapons, financial assistance and a safe haven. The use of domestic terrorism is not limited to non-governmental groups as state terrorism forms an integral part of domestic terrorism. Governments, their armies, secret police and intelligence services may be labelled as terrorists when they are involved in terrorist activities. Autocratic governments often resort to violence (associated with terrorism) to limit legitimate dissent.

POLITICAL TERRORISM

Political terrorism can be defined as the use or threat of terror by a state or a group outside government in pursuit of a set of ideological objectives that ignore the objectives of domestic and international law. "The intimate connection between terrorism and ideological politics is vital for present purposes, since it is precisely this connection that distinguishes modern terrorism from earlier forms of political violence." This form of terrorism is used primarily for political ends. Terrorism used as a modus operandi by political groups reflects their inability to achieve their political objectives through legitimate means. Political terrorism cannot be understood outside the context of the development of terrorist, or potentially terrorist, ideologies, beliefs and lifestyles. Thus, political terrorism embodies violence or the threat of violence against non-combatants in order to achieve political goals. In fact, as is argued by Stohl and Lopez, there is no clear classification for political terrorism across regional and ideological lines. The use of violence by states has been accepted as a standard operating procedure since the 1960s, in response to liberation struggles.

CRIME-RELATED TERRORISM

Criminal terrorism is defined as "the systematic use of terror for ends of material gain". The primary manifestations of force in this form of terrorism include kidnapping, extortion, assassination and murder. Targets are selected primarily on considerations of personal and material gain. If a member of a state structure is selected at all, it is either for direct personal gain or to reduce interference by governmental authorities in their efforts to put an end to criminal activity. For example, with the dissolution of the Soviet Union, 15 independent states came into being. Poor socio-economic conditions contributed to a deterioration of law enforcement, border forces and to general unemployment.

Control over weapons and explosives (conventional and unconventional) weakened, which threatened not only national, but also regional and international security. The national security of states in the region was threatened by the escalation of criminal gangs and organised crime syndicates. Political and criminal terrorism are regarded as a major threat to security within the territory of the former Soviet Union. Criminal terrorism has taken the form of contract assassinations, kidnappings and intimidation bombings. Targets include business pe1ent minibus owners and drivers, against buses of the Golden Arrow Bus Company.

NARCO-TERRORISM

Narco-terrorism can be described as terrorism conducted to further the aims of drug traffickers. It may take the form of assassination, extortion, hijacking, bombing, and kidnapping directed at judges, prosecutors, elected officials, or law enforcement agents, and the general disruption of government, to divert attention from drug operations. Although narco-terrorism is a sub-element of crime-related terrorism, it is significant enough to be considered in its own right. Narco-terrorism, in the first instance, includes narcotics trafficking by terrorist groups in return for the funds with which to conduct terror. In the Asia/Pacific region, narco-terrorism is linked to political terrorism. The objective is to force governments or their agents (such as law enforcement agencies) to scale down their activities against drug syndicates.

In other words, narco-terrorism refers to the use of extreme pressure and violence by the growers, producers, or distributors of narcotics to force a government agency to modify its opinion with regard to curtailing the sale and the use of narcotics. Although violence has always been an inevitable part of the drug trade, narco-battles have increasingly spilled over into the non-criminal world. Today's narco-terrorism involves the assassination of political leaders, the bombing of civilian aeroplanes, alliances between armed guerrillas and narco-traffickers, widespread gunrunning, and may even involve attempts to overthrow a government that is attempting to curtail the drug trade.

Colombia is one of the best examples of a state where narcotics introduced not only terrorism, but also an illegal international arms-trade network. State-sponsored terrorism also plays a role as a destabilisation factor. For example, all four major terrorist groups in Colombia have received arms and training from Cuba and aid from Libya. The involvement of Cuba and Libya (although indirectly) supports the conclusion that an international network exists, linking terrorist groups and individual role-players.

Colombia has historical ties with Cuba, organised crime organisations (which are active in drugs, guns and illegal alien smuggling in Panama) and the Russian Mafia responsible for supplying weapons to Colombian narco-terrorist forces. China's flagship commercial shipping fleet, China Ocean Shipping Company (COSCO), is directly connected to the Chinese armed forces, the People's Liberation Army, and the Chinese government. COSCO ships have served as carriers for massive smuggling operations of weapons, drugs and illegal aliens around the world. In addition, the Chinese government has used COSCO in undertakings to ship missiles – and components of weapons of mass destruction – to rogue nations such as Pakistan and Iran.

ISSUE-MOTIVATED TERRORISM

Groups that coalesce around various social issues (such as racial equality, pro and anti-abortion, animal rights, and nuclear issues), environmental concerns, land and economic rights, and other matters impinging on the public conscience, generally operate within the bounds of legitimate democratic dissent. However, in certain cases these pressure groups exceed the bounds of legitimate protest. This form of terrorism can be considered as the least serious form of random violence against the public. In some cases issue-motivated terrorism may also include elements of religiously motivated terrorism, with reference to fundamental interpretations of religious doctrines (for example, the debate about the 'right' to take a life).

ECO-TERRORISM

Many developed countries have experienced forms of eco-terrorism. For example, multinational corporations such as Tarmac, Costain and ARC (a unit of the Hanson conglomerate) have been targeted by ecological activists. Companies not only face financial threats from highly sophisticated, well organised eco-organisations, but are also subjected to terrorist tactics, such as bomb threats, and the intimidation of their staff. British police are, for example, investigating the tactics used by underground eco-groups, which distribute leaflets with instructions on how to assemble home-made explosives. In the United States 'Earth First' was established in the 1980s, focusing on nuclear facilities and associated electrical systems. In 1986, this group was responsible for a successful attack on the Palo Verdes nuclear facility transmission lines in the United States. Radical environmental movements, and acts of terrorism associated with them, are on the increase.

INTERNATIONAL TERRORISM

Alexander and Gleason make a distinction between domestic and international terrorism: "Terrorist activities may be regarded as international when the interests of more than one state are involved, for example, when the perpetrator or the victim is a foreigner in the country where the act is done or the perpetrator has fled to another country [in contrast to domestic terrorism]." The international character is highlighted with the participation of foreign nationals in "international terrorist organisations", such as the activities of the Abu Nidal Organisation in the United States. The activities of this group (as well as others with the same modus operandi) include the smuggling and transfer of currency, and providing information and intelligence to other members inside the United States and throughout the world. The Abu Nidal group has also obstructed investigations, fraudulently obtained passports, bought weapons, recruited new members and collected information in a clandestine manner.

The international political system has contributed to the increase in international terrorism in a number of ways. During the Cold War unconventional modes of warfare, such as terrorism, became more attractive as instruments of policy for states and non-state organisations such as national liberation movements. "Such methods are low-cost, relatively low-risk and yet afford the possibilities of high yield in terms of weakening, penetrating or even gaining control through covert means. State-sponsored international terrorism carries the added attraction for its perpetrators that it can be carried out secretly, and, if suspicions are voiced, plausibly denied."

Israel's occupation of the West Bank and the Gaza Strip contributed to religiously motivated terrorism and the establishment of several terrorist organisations with a network all over the world. The Middle East problem has never been purely local since its original cause – the creation of the state of Israel – was an act of the international community rather than an outcome of the domestic balance of forces between local Jews and Arabs. Socio-economic problems, which are sometimes aggravated by a government's action or inaction, contribute to communities' feelings of frustration with and alienation from the government. Unattended grievances of various ethnic and religious minorities have led to the establishment of terrorist groups set up to counter the inadequacies of regimes. For example, the division between the rich northern hemisphere and poor southern hemisphere has contributed to the development of terrorist groups. Islamic revivalism and extremism go hand in hand with poor socio-economic conditions. Since the 18th century periods of Islamic revivalism, religio-political movements have developed in response to political fragmentation and economic, social and moral decline. International terrorism, in other words, comprises acts that have clear international consequences. These acts include incidents where terrorists cross national borders to strike foreign targets, select victims or targets because of their connections to a foreign country (for example, diplomats, local executives), attack airliners on international flights, or force airliners to fly to other countries. International terrorism does not include the activities of dissident groups when carried out against a local government or citizens in their own country if no foreign connection is involved.

STATE-SPONSORED TERRORISM

State-sponsored terrorism involves the employment of lethal force across international borders for the purpose of destroying or weakening the political cohesion of a targeted political entity. The state that resorts to terrorism does not use its own military instruments to deliver the lethal force, but harnesses social elements within the targeted entity to do so. States sponsor terrorism for three basic reasons:

- it is safer for the agent state;
- it is cheap; and
- the current interstate infrastructure enhances and supports the use of terrorism for political goals through modern technology.

Within state-sponsored terrorism, Hanle has identified three basic types of terrorism employed by social forces that lend themselves to outside sponsorship:

National revolutionary terrorism (so-called 'homofighters', or terrorists operating against their fellow countrymen). For example, both sides during the anti-apartheid struggle used terror tactics against fellow South Africans.

International revolutionary terrorism ('xeno-fighters' who employ terrorism against targets controlled and operated by persons other than the terrorists' fellow countrymen, including colonial terrorist organisations). These organisations include, for example, the Palestine Liberation Organisation (PLO) fighting those who control their homelands and those who are allied with them; and ideologically motivated terrorists that have widespread popular support, for example, Islamic Jihad and other radical Islamic terrorist groups. International terrorists need and receive more support from the outside than do domestic terrorist groups.

This, in turn, gives them a greater technical ability to operate at a higher level of violence than their domestic counterparts. State sponsorship puts resources such as intelligence, money, sophisticated munitions and technical expertise at the disposal of the terrorists, thus reducing the constraints on the terrorists. States supporting international revolutionary terrorists are usually those with the same ideology as the terrorists or those wishing to destabilise and weaken the targeted entity politically.

The difference between homo-fighters and xeno-fighters is that the latter tend to adopt more indiscriminate tactics. This explains the indiscriminate nature of force used by international terrorists as opposed to national revolutionary terrorists. Minute, political terrorist gangs or so-called micro-political terrorist gangs that seldom have a membership of more than a dozen people (including the Baader-Meinhof gang and the Japanese Red Army of the 1970s). State-sponsored terrorism may be expected to continue as a form of limited conflict used by marginalised states. State-sponsored international terrorism can also be used as a tool of domestic or foreign policy.

Iran, even with US sanctions, continues to use terrorism as a weapon of foreign policy to kill dissidents and to disrupt peace processes through its support for Hamas, the Palestinian Islamic Jihad (PIJ) and the Popular Front for the Liberation of Palestine – General Command (PFLP-GC). It also provides a safe haven for the Kurdistan Workers Party (PKK). Sudan supports the armed opposition groups of all its neighbouring countries and was even involved in the planning and training of the assailants involved in the attempted assassination of President Hosni Mubarak in Addis Ababa. Thus, Sudan could be considered to be a destabilising factor in Northern Africa. Before the assassination attempt, the Egyptian government accused the fundamentalist government in Khartoum of instigating militant Islamic violence inside Egypt. In addition, Sudan also harboured Osama Bin Laden and members of the world's most violent groups such as the Abu Nidal Organisation, Hizbollah and Hamas. Khartoum is known as a major transit point and base for a number of terrorist groups.

The growth of international terrorist movements has been linked to the willingness of some nations to sponsor campaigns of terror directly or indirectly, often through proxies and other means. States sponsor terrorism by providing funding, training, a safe haven, weapons and logistical support to terrorists. State sponsorship increases the danger of terrorism because it provides the client group with far greater firepower than they would ever be likely to obtain in the normal arms-market.

TRANSNATIONAL TERRORISM

A shift has been detected since the 1990s from state-sponsored international terrorism that is generally more structured with well-established hierarchies and infrastructure, towards international radical terrorists that operate in a decentralised fashion. This trend is regarded as a significant internationalisation of terrorist activities. In the past, it would have been correct to say that in general terms most terrorist organisations were readily identifiable from their constitution, which was often organised on quasi-military lines, with a definable command structure, a strategy and an identifiable political aim.

According to Anderson, transnational terrorism is "... the use, or threat of use, of anxiety – including, extra normal violence for political purposes by any individual or group, whether acting for or in opposition to established governmental authority, when such action is intended to influence the attitudes and behaviour of a target group wider than the immediate victims and when, through the nationality or foreign ties of its perpetrators, through its location, through the nature of its institutional or human victims, or through the mechanics of its resolution, its ramifications transcend national boundaries".

The Central Intelligence Agency (CIA) distinguishes between international terrorism and transnational terrorism, stating that the latter is terrorism "carried out by basically autonomous non-state actors, whether or not they enjoy some degree of support from sympathetic states", as opposed to "international terrorism, which is terrorism carried out by individuals or groups controlled by a sovereign state".

Transnational terrorism refers to groups comprised of individuals of various nationalities, all united under the dual banner of religion and violence. According to Mickolus: "terror is transnational when, through the nationality or foreign ties of its perpetrators, its location, the nature of its institutional or human victims, or the mechanics of its resolution and its ramifications transcend national boundaries". In other words, adherents of international radical terrorism generally overcome traditional national differences by concentrating on a common goal of achieving social change, under the banner of personal beliefs, through violence. These individuals may not consider themselves to be citizens of any particular country, but instead seek common political, social, economic or personal objectives that transcend nation-state boundaries. The World Trade Centre bombing may be considered as an act of transnational terrorism, because of the different nationalities of the terrorists involved. The suspected bombers include Egyptians, Iraqis, Jordanians, Palestinians and US citizens.

Although not all of the above-mentioned categories of terrorism exist in South Africa, terrorism is an international phenomenon. The implication for South Africa is that transnational terrorism, in association with transnational crime, presents a real threat to national, regional and international security. South Africa is an open society with a large number of illegal immigrants and a well-established infrastructure. This presents a fertile ground for individuals and groups who want to engage in terrorist activities. South Africa is regarded as the gateway to the rest of Africa, especially to southern Africa. However, as with other African countries, the threat presented by terrorism is on the increase. The threat can be seen to exist on two levels, namely as an external threat and as an internal threat.

A Nation of more than 1 billion citizens contains many grievances. India's democracy allows freedom of expression of such grievances, but many times in the past the impatient and ruthless few have used violence to make their point. The US State Department estimates that about 2300 people died in attacks by various groups in India last year. Mumbai, the nation's financial capital, has suffered six major terrorist strikes since 1993, including a campaign of bombings in 2006 that killed more than 200 people.

This week's coordinated terrorist attacks on India's largest city came suddenly, but not without warning. Police had earlier been warned by self-declared Islamists that

Mumbai would be attacked in reprisal for the country's alleged failure to protect the human rights of its Muslim citizens. Terrorism, of course, has no religion, but for at least a quarter of a century now, political extremists professing religious piety have staged attacks in different parts of the country: Kashmir, Gujarat, Punjab, and Orissa - the list is long. At the same time this week's atrocity bears the hallmarks of the global jihad that brought us the September 11, 2001 attacks and the Bali, London and Madrid bombings. Targets included transport infrastructure, five-star hotels and restaurants frequented by westerners, as well as a Jewish centre. The assailants were young men, heavily armed and well trained.

It is not yet known if they were imported for this purpose or were home-grown terrorists. India has known both in the 62 years since independence. At times, Pakistan has done its best to pour fuel on India's internal fires, and India's Prime Minister, Manmohan Singh, has been quick to warn of serious consequences if the latest attacks are linked to neighbouring countries. Indian naval vessels have boarded two Pakistani merchant ships in the Arabian Sea amid claims the attackers arrived in Mumbai by boat and spoke a dialect of Punjabi unique to Pakistan. But these are early days. It is to be hoped that a rush to judgment - egged on by India's highly competitive news media - will be avoided. The terrorists' modus operandi was similar, for example, to previous attacks by the Liberation Tigers of Tamil Eelam, or Tamil Tigers, in Sri Lanka, who have in the past cooperated with other terrorist groups. The world needs to know the identities, motivations and connections of the perpetrators of these latest attacks, and a patient, methodical and open-minded investigation based on hard, publicly-available evidence has the best chance of success.

Like al-Qaeda, the aim of terrorists everywhere is to sow insecurity and hatred in free societies. Those who have attacked Mumbai would like nothing better than to ignite a new and destabilising round of enmities between India and Pakistan. They will also be gratified if their handiwork should trigger sectarian violence between Hindus and Muslims, and as India heads for national elections in the first half of next year the scope for political polarisation is obvious. In the twilight of the Bush Administration it is worth remembering that while terrorists can temporarily disrupt life in democratic nations, they can never destroy us. But democracies that lash out blindly in retaliation can do great damage to their own social and political fabric. India has demonstrated in the past a capacity for restraint in the face of extreme provocation. It deserves our strong support in this difficult time.

Australians are among the dead in Mumbai and their loss should cement our determination to fight shoulder to shoulder with the nation under attack. The Australian Government has a legal obligation to warn its citizens about security threats prevailing in India, but it would be perverse if such warnings serve the terrorists' purpose of damaging confidence in India. Many Australians know the risks and are still prepared to continue visiting and doing business there. Before and since independence, Indians have paid a heavy price for their freedom. Their nation has been called a functioning anarchy, the land of a million mutinies, but there is something miraculous and important about its progress. Australia must show solidarity with India's cause, and be ready to share the sacrifices necessary to ensure its ultimate victory.

If your sore limb looks big, it will hurt more, according to a researcher at the Prince of Wales Medical Research Institute. It is part of a complex interaction within the brain between information from nerve endings in the affected limb, and the brain's perception of how sore the limb appears. The researcher, Lorimer Moseley, describes it as possibly a response to danger: if it looks bigger, it looks more swollen, and therefore the brain acts to protect it. Actually we think there may be another explanation. Let's be frank: the brain is bunging it on. Having been silly enough to fold the ladder up on its arm, say, after clearing out the gutters, the brain is trying to milk the situation for sympathy. The brain is clearly angling for a sickie here. Well, it's not going to get it. The rest of us have to work for a living; what's so special about the brain? Let us make things clear: the brain should get a haircut and get a job.

INDIA'S DAY OF RECKONING

There was a one-day cricket match on television, and the streets were quite empty in the old part of Mumbai, down on the peninsula that juts into the Arabian Sea, where shops, restaurants and small hotels are crammed into once-gracious stone apartment blocks built for the former British commercial class and their local partners. About 9.15pm, Bharat Tamore stepped out from his small apartment to walk to the Taj Mahal Palace Hotel where his night shift as a junior manager was due to start at 10 pm. diverting to the waterfront to enjoy the sea breeze, he noticed something unusual.

"It was a small inflatable raft, not usually seen in our parts where fishermen ply only small boats," Tamore told *The Times of India*. "In the darkness, I saw eight young men stepping out of the raft, two at a time. They jumped into the waters, and picked up a haversack. They bent down again, and came up carrying two more haversacks, one in each hand."

Tamore approached the men, who looked in their 20s and were wearing jeans and jackets, and asked them what they were doing. "We're students," one said. Tamore accepted the explanation. Six of the young men went off, carrying the haversacks that seemed to be very heavy. Two got back in the dinghy, started the outboard, and shot off into the darkness.

The hotel staffer walked to the back entrance of the Taj, the luxury century-old stone pile facing the harbour near the triumphal Gateway of India built for King George V's tour of his empire's jewel, and started changing into his uniform. Soon after he heard gunshots coming from the fashionable Shamiana restaurant, where Mumbai's business and financial wizards mix with wealthy tourists and Bollywood film figures for late suppers. It began a night of terror that ended when Tamore was guided from his hiding place by police at 4am.

For the attackers, Wednesday night was the culmination of careful preparation that must have begun months earlier, possibly in neighbouring Pakistan. It now appears that some time in the 12 days before the attack, up to 20 young fanatics had overwhelmed the crew of a 14-metre trawler called the Kuber after it sailed on November 14 from the Gujarat port of Porbandar for a 10-day fishing trip.

Capable of only seven or eight nautical miles an hour, the trawler chugged down the coast towards Mumbai, mingling with the hundreds of fishing and trading boats plying the generally calm seas. Several kilometres off the brightly lit "Maximum City", as dubbed by the writer Suketu Mehta, the little vessel stopped, and two inflatables were launched. The attackers sped into the metropolis of 15 million inhabitants, leaving a dead captain on the bobbing trawler and no sign of the four other crews. Carrying their rucksacks of metal ammunition clips, grenades and concealed Kalashnikov automatic rifles, the men were dropped at jetties around the peninsula, close to their targets.

A bit after 9.30, two gunmen went to the Leopold Cafe. Once a haunt of minor underworld figures, Somali traders and wizened Western hippies and made famous in the Australian jail escapee Gregory David Roberts's novel *Shantaram*, the cafe is now a self-consciously "low-life" locale for backpackers, professionals and aircrews. It even sells its own T-shirt. From the pavement outside, where vendors were closing up their stalls and laying down mats to sleep, the gunmen opened up with their automatic rifles through the open sides, before tossing in grenades. Two young Australians were among the many injured, lying with about eight dead customers and waiters.

The two then fled down the side street, which leads to the Taj, and joined others to enter via a door normally kept locked but open that night because of weddings and corporate functions. They walked into the lobby, a wide expanse of marble and fountains, and opened fire. Some headed into the Shamiana, spraying gunfire, and trying to single out American and British citizens as captives. Then they headed up to the residential suite of the hotel general manager, Karambir Kang, showing a familiarity with the detailed layout and passageways of the old building. Kang's wife and two children have been reported killed during the siege and fire that then started.

Among the dead left by the mayhem was the Greek millionaire Andreas Liveras, the owner of a luxury yacht charter business who had come to scout for opportunities. The French nuclear scientist Georges Vendryes, known as the father of the fast-breeder reactor, managed to escape with his wife, as did the Australian cricket lawyer Dean Kino who had come to help prepare the Champions League T20 competition, now postponed.

Another group stormed the lobby of the Oberoi Trident, another luxury hotel on the other side of the peninsula, where guests included a 25-member NSW trade delegation. The gunmen sprayed the lobby with gunfire and tossed grenades as staff and guests fled through the kitchens, before holing up on the 19th floor with foreign and local hostages. Midway up the peninsula, four gunmen walked into the concourse of the Chhatrapati Shivaji Terminus, the vast neo-Saracenic railway station once named after Queen Victoria.

Pulling out their guns, they opened fire at random among commuters getting late trains home, killed about 10 people and left the polished floors awash with gore. The attackers ran off towards the nearby Cama Hospital. Hemant Karkare, the head of Maharashtra state's anti-terrorism squad, had been summoned from his official flat. A veteran of the elite national police service, he'd taken up the key Mumbai-based position after seven years in Vienna working under diplomatic cover for the Indian external intelligence service, the Research and Analysis Wing or RAW.

Already he'd shown a fearless disregard for political pressure, arresting a Hindu holy man and a serving army lieutenant-colonel for a recent bombing in the inland city of Malegaon which had been portrayed initially as an Islamist plot. Arriving at the railway station, Karkare put on a bullet-proof vest and helmet, and set off in pursuit of the attackers. But he removed them some time before he got to the Cama Hospital and, in a close-quarter clash, died with three bullets in the chest, while two other senior police died alongside him.

The night of slaughter went on, with attackers killing two security guards at the hospital, some seizing a police vehicle and driving through the city shooting at random, and others trying to keep police bailed up inside their headquarters and shooting up the popular Regal cinema. A separate attack caught a rabbi, his family and several Jewish worshippers at the small Chabad Lubavitch centre, back down the peninsula. As Thursday dawned, police were reinforced with truckloads of army and navy commandos from nearby barracks, and elite Special Forces from the National Security Guard.

As operations proceeded to isolate and overwhelm gunmen and save hotel guests, police and intelligence officials began interrogating three of the captured attackers. Indian press reports quoted Major-General R. K. Hooda, the leader of the operations, as saying the attackers had pretended to come from Hyderabad, an ancient city with a big Muslim population in central India, but they had captured one man who spoke with a Punjabi accent and appeared to be from Pakistan. Some reports named the man as Ajmal Amir Kamal, a resident of Multan in Pakistan.

Even before this information, the precision and planning of the concerted attacks pointed to an expertise beyond the scope of India's domestic extremists. As Jane's Information Group in Britain reported in its *Country Risk Daily Report*: "From a tactical perspective, most terrorist attacks in India have been carried out through the use of improvised explosive devices planted on bicycles, motorcycles and cars, and triggered by timers or mobile telephones." To Yogesh Pratap Singh, a former senior policeman now a Mumbai barrister, the sea approach to bring a large number of men and weapons, around the normal surveillance screening, pointed to a link with Pakistan-based organisations. "It seems to be a highly trained operation," he says. "They kept it very secret, they don't allow any information to come out, and they're ready to die: such a wide, comprehensive and immaculate modus operandi is that of al-Qaeda."

The assessment by Jane's Information Group also emphasised that the apparent focus on killing or capturing foreign businesspeople, specifically US and British nationals, had not occurred previously and suggested "a wider global anti-Western agenda" in contrast to national issues that appeared to motivate recent Indian incidents.

A leading Indian intelligence and terrorism expert, the former senior RAW official B. Raman, says sheer expense points to assistance from Pakistan, either its intelligence service, exiled Mumbai mafia figures such as the gang boss Dawood Ibrahim, or al-Qaeda and its Pakistani affiliates. "Indian boys who had taken to terrorism in the name of Indian Mujahideen, they do not have that kind of money at their disposal," Raman says. "I personally feel this has the clear stamp of al-Qaeda."

The Indian Prime Minister, Manmohan Singh, also pointed the finger after an emergency cabinet meeting. "The well-planned and well-orchestrated attacks, probably with external linkages, were intended to create a sense of panic, by choosing high-profile targets and indiscriminately killing foreigners," Singh said in a national TV address.

"It is evident that the group which carried out these attacks, based outside the country, had come with single-minded determination to create havoc in the commercial capital of the country. We will take up strongly with our neighbours that the use of their territory for launching attacks on us will not be tolerated, and that there would be a cost if suitable measures are not taken by them."

This would point to terrorist groups based in Pakistan, such as the Lashkar-e-Toiba, which transferred their attention and deadly expertise from the anti-Soviet war in Afghanistan to undermining Indian rule in its part of Kashmir during the 1990s, with active assistance from Pakistan's Inter-Services Intelligence, at least up until September 11, 2001. These groups have a record of suicide attacks, in Kashmir and more widely in India, including the December 2001 assault on the Indian parliament.

Yet the only early claimant to responsibility for attack was a hitherto-unknown group, the "Deccan Mujahideen", which emailed claims to Indian media via a Russian server. Deccan, located in Hyderabad seemed to link to the attackers' cover story, while Mujahideen linked to a new terrorist group, the Indian Mujahideen, which had emerged after serial blasts in three northern Indian cities last November. It later claimed to have carried out the July 2006 train bombings in Mumbai, as well as bombings this year in Jaipur, Ahmedabad, and New Delhi. But the Indian Mujahideen is in many ways even more of a danger for India than groups such as Lashkar-e-Toiba.

It appears to draw on alienated elements among India's vast population of Muslims, numbering 140 million. Its recruits include some young people whose family members suffered in the vicious anti-Muslim pogroms that swept Mumbai and some other centres at the end of 1992, after the destruction of the disputed Ayodhya mosque by Hindu zealots, and in Gujarat in 2002. A wider pool is the Students Islamic Movement of India, a banned organisation of religious purists.

They include many well-educated and well-travelled people, able to find their way around the upper echelons of the global economy and India. Among suspected members arrested in Mumbai not long before this attack were three IT professionals, including one with a senior position in yahoo.com, who had visited the United States. This would suggest that as well as a sharpened counter-terrorist intelligence performance, India has a huge task of rebuilding faith in its secular politics. This faith has been eroded by the desultory efforts to sheet home blame for the 1992 Mumbai pogrom against complicit police and politicians, and by the impunity of Gujarat's chief minister, Narendra Modi, and his police for their role in whipping up that state's horrific violence in 2002. As national elections approach in the first half of next year, Singh's Congress Party Government is struggling to find balance between a Hindu-nationalist opposition, the Bharatiya Janata Party, baying for a crackdown on terrorism and its duty to protect Muslims from oppressive surveillance.

Violence between Hindu extremists and Christian converts in eastern states, the growing Maoist insurgency in central regions and the delicate Kashmir situation add to the precarious security mix. Yet so far the Indian Mujahideen may just be local cover for outside groups. The attackers, who have been in limited contact with the Indian media, seem motivated by concerns dealing with Kashmir and India's strategic position. "Are you aware how many people have been killed in Kashmir?" asked one attacker naming himself as Imran, who called a TV station from the Jewish centre seige. "Are you aware how your army has killed Muslims?"

In May the Lashkar-e-Toiba head, Abdul Subhan Qureshi, threatened to attack tourist sites unless the Government withdrew its support for the United States, and it has claimed responsibility for the recent bombings in Bangalore, Ahmedabad and Delhi. This suggests that by striking at India's investment and inflows, the attackers want India to pay a heavy price for its backing of the Karzai Government in Kabul and its detente with Pakistan over Kashmir.

Although fragile, the reduction in tension between the two countries allows the Pakistan army to divert forces to fighting the Taliban along the North-West Frontier. If one result is also a boost to the Hindu nationalists in India's politics and harsher monitoring of India's Muslims, that is not just collateral damage but another wedge into the secular structures that have kept India together for more than 60 years.

TRACKING DOWN THE TERRORISTS

At 3:15 p.m. local time on Friday, a massive blast went off inside the hotel, loud enough to startle the hundreds of journalists gathered at the security cordon hundreds of yards behind the hotel. An officer who ran out of the hotel, carrying a pistol, said; "Now everything is burned. The stairs are burned. The woodwork is all spoiled." What did this blast mean? "They are getting desperate," he said. "You can tell by their actions."

The officer reported that commandos had trapped three terrorists on the top floor of the hotel. The rest of the suspects were on the ground floor, but he was not sure how many were in the building altogether, estimating between seven and 10. When asked whether they were trying to take any of the suspects alive, he almost smiled at the question. "The Taj is a beloved landmark in this city, and its residents will have to get used to the idea that the Taj will never be the same. Disbelieving Mumbaikars have been watching as their city of 12 million has been paralyzed – shops closed, streets emptied – by just two dozen attackers in the past two days.

How could this happen? The unwelcome truth is that this grand cosmopolitan city, one that has survived two even deadlier terrorists' bombings in 2003 and 2006, was caught completely unprepared.

The scale and sophistication of the attacks, which began at about 9:30 p.m. local time on Wednesday as gunmen stormed hotels with AK-47s and grenades became clear on Thursday and Friday: over 155 people are reported dead, and more than 300 are injured. The injured were brought to local hospitals from the sites of the attacks, which included the Taj and another luxury hotel, the main railway terminus, a cafe and two hospitals. Among the police, 14 were killed and 25 injured. The Maharashtra chief minister, Vilasrao Deshmukh, estimates that there were 20 to 25 terrorists involved seven of them now dead.

Unlike most of the recent simultaneous bomb attacks in India, this one continued to do its damage after the initial shock wore off, gathering strength and changing form as the smoke and noise from the blasts cleared. In this case, the attackers turned hostage takers at three of the sites: the two hotels and a residential building called Nariman House. Those stranded in hotels might have had a shorter ordeal if the hotel management had put into place at least some kind of emergency plan in case of a terrorist attack. About 100 people, including one man with a gunshot wound, took refuge in a conference center at the Taj when they heard shooting but were left there all night, with no communication from anyone, let alone any instructions on how to exit the building safely.

Hotel managers at the Taj are given some crisis-management training, but nothing that would prepare them for a situation in which the attackers were running "free and loose" inside the hotel, says Anupam Amrohi, 23, an employee of Taj hotels in Bangalore. Amrohi was on the phone with his friends trapped inside the conference center all night. "They should have pulled the alarm," he says. Instead, hotel staff advised people already inside to stay where they were. People in their rooms were told to stay put even after the firing between the police and the suspects began. Hotel operators would call them periodically to remind them to keep the lights off and the volume on the TV down.

The lack of any prior local police intelligence about the attacks — a complaint voiced by many Mumbaikars today — is particularly alarming given the meticulous planning and unusual modus operandi of the attackers. For example, an Indian navy spokesman confirmed that the terrorists entered Mumbai without detection by taking a sea route. Starting from a base in Gujarat to the north of Mumbai, they made their way to the Gateway of India at Mumbai's southern tip and another landing point on the peninsula 14 nautical miles away; they killed one boatman in the process.

The attack on the Leopold Cafe and Restaurant also shows intimate local knowledge. Like the Oberoi and Taj hotels, it is a favorite of foreigners, mostly backpackers and fans of the best-selling novel *Shantaram,* in which the Leopold is a key setting. As you come out from the Leopold, a hard right takes you into a narrow lane, which leads directly to the back entrance of the Taj. Several people in the Apna Bidi shop, around the corner from the Leopold, reported that at about 9:30 p.m. Wednesday, immediately after the blasts, they saw two of the attackers with AK-47s running from the Leopold into the narrow lane that leads to the Taj. Either the terrorists were natives to the city or they had time to practice, prepare and carefully plot their targets and the path they would take between them. As the three simultaneous hostage dramas began to unfold, onlookers gathered. "It's like watching 24 in slow motion," said Vineet Pandit, 22, who lives near the Oberoi. What they would see at each of these sites was a parade of hundreds of uniformed troops over the course of several hours: the Mumbai police, the Indian army and paramilitary groups including the Rapid Action Force and the National Security Guard's elite "Black Cat" commandos, distinctive in their all-black uniforms. It was not always clear who was in charge. On Thursday at the Taj, police officers waited idly in their jeeps as 100 army personnel tried to take control of the hotel. At the Oberoi, the police commissioner appeared to be taking the lead.

In Colaba market, a handful of terrorists stormed one of the apartment buildings at about 10 p.m. on Wednesday and then began randomly shooting and lobbing grenades into the street and at neighboring buildings, according to residents of the area. From the vantage point of three Black Cat snipers watching the building, I could see Nariman House's shattered windows. The couples who own the building are Jewish, giving rise to rumors throughout the day that "Israelis" were somehow involved in the attacks. The other people in the building, inclu ding an infant wearing a pink bonnet and green blanket, were held as hostages but released early Thursday. The last person to leave, a young woman, told authorities that the only remaining hostages were the couple, who had made no sound or movement since the night before.

By 5 p.m., they were presumed to be dead, and the Black Cat commandos moved in half an hour later, unleashing a volley of gunshots into the building. By 9:30 p.m. local time, the firing was still going on, and it was not clear whether the four to five suspects inside had been killed or captured. So who are the terrorists? That too is unclear. A group calling itself the Deccan Mujahideen sent an e-mail to news organizations early Thursday morning claiming responsibility for the attacks. Two of the terrorists spoke to a local news channel, India TV, to air their grievances: "When so many of us were killed, who did anything for us?" a man called Shadullah asked, referring to anti-Muslim riots in northern India in 1992 and '93.

He said he was among seven people holding hostages at the Oberoi but didn't make any specific demands other than for the release of other *mujahedin* jailed in India and for an end to the persecution of Muslims. He did not reveal where the group comes from, though the Deccan in its name presumably refers to the plateau that stretches across southern India. Officials have suggested that there may have been a foreign power involved, rejecting the widespread belief among defense and political analysts that there is an able network of homegrown terrorists in India. (Major General R.K. Hooda, an army officer who was the commander for today's military operations, hinted that their accents might have been Pakistani.)

So far, there have been little more than hints and platitudes from the steady stream of high-profile visitors to south Mumbai: the local strongman Raj Thackeray, Maharashtra state chief minister Vilasrao Deshmukh, Member of Parliament Milind Deora. Prime Minister Manmohan Singh and Congress President Sonia Gandhi are said to be on their way to the city, as is opposition BJP leader L.K. Advani. The question is will they do anything to better prepare this city, and the rest of India, for the next time?

The men came wearing black hoods, firing automatic weapons and throwing grenades, taking hostages, attacking two hotels, a cinema, a café, a train station and other popular and undefended "soft targets." An e-mail message to Indian media outlets that claimed responsibility for the bloody attacks in Mumbai on Wednesday night said the militants were from the Deccan Mujahideen. Global terrorism experts said Thursday they had never heard of the group. And based on its tactics, they said, it was probably not a cell or group linked to Al Qaeda. "It's even unclear whether it's a real group or not," said Bruce Hoffman, a professor at the School of Foreign Service at Georgetown University and the author of the book "Inside Terrorism." "It could be a cover name for another group, or a name adopted just for this particular incident."

Chrtistine Fair, senior political scientist and a South Asia expert at the RAND Corporation, was careful to say that the identity of the terrorists could not yet be known. But she insisted the style of the attacks and the targets in Mumbai suggested that the militants were likely to be Indian Muslims - and not linked to Al Qaeda or the violent South Asian terrorist group Lashkar-e-Taiba.

"There's absolutely nothing Al Qaeda-like about it," she said of the attack. "Did you see any suicide bombers? And there are no fingerprints of Lashkar. They don't do hostage taking, and they don't do grenades." Hoffman agreed that the assault was "not exactly Al Qaeda's modus operandi, which is suicide, attacks."

But he said the timed attacks, which he called "tactical, sophisticated and coordinated," perhaps pointed to a broader organization behind the perpetrators. Fair also noted that the fact the group had not proclaimed its ideology in a manifesto was "not at all unusual." "You don't see these types of terrorist operations very often, if at all," Hoffman said. "These aren't just a bunch of radical guys coming together to cause mayhem.

"This takes a different skill set. It doesn't take much skill to make a bomb. This is not just pressing a button as a suicide bomber and dying. You don't learn this over the Internet." The word Deccan describes the middle and south of India, which is dominated by the Deccan Plateau. Mujahideen, of course, is the commonly used Arabic word for holy fighters. The very name - if it is a real group - suggests a domestic agenda.

"It's maybe not so much a group as a cell that will take on a name for a specific operation," said Fair. "In India you hear these unusual names." Fair did not agree that the attacks on Wednesday necessarily required deep planning and training. "This wasn't something that required a logistical mastermind," she said. "These were not hardened targets. A huge train station with zero security. Two hotels owned by Indians Leopold's Café with no security. How hard is it, really? It's not rocket science."

Fair believes the attacks could be "yet another manifestation of domestic terrorism" that has its genesis in a longstanding institutional discrimination against Muslims. "There are a lot of very, very angry Muslims in India," she said, "The economic disparities are startling, and India has been very slow to publicly embrace its rising Muslim problem.

You cannot put lipstick on this pig. This is a major domestic political challenge for India."

The CIA puts the population of India at 1.15 billion, with Hindus making up about 80 percent of the total and Muslims 13.4 percent. Fair said one incident - "a watershed event" - that continues to anger Muslims were the riots that swept nearby Gujarat State in 2002. The violence killed between 1,000 and 2,000 people, most of them Muslims.

"The public political face of India says, 'Our Muslims have not been radicalized.' But the Indian intelligence apparatus knows that's not true. India's Muslim communities are being sucked into the global landscape of Islamist jihad. "Indians will have a strong incentive to link this to Al Qaeda.'Al Qaeda's in your toilet!' But this is a domestic issue. This is not India's 9/11." For Hoffman, who has studied terrorism for more than 30 years, the Mumbai attacks are "alarming on a number of levels."

"It's not often that things in terrorism alarm me. So much is a repeat of what we see almost every day, like suicide bombings. There's no real innovation in terrorism, which is why 9/11 was so terrifying, because it was so innovative and heinously clever. "But these attacks show how a handful of men, basically using weapons off the shelf, can paralyze a city and frustrate highly trained security forces. These attacks were calculated to spread alarm and anxiety - to put it quite frankly, to unhinge things - and that's exactly what they've done."

TALIBAN VS US

On the face of it, there is no basic change in the situation on the ground in the war theater in Afghanistan and Pakistan. The United States-led war machine is the same, the pattern of the Taliban's attacks is the same and Islamabad is still an ally of the US. Nevertheless, the players are already raising the level of their struggle in an effort to win the war when battle resumes in full come next spring. The Taliban decided to target the supply lines of the North Atlantic Treaty Organization (NATO) as it passed through Pakistan - as much as 90% of NATO's needs take this route, with no viable alternative. This has had some success, but over the past 10 days attacks on Kabul-bound convey in the Khyber Agency has reached unprecedented levels. Thirteen containers full of arms and ammunition, military vehicles and food were looted by the Taliban, forcing an entire NATO convoy from the southern port city of Karachi to stop in Peshawar, the capital of North-West Frontier Province.

Under an emergency arrangement, safe warehouses were hired for the supply trucks and containers to park. It was not until Monday, under extraordinary government-enabled security measures, that the convoy was able to resume its journey. The attacks have been so incessant that Asia Times Online has learned that 530 containers loaded with armored personnel vehicles, military trucks, Humvees, arms and ammunition have not yet been delivered. They were sent four months ago from Jabal-i-Ali in the United Arab Emirates to Karachi. Clearly, if this continues, NATO's war effort will be severely compromised. This is not the only area in which the Taliban have successfully expanded the scope of their activities.

In an important development, they are now active in and around Peshawar, where they are engaging the Pakistani security forces. In recent days they have also conducted a high-profile abduction of an Iranian diplomat and attacked foreign journalists and government functionaries. They are also killing pro-government tribal chiefs in Bajaur and Mohamand Agencies, while all the time attracting more and more recruits. The aim is to establish such a presence that Pakistan will be forced to retreat and leave the Taliban alone to wage their war against NATO in neighboring Afghanistan.

Meanwhile, in NATO headquarters in Kabul and Brussels it has been realized that the level of the Taliban's control in Afghanistan is such that they are inching towards a serious escalation of the violence which could create serious turmoil right in the heart of Kabul. The provinces of Wardak, Logar, Kapisa and Parwan, all relatively close to Kabul, are either partially controlled by the Taliban or the Taliban have a sufficiently significant presence to make them no-go areas for anti-Taliban forces. In this scenario, especially over concerns about its supply lines, NATO is reluctant to entrust Pakistan with tackling the problem. Although relations between the two countries are good; even low-profile Pakistani support for the Taliban could turn the tables in Afghanistan.

NATO will therefore lead all actions, whether in Afghanistan or Pakistan. This is not too popular in Pakistan. Last week, the NATO commander in Afghanistan, General David McKiernan, visited Islamabad to brief parliamentarians, but several of them, including those of the dominant Pakistan People's Party and Federal Minister Raza Rabbani, refused to attend. They called the meeting a serious breach of Pakistan's sovereignty as no military official of another country is supposed to approach parliamentarians without the Foreign Office's mediation.

McKiernan wanted to take Pakistani lawmakers into his confidence over a new NATO initiative to increase the scope of Operation Lion Heart, which involves US strikes on insurgent targets in the Kunar region of Afghanistan and a full-scale Pakistani campaign in the region of Bajaur Agency. In the latter sphere, air attacks would be bolstered by land assaults. Asia Times Online has learned that Qari Ziaur Rahman, the chief commander of Kunar and Bajaur, has admitted that the escalation in Kunar has already caused temporary problems, such as restricting militants from traveling from Kunar to aid their colleagues in Bajaur just across the border.

Nevertheless, the militants claim to have defeated the Pakistan military in Bajaur and plan to release a celebratory video to this effect in the near future. Pakistan army Chief General Parvez Ashfaq Kiani plans to visit Brussels to discuss the exact modus operandi of the new phase of Operation Lion Heart. High-level meetings between US intelligence and Pakistan's Inter-Services Intelligence (ISI) have already been held at different levels to devise plans to cripple the support systems of the Taliban and al-Qaeda in Pakistan.

Two prominent names came under discussion at these meetings: retired Lieutenant-General Hamid Gul and a former ISI official retired Squadron Leader Khalid Khawaja. Gul, a former head of the ISI, is suspected of providing political and moral support to the Taliban-led resistance in Afghanistan. Last year, former premier Benazir Bhutto named him as a suspect for the October 18 attack on her life in Karachi. She was subsequently assassinated in December. Khawaja was the first person in the country to assist the displaced families of Arab fighters who fled to Pakistan after the US invasion of Afghanistan in 2001. He fought their cases in court, arranged temporary housing for them and assisted them in departing to their countries. Khawaja is active in the cause of missing people (those detained without trial for years) and wants to register cases against the former chief of army staff and president, General Pervez Musharraf, and his military aides for abuses allegedly committed during their eight years in power. Tightening the noose around people such as Gul and Khawaja and the like is one way to cut off support for the Taliban. The battle has begun in earnest in preparation for next year's showdown.

2

The Changing Meaning of Terrorism

The word 'terrorism' was first popularized during the French Revolution. In contrast to its contemporary usage, at that time terrorism had a decidedly positive connotation. The system or regime de la terreur of 1793-4 – from which the English word came – was adopted as a means to establish order during the transient anarchical period of turmoil and upheaval that followed the uprisings of 1789, as it has followed in the wake of many other revolutions. Hence, unlike terrorism as it is commonly understood today, to mean a revolutionary or anti-government activity undertaken by non-state or subnational entities, the regime de la terreur was an instrument of governance wielded by the recently established revolutionary state. It was designed to consolidate the new government's power by intimidating counter-revolutionaries, subversives and all other dissidents whom the new regime regarded as 'enemies of the people'. The Committee of General Security and the Revolutionary Tribunal ('People's Court' in the modern vernacular) were thus accorded wide powers of arrest and judgement, publicly putting to death by guillotine persons convicted of treasonous (i.e. reactionary) crimes. In this manner, a powerful lesson was conveyed to any and all who might oppose the revolution or grow nostalgic for the ancient regime.

Ironically, perhaps, terrorism in its original context was

also closely associated with the ideals of virtue and democracy. The revolutionary leader Maximilien Robespierre firmly believed that virtue was the mainspring of a popular government at peace, but that during the time of revolution must be allied with terror in order for democracy to triumph. He appealed famously to 'virtue, without which terror is evil; terror, without which virtue is helpless', and proclaimed: 'Terror is nothing but justice, prompt, severe and inflexible; it is therefore an emanation of virtue.'

Despite this divergence from its subsequent meaning, the French Revolution's 'terrorism' still shared at least two key characteristics in common with its modern-day variant. First, the regime de la terreur was neither random nor indiscriminate, as terrorism is often portrayed today, but was organized, deliberate and systematic. Second, its goal and its very justification – like that of contemporary terrorism – was the creation of a 'new and better society' in place of a fundamentally corrupt and undemocratic political system. Indeed, Robespierre's vague and utopian exegeses of the revolution's central goals are remarkably similar in tone and content to the equally turgid, millenarian manifestos issued by many contemporary revolutionary - primarily left-wing, Marxist-oriented – terrorist organizations. For example, in 1794 Robespierre declared, in language eerily presaging the communiques issued by groups such as Germany's Red Army Faction and Italy's Red Brigades nearly two centuries later:

> We want an order of things ... in which the arts are an adornment to the liberty that ennobles them, and commerce the source of wealth for the public and not of monstrous opulence for a few families ... In our country we desire morality instead of selfishness, honesty and not mere 'honor', principle and not mere custom, duty and not mere propriety, the sway of reason rather than the tyranny of fashion, a scorn for vice and not a contempt for the unfortunate...

Like many other revolutions, the French Revolution eventually began to consume itself. On 8 Thermidor, year two of the new calendar adopted by the revolutionaries (26

July 1794), Robespierre announced to the National Convention that he had in his possession a new list of traitors. Fearing that their own names might be on that list, extremists joined forces with moderates to repudiate both Robespierre and his regime de la terreur. Robespierre and his closest followers themselves met the same fate that had befallen some 40,000 others: execution by guillotine. The Terror was at an end; thereafter terrorism became a term associated with the abuse of office and power – with overt 'criminal' implications. Within a year of Robespierre's demise, the word had been popularized in English by Edmund Burke who, in his famous polemic against the French Revolution, described the 'Thousands of those Hell hounds called Terrorists ... let loose on the people'.

One of the French Revolution's more enduring repercussions was the impetus it gave to anti-monarchical sentiment elsewhere in Europe. Popular subservience to rulers who derived their authority from God through 'divine right of rule', not from their subjects, was increasingly questioned by a politically awakened continent. The advent of nationalism, and with it notions of statehood and citizenship based on the common identity of a people rather than the lineage of a royal family, were resulting in the unification and creation of new nation-states such as Germany and Italy.

Meanwhile, the massive socio-economic changes engendered by the industrial revolution were creating new 'universalist' ideologies (such as communism/Marxism), born of the alienation and exploitative conditions of nineteenth-century capitalism. From this milieu a new era of terrorism emerged, in which the concept had gained many of the familiar revolutionary, anti-state connotations of today. Its chief progenitor was arguably the Italian republican extremist, Carlo Pisacane, who had forsaken his birthright as duke of San Giovanni only to perish in 1857 during an illfated revolt against 'Bourbon rule, A passionate advocate of federalism and mutualism, Pisacane is remembered less on this account than for the theory of 'propaganda by deed', which he is credited with defining – an idea that has exerted a compelling influence on rebels and terrorists alike ever since. 'The propaganda of the idea is a chimera,' Pisacane wrote. 'Ideas result from deeds, not the latter from the former, and the people will not be free when they are educated, but educated when they are free.' Violence, he argued, was necessary not only to draw attention to, or generate publicity for, a cause, but to inform, educate and ultimately rally the masses behind the revolution. The didactic purpose of violence, Pisacane argued, could never be effectively replaced by pamphlets, wall posters or assemblies.

Perhaps the first organization to put into practice Pisacane's dictum was the Narodnaya Volya, or People's Will (sometimes translated as People's Freedom), a small group of Russian constitutionalists that had been founded in 1878 to challenge tsarist rule. For the Narodnaya Volya, the apathy and alienation of the Russian masses afforded few alternatives to the resort to daring and dramatic acts of violence designed to attract attention to the group and its cause. However, unlike the many late twentieth-century terrorist organizations who have cited the principle of 'propaganda by deed' to justify the wanton targeting of civilians in order to assure them publicity through the shock and horror produced by wholesale bloodshed, the Narodnaya Volya displayed an almost quixotic attitude to the violence they wrought. To them, 'propaganda by deed' meant the selective targeting of specific individuals whom the group considered the embodiment of the autocratic, oppressive state. Hence their victims – the tsar, leading members of the royal family, senior government officials – were deliberately chosen for their 'symbolic' value as the dynastic heads and subservient agents of a corrupt and tyrannical regime. An intrinsic element in the group's collective beliefs was that 'not one drop of superfluous blood' should be shed in pursuit of aims, however noble or utilitarian they might be. Even having selected their targets with great care and the utmost deliberation, group members still harboured profound regrets about taking the life of a fellow human being. Their unswerving adherence to this principle is perhaps best illustrated by the failed attempt on the life of the Grand Duke Serge Alexandrovich made by a successor organization to the Narodnaya Volya in 1905. As the royal carriage came into view, the terrorist tasked with the assassination saw that the duke was unexpectedly accompanied by his children and therefore aborted his mission rather than risk harming the intended victim's family (the duke was killed in a subsequent attack). By comparison, the mid-air explosion caused by a terrorist bomb on Pan Am flight 103 over Lockerbie, Scotland, in December 1988 indiscriminately claimed the lives of all 259 persons on board – innocent men, women and children alike – plus eleven inhabitants of the village where the plane crashed.

Ironically, the Narodnaya Volya's most dramatic accomplishment also led directly to its demise. On 1 March 1881 the group assassinated Tsar Alexander II. The failure of eight previous plots had led the conspirators to take extraordinary measures to ensure the success of this attempt. Four volunteers were given four bombs each and deployed along the alternative routes followed by the tsar's cortege. As two of the bomber-assassins stood in wait on the same street, the sleighs carrying the tsar and his Cossack escort approached the first terrorist, who hurled his bomb at the passing sleigh, missing it by inches. The whole entourage came to a halt as soldiers seized the hapless culprit and the tsar descended from his sleigh to check on a bystander wounded by the explosion. 'Thank God, I am safe,' the tsar reportedly declared – just as the second bomber emerged from the crowd and detonated his weapon, killing both himself and his target. The full weight of the tsarist state now fell on the heads of the Narodnaya Volya. Acting on information provided by the arrested member, the secret police swept down on the group's safe houses and hideouts, rounding up most of the plotters, who were quickly tried, convicted and hanged. Further information from this group led to subsequent arrests, so that within a year of the assassination only one member of the original executive committee was still at large. She too was finally apprehended in 1883, at which point the first generation of Narodnaya Volya terrorists ceased to exist, although various successor organizations subsequently emerged to carry on the struggle.

At the time, the repercussions of the tsar's assassination could not have been known or appreciated by either the condemned or their comrades languishing in prison or exiled to Siberia. But in addition to precipitating the beginning of the end of tsarist rule, the group also deeply influenced individual revolutionaries and subversive organizations elsewhere. To the nascent anarchist movement, the 'propaganda by deed' strategy championed by the Narodnaya Volya provided a model to be emulated. Within four months of the tsar's murder, a group of radicals in London convened an 'anarchist conference' which publicly applauded the assassination and extolled tyrannicide as a means to achieve revolutionary change. In hopes of encouraging and coordinating worldwide anarchist activities, the conferees decided to establish an 'Anarchist International' (or 'Black International'). Although this idea, like most of their ambitious plans, came to nought, the publicity generated by even a putative 'Anarchist International' was sufficient to create a myth of global revolutionary pretensions and thereby stimulate fears and suspicions disproportionate to its actual impact or political achievements. Disparate and uncoordinated though the anarchists' violence was, the movement's emphasis on individual action or operations carried out by small cells of like-minded radicals made detection and prevention by the police particularly difficult, thus further heightening public fears. For example, following the assassination of US President William McKinley in 1901 (by a young Hungarian refugee, Leon Czolgocz, who, while not a regular member of any anarchist organization, was nonetheless influenced by the philosophy), Congress swiftly enacted legislation barring known anarchists or anyone 'who disbelieves in or is opposed to all organized government' from entering the United States. However, while anarchists were responsible for an impressive string of assassinations of heads of state and a number of particularly notorious bombings from about 1878 until the second decade of the twentieth century, in the final analysis, other than stimulating often exaggerated fears, anarchism made little tangible impact on either the domestic or the international politics of the countries affected. It does, however, offer an interesting historical footnote: much as the 'information revolution' of the late twentieth century is alleged to have made the means and methods of bomb-making and other types of terrorist activity more readily available via the Internet, on CD-ROM, and through ordinary libraries and bookstores, one of anarchism's flourishing 'cottage industries' more than a century earlier was the widespread distribution of similar 'how-to' or DIY-type manuals and publications of violence and mayhem.

On the eve of the First World War, terrorism still retained its revolutionary connotations. By this time, growing unrest and irredentist ferment had already welled up within the decaying Ottoman and Habsburg Empires. In the 1880s and 1890s, for example, militant Armenian nationalist movements in eastern Turkey pursued a terrorist strategy against continued Ottoman rule of a kind that would later be adopted by most of the post-Second World War ethnonationalist/separatist movements. The Armenians' objective was simultaneously to strike a blow against the despotic 'alien' regime through repeated attacks on its colonial administration and security forces, in order to rally indigenous support, as well as to attract international attention, sympathy and support. Around the same time, the Inner Macedonian Revolutionary Organization (IMRO) was active in the region overlapping present-day Greece, Bulgaria and Serbia. Although the Macedonians did not go on to suffer the catastrophic fate that befell the Armenians during the First World War (when an estimated one million persons perished in what is considered to be the first officially implemented genocide of the twentieth century), IMRO never came close to achieving its aim of an independent Macedonia and thereafter degenerated into a mostly criminal organization of hired thugs and political assassins.

The events immediately preceding the First World War in Bosnia are of course more familiar because of their subsequent cataclysmic impact on world affairs. There, similar groups of disaffected nationalists – Bosnian Serb intellectuals, university students and even schoolchildren, collectively known as Mlada Bosna, or Young Bosnians – arose against continued Habsburg suzerainty. While it is perhaps easy to dismiss the movement, as some historians have, as comprised of 'frustrated, poor, dreary and maladjusted' adolescents – much as many contemporary observers similarly denigrate modern-day terrorists as mindless, obsessive and maladjusted – it was a member of Young Bosnia, Gavrilo Princip, who is widely credited with having set in motion the chain of events that began on 28 June 1914, when he assassinated the Habsburg Archduke Franz Ferdinand in Sarajevo, and culminated in the First World War. Whatever its superficially juvenile characteristics, the group was nonetheless passionately dedicated to the attainment of a federal South Slav political entity – uniting Slovenes, Croats and Serbs – and resolutely committed to assassination as the vehicle with which to achieve that aim. In this respect, the Young Bosnians perhaps had more in common with the radical republicanism of Giuseppe Mazzini, one of the most ardent exponents of Italian unification in the nineteenth century, than with groups such as the Narodnaya Volya – despite a shared conviction in the efficacy of tyrannicide. An even more significant difference, however, was the degree of involvement in, and external support provided to, Young Bosnian activities by various shadowy Serbian nationalist groups. Principal among these was the pan-Serb secret society, the Narodna Obrana ('The People's Defence' or 'National Defence').

The Narodna Obrana had been established in 1908 originally to promote Serb cultural and national activities. It subsequently assumed a more subversive orientation as the movement became increasingly involved with anti-Austrian activities – including terrorism – mostly in neighbouring Bosnia and Hercegovina. Although the Narodna Obrana's exclusionist pan-Serbian aims clashed with the Young Bosnians' less parochial South Slav ideals, its leadership was quite happy to manipulate and exploit the Bosnians' emotive nationalism and youthful zeal for their own purposes. To this end, the Narodna Obrana actively recruited, trained and armed young Bosnians and Hercegovinians from movements such as the Young Bosnians who were then deployed in various seditious activities against the Habsburgs. As early as four years before the archduke's assassination, a Hercegovinian youth, trained by a Serb army officer with close ties to the Narodna Obrana, had attempted to kill the governor of Bosnia. But, while the Narodna Obrana included among its members senior Serbian government officials, it was not an explicitly government-controlled or directly state-supported entity.

Whatever hazy government links it maintained were further and deliberately obscured when a radical faction left the Narodna Obrana in 1911 and established the Ujedinjenje ili Start, 'The Union of Death' or 'Death or Unification' – more popularly known as the Crna Ruka, or the 'Black Hand'. This more militant and appreciably more clandestine splinter has been described by one historian as combining the more unattractive features of the anarchist cells of earlier years – which had been responsible for quite a number of assassinations in Europe and whose methods had a good deal of influence via the writings of Russian anarchists upon Serbian youth – and of the [American] Ku Klux Klan. There were gory rituals and oaths of loyalty, there were murders of backsliding members, there was identification of members by number, there were distributions of guns and bombs. And there was a steady traffic between Bosnia and Serbia.

This group, which continued to maintain close links with its parent body, was largely composed of serving Serbian military officers. It was led by Lieutenant-Colonel Dragutin Dmitrievich (known by his pseudonym, Apis), himself the chief of the Intelligence Department of the Serbian general staff. With this key additional advantage of direct access to military armaments, intelligence and training facilities, the Black Hand effectively took charge of all Serb-backed clandestine operations in Bosnia.

Although there were obviously close links between the Serbian military, the Black Hand and the Young Bosnians, it would be a mistake to regard the relationship as one of direct control, much less outright manipulation. Clearly, the Serbian government was well aware of the Black Hand's objectives and the violent means the group employed in pursuit of them; indeed, the Serbian Crown Prince Alexander was one of the group's benefactors. But this does not mean that the Serbian government was necessarily as committed to war with Austria as the Black Hand's leaders were, or that it was prepared to countenance the group's more extreme plans for fomenting cross-border, anti-Habsburg terrorism. There is some evidence to suggest that the Black Hand may have been trying to force Austria's hand against Serbia and thereby plunge both countries into war by actively abetting the Young Bosnians' plot to assassinate the archduke. Indeed, according to one revisionist account of the events leading up to the murder, even though the pistol used by Princip had been supplied by the Black Hand from a Serb military armoury in Kragujevac, and even though Princip had been trained by the Black Hand in Serbia before being smuggled back across the border for the assassination, at the eleventh hour Dmitrievich had apparently bowed to intense government pressure and tried to stop the assassination.

According to this version, Princip and his fellow conspirators would hear nothing of it and stubbornly went ahead with their plans. Contrary to popular assumption, therefore, the archduke's assassination may not have been specifically ordered or even directly sanctioned by the Serbian government. However, the obscure links between high government officials and their senior military commanders and ostensibly independent, transnational terrorist movements, and the tangled web of intrigue, plots, clandestine arms provision and training, intelligence agents and cross-border sanctuary these relationships inevitably involved, provide a pertinent historical parallel to the contemporary phenomenon known as 'state-sponsored' terrorism (that is, the active and often clandestine support, encouragement and assistance provided by a foreign government to a terrorist group), which is discussed below.

By the 1930s, the meaning of 'terrorism' had changed again. It was now used less to refer to revolutionary movements and violence directed against governments and their leaders, and more to describe the practices of mass repression employed by totalitarian states and their dictatorial leaders against their own citizens. Thus the term regained its former connotations of abuse of power by governments, and was applied specifically to the authoritarian regimes that had come to power in Fascist Italy, Nazi Germany and Stalinist Russia. In Germany and Italy respectively, the accession to office of Hitler and Mussolini had depended in large measure on the 'street' – the mobilization and deployment of gangs of brown- or black-shifted thugs to harass and intimidate political opponents and root out other scapegoats for public vilification and further victimization. 'Terror? Never,' Mussolini insisted, demurely dismissing such intimidation as 'simply ... social hygiene, taking those individuals out of circulation like a doctor would take out a bacillus'. The most sinister dimension of this form of 'terror' was that it became an intrinsic component of Fascist and Nazi governance, executed at the behest of, and in complete subservience to, the ruling political party of the land – which had arrogated to itself complete, total control of the country and its people. A system of government-sanctioned fear and coercion was thus created whereby political brawls, street fights and widespread persecution of Jews, communists and other declared 'enemies of the state' became the means through which complete and submissive compliance was ensured. The totality of party control over and perversion of, government was perhaps most clearly evinced by a speech given by Hermann Goering, the newly appointed Prussian minister of the interior, in 1933. 'Fellow Germans,' he declared,

My measures will not be crippled by any judicial thinking. My measures will not be crippled by any bureaucracy. Here I don't have to worry about Justice; my mission is only to destroy and exterminate nothing more. This struggle will be a struggle against chaos, and such a struggle I shall not conduct with the power of the police. A bourgeois State might have done that. Certainly, I shall use the power of the State and the police to the utmost, my dear Communists, so don't draw any false conclusions; but the struggle to the death, in which my fist will grasp your necks, I shall lead with those there the Brown Shirts.

The 'Great Terror' that Stalin was shortly to unleash in Russia both resembled and differed from that of the Nazis. On the one hand, drawing inspiration from Hitler's ruthless elimination of his own political opponents, the Russian dictator similarly transformed the political party he led into a servile instrument responsive directly to his personal will, and the state's police and security apparatus into slavish organs of coercion, enforcement and repression. But conditions in the Soviet Union of the 1930s bore little resemblance to the turbulent political, social and economic upheaval afflicting Germany and Italy during that decade and the previous one.

On the other hand, therefore, unlike either the Nazis or the Fascists, who had emerged from the political free-for-alls in their own countries to seize power and then had to struggle to consolidate their rule and retain their unchallenged authority, the Russian Communist Party had by the mid-1930s been firmly entrenched in power for more than a decade. Stalin's purges, in contrast to those of the French Revolution, and even to Russia's own recent experience, were not 'launched in time of crisis, or revolution and war ... [but] in the coldest of cold blood, when Russia had at last reached a comparatively calm and even moderately prosperous condition'. Thus the political purges ordered by Stalin became, in the words of one of his biographers, a 'conspiracy to seize total power by terrorist action', resulting in the death, exile, imprisonment or forcible impressment of millions.

Certainly, similar forms of state-imposed or state-directed violence and terror against a government's own citizens continue today. The use of so-called 'death squads' (often off-duty or plain-clothes security or police officers) in conjunction with blatant intimidation of political opponents, human rights and aid workers, student groups, labour organizers, journalists and others has been a prominent feature of the right-wing military dictatorships that took power in Argentina, Chile and Greece during the 1970s and even of elected governments in El Salvador, Guatemala, Colombia and Peru since the mid-1980s. But these state-sanctioned or explicitly ordered acts of internal political violence directed mostly against domestic populations – that is, rule by violence and intimidation by those already in power against their own citizenry – are generally termed 'terror' in order to distinguish that phenomenon from 'terrorism', which is understood to be violence committed by non-state entities.

Following the Second World War, in another swing of the pendulum of meaning, 'terrorism' regained the revolutionary connotations with which is it most commonly associated today. At that time, the term was used primarily in reference to the violent revolts then being prosecuted by the various indigenous nationalist/anti-colonialist groups that emerged in Asia, Africa and the Middle East during the late 1940s and 1950s to oppose continued European rule. Countries as diverse as Israel, Kenya, Cyprus and Algeria, for example, owe their independence at least in part to nationalist political movements that employed terrorism against colonial powers. It was also during this period that the 'politically correct' appellation of 'freedom fighters' came into fashion as a result of the political legitimacy that the international community (whose sympathy and support was actively courted by many of these movements) accorded to struggles for national liberation and self-determination. Many newly independent

Third World countries and communist bloc states in particular adopted this vernacular, arguing that anyone or any movement that fought against 'colonial' oppression and/or Western domination should not be described as 'terrorists', but were properly deemed to be 'freedom fighters'. This position was perhaps most famously explained by the Palestine Liberation Organization (PLO) chairman Yassir Arafat, when he addressed the United Nations General Assembly in November 1974. 'The difference between the revolutionary and the terrorist,' Arafat stated, 'lies in the reason for which each fights. For whoever stands by a just cause and fights for the freedom and liberation of his land from the invaders, the settlers and the colonialists, cannot possibly be called terrorist ...'

During the late 1960s and 1970s, terrorism continued to be viewed within a revolutionary context. However, this usage now expanded to include nationalist and ethnic separatist groups outside a colonial or neo-colonial framework as well as radical, entirely ideologically motivated organizations. Disenfranchised or exiled nationalist minorities – such as the PLO, the Quebecois separatist group FLQ (Front de Liberation du Quebec), the Basque ETA (Euskadi ta Askatasuna, or Freedom for the Basque Homeland) and even a hitherto unknown South Moluccan irredentist group seeking independence from Indonesia – adopted terrorism as a means to draw attention to themselves and their respective causes, in many instances with the specific aim, like their anti-colonial predecessors, of attracting international sympathy and support. Around the same time, various left-wing political extremists – drawn mostly from the radical student organizations and Marxist/Leninist/Maoist movements in Western Europe, Latin America and the United States – began to form terrorist groups opposing American intervention in Vietnam and what they claimed were the irredeemable social and economic inequities of the modern capitalist liberal-democratic state.

Although the revolutionary cum ethno-nationalist/separatist and ideological exemplars continue to shape our most basic understanding of the term, in recent years 'terrorism' has been used to denote broader, less distinct phenomena. In the early 1980s, for example, terrorism came to be regarded as a calculated means to destabilize the West as part of a vast global conspiracy. Books like The Terror Network by Claire Sterling propagated the notion to a receptive American presidential administration and similarly susceptible governments elsewhere that the seemingly isolated terrorist incidents perpetrated by disparate groups scattered across the globe were in fact linked elements of a massive clandestine plot, orchestrated by the Kremlin and implemented by its Warsaw Pact client states, to destroy the Free World. By the middle of the decade, however, a series of suicide bombings directed mostly against American diplomatic and military targets in the Middle East was focusing attention on the rising threat of state-sponsored terrorism. Consequently, this phenomenon – whereby various renegade foreign governments such as the regimes in Iran, Iraq, Libya and Syria became actively involved in sponsoring or commissioning terrorist acts – replaced communist conspiracy theories as the main context within which terrorism was viewed. Terrorism thus became associated with a type of covert or surrogate warfare whereby weaker states could confront larger, more powerful rivals without the risk of retribution.

In the early 1990s the meaning and usage of the term 'terrorism' were further blurred by the emergence of two new buzzwords: `narco-terrorism' and the so-called `gray area phenomenon'. The former term revived the Moscow-orchestrated terrorism conspiracy theories of previous years while introducing the critical new dimension of narcotics trafficking. Thus `narco-terrorism' was defined by one of the concept's foremost propagators as the `use of drug trafficking to advance the objectives of certain governments and terrorist organizations' – identified as the `Marxist-Leninist regimes' of the Soviet Union, Cuba, Bulgaria and Nicaragua, among others. The emphasis on `narco-terrorism' as the latest manifestation of the communist plot to undermine Western society, however, had the unfortunate effect of diverting official attention away from a bona fide emerging trend. To a greater extent than ever in the past, entirely criminal (that is, violent, economically motivated) organizations were now forging strategic alliances with terrorist and guerrilla organizations or themselves employing violence for specifically political ends. The growing power of the Colombian cocaine cartels, their close ties with left-wing terrorist groups in Colombia and Peru, and their repeated attempts to subvert Colombia's electoral process and undermine successive governments constitute perhaps the best-known example of this continuing trend.

Those who drew attention to this 'gray area phenomenon' were concerned less with grand conspiracies than with highlighting the increasingly fluid and variable nature of subnational conflict in the post-Cold War era. Accordingly, in the 1990s terrorism began to be subsumed by some analysts within the 'gray area phenomenon'. Thus the latter term came to be used to denote 'threats to the stability of nation states by non-state actors and non-governmental processes and organizations'; to describe violence affecting 'immense regions or urban areas where control has shifted from legitimate governments to new half-political, half-criminal powers'; or simply to group together in one category the range of conflicts across the world that no longer conformed to traditionally accepted notions of war as fighting between the armed forces of two or more established states, but instead involved irregular forces as one or more of the combatants. Terrorism had shifted its meaning again from an individual phenomenon of subnational violence to one of several elements, or part of a wider pattern, of non-state conflict.

TERRORISM SO DIFFICULT TO DEFINE? WHY

Not surprisingly, as the meaning and usage of the word have changed over time to accommodate the political vernacular and discourse of each successive era, terrorism has proved increasingly elusive in the face of attempts to construct one consistent definition. At one time, the terrorists themselves were far more cooperative in this endeavour than they are today. The early practitioners didn't mince their words or hide behind the semantic camouflage of more anodyne labels such as 'freedom fighter' or 'urban guerrilla'. The nineteenth-century anarchists, for example, unabashedly proclaimed themselves to be terrorists and frankly proclaimed their tactics to be terrorism. The members of Narodnaya Volya similarly displayed no qualms in using these same words to describe themselves and their deeds. However, such frankness did not last. The Jewish terrorist group of the 1940s known as Lehi (the Hebrew acronym for Lohamei Herut Yisrael, the Freedom Fighters for Israel, more popularly known simply as the Stern Gang after their founder and first leader, Abraham Stern) is thought to be one of the last terrorist groups actually to describe itself publicly as such. It is significant, however, that even Lehi, while it may have been far more candid than its latter-day counterparts, chose as the name of the organization not 'Terrorist Fighters for Israel', but the far less pejorative 'Freedom Fighters for Israel'.

Similarly, although more than twenty years later the Brazilian revolutionary Carlos Marighela displayed few compunctions about openly advocating the use of 'terrorist' tactics, he still insisted on depicting himself and his disciples as 'urban guerrillas' rather than 'urban terrorists'. Indeed, it is clear from Marighela's writings that he was well aware of the word's undesirable connotations, and strove to displace them with positive resonances. 'The words "aggressor" and "terrorist"', Marighela wrote in his famous Handbook of Urban Guerrilla War (also known as the 'Mini-Manual'), 'no longer mean what they did. Instead of arousing fear or censure, they are a call to action. To be called an aggressor or a terrorist in Brazil is now an honour to any citizen, for it means that he is fighting, with a gun in his hand, against the monstrosity of the present dictatorship and the suffering it causes.'

This trend towards ever more convoluted semantic obfuscations to side-step terrorism's pejorative overtones has, if anything, become more entrenched in recent decades. Terrorist organizations almost without exception now regularly select names for themselves that consciously eschew the word 'terrorism' in any of its forms. Instead these groups actively seek to evoke images of:

- Freedom and liberation (e.g. the National Liberation Front, the Popular Front for the Liberation of Palestine, Freedom for the Basque Homeland, etc.);
- Armies or other military organizational structures (e.g. the National Military Organization, the Popular Liberation Army, the Fifth Battalion of the Liberation

Army, etc.);

- Actual selfdefence movements (e.g. the Afrikaner Resistance Movement, the Shankhill Defence Association, the Organization for the Defence of the Free People, the Jewish Defense Organization, etc.);
- Righteous vengeance (the Organization for the Oppressed on Earth, the Justice Commandos of the Armenian Genocide, the Palestinian Revenge Organization, etc.); – or else deliberately choose names that are decidedly neutral and therefore bereft of all but the most innocuous suggestions or associations (e.g. the Shining Path, Front Line, al-Dawa ('The Call'), Alfaro Lives – Damn It!, Kach ('Thus'), al-Gamat al-Islamiya ('The Islamic Organization'), the Lantero Youth Movement, etc.).

What all these examples suggest is that terrorists clearly do not see or regard themselves as others do. 'Above all I am a family man,' the arch-terrorist Carlos, 'The Jackal', described him to a French newspaper following his capture in 1994. Cast perpetually on the defensive and forced to take up arms to protect themselves and their real or imagined constituents only, terrorists perceive themselves as reluctant warriors, driven by desperation – and lacking any viable alternative – to violence against a repressive state, a predatory rival ethnic or nationalist group, or an unresponsive international order. This perceived characteristic of self-denial also distinguishes the terrorist from other types of political extremists as well as from persons similarly involved in illegal, violent avocations. A communist or a revolutionary, for example, would likely readily accept and admit that he is in fact a communist or a revolutionary. Indeed, many would doubtless take particular pride in claiming either of those appellations for themselves. Similarly, even a person engaged in illegal, wholly disreputable or entirely selfish violent activities, such as robbing banks or carrying out contract killings, would probably admit to being a bank robber or a murderer for hire. The terrorist, by contrast, will never acknowledge that he is a terrorist and moreover will go to great lengths to evade and obscure any such inference or connection. Terry Anderson, the American journalist who was held hostage for almost seven years by the Lebanese terrorist organization Hezbollah, relates a telling conversation he had with one of his guards. The guard had objected to a newspaper article that referred to Hezbollah as terrorists.

'We are not terrorists,' he indignantly stated, 'we are fighters. ' Anderson replied, 'Hajj, you are a terrorist, look it up in the dictionary. You are a terrorist, you may not like the word and if you do not like the word, do not do it.' The terrorist will always argue that it is society or the government or the socio-economic 'system' and its laws that are the real 'terrorists', and moreover that if it were not for this oppression, he would not have felt the need to defend either himself or the population he claims to represent. Another revealing example of this process of obfuscation-projection may be found in the book Invisible Armies, written by Sheikh Muhammad Hussein Fadlallah, the spiritual leader of the Lebanese terrorist group responsible for Anderson's kidnapping. 'We don't see ourselves as terrorists,' Fadlallah explains, 'because we don't believe in terrorism. We don't see resisting the occupier as a terrorist action. We see ourselves as mujihadeen [holy warriors] who fight a Holy War for the people.'

On one point, at least, everyone agrees: terrorism is a pejorative term. It is a word with intrinsically negative connotations that is generally applied to one's enemies and opponents, or to those with whom one disagrees and would otherwise prefer to ignore. 'What is called terrorism', Brian Jenkins has written, 'thus seems to depend on one's point of view. Use of the term implies a moral judgement; and if one party can successfully attach the label terrorist to its opponent, then it has indirectly persuaded others to adopt its moral viewpoint.' Hence the decision to call someone or label some organization 'terrorist' becomes almost unavoidably subjective, depending largely on whether one sympathizes with or opposes the person/group/cause concerned. If one identifies with the victim of the violence, for example, then the act is terrorism. If, however, one identifies with the perpetrator, the violent act is regarded in a more sympathetic, if not positive (or, at the worst, an ambivalent) light; and it is not terrorism.

The implications of this associational logic were perhaps most clearly demonstrated in the exchanges between Western and non-Western member states of the United Nations following the 1972 Munich Olympics massacre, in which eleven Israeli athletes were killed. The debate began with the proposal by the then UN Secretary-General, Kurt Waldheim, that the UN should not remain a 'mute spectator' to the acts of terrorist violence then occurring throughout the world but should take practical steps that might prevent further bloodshed. While a majority of the UN member states supported the Secretary-General, a disputatious minority – including many Arab states and various African and Asian countries – derailed the discussion, arguing (much as Arafat would do two years later in his own address to the General Assembly) that 'people who struggle to liberate themselves from foreign oppression and exploitation have the right to use all methods at their disposal, including force'.

The Third World delegates justified their position with two arguments. First, they claimed that all bona fide liberation movements are invariably decried as 'terrorists' by the regimes against which their struggles for freedom are directed. The Nazis, for example, labelled as terrorists the resistance groups opposing Germany's occupation of their lands, Moulaye el-Hassen, the Mauritanian ambassador, pointed out, just as 'all liberation movements are described as terrorists by those who have reduced them to slavery'. Therefore, by condemning 'terrorism' the UN was endorsing the power of the strong over the weak and of the established entity over its non-established challenger – in effect, acting as the defender of the status quo. According to Chen Chu, the deputy representative of the People's Republic of China, the UN thus was proposing to deprive 'oppressed nations and peoples' of the only effective weapon they had with which to oppose 'imperialism, colonialism, neo-colonialism, racism and Israeli Zionism'. Second, the Third World delegates argued forcefully that it is not the violence itself that is germane, but its 'underlying causes': that is, the 'misery, frustration, grievance and despair' that produce the violent acts. As the Mauritanian representative again explained, the term 'terrorist' could 'hardly be held to apply to persons who were denied the most elementary human rights, dignity, freedom and independence, and whose countries objected to foreign occupation'. When the issue was again raised the following year, Syria objected on the grounds that 'the international community is under legal and moral obligation to promote the struggle for liberation and to resist any attempt to depict this struggle as synonymous with terrorism and illegitimate violence'. The resultant definitional paralysis subsequently throttled UN efforts to make any substantive progress on international cooperation against terrorism beyond very specific agreements on individual aspects of the problem (concerning, for example, diplomats and civil aviation).

The opposite approach, where identification with the victim determines the classification of a violent act as terrorism, is evident in the conclusions of a parliamentary working group of NATO (an organization comprised of long-established, status quo Western states). The final report of the 1989 North Atlantic Assembly's Subcommittee on Terrorism states: 'Murder, kidnapping, arson and other felonious acts constitute criminal behavior, but many non-Western nations have proved reluctant to condemn as terrorist acts what they consider to be struggles of national liberation.' In this reasoning, the defining characteristic of terrorism is the act of violence itself, not the motivations or justification for or reasons behind it. This approach has long been espoused by analysts such as Jenkins who argue that terrorism should be defined 'by the nature of the act, not by the identity of the perpetrators or the nature of their cause'. But this is not an entirely satisfactory solution either, since it fails to differentiate clearly between violence perpetrated by states and by non-state entities, such as terrorists. Accordingly, it plays into the hands of terrorists and their apologists who would argue that there is no difference between the 'low-tech' terrorist pipe-bomb placed in the rubbish bin at a crowded market that wantonly and indiscriminately kills or maims everyone within a radius measured in tens of feet and the 'high-tech' precision-guided ordnance dropped by air force fighter-bombers from a height of 20,000 feet or more that achieves the same wanton and indiscriminate effects on the crowded marketplace far below. This rationale thus equates the random violence inflicted on enemy population centres by military forces – such as the Luftwaffe's raids on Warsaw and Coventry, the Allied fire-bombings of Dresden and Tokyo, and the atomic bombs dropped by the United States on Hiroshima and Nagasaki during the Second World War, and indeed the countervalue strategy of the post-war superpowers' strategic nuclear policy, which deliberately targeted the enemy's civilian population – with the violence committed by substate entities labelled 'terrorists', since both involve the infliction of death and injury on noncombatants. Indeed, this was precisely the point made during the above-mentioned UN debates by the Cuban representative, who argued that 'the methods of combat used by national liberation movements could not be declared illegal while the policy of terrorism unleashed against certain peoples [by the armed forces of established states] was declared legitimate'.

It is a familiar argument. Terrorists, as we have seen, deliberately cloak themselves in the terminology of military jargon. They consciously portray themselves as bona fide (freedom) fighters, if not soldiers, who – though they wear no identifying uniform or insignia – are entitled to treatment as prisoners of war (POWs) if captured and therefore should not be prosecuted as common criminals in ordinary courts of law. Terrorists further argue that, because of their numerical inferiority, far more limited firepower and paucity of resources compared with an established nation-state's massive defence and national security apparatus, they have no choice but to operate clandestinely, emerging from the shadows to carry out dramatic (in other words, bloody and destructive) acts of hit-and-run violence in order to attract attention to, and ensure publicity for, themselves and their cause. The bomb-in-the-rubbish-bin, in their view, is merely a circumstantially imposed 'poor man's air force': the only means with which the terrorist can challenge – and get the attention of – the more powerful state. 'How else can we bring pressure to bear on the world?' one of Arafat's political aides once enquired. 'The deaths are regrettable, but they are a fact of war in which innocents have become involved. They are no more innocent than the Palestinian women and children killed by the Israelis and we are ready to carry the war all over the world.

But rationalizations such as these ignore the fact that, even while national armed forces have been responsible for far more death and destruction than terrorists might ever aspire to bring about, there nonetheless is a fundamental qualitative difference between the two types of violence. Even in war there are rules and accepted norms of behaviour that prohibit the use of certain types of weapons (for example, hollow-point or 'dum-dum' bullets, CS 'tear' gas, chemical and biological warfare agents), proscribe various tactics and outlaw attacks on specific categories of targets. Accordingly, in theory, if not always in practice, the rules of war – as observed from the early seventeenth century when they were first proposed by the Dutch jurist Hugo Grotius and subsequently codified in the famous Geneva and Hague Conventions on Warfare of the 1860s, 1899, 1907 and 1949 – not only grant civilian noncombatants immunity from attack, but also

- Prohibit taking civilians as hostages;
- Impose regulations governing the treatment of captured or surrendered soldiers (POWs);
- Outlaw reprisals against either civilians or POWs;
- Recognize neutral territory and the rights of citizens of neutral states; and
- Uphold the inviolability of diplomats and other accredited representatives.

Even the most cursory review of terrorist tactics and targets over the past quarter-century reveals that terrorists have violated all these rules. They not infrequently have

- Taken hostage civilians, whom in some instances they

have then brutally executed (e.g. the former Italian prime minister Aldo Moro and the German industrialist Hans Martin Schleyer, who were respectively taken captive and later murdered by the Red Brigades and the Red Army Faction);

- Similarly abused and murdered kidnapped military officers — even when they were serving on UN-sponsored peacekeeping or truce supervisory missions (e.g. the American Marine Lieutenant-Colonel William Higgins, the commander of a UN truce monitoring detachment, who was abducted by Lebanese Shi'a terrorists in 1989 and subsequently hanged);
- Undertaken reprisals against wholly innocent civilians, often in countries far removed from the terrorists' ostensible 'theatre of operation', thus disdaining any concept of neutral states or the rights of citizens of neutral countries (e.g. the brutal 1986 machine-gun and hand-grenade attack on Turkish Jewish worshippers at an Istanbul synagogue carried out by the Palestinian Abu Nidal Organization in retaliation for a recent Israeli raid on a guerrilla base in southern Lebanon); and
- Repeatedly attacked embassies and other diplomatic installations (e.g. the bombings of the US embassies in Beirut and Kuwait City in 1983 and 1984, and the mass hostage-taking at the Japanese ambassador's residence in Lima, Peru, in 1996-7), as well as deliberately targeting diplomats and other accredited representatives (e.g. the British ambassador to Uruguay, Sir Geoffrey Jackson, who was kidnapped by leftist terrorists in that country in 1971, and the fifty-two American diplomats taken hostage at the Tehran legation in 1979).

Admittedly, the armed forces of established states have also been guilty of violating some of the same rules of war. However, when these transgressions do occur — when civilians are deliberately and wantonly attacked in war or taken hostage and killed by military forces — the term 'war crime' is used to describe such acts and, imperfect and flawed as both international and national judicial remedies may be, steps nonetheless are often taken to hold the perpetrators accountable for these crimes. By comparison, one of the fundamental raisons d'etre of international terrorism is a refusal to be bound by such rules of warfare and codes of conduct. International terrorism disdains any concept of delimited areas of combat or demarcated battlefields, much less respect of neutral territory. Accordingly, terrorists have repeatedly taken their often parochial struggles to other, sometimes geographically distant, third party countries and there deliberately enmeshed persons completely unconnected with the terrorists' cause or grievances in violent incidents designed to generate attention and publicity.

The reporting of terrorism by the news media, which have been drawn into the semantic debates that divided the UN in the 1970s and continue to influence all discourse on terrorism, has further contributed to the obfuscation of the terrorist/'freedom fighter' debate, enshrining imprecision and implication as the lingua franca of political violence in the name of objectivity and neutrality. In striving to avoid appearing either partisan or judgemental, the American media, for example, resorted to describing terrorists – often in the same report – as variously guerrillas, gunmen, raiders, commandos and even soldiers. A random sample of American newspaper reports of Palestinian terrorist activities between June and December 1973, found in the terrorism archives and database maintained at the University of St Andrews in Scotland, provided striking illustrations of this practice. Out of eight headlines of articles describing the same incident, six used the word 'guerrillas' and only two 'terrorists' to describe the perpetrators. An interesting pattern was also observed whereby those accounts that immediately followed a particularly horrific or tragic incident – that is, involving the death and injury of innocent persons (in this instance, the attack on a Pan Am airliner at Rome airport, in which thirty-two passengers were killed) – tended to describe the perpetrators as 'terrorists' and their act as 'terrorism' (albeit in one case only in the headline, before reverting to the more neutral terminology of 'commando', 'militants', and 'guerrilla attack' in the text) more frequently than did reports of less serious or non-lethal incidents. One New York Times leading article, however, was far less restrained than the stories describing the actual incident, describing it as 'bloody' and 'mindless' and using the words 'terrorists' and 'terrorism' interchangeably with 'guerrillas' and 'extremists'. Only six months previously, however, the same newspaper had run a story about another terrorist attack that completely eschewed the terms 'terrorism' and 'terrorist', preferring 'guerrillas' and 'resistance' (as in 'resistance movement') instead. The Christian Science Monitor's reports of the Rome Pan Am attack similarly avoided 'terrorist' and 'terrorism' in favour of 'guerrillas' and 'extremists'; an Associated Press story in the next day's Los Angeles Times also stuck with 'guerrillas', while the two Washington Post articles on the same incident opted for the terms 'commandos' and 'guerrillas'.

This slavish devotion to terminological neutrality, which David Rapoport first observed over twenty years ago, is still in evidence today. A recent article appearing in the International Herald Tribune (a Paris-based newspaper published in conjunction with the New York Times and Washington Post) reported an incident in Algeria where thirty persons had been killed by perpetrators who were variously described as 'terrorists' in the article's headline, less judgementally as 'extremists' in the lead paragraph and as the still more ambiguous 'Islamic fundamentalists' in the article's third paragraph. In a country that since 1992 has been afflicted with an unrelenting wave of terrorist violence and bloodshed that has claimed the lives of an estimated 75,000 persons, one might think that the distinctions between 'terrorists', mere 'extremists' and ordinary 'fundamentalists' would be clearer. Yet fifty years ago the same newspaper apparently had fewer qualms about using the word 'terrorists' to describe the two young Jewish men in pre-independence Israel who, while awaiting execution after having been convicted of attacking British military targets, committed suicide. Other press accounts of the same period in The Times of London and the Palestine Post similarly had no difficulties, for example, in describing the 1946 bombing by Jewish terrorists of the British military headquarters and government secretariat located in Jerusalem's King David Hotel as a 'terrorist' act perpetrated by 'terrorists'. Similarly, in perhaps the most specific application of the term, the communist terrorists against whom the British fought in Malaya throughout the late 1940s and 1950s were routinely referred to as 'CTs' – for 'Communist terrorists'. As Rapoport warned in the 1970s, 'In attempting to correct the abuse of language for political purposes, our journalists may succeed in making language altogether worthless.'

The cumulative effect of this proclivity towards equivocation is that today there is no one widely accepted or agreed definition for terrorism. Different departments or agencies of even the same government will themselves often have very different definitions for terrorism. The US State Department, for example, uses the definition of terrorism contained in Title 22 of the United States Code, Section 2656f (d): Premeditated, politically motivated violence perpetrated against noncombatant targets by subnational groups or clandestine agents, usually intended to influence an audience.

While the US Federal Bureau of Investigation (FBI) defines terrorism as.

The unlawful use of force or violence against persons or property to intimidate or coerce a Government, the civilian population, or any segment thereof, in furtherance of political or social objectives, and the US Department of Defense defines it as

> The unlawful use of – or threatened use of – force or violence against individuals or property to coerce or intimidate governments or societies, often to achieve political, religious, or ideological objectives.

Not surprisingly, each of the above definitions reflects the priorities and particular interests of the specific agency involved. The State Department's emphasis is on the premeditated and planned or calculated nature of terrorism in contrast to more spontaneous acts of political violence. Its definition is also the only one of the three to emphasize both the ineluctably political nature of terrorism and the perpetrators' fundamental 'subnational' characteristic. The State Department definition, however, is conspicuously deficient in failing to consider the psychological dimension of terrorism. Terrorism is as much about the threat of violence as the violent act itself and, accordingly, is deliberately conceived to have far-reaching psychological repercussions beyond the actual target of the act among a wider, watching, 'target' audience. As Jenkins succinctly observed two decades ago, 'Terrorism is theatre.'

Given the FBI's mission of investigating and solving crimes – both political (e.g. terrorism) and other – it is not surprising that its definition focuses on different elements. Unlike the State Department, this definition does address the psychological dimensions of the terrorist act described above, laying stress on terrorism's intimidatory and coercive aspects. The FBI definition also identifies a much broader category of terrorist targets than only 'noncombatants', specifying not only governments and their citizens, but also inanimate objects, such as private and public property. The FBI definition further recognizes social alongside political objectives as fundamental terrorist aims – though it offers no clearer elucidation of either.

The Department of Defense definition of terrorism is arguably the most complete of the three. It highlights the terrorist threat as much as the actual act of violence and focuses on terrorism's targeting of whole societies as well as governments. The Defense Department definition further cites the religious and ideological aims of terrorism alongside its fundamental political objectives – but curiously omits the social dimension found in the FBI's definition.

It is not only individual agencies within the same governmental apparatus that cannot agree on a single definition of terrorism. Experts and other long-established scholars in the field are equally incapable of reaching a consensus. In the first edition of his magisterial survey, Political

Terrorism: A Research Guide, Alex Schmid devoted more than a hundred pages to examining more than a hundred different definitions of terrorism in an effort to discover a broadly acceptable, reasonably comprehensive explication of the word. Four years and a second edition later, Schmid was no closer to the goal of his quest, conceding in the first sentence of the revised volume that the 'search for an adequate definition is still on'. Walter Laqueur despaired of defining terrorism in both editions of his monumental work on the subject, maintaining that it is neither possible to do so nor worthwhile to make the attempt. 'Ten years of debates on typologies and definitions', he responded to a survey on definitions conducted by Schmid, 'have not enhanced our knowledge of the subject to a significant degree.'

At the end of this exhaustive exercise, Schmid asks 'whether the above list contains all the elements necessary for a good definition. The answer', he suggests, 'is probably "no".' If it is impossible to define terrorism, as Laqueur argues, and fruitless to attempt to cobble together a truly comprehensive definition, as Schmid admits, are we to conclude that terrorism is impervious to precise, much less accurate definition? Not entirely. If we cannot define terrorism, then we can at least usefully distinguish it from other types of violence and identify the characteristics that make terrorism the distinct phenomenon of political violence that it is.

3

Distinctions as a Path to Definition

Guerrilla warfare is a good place to start. Terrorism is often confused or equated with, or treated as synonymous with, guerrilla warfare. This is not entirely surprising, since guerrillas often employ the same tactics (assassination, kidnapping, bombings of public gathering-places, hostage-taking, etc.) for the same purposes (to intimidate or coerce, thereby affecting behaviour through the arousal of fear) as terrorists. In addition, both terrorists and guerrillas wear neither uniform nor identifying insignia and thus are often indistinguishable from noncombatants. However, despite the inclination to lump both terrorists and guerrillas into the same catch-all category of 'irregulars', there are nonetheless fundamental differences between the two. 'Guerrilla', for example, in its most widely accepted usage, is taken to refer to a numerically larger group of armed individuals, who operate as a military unit, attack enemy military forces, and seize and hold territory (even if only ephemerally during daylight hours), while also exercising some form of sovereignty or control over a defined geographical area and its population. Terrorists, however, do not function in the open as armed units, generally do not attempt to seize or hold territory, deliberately avoid engaging enemy military forces in combat and rarely exercise any direct control or sovereignty either over territory or population. It is also useful to distinguish terrorists from ordinary criminals. Like terrorists, criminals use violence as a means to attaining a specific end. However, while the violent act itself may be similar – kidnapping, shooting, arson, for example – the purpose or motivation clearly is not. Whether the criminal employs violence as a means to obtain money, to acquire material goods, or to kill or injure a specific victim for pay, he is acting primarily for selfish, personal motivations (usually material gain). Moreover, unlike terrorism, the ordinary criminal's violent act is not designed or intended to have consequences or create psychological repercussions beyond the act itself.

The criminal may of course use some short-term act of violence to 'terrorize' his victim, such as waving a gun in the face of a bank clerk during a robbery in order to ensure the clerk's expeditious compliance. In these instances, however, the bank robber is conveying no 'message' (political or otherwise) through his act of violence beyond facilitating the rapid handing over of his 'loot'. The criminal's act therefore is not meant to have any effect reaching beyond either the incident itself or the immediate victim. Further, the violence is neither conceived nor intended to convey any message to anyone other than the bank clerk himself, whose rapid cooperation is the robber's only objective. Perhaps most fundamentally, the criminal is not concerned with influencing or affecting public opinion: he simply wants to abscond with his money or accomplish his mercenary task in the quickest and easiest way possible so that he may reap his reward and enjoy the fruits of his labours. By contrast, the fundamental aim of the terrorist's violence is ultimately to change 'the system' – about which the ordinary criminal, of course, couldn't careless.

The terrorist is also very different from the lunatic assassin, who may use identical tactics (e.g. shooting, bombing) and perhaps even seeks the same objective (e.g. the death of a political figure). However, while the tactics and targets of terrorists and lone assassins are often identical, their purpose is not. Whereas the terrorist's goal is again ineluctably political (to change or fundamentally alter a political system through his violent act), the lunatic assassin's goal is more often intrinsically idiosyncratic, completely egocentric and deeply personal. John Hinckley, who tried to kill President Reagan in 1981 to impress the actress Jodie Foster, is a case in point. He acted not from political motivation or ideological conviction but to fulfil some profound personal quest (killing the president to impress his screen idol). Such entirely apolitical motivations can in no way be compared to the rationalizations used by the Narodnaya Volya to justify its campaign of tyrannicide against the tsar and his minions, nor even to the Irish Republican Army's efforts to assassinate Prime Minister Margaret Thatcher or her successor, John Major, in hopes of dramatically changing British policy towards Northern Ireland. Further, just as one person cannot credibly claim to be a political party, so a lone individual cannot be considered to constitute a terrorist group. In this respect, even though Sirhan Sirhan's assassination of presidential candidate and US Senator Robert Kennedy in 1968 had a political motive (to protest against US support for Israel), it is debatable whether the murder should be defined as a terrorist act since Sirhan belonged to no organized political group and acted entirely on his own, out of deep personal frustration and a profound animus that few others shared. To qualify as terrorism, violence must be perpetrated by some organizational entity with at least some conspiratorial structure and identifiable chain of command beyond a single individual acting on his or her own.

Finally, the point should be emphasized that, unlike the ordinary criminal or the lunatic assassin, the terrorist is not pursuing purely egocentric goals – he is not driven by the wish to line his own pocket or satisfy some personal need or grievance. The terrorist is fundamentally an altruist: he believes that he is serving a 'good' cause designed to achieve a greater good for a wider constituency – whether real or imagined – which the terrorist and his organization purport to represent. The criminal, by comparison, serves no cause at all, just his own personal aggrandizement and material satiation. Indeed, a 'terrorist without a cause (at least in his own mind)', Konrad Kellen has argued, 'is not a terrorist'. Yet the possession or identification of a cause is not a sufficient criterion for labelling someone a terrorist. In this key respect, the difference between terrorists and political extremists is clear.

Many persons, of course, harbour all sorts of radical and extreme beliefs and opinions, and many of them belong to radical or even illegal or proscribed political organizations. However, if they do not use violence in the pursuance of their beliefs, they cannot be considered terrorists. The terrorist is fundamentally a violent intellectual, prepared to use and indeed committed to using force in the attainment of his goals.

By distinguishing terrorists from other types of criminals and terrorism from other forms of crime, we come to appreciate that terrorism is

* Ineluctably political in aims and motives;
* Violent — or, equally important, threatens violence;
* Designed to have far-reaching psychological repercussions beyond the immediate victim or target;
* Conducted by an organization with an identifiable chain of command or conspiratorial cell structure (whose members wear no uniform or identifying insignia); and
* Perpetrated by a subnational group or non-state entity.

We may therefore now attempt to define terrorism as the deliberate creation and exploitation of fear through violence or the threat of violence in the pursuit of political change. All terrorist acts involve violence or the threat of violence. Terrorism is specifically designed to have far-reaching psychological effects beyond the immediate victim(s) or object of the terrorist attack. It is meant to instil fear within, and thereby intimidate, a wider 'target audience' that might include a rival ethnic or religious group, an entire country, a national government or politicaparty, or public opinion in general. Terrorism is designed to create power where there is none or to consolidate power where there is very little. Through the publicity generated by their violence, terrorists seek to obtain the leverage, influence and power they otherwise lack to effect political change on either a local or an international scale.

4

Terrorist Organisations

TERRORIST ORGANISATIONS

Abu Nidal Organization (ANO)
Abu Sayyaf Group (ASG)
Al-Aqsa Martyrs Brigade
Ansar al-Sunna (AS)
Armed Islamic Group (GIA)
Asbat al-Ansar
Aum Shinrikyo (Aum)
Basque Fatherland and Liberty (ETA)
Communist Party of Philippines/New People's Army (CPP/NPA)
Continuity Irish Republican Army (CIRA)
Gama'a al-Islamiyya (IG)
HAMAS
Harakat ul-Mujahedin (HUM)
Hizballah
Islamic Jihad Union (IJU)
Islamic Movement of Uzbekistan (IMU)
Jaish-e-Mohammed (JEM)
Jemaah Islamiya Organization (JI)
Al-Jihad (AJ)

Kahane Chai (Kach)

Kongra-Gel (KGK/PKK)

Lashkar e-Tayyiba (LT)

Lashkar i Jhangvi (LJ)

Liberation Tigers of Tamil Eelam (LTTE)

Libyan Islamic Fighting Group (LIFG)

Moroccan Islamic Combatant Group (GICM)

Mujahedin-e Khalq Organization (MEK)

National Liberation Army (ELN)

Palestine Liberation Front (PLF)

Palestinian Islamic Jihad (PIJ)

Popular Front for the Liberation of Palestine (PFLP)

Popular Front for the Liberation of Palestine-General Command (PFLP-GC)

Al-Qaida (AQ)

Al-Qaida in Iraq (AQI)

Al-Qaida in the Islamic Maghreb (AQIM) [Formerly Salafist Group for Call and Combat (GSPC)]

Real IRA (RIRA)

Revolutionary Armed Forces of Colombia (FARC)

Revolutionary Nuclei (RN)

Revolutionary Organization 17 November

Revolutionary People's Liberation Party/Front (DHKP/C)

Shining Path (SL)

United Self-Defense Forces of Colombia (AUC)

ABU NIDAL ORGANIZATION (ANO)

a.k.a. Arab Revolutionary Brigades; Arab Revolutionary Council; Black September; Fatah Revolutionary Council; Revolutionary Organization of Socialist Muslims.

Discription

The ANO international terrorist organization was

founded by Sabri al-Banna (a.k.a. Abu Nidal) after splitting from the Palestine Liberation Organization (PLO) in 1974. The group's previous known structure consisted of various functional committees, including political, military, and financial. In August 2002, Abu Nidal died in Baghdad; the new leadership of the organization remains unclear.

Activities

The ANO has carried out terrorist attacks in 20 countries, killing or injuring almost 900 persons; however, the group has not staged a major attack against Western targets since the late 1980s. Major attacks included the Rome and Vienna airports in 1985, the Neve Shalom synagogue in Istanbul, the hijacking of Pan Am Flight 73 in Karachi in 1986, and the City of Poros day-excursion ship attack in Greece in 1988. The ANO is suspected of assassinating PLO deputy chief Abu Iyad and PLO security Chief Abu Hul in Tunis in 1991. The ANO was responsible for the December 1985 simultaneous Rome and Vienna airport attacks in which 12 people died, including five American citizens.

Strength

Current strength and operational status are unknown.

Location/Area of Operation

Although former and possibly current ANO associates may be in Iraq and Lebanon, the group is largely considered inactive.

EXTERNAL AID

The ANO received considerable support, including safe haven, training, logistical assistance, and funding from Iraq, Libya, and Syria (until 1987). The ANO's current access to resources is unclear, but it is likely severely impacted by the decline in state support.

ABU SAYYAF GROUP (ASG)

a.k.a. Al Harakat al Islamiyya.

Description

The ASG is a violent Muslim terrorist group operating in the southern Philippines. Some ASG leaders allegedly fought in Afghanistan during the Soviet invasion and are students and proponents of radical Islamic teachings. The group split from the much larger Moro National Liberation Front in the early 1990s under the leadership of Abdurajak Abubakar Janjalani, who was killed in a clash with Philippine police in December 1998. His younger brother, Khadaffy Janjalani, replaced him as the nominal leader of the group. In September 2006, Janjalani was killed in a gun battle with the Armed Forces of the Philippines. Radullah Sahiron is assumed to be the new ASG leader.

Activities

The ASG engages in kidnappings for ransom, bombings, beheadings, assassinations, and extortion. The group's stated goal is to promote an independent Islamic state in western Mindanao and the Sulu Archipelago, areas in the southern Philippines heavily populated by Muslims, but the ASG primarily has used terror for financial profit. Recent bombings may herald a return to a more radical, politicized agenda, at least among certain factions. In August 2006, the Armed Forces of the Philippines began "Operation Ultimatum," a sustained campaign that has disrupted ASG forces in safe havens on Jolo Island in the Sulu archipelago, and resulted in the killing of ASG leader Khadafy Janjalani in September 2006.

The group's first large-scale action was a raid on the town of Ipil in Mindanao in April 1995. In April 2000, an ASG faction kidnapped 21 persons, including ten Western tourists, from a resort in Malaysia. In May 2001, the ASG kidnapped three U.S. citizens and 17 Filipinos from a tourist resort in Palawan, Philippines. Several of the hostages, including U.S. citizen Guillermo Sobero, were murdered. A Philippine military hostage rescue operation in June 2002 freed U.S. hostage Gracia Burnham, but her husband Martin Burnham and Filipina Deborah Yap were killed. U.S. and Philippine authorities blame the ASG for exploding a bomb near a Philippine military base in Zamboanga in October 2002 that killed a U.S. serviceman. In February 2004, Khadaffy Janjalani's faction bombed SuperFerry 14 in Manila Bay, killing 132. In March 2004, Philippine authorities arrested an ASG cell whose bombing targets included the U.S. Embassy in Manila. The ASG also claimed responsibility for the 2005 Valentine's Day bombings in Manila, Davao City, and General Santos City, which killed eight and injured more than 150.

Strength

ASG is estimated to have 200 to 500 members.

Location/Area of Operation

The ASG was founded in Basilan Province and operates primarily in the provinces of the Sulu Archipelago, namely Basilan, Sulu, and Tawi-Tawi. The group also operates on the Zamboanga peninsula and members occasionally travel to Manila. In mid-2003, the group started operating in Mindanao's city of Cotobato and on the provincial coast of Sultan Kudarat, Mindanao. The ASG was expelled from Mindanao proper by the Moro Islamic Liberation Front (MILF) in mid-2005. The group expanded its operational reach to Malaysia in 2000 with the abduction of foreigners from a tourist resort there.

External Aid

The ASG is funded through acts of ransom and extortion, and receives funding from both regional terrorist groups such as Jemaah Islamiya (JI), which is based mainly in Indonesia, and Middle Eastern Islamic extremists.

AL-AQSA MARTYRS BRIGADE (AL-AQSA)

a.k.a. al-Aqsa Martyrs Battalion; Fatah Tanzim.

Description

The al-Aqsa Martyrs Brigades consist of localized cells of Palestinian militants loyal to the secular-nationalist Fatah movement. Al-Aqsa emerged at the outset of the 2000

Palestinian al-Aqsa Intifadah, splitting from the Fatah party to attack Israeli military targets and settlers with the aim of driving Israel from the West Bank and Gaza Strip and establishing a Palestinian state. Al-Aqsa has no central leadership; the cells operate with autonomy, although they remained ideologically loyal to Palestinian Authority (PA) President and Fatah party head Yassir Arafat until his death in 2004.

Activities

Al-Aqsa initially focused on small arms attacks against Israeli military personnel and settlers in the West Bank. In 2002, the group began to conduct suicide bombings against Israeli civilians. After a March 2002 bombing, the U.S. State Department designated Al-Aqsa a foreign terrorist organization. Al-Aqsa suspended most anti-Israel attacks as part of the broader unilateral Palestinian ceasefire agreement during 2004 but resumed them following HAMAS's electoral victory in January 2006. Al-Aqsa members have continued anti-Israeli as well as intra-Palestinian violence and contribute to the overall chaotic security environment inside the Palestinian territories. Al-Aqsa has not targeted U.S. interests as a policy, although its anti-Israeli attacks have killed some dual U.S.-Israel citizens.

Strength

Current strength is unknown.

Location/Area of Operation

Al-Aqsa operates mainly in the West Bank but has conducted attacks inside Israel and the Gaza Strip. The group has members in refugee camps in southern Lebanon and overseas, although it has not demonstrated transnational capability.

External Aid

Iran has exploited Al-Aqsa's lack of leadership and funds by providing aid and exerting influence over the organization.

Ansar al-Sunna (AS)

a.k.a. Ansar al-Islam; Ansar Al-Sunna Army; Devotees of Islam; Followers of Islam in Kurdistan; Helpers of Islam; Jaish Ansar Al-Sunna; Jund Al-Islam; Kurdish Taliban; Kurdistan Supporters of Islam; Partisans of Islam; Soldiers of God; Soldiers of Islam; Supporters of Islam in Kurdistan.

Description

Ansar al-Sunna (AS) is a Salafi terrorist group whose goals include expelling the U.S.- led Coalition from Iraq and establishing an independent Islamic Iraqi state. This amorphous group has changed its name several times over the years and was last known as Ansar al-Islam. AS announced its creation in 2003 by posting a statement to the Internet calling all extremists in Iraq to unite under the new name. The bid to become a jihadist umbrella organization failed, but the name AS stuck. AS has ties to the al-Qaida central leadership and al-Qaida in Iraq (AQI); it has a competitive relationship with AQI, and did not join the AQI-dominated "Islamic State of Iraq."

Some members of AS trained in al-Qaida camps in Afghanistan, and the group provided safe haven to al-Qaida fighters before Operation Iraqi Freedom (OIF). Since OIF, AS has become the second-most prominent group engaged in anti-Coalition attacks in Iraq behind AQI and has maintained a strong propaganda campaign.

Activities

Continues to conduct attacks against a wide range of targets that includes Coalition Forces, the Iraqi government and security forces, and Kurdish and Shia figures. AS has claimed responsibility for many high profile attacks, including the simultaneous suicide bombings of the Patriotic Union of Kurdistan and Kurdistan Democratic Party offices in Irbil in February 2004, the bombing of the U.S. military dining facility in Mosul in December 2004, and numerous kidnappings, executions, and assassinations.

Strength

Precise numbers are unknown, but AS is the second largest Sunni jihadist group in Iraq, behind AQI.

Location/Area of Operation

Primarily central, western, and northern Iraq.

External Aid

Receives assistance from a loose network of associates in Europe and the Middle East.

Armed Islamic Group (GIA)

a.k.a. Al-Jama'ah al-Islamiyah al-Musallah; Groupement Islamique Arme .

Description

An Islamic extremist group, the GIA aims to overthrow the Algerian regime and replace it with a fundamentalist Islamic state. The GIA began its violent activity in 1992 after the military government suspended legislative elections in anticipation of an overwhelming victory by the Islamic Salvation Front, the largest Islamic opposition party.

Activities

The GIA has engaged in attacks against civilians and government workers. The GIA began conducting a terrorist campaign of civilian massacres in 1992, sometimes wiping out entire villages and killing tens of thousands of Algerians, thus alienating itself from the Algerian populace in the process.

Since announcing its campaign against foreigners living in Algeria in 1992, the GIA killed more than 100 expatriate men and women, mostly Europeans, in the country. Many of the GIA's members have joined other Islamist groups or have been killed or captured by the Algerian government. The government's September 2005 reconciliation program led to an increase in the number of GIA terrorist suspects who surrendered to security forces. The GIA's most recent significant attacks occurred in August 2001.

Strength

Precise numbers are unknown, but probably fewer than 100.

Location/Area of Operation

Algeria, the Sahel, and Europe.

External Aid

The GIA has members in Europe that provide funding but mostly the group engages in criminal activity to finance activities and raise funds.

Asbat al-Ansar

a.k.a. League of the Followers; Partisans' League.

Description

Asbat al-Ansar, the League of the Followers or Partisans' League, is a Lebanon-based Sunni extremist group composed primarily of Palestinians with links to Usama bin Ladin's al-Qaida organization and other Sunni extremist groups. Asbat is well positioned to play an important role should al-Qaida attempt to expand further its terrorist operations to Lebanon. The group follows an extremist interpretation of Islam that justifies violence against civilian targets to achieve political ends. Some of the group's goals include overthrowing the Lebanese government and thwarting perceived anti-Islamic and pro-Western influences in the country.

Activities

Asbat al-Ansar maintains close ties with the al-Qaida network, and had a "front-line" command post relatively close to Israel's border in the Ain al-Hilwah (Palestinian) refugee camp. In early to mid-March, Lebanese authorities arrested several members of the group. Some were Palestinians, some were Lebanese. Members of this group were believed by some to have been responsible for a Katyusha rocket attack on the Galilee (Israel) in December 2005. On April 3, 2006, a video was posted to an Islamic website claiming that five members of Asbat al-Ansar were killed fighting in Iraq; the date of death was not provided. Asbat al-Ansar members have been involved in fighting Coalition Forces in Iraq since at least 2005 and several members of the group have been killed in anti-Coalition operations.

Since it first emerged in the early 1990s, Asbat al-Ansar has carried out multiple terrorist attacks in Lebanon; in the mid-1990s the group assassinated Lebanese religious leaders and bombed nightclubs, theaters, and liquor stores. It was involved in clashes in northern Lebanon in December 1999, and carried out a rocket-propelled grenade attack on the Russian Embassy in Beirut in January 2000. Asbat al-Ansar's leader, Ahmad Abd al-Karim al-Sa'di a.k.a. Abu Muhjin, remains at large despite being sentenced to death in absentia for the 1994 murder of a Muslim cleric. In September 2004, operatives with links to the group were believed to be involved in a planned terrorist operation targeting the Italian Embassy, the Ukrainian Consulate General, and Lebanese government offices. In October 2004, Mahir al-Sa'di, a member of Asbat al-Ansar, was sentenced in absentia to life imprisonment for plotting to assassinate then U.S. Ambassador to Lebanon David Satterfield in 2000. Al-Sa'di was working in cooperation with Abu Muhammad al-Masri, the head of al-Qaida at the 'Ayn al-Hilwah refugee camp, where fighting has occurred between Asbat al-Ansar and Fatah elements.

Strength

The group commands about 300 fighters in Lebanon.

Location/Area of Operation

The group's primary base of operations is the 'Ayn al-Hilwah Palestinian refugee camp near Sidon in southern Lebanon.

External Aid

Probably receives money through international Sunni extremist networks.

AUM SHINRIKYO (AUM)

a.k.a. A.I.C. Comprehensive Research Institute; A.I.C. Sogo Kenkyusho; Aleph; Aum Supreme Truth.

Description

Shoko Asahara established Aum in 1987, and the cult received legal status as a religious entity in 1989. At first, Aum aimed to take over Japan and then the world, but over time it began to emphasize the imminence of the end of the world. Asahara predicted 1996, and 1999 to 2003, as likely dates and said that the United States would initiate Armageddon by starting World War III with Japan. The Japanese government revoked its recognition of Aum as a religious organization following Aum's deadly sarin gas attack in Tokyo in March 1995.

In 1997, however, a government panel decided not to invoke the Operations Control Law against the group that would have outlawed it. A 1999 law authorized the Japanese government to maintain police surveillance over the group because of concerns that Aum might launch future terrorist attacks. Under the leadership of Fumihiro Joyu, the chief of Aum's once thriving Moscow operation, Aum changed its name to Aleph in January 2000 and tried to distance itself from the violent and apocalyptic teachings of its founder. In late 2003, however, Joyu stepped down under pressure from members who wanted to return fully to the worship of Asahara. A growing divide between members supporting Joyu and those who remain loyal to Asahara is splitting the cult into factions. In 2006, Joyu officially split from Aleph over recognizing Shoko Asahara as the sole authority.

Activities

In March 1995, Aum members simultaneously released the chemical nerve agent sarin on several Tokyo subway trains, killing 12 persons and causing up to 6,000 to seek medical treatment. Subsequent investigations by the Japanese government revealed the group was responsible for other mysterious chemical incidents in Japan in 1994, including a sarin gas attack on a residential neighborhood in Matsumoto that killed seven and hospitalized approximately 500. The group's attempts to conduct attacks using biological agents were unsuccessful. Japanese police arrested Asahara in May 1995, and in February 2004 authorities sentenced him in to death for his role in the 1995 attacks. In September 2006, Asahara lost his final appeal against the death penalty.

Since 1997, the cult has recruited new members, engaged in commercial enterprises, and acquired property, although it scaled back these activities significantly in 2001 in response to a public outcry. In July 2001, Russian authorities arrested a group of Russian Aum followers who had planned to set off bombs near the Imperial Palace in Tokyo as part of an operation to free Asahara from jail and smuggle him to Russia.

Strength

Aum's current membership in Japan is estimated to be about 1,650 persons. At the time of the Tokyo subway attack, the group claimed to have as many as 40,000 members worldwide, including 9,000 in Japan and 30,000 members in Russia.

Location/Area of Operation

Aum's principal membership is located in Japan, while a residual branch comprising about 300 followers lives in Russia.

External Aid

None.

BASQUE FATHERLAND AND LIBERTY (ETA)

a.k.a. Askatasuna; Batasuna; Ekin; Epanastatiki Pirines; Euskal Herritarrok; Euzkadi Ta Askatasuna; Herri Batasuna; Jarrai-Haika-Segi; K.A.S.; Popular Revolutionary Struggle; XAKI.

Description

ETA was founded in 1959 with the aim of establishing an independent homeland based on Marxist principles encompassing the Spanish Basque provinces of Vizcaya,

Guipuzcoa, and Alava, as well as the autonomous region of Navarra and the southwestern French territories of Labourd, Basse-Navarre, and Soule. Spain and the European Union both have listed ETA as a terrorist organization, and in 2002 the Spanish parliament banned the political party Batasuna, ETA's political wing, charging its members with providing material support to the terrorist group.

In 2004, Spain and France formed a joint counterterrorism and judicial unit to combat ETA and Islamic terrorist groups. During 2005 and 2006, police in both countries together arrested around 100 individuals associated with ETA, dismantled several of the group's cells, and dealt a significant blow to its operational capability. Spanish and French prisons are estimated to hold a total of more than 500 ETA members. In March 2006, ETA announced that it would implement a "permanent" ceasefire. On December 30, ETA exploded a massive car-bomb that destroyed much of the covered parking garage outside the new Terminal 4 of Madrid's Barajas International Airport and effectively broke its nine-month "permanent ceasefire." Two individuals killed in the blast became ETA's first fatalities in more than three years. The Government of Spain suspended talks with ETA, and government officials subsequently said political negotiations with the group had ended.

Activities

ETA primarily conducts bombings and assassinations; targets are typically Spanish government officials, security and military forces, politicians, and judicial figures, but the group also has targeted journalists and tourist areas. The group is responsible for killing more than 800 and injuring thousands more since it began its lethal attacks in the late 1960s. Security service scrutiny and a public outcry after the Islamic extremist train bombings in Madrid in March 2004, have limited ETA's capability and willingness to inflict casualties. ETA conducted no fatal attacks in 2005, but did mount more than 30 low-level bombings, most preceded by a warning call, that caused minor injuries and property damage. In February 2005, ETA detonated a car bomb in Madrid at a convention center where Spanish King Juan Carlos and then Mexican President Vicente Fox were scheduled to appear, wounding more than 20 people.

In June 2005, ETA launched grenades at the airport that serves the city of Zaragoza, shutting down the airport but causing no damage or injuries. ETA also detonated an explosive device at a stadium constructed as part of Madrid's bid to host the 2012 Olympic Games; there were no injuries in that attack. Just days before its March 2006 cease-fire announcement, ETA claimed responsibility for a spate of roadside blasts in northern Spain that caused no injuries. Its late 2006 attack at Madrid's airport is the group's first fatal attack since March 2003. ETA finances its activities primarily through bribery and extortion.

Strength

Not precisely known, but believed to number in the low hundreds.

Location/Area of Operation

Operates primarily in the Basque autonomous regions of northern Spain and southwestern France, but also has attacked Spanish and French interests elsewhere.

External Aid

Has received training at various times in the past in Libya, Lebanon, and Nicaragua. Some ETA members allegedly fled to Cuba and Mexico, while others reside in South America. ETA members have operated and been arrested in other European countries, including Belgium, the Netherlands, and Germany.

COMMUNIST PARTY OF PHILIPPINES/NEW PEOPLE'S ARMY (CPP/NPA)

a.k.a. Communist Party of the Philippines; CPP; New People's Army; NPA.

Description

The military wing of the Communist Party of the Philippines (CPP), the NPA is a Maoist group formed in March 1969 with the aim of overthrowing the government through protracted guerrilla warfare. Jose Maria Sison, the chairman of the CPP's Central Committee and the NPA's founder, reportedly directs CPP and NPA activity from the Netherlands, where he lives in self-imposed exile. Luis Jalandoni, a fellow Central Committee member and director of the CPP's overt political wing, the National Democratic Front (NDF), also lives in the Netherlands and has become a Dutch citizen. Although primarily a rural-based guerrilla group, the NPA has an active urban infrastructure to support its terrorist activities and at times uses city-based assassination squads.

Activities

The NPA primarily targets Philippine security forces, government officials, local infrastructure, and businesses that refuse to pay extortion, or "revolutionary taxes." The NPA extorts politicians running for office in NPA-influenced areas, charging them for "campaign permits." The group opposes any U.S. military presence in the Philippines and in the past has attacked U.S. military interests; it killed several U.S. service personnel before the U.S. base closures in 1992. The NPA claimed responsibility for the assassination of two congressmen, from Quezon in May 2001 and Cagayan in June 2001, among other killings. Periodic peace talks with the Philippine government stalled after these incidents. In December 2005, the NPA publicly expressed its intent to target U.S. personnel if they were discovered in NPA operating areas.

Strength

Estimated at less than 9,000 in number significantly lower than its peak strength of approximately 25,000 in the 1980s.

Location/Area of Operations

Operates in rural Luzon, Visayas, and parts of northern

and eastern Mindanao. Has cells in Manila and other metropolitan centers.

External Aid

Unknown

CONTINUITY IRISH REPUBLICAN ARMY (CIRA)

a.k.a. Continuity Army Council; Continuity IRA; Republican Sinn Fein.

Description

CIRA is a terrorist splinter group formed in 1994 as the clandestine armed wing of Republican Sinn Fein, which split from Sinn Fein in 1986. "Continuity" refers to the group's belief that it is carrying on the original Irish Republican Army's (IRA) goal of forcing the British out of Northern Ireland. CIRA's aliases, Continuity Army Council and Republican Sinn Fein, are included in its FTO designation. CIRA cooperates with the larger Real IRA (RIRA).

Activities

CIRA has been active in Belfast and the border areas of Northern Ireland, where it has carried out bombings, assassinations, kidnappings, hijackings, extortion, and robberies. On occasion, it has provided advance warning to police of its attacks. Targets have included the British military, Northern Ireland security forces, and Loyalist paramilitary groups. CIRA did not join the Provisional IRA in the September 2005 decommissioning and remains capable of effective, if sporadic, terrorist attacks. In late 2006 CIRA members issued a list of up to 20 individuals they were targeting for paramilitary attacks, several of whom were wounded in subsequent shootings.

Strength

Membership is small, with possibly fewer than 50 hardcore activists. Police counterterrorist operations have reduced the group's strength, but CIRA continues to recruit, train, and plan operations.

Location/Area of Operation

Northern Ireland and the Irish Republic. Does not have an established presence in Great Britain.

External Aid

Suspected of receiving funds and arms from sympathizers in the United States. May have acquired arms and material from the Balkans in cooperation with the Real IRA.

GAMA'A AL-ISLAMIYYA (IG)

a.k.a. Al-Gama'at; Egyptian al-Gama'at al-Islamiyya; Islamic Gama'at (IG); Islamic Group.

DESCRIPTION

The IG, Egypt's largest militant group, has been active since the late 1970s and is a loosely organized network, whose primary goal is to overthrow the Egyptian government and replace it with an Islamic state. It has an external wing with supporters in several countries. The group's issuance of a ceasefire in 1997 led to a split into two factions: one, led by Mustafa Hamza, supported the ceasefire; the other, led by Rifa'i Taha Musa, called for a return to armed operations. The IG issued another ceasefire in March 1999, but its spiritual leader, Shaykh Umar Abd al-Rahman, sentenced to life in prison in January 1996 for his involvement in the 1993 World Trade Center bombing and incarcerated in the United States, and rescinded his support for the ceasefire in June 2000. IG has not conducted an attack inside Egypt since the 1997 Luxor attack, which killed 58 tourists, four Egyptians, and wounded dozens more. In February 1998, a senior member signed Usama bin Ladin's fatwa calling for attacks against the United States.

In early 2001, Taha Musa published a book in which he attempted to justify terrorist attacks that would cause mass casualties. Taha Musa disappeared several months thereafter, and there is no information as to his current whereabouts. In

March 2002, members of the group's historic leadership in Egypt declared use of violence misguided and renounced its future use, prompting denunciations by much of the leadership abroad. The Egyptian government continues to release IG members from prison; approximately 900 were released in 2003, and most of the 700 persons released in 2004 at the end of the Muslim holy month of Ramadan were IG members. Ayman al-Zawahiri announced in August 2006 that IG had merged with al-Qaida, but the group quickly denied this claim.

Activities

IG conducted armed attacks against Egyptian security and other government officials, Coptic Christians, and Egyptian opponents of Islamic extremism before the 1997 ceasefire; after the ceasefire, the faction led by Taha Musa launched attacks on tourists in Egypt, most notably the 1997 Luxor attack. IG claimed responsibility for the June 1995 assassination attempt on Egyptian President Hosni Mubarak in Addis Ababa, Ethiopia.

Strength

Unknown and at its peak IG probably commanded several thousand hardcore members and a like number of sympathizers. The 1999 ceasefire, security crackdowns following the 1997 attack in Luxor, and post-September 11 security efforts, have probably resulted in a substantial decrease in the group's numbers.

Location/Area of Operation

IG Operates mainly in the Al-Minya, Asyut, Qina, and Sohaj Governorates of southern Egypt. It also appears to have support in Cairo, Alexandria, and other urban locations, particularly among unemployed graduates and students. The IG has an external presence, including in the United Kingdom, Afghanistan, Yemen, and in various locations in Europe.

External Aid

Unknown. Usama Bin Ladin and Afghan militant groups

support the organization. IG also may obtain some funding through various Islamic non-governmental organizations.

THE ISLAMIC RESISTANCE MOVEMENT (HAMAS)

a.k.a. Harakat al-Muqawama al-Islamiya; Izz al-Din al Qassam Battalions; Izz al-Din al Qassam Brigades; Students of Ayyash; Students of the Engineer; Yahya Ayyash Units.

Description

HAMAS, which includes military and political wings, was formed at the onset of the first Palestinian uprising or Intifadah in late 1987, as an outgrowth of the Palestinian branch of the Muslim Brotherhood. The armed element, called the Izz al-Din al-Qassam Brigades, conducts anti-Israeli attacks, including suicide bombings against civilian targets inside Israel. Social-political elements engage in "Dawa" or ministry activities, includes running charities and schools, fund-raising and political activities. A Shura council based in Damascus, Syria, sets overall policy. Since winning Palestinian Authority (PA) elections in 2006, HAMAS has taken control of significant PA ministries, including the Ministry of Interior. HAMAS formed an expanded, overt militia called the Executive Force, subordinate to the Ministry.

Activities

Prior to 2005, HAMAS conducted numerous anti-Israeli attacks including suicide bombings, rocket attacks, IED attacks, and shootings. The group curtailed terrorist attacks in February 2005 after agreeing to a temporary period of calm brokered by the PA, and ceased most violence after winning control of the PA legislature and cabinet in 2006. After HAMAS staged a June 25 attack on IDF soldiers near Kerem Shalom that resulted in two deaths and the abduction of Corporal Gilad Shalit, Israel took steps that severely limited the operation of the Rafah crossing. HAMAS maintained and expanded its military capabilities during this time. HAMAS has not directly targeted U.S. interests, although the group makes little or no effort to avoid targets frequented by foreigners.

Strength

HAMAS probably has several hundred members in its armed wing, the al-Qassam Brigades, along with its reported 6,000-man Executive Force and tens of thousands of supporters and sympathizers.

Location/Area of Operation

HAMAS has an operational presence in every major city within the Palestinian territories and has focused its anti-Israeli attacks on targets in those territories and Israel. The group retains a cadre of leaders and facilitators that conduct diplomatic, fundraising, and arms smuggling activities in Lebanon, Syria, and other states.

External Aid

Receives some funds, weapons and training from Iran. Also receives donations from Palestinian expatriates around the world and private benefactors in Arab states. Some fundraising and propaganda activity takes place in Western Europe and North America.

HARADAT UL-MUJAHEDIN (HUM)

a.k.a. Al-Faran; Al-Hadid; Al-Hadith; Harakat ul-Ansar; Harakat ul-Mujahideen; HUA; Jamiat ul-Ansar (JUA).

Description

HUM, an Islamic militant group based in Pakistan, is politically aligned with the radical political party Jamiat Ulema-i-Islam's Fazlur Rehman faction (JUI-F), and operates primarily in Kashmir. Reportedly under pressure from the Government of Pakistan, HUM's long time leader Fazlur Rehman Khalil stepped down and, in January 2005, was replaced by Dr. Badr Munir as the head of HUM. Khalil has been linked to Usama bin Ladin, and his signature was found on Bin Ladin's fatwa in

February 1998 calling for attacks on U.S. and Western interests.

HUM operated terrorist training camps in eastern Afghanistan until Coalition air strikes destroyed them in autumn 2001. Khalil was detained by Pakistani authorities in mid-2004 and subsequently released in late December. In 2003, HUM began using the name Jamiat ul-Ansar (JUA). Pakistan banned JUA in November 2003.

Activities

HUM has conducted a number of operations against Indian troops and civilian targets in Kashmir. It is linked to the Kashmiri militant group al-Faran that kidnapped five Western tourists in Kashmir in July 1995; one was killed in August, and the other four reportedly were killed in December of the same year. HUM was responsible for the hijacking of an Indian airliner in December 1999 that resulted in the release of Masood Azhar, an important leader in the former Harakat ul-Ansar who was imprisoned by India in 1994 and founded Jaish-e-Mohammed (JEM) after his release. Ahmed Omar Sheik also was released in 1999, and was later convicted of the abduction and murder in 2002 of U.S. journalist Daniel Pearl.

Strength

HUM has several hundred armed supporters located in Azad Kashmir, Pakistan, and India's southern Kashmir and Doda regions and in the Kashmir valley. Supporters are mostly Pakistanis and Kashmiris, but also include Afghans and Arab veterans of the Afghan war. HUM uses light and heavy machine guns, assault rifles, mortars, explosives, and rockets. In 2000, HUM lost a significant share of its membership in defections to the JEM.

Location/Area of Operation

Based in Muzaffarabad, Rawalpindi, and several other towns in Pakistan, HUM conducts insurgent and terrorist operations primarily in Kashmir, but members have also been found operating in Afghanistan. HUM trains its militants in Afghanistan and Pakistan.

External Aid

Collects donations from wealthy and grassroots donors in Pakistan, Kashmir, Saudi Arabia, and other Gulf and Islamic states. HUM's financial collection methods also include soliciting donations in magazine ads and pamphlets. The sources and amount of HUM's military funding are unknown. Its overt fundraising in Pakistan has been constrained since the government clampdown there on extremist groups and the freezing of terrorist assets.

HIZBALLAH

(Common alternate spellings: Hezbollah, Hizbullah, Hizb'allah)

a.k.a. Party of God; Islamic Jihad.

Description

Formed in 1982 in response to the Israeli invasion of Lebanon, this Lebanese-based radical Shia group takes its ideological inspiration from the Iranian revolution and the teachings of the late Ayatollah Khomeini. The group follows the religious guidance of Khomeini's successor, Iranian Supreme Leader Ali Khamenei. Hizballah is closely allied with Iran and often acts at its behest, but it also can and does act independently. Although Hizballah does not share the Syrian regime's secular orientation, the group has been a strong ally in helping Syria advances its political objectives in the region. The Majlis al-Shura, or Consultative Council, is the group's highest governing body and has been led by Secretary General Hasan Nasrallah since 1992.

Hizballah remains the most technically capable terrorist group in the world. It has strong influence in Lebanon's Shia community, which comprises about one-third of Lebanon's population. The Lebanese government still recognizes Hizballah as a legitimate "resistance group" and political party. Hizballah maintains offices in Beirut and elsewhere in the country, has official liaison officers to the security services, claims 14 elected officials in the 128-seat

Lebanese National Assembly and was represented in the Cabinet for the first time, by the Minister of Water and Electricity Mohammed Fneish, until his resignation, along with other Shia ministers on November 11, 2006. Hizballah has largely withdrawn its military presence from southern Lebanon in accordance with UNSCR 1701, although likely maintains weapons caches in southern Lebanon and justifies its continued arms status by claiming to act in defense of Lebanon against acts of Israeli aggression, such as regular Israeli overflights of Lebanese airspace. Hizballah alleges that Israel has not withdrawn completely from Lebanese territory because, in Hizballah's view, the Shebaa Farms and other areas belong to Lebanon. Hizballah supports a variety of violent anti-Western groups, including Palestinian terrorist organizations. This support includes the covert provision of weapons, explosives, training, funding, and guidance, as well as ov.ert political support.

Activities

In 2006, Hizballah launched a number of attacks on Israel, including the May 28 and July 12 attack, which resulted in the capture and kidnapping of two Israeli soldiers. Hizballah continued to call for the destruction of Israel and provided support to select Palestinian groups to augment their capacity to conduct attacks against Israel. Since at least 2004, Hizballah has provided training and logistics to select Iraqi Shia militants, including for the construction and use of shaped charge IEDs, which Hizballah developed against Israeli forces in southern Lebanon during the late 1990s and which can penetrate heavily armored vehicles. Hizballah is known to have been involved in numerous anti-U.S. and anti-Israeli terrorist attacks, and prior to September 11, 2001, was responsible for more American deaths than any other terrorist group; its terrorist attacks have included the suicide truck bombings of the U.S. Embassy and U.S. Marine barracks in Beirut in 1983 and the U.S. Embassy annex in Beirut in 1984. Four members of Hizballah, Imad Mughniyah, Hasan Izz-al-Din, Mohammed Hamadei, and Ali Atwa, are on the FBI's list of most wanted terrorists for the 1985 hijacking of TWA flight 847, during which a U.S. Navy diver was murdered. Elements of the group were responsible for the kidnapping, detention, and murder of Americans and other Westerners in Lebanon in the 1980s. Hizballah also has been implicated in the attacks on the Israeli Embassy in Argentina in 1992 and the Argentine-Israeli Mutual Association (AMIA) in Buenos Aires in 1994.

The U.S. Government has indicted a member of Lebanese Hizballah for his participation in the June 1996 truck bomb attack of the U.S. Air Force dormitory at Khobar Towers in Saudi Arabia. In 2000, Hizballah operatives captured three Israeli soldiers in the Sheba'a Farms area and kidnapped an Israeli non-combatant.

Strength

Thousands of supporters and members, and few hundred terrorist operatives.

Location/Area of Operation

Operates in the southern suburbs of Beirut, the Beka'a Valley, and southern Lebanon and has established cells in Europe, Africa, South America, North America, and Asia.

External Aid

Receives training, weapons, and explosives, as well as political, diplomatic, and organizational aid from Iran, and diplomatic, political, and logistical support from Syria. Hizballah also receives funding from religious donations, and profits from legal and illegal businesses.

ISLAMIC JIHAD UNION (IJU)

a.k.a. Al-Djihad al-Islami; Dzhamaat Modzhakhedov; Islamic Jihad Group of Uzbekistan;

Jama'at al-Jihad; Jamiat al-Jihad al-Islami; Jamiyat; The Jamaat Mujahedin; The Kazakh Jama'at; The Libyan Society.

Description

The IJU is an extremist organization which splintered from the Islamic Movement of Uzbekistan. They oppose secular rule in Uzbekistan and seek to replace it with a government based on Islamic law.

Activities

The IJU issued a statement in May 2004 fully supporting the armed attacks on Uzbek police and military personnel in Andijon, Uzbekistan, and called for the overthrow of the Uzbekistani regime. The group first conducted attacks in March-April 2004 targeting a popular bazaar and police at several roadway checkpoints. These attacks killed approximately 47 people, including 33 terrorists, some of whom were suicide bombers. The IJU's claim of responsibility, which was posted to multiple militant Islamic websites, denounced the leadership of Uzbekistan. These attacks marked the first use of suicide bombers in Central Asia. In July 2004, the group struck again with near-simultaneous suicide bombings of the U.S. and Israeli Embassies and the Uzbekistani Prosecutor General's office in Tashkent. The IJU again claimed responsibility via an Islamic website and stated that martyrdom operations by the group would continue. The statement also indicated that the attacks were done in support of IJU's Palestinian, Iraqi, and Afghan brothers in the global insurgency. The date of the July attack corresponded with the trial of individuals arrested for their alleged participation in the March-April attacks.

Strength

Unknown

Location/Area of Operation

Militants are scattered throughout Central Asia and probably parts of South Asia.

External Aid

Unknown

ISLAMIC MOVEMENT OF UZBEKISTAN (IMU)

Description

The IMU is a group of Islamic militants from Uzbekistan and other Central Asian states. The IMU's goal is to overthrow Uzbekistani President Islam Karimov and establishing an Islamic state in Uzbekistan. The IMU is affiliated with al-Qaida and, under the leadership of Tohir Yoldashev, has embraced Usama bin Ladin's ideology.

Activities

Since Operation Enduring Freedom, the IMU has been predominantly occupied with attacks on U.S. and Coalition soldiers in Afghanistan. Although it is difficult to differentiate between IMU and Islamic Jihad Union members, Pakistani security forces continue to arrest probable IMU operatives in the Federally Administered Tribal Areas (FATA).

The IMU was active in terrorist operations in Central Asia. Tajikistan arrested several IMU members in 2005. In November 2004, the IMU was blamed for an explosion in the southern Kyrgyz city of Osh that killed one police officer and one terrorist. In May 2003, Kyrgyz security forces disrupted an IMU cell that was seeking to bomb the U.S. Embassy and a nearby hotel in Bishkek, Kyrgyzstan. The IMU was also responsible for explosions in Bishkek in December 2002 and Osh in May 2003 that killed eight people. The IMU primarily targeted Uzbekistani interests before October 2001, and is believed to have been responsible for several explosions in Tashkent in February 1999. IMU militants took foreigners hostage in Kyrgyzstan for two consecutive years: in August 1999, IMU militants took four Japanese geologists and eight Kyrgyz soldiers hostage, and in August 2000, they took four U.S. mountain climbers hostage.

Strength

Approximately 500 members.

Location/Area of Operation

IMU militants are scattered throughout South Asia,

Central Asia, and Iran. Their area of operation includes Afghanistan, Iran, Kyrgyzstan, Pakistan, Tajikistan, Kazakhstan, and Uzbekistan.

External Aid

The IMU receives support from a large Uzbek diaspora, Islamic extremist groups and patrons in the Middle East, Central Asia, and South Asia.

JAISH-E-MOHAMMED (JEM)

a.k.a. Army of Mohammed; Jaish-i-Mohammed; Khudamul Islam; Khuddam-ul-Islam; Kuddam e Islami; Mohammed's Army; Tehrik ul-Furqaan.

Description

Jaish-e-Mohammed is an Islamic extremist group based in Pakistan founded by Masood Azhar, a former senior leader of Harakat ul-Ansar, upon his release from prison in India in early 2000. The group's aim is to unite Kashmir with Pakistan, and it has openly declared war against the United States. It is politically aligned with the radical political party Jamiat Ulema-i-Islam's Fazlur Rehman faction (JUI-F). Pakistan outlawed JEM in 2002. By 2003, JEM had splintered into Khuddam ul-Islam (KUI),headed by Azhar, and Jamaat ul-Furqan (JUF), led by Abdul Jabbar, who was released from Pakistani custody in August 2004 after being detained for suspected involvement in the December 2003 assassination attempts against President Pervez Musharraf. Pakistan banned KUI and JUF in November 2003.

Activities

Jaish-e-Mohammed continues to operate openly in parts of Pakistan despite President Musharraf's 2002 ban on its activities. The group is well-funded, and is said to have tens of thousands of followers who support attacks against Indian targets, the Pakistani government, and sectarian minorities.

Since Masood Azhar's 2000 release from Indian custody in exchange for 155 hijacked Indian Airlines hostages, JEM has conducted many fatal terrorist attacks in the area. JEM continues to claim responsibility for several suicide car bombings in Kashmir, including a suicide attack on the Jammu and Kashmir legislative assembly building in Srinagar in October 2001 that killed more than 30. The Indian government has publicly implicated the JEM, along with Lashkar e-Tayyiba, for the December 2001 attack on the Indian Parliament that killed nine and injured 18. Pakistani authorities suspect that JEM members may have been involved in the 2002 anti-Christian attacks in Islamabad, Murree, and Taxila that killed two Americans. In December 2003, Pakistan implicated elements of JEM in the two assassination attempts against President Musharraf. In July 2004, Pakistani authorities arrested a JEM member wanted in connection with the 2002 abduction and murder of U.S. journalist Daniel Pearl. In 2006, JEM claimed responsibility for a number of attacks, including the killing of several Indian police officials in the Indian-administered Kashmir capital of Srinagar.

Strength

JEM has at least several hundred armed supporters, including a large cadre of former HUM members, located in Pakistan, in India's southern Kashmir and Doda regions, and in the Kashmir Valley. Supporters are mostly Pakistanis and Kashmiris, but also include Afghans and Arab veterans of the Afghan war. The group uses light and heavy machine guns, assault rifles, mortars, improvised explosive devices, and rocket-propelled grenades.

Location/Area of Operation

Pakistan and Kashmir and until autumn 2001, JEM maintained training camps in Afghanistan.

External Aid

Most of JEM's cadre and material resources have been drawn from the Pakistani militant groups Harakat ul-Jihad-i-Islami (HUJI) and the Harakat ul-Mujahedin (HUM). In anticipation of asset seizures by the Pakistani government,

JEM withdrew funds from bank accounts and invested in legal businesses, such as commodity trading, real estate, and production of consumer goods. In addition, JEM collects funds through donation requests in magazines and pamphlets, and al-Qaida is suspected of providing funding.

JEMAAH ISLAMIYA (JI)

Description

The Southeast Asia-based Jemaah Islamiya (JI) is a terrorist group that seeks the establishment of an Islamic caliphate spanning Indonesia, Malaysia, southern Thailand, Singapore, Brunei, and the southern Philippines. More than 300 JI operatives, including operations chief Hambali, have been captured since 2002.

Several are no longer incarcerated, however, including JI emir Abu Bakar Bashir who was released from prison in 2006 after serving a 25-month sentence for his involvement in the 2002 Bali bombings. The death of top JI bombmaker Azahari bin Husin in November 2005, and further arrests of several close associates of senior JI operative Noordin Mat Top in 2006 likely disrupted JI's anti-Western attacks- that occurred annually from 2002-2005.

Activities

The group's most recent high-profile attack occurred in Bali on October 1, 2005 and left 26 persons dead. Other major JI attacks include the September 2004 bombing outside the Australian Embassy in Jakarta, the August 2003 bombing of the J. W. Marriott Hotel in Jakarta, and the October 2002 Bali bombing. The 2002 Bali attack, which killed more than 200, remains one of the deadliest terrorist attacks since 9/11. In December 2001, Singaporean authorities uncovered a JI plot to attack the U.S. and Israeli Embassies and British and Australian diplomatic buildings in Singapore. JI is also responsible for the coordinated bombings of numerous Christian churches in Indonesia in December 2000 and was involved in the bombings of several targets in Manila the same month.

Strength

Exact numbers currently are unknown. Estimates of total JI members vary from the hundreds to one thousand.

Location/Area of Operation

JI is based in Indonesia and believed to have cells in Indonesia, Malaysia, and the Philippines.

External Aid

Investigations indicate that JI is fully capable of its own fundraising, although it also receives financial, ideological, and logistical support from Middle Eastern contacts, and non-governmental organizations.

AL-JIHAD (AJ)

Egyptian Islamic Jihad (EIJ); Egyptian al-Jihad; New Jihad; The Jihad Group

Description

This Egyptian Islamic extremist group merged with Usama Bin Ladin's al-Qaida organization in 2001. Usama Bin Ladin's deputy, Ayman al-Zawahiri, was the former head of AJ. Active since the 1970s, AJ's primary goal has been the overthrow of the Egyptian government and the establishment of an Islamic state. The group's targets, historically, have been high-level Egyptian government officials as well as U.S. and Israeli interests in Egypt and abroad. Regular Egyptian crackdowns on extremists have greatly reduced AJ capabilities in Egypt.

Activities

The original AJ was responsible for the 1981 assassination of Egyptian President Anwar Sadat. It claimed responsibility for the attempted assassinations in 1993 of Interior Minister Hassan al-Alfi and Prime Minister Atef Sedky. AJ has not conducted an attack inside Egypt since 1993 and has never successfully targeted foreign tourists there. The group was responsible for the Egyptian Embassy bombing in Islamabad in 1995 and a disrupted plot against the U.S. Embassy in Albania in 1998.

Strength

Believed to have several hundred hard-core members inside and outside of Egypt.

Location/Area of Operation

Most AJ members today are outside Egypt in countries such as Afghanistan, Pakistan, Lebanon, the United Kingdom, and Yemen. AJ activities have been centered outside Egypt for several years under the auspices of al-Qaida.

External Aid

Since 1998 AJ has received most of its funding from al-Qaida; these close ties culminated in the eventual merger of the groups in June 2001. Some funding may come from various Islamic non-governmental organizations, cover businesses, and criminal acts.

KAHANE CHAI (KACH)

a.k.a. American Friends of the United Yeshiva; American Friends of Yeshivat Rav Meir;

Committee for the Safety of the Roads; Dikuy Bogdim; DOV; Forefront of the Idea;

Friends of the Jewish Idea Yeshiva; Jewish Idea Yeshiva; Jewish Legion; Judea Police;

Judean Congress; Kach; Kahane; Kahane Lives; Kahane Tzadak; Kahane.org; Kahanetzadak.com; Kfar Tapuah Fund; Koach; Meir's Youth; New Kach Movement;

Newkach.org; No'ar Meir; Repression of Traitors; State of Judea; Sword of David; The Committee Against Racism and Discrimination (CARD); The Hatikva Jewish Identity Center;

The International Kahane Movement; The Jewish Idea Yeshiva; The Judean Legion; The Judean Voice; The

Gomemiyut Movement; The Rabbi Meir David Kahane Memorial Fund; The Voice of Judea; The Way of the Torah; The Yeshiva of the Jewish Idea; Yeshivat Harav Meir.

Description

Kach's stated goal is to restore the biblical state of Israel. Kach was founded by radical Israeli-American rabbi Meir Kahane. Its offshoot Kahane Chai, (translation: "Kahane Lives") was founded by Meir Kahane's son Binyamin following his father's 1990 assassination in the United States. Both Kach and Kahane Chai were declared terrorist organizations in 1994 by the Israeli Cabinet under its 1948 Terrorism Law. This designation followed the groups' statements in support of Dr. Baruch Goldstein's attack in February 1994 on the Ibrahimi Mosque (Goldstein was affiliated with Kach) and their verbal attacks on the Israeli government. Palestinian gunmen killed Binyamin Kahane and his wife in a drive-by shooting in December 2000 in the West Bank.

Activities

Kach has harassed and threatened Arabs, Palestinians, and Israeli government officials, and has vowed revenge for the death of Binyamin Kahane and his wife. Kach is suspected of involvement in a number of low-level attacks since the start of the al-Aqsa intifada in 2000.

Strength

Unknown

Location/Area of Operation

Israel and West Bank settlements, particularly Qiryat Arba' in Hebron.

External Aid

Receives support from sympathizers in the United States and Europe.

KONGRA-GEL(KGK/PKK)

(Despite name changes, the group is still most commonly

referred to as the PKK; for the purposes of this report we refer to the group as Kongra-Gel/PKK or KGK/PKK.)

a.k.a. Kurdish Freedom Hawks (TAK); Kurdistan Workers' Party (PKK); Freedom and Democracy Congress of Kurdistan (KADEK); Halu Mesru Savunma Kuvveti (HSK); Kurdistan Freedom and Democracy Congress; Kurdistan People's Congress (KHK); Partiya Karkeran Kurdistan; People's Congress of Kurdistan; The People's Defense Force.

Description

The KGK/PKK was founded by Abdullah Ocalan in 1974 as a Marxist-Leninist separatist organization. The group, composed primarily of Turkish Kurds, launched a campaign of violence in 1984. The KGK/PKK aspired to establish an independent Kurdish state in southeastern Turkey, but in recent years has spoken more often about cultural or linguistic rights. In the early 1990s, the KGK/PKK moved beyond rural-based insurgent activities to include urban terrorism.

In the 1990s south-eastern Anatolia was the scene of significant violence; some estimates place casualties at approximately 30,000 persons. Following his capture in 1999, Ocalan announced a "peace initiative," ordering members to refrain from violence and requesting dialogue with Ankara on Kurdish issues. Ocalan's death-sentence was commuted to life-imprisonment; he remains the symbolic leader of the group. The group foreswore violence until June 2004, when the group's hard-line militant wing took control and renounced the self-imposed ceasefire of the previous five years. Striking over the border from bases within Iraq the KGK/PKK engaged in terrorist attacks in eastern and western Turkey.

Activities

Primary targets have been Turkish government security forces, local Turkish officials, and villagers who oppose the organization in Turkey. The group conducted attacks on Turkish diplomatic and commercial facilities in West European cities in 1993 and again in spring 1995. In an attempt to damage

Turkey's tourist industry, the KGK/PKK bombed tourist sites and hotels and kidnapped foreign tourists in the early-to-mid-1990s. Turkish authorities have confirmed or suspect that the group is responsible for dozens of bombings since 2004 in western Turkey, particularly in Istanbul and increasingly in resort areas on the western coast where foreign tourists, among others, have been killed. There have also been dozens of military clashes between Turkish security forces and KGK/PKK militants.

Strength

Approximately 4,000 to 5,000; 3,000 to 3,500 are currently located in northern Iraq.

Location/Area of Operation

Operates primarily in Turkey, Iraq, Europe, and the Middle East.

External Aid

Kongra-Gel/PKK has historically received safe haven and modest aid from Syria, Iraq, and Iran. Since 1999, Syria and Iran have cooperated with Turkey against the PKK, in a limited fashion. The KGK/PKK funds rise in Europe.

LASHKAR E-TAYYIBA (LT)

a.k.a. Al Mansooreen; Al Mansoorian; Army of the Pure; Army of the Pure and Righteous;

Army of the Righteous; Jamaat ud-Dawa and Al Monsooreen; Lashkar e-Toiba; Lashkar-i-Taiba; Paasban-e-Ahle-Hadis; Paasban-e-Kashmir; Paasban-i-Ahle-Hadith; Pasban-e-Ahle-Hadith; Pasban-e-Kashmir.

Description

LT began as the militant wing of the Islamic extremist organization Markaz Dawa ul-Irshad (MDI), which was formed in the mid-1980s. MDI changed its name to Jamaat ul-Dawa (JUD) in 2001, probably in an effort to avoid Pakistan government restrictions. LT, which is not connected to any political party, is led by Hafiz Muhammad Saeed and is one of the three largest and best-trained groups fighting in Kashmir against India. The Pakistani government banned the group and froze its assets in January 2002. Elements of LT and Jaish-e-Muhammad combined with other groups to mount attacks as "The Save Kashmir Movement."

Activities

LT has conducted a number of operations against Indian troops and civilian targets in Jammu and Kashmir since 1993. LT claimed responsibility for numerous attacks in 2001, including an attack in January on Srinagar airport that killed five Indians; an attack on a police station in Srinagar that killed at least eight officers and wounded several others; and an attack in April against Indian border security forces that left at least four dead. The Indian government publicly implicated LT, along with JEM, for the December 2001 attack on the Indian Parliament building, although concrete evidence is lacking. LT is also suspected of involvement in May 2002 attack on an Indian Army base in Kaluchak that left 36 dead. India blamed LT for an October 2005 attack in New Delhi and a December 2005 Bangalore attack. Senior al-Qaida lieutenant Abu Zubaydah was captured at an LT safe house in Faisalabad in March 2002, which suggested that some members were facilitating the movement of al-Qaida members in Pakistan and Government of India officials hold LT responsible for the July 11, 2006 train attack in Mumbai.

Strength

LT has several thousand members in Azad Kashmir, Pakistan, in the southern Jammu and Kashmir and Doda regions, and in the Kashmir Valley. Almost all LT members are Pakistanis from madrassas across Pakistan or Afghan veterans of the Afghan wars.The group uses assault rifles, light and heavy machine guns, mortars, explosives, and rocket-propelled grenades.

Location/Area of Operation

Based in Muridke (near Lahore) and Muzaffarabad.

External Aid

Collects donations from the Pakistani expatriate communities in the Middle East and United Kingdom, Islamic NGOs, and Pakistani and other Kashmiri business people. LT also maintains a website under the name Jamaat ud-Daawa through which it solicits funds and provides information on the group's activities. The precise amount of LT funding is unknown.

LASH KARI JHANGVI (LJ)

a.k.a. Lashkar e Jhangvi; Lashkari-i-Jhangvi.

Description

Lashkar i Jhangvi (LJ) is the militant offshoot of the Sunni Deobandi sectarian group Sipahi-Sahaba Pakistan. LJ focuses primarily on anti-Shia attacks and was banned by Pakistani President Musharraf in August 2001 as part of an effort to rein in sectarian violence. Many of its members then sought refuge in Afghanistan with the Taliban, with whom they had existing ties. After the collapse of the Taliban, LJ members became active in aiding other terrorists with safe houses, false identities, and protection in Pakistani cities, including Karachi, Peshawar, and Rawalpindi. In January 2003, the United States added LJ to the list of designated Foreign Terrorist Organizations.

Activities

LJ specializes in armed attacks and bombings and has admitted responsibility for numerous killings of Shia religious and community leaders in Pakistan. In January 1999, the group attempted to assassinate former Prime Minister Nawaz Sharif and his brother Shabaz Sharif, Chief Minister of Punjab Province. Pakistani authorities have publicly linked LJ members to the 2002 abduction and murder of U.S. journalist

Daniel Pearl. Media reports linked LJ to attacks on Christian targets in Pakistan, including a March 2002 grenade assault on the Protestant International Church in Islamabad that killed two U.S. citizens, but no formal charges were filed against the group. Pakistani authorities believe LJ was responsible for the July 2003 bombing of a Shiite mosque in Quetta, Pakistan. Authorities also implicated LJ in several sectarian incidents in 2004, including the May and June bombings of two Shiite mosques in Karachi that killed more than 40 people. In May 2006, Pakistani police arrested two LJ militants suspected of involvement in the April bombing outside the U.S. Consulate in Karachi that killed one U.S. official; investigations are ongoing. In late 2006, Pakistani security agencies arrested eight suspects allegedly involved in the October blast at the Ayub Park in Rawalpindi and in planting anti-tank rockets at several locations in Islamabad. The Pakistani Interior Minister claimed these suspects have links to LJ and al-Qaida.

Strength

Probably fewer than 100

Location/Area of Operation

LJ is active primarily in Punjab and Karachi. Some members travel between Pakistan and Afghanistan.

External Aid

Unknown

LIBERATION TIGERS OF TAMIL EELAM (LTTE)

a.k.a. Ellalan Force; The Tamil Tigers.

Description

Founded in 1976, LTTEis the most powerful Tamil secessionist group in Sri Lanka. LTTE wants to establish an independent Tamil state in the island's north and east. It began its insurgency against the Sri Lankan government in 1983 and has relied on a guerrilla strategy that includes the use of terrorist tactics. LTTE nominally has observed a ceasefire agreement with the Sri Lankan government since 2002. The United States designated LTTE as a Foreign Terrorist Organization in October 1997.

Activities

LTTE has integrated a battlefield insurgent strategy with a terrorist program that targets key personnel in the countryside and senior Sri Lankan political and military leaders in Colombo and other urban centers. It also has conducted a sustained campaign targeting rival Tamil groups and figures, and assassinated the head of government of two countries:

Prime Minister Rajiv Gandhi of India in 1991 and President Premadasa of Sri Lanka in 1993. LTTE is most notorious for the Black Tigers, its cadre of suicide bombers. Political assassinations and bombings were commonplace tactics prior to the ceasefire and have increased again since mid-2005. Fighting between LTTE and the Sri Lanka government escalated in 2006.

Strength

Exact strength is unknown, but LTTE is estimated to have 8,000 to 10,000 armed combatants in Sri Lanka, with a core of 3,000 to 6,000 trained fighters.LTTE also has a significant overseas support structure for fundraising, weapons procurement, and propaganda activities.

Location/Area of Operations

Headquartered in northern Sri Lanka, LTTE controls portions of the northern and eastern coastal areas of Sri Lanka, where it has set up a comprehensive administrative structure, but also has conducted operations throughout the island. LTTE leader Velupillai Prabhakaran has established an extensive network of checkpoints and informants to keep track of any outsiders who enter the group's area of control.

External Aid

LTTE's overt organizations support Tamil separatism by lobbying foreign governments and the United Nations. LTTE also uses its international contacts and the large Tamil Diaspora in North America, Europe, and Asia to procure weapons, communications, funding, and other needed supplies.

LIBYAN ISLMIC FIGHTING GROUP (LIFG)

Description

The Libyan Islamic Fighting Group (LIFG) emerged in the early 1990s among Libyans who had fought Soviet forces in Afghanistan and the Qadhafi regime in Libya. The LIFG declared Libyan President Muammar Qadhafi unIslamic and pledged to overthrow him. Some members maintain a strictly anti-Qadhafi focus and organize against Libyan government interests, but others, such as Abu al-Faraj al-Libi, who was arrested in Pakistan in 2005, are aligned with Usama bin Ladin and believed to be part of al-Qaida's leadership structure or active in the international terrorist network. The United States designated the LIFG a Foreign Terrorist Organization in December 2004.

Activities

Libyans associated with the LIFG are part of the broader international terrorist movement. Spanish media in August 2005 linked Ziyad Hashem, an alleged member of the LIFG's media committee, as well as the imprisoned amir Abdullah al-Sadeq, with the Tunisian Islamist Serhane Ben Abdelmajid Fakhet, the suspected ringleader in the 2004 Madrid attacks. The LIFG is one of the groups believed to have planned the Casablanca suicide bombings in May 2003. The LIFG continues to target Libyan interests, and attempted to assassinate Qadhafi a total of four times; the last attempt was in 1998. The LIFG engaged Libyan security forces in armed clashes during the 1990s.

Strength

Probably have several hundred active members or supporters.

Location/Area of Operation

Since the late 1990s many members have fled to various Asian, Arabian Gulf, African, and European countries, particularly the United Kingdom. It is likely that LIFG maintains a clandestine presence in Libya.

External Aid

Unknown and has used Islamic charitable organizations as cover for raising and transferring money and documents.

MOROCCAN ISLAMIC COMBATANT GROUP (GICM)

a.k.a. Groupe Islamique Combattant Marocain.

Description

The Moroccan Islamic Combatant Group (GICM) is a clandestine transnational terrorist group currently centered in the Moroccan diaspora communities of Western Europe. Its goals include establishing an Islamic state in Morocco and supporting al-Qaida's war against the West by assisting in the assimilation of al-Qaida operatives into Moroccan and then European society. The group appears to have emerged in the 1990s and is comprised of Moroccan recruits who trained in armed camps in Afghanistan, including some who fought in the Soviet Afghan war. GICM members interact with other North African extremists, particularly in Europe. In November 2002, the United States designated the GICM for asset freeze under EO 13224 following the group's submission to the UNSCR 1267 Sanctions Committee. The United States designated GICM as a Foreign Terrorist Organization on October 11, 2005.

Activities

The GICM carried out its first attack in Casablanca, Morocco on May 16, 2003, and GICM members were responsible for the Madrid attack. Moroccans associated with the GICM are part of the broader international terrorist movement; GICM members have been implicated in the recruitment network of individuals for Iraq, and at least one GICM member has carried out a suicide attack against Coalition Forces in Iraq.

Strength

Much of the GICM's leadership in Morocco and Europe have been killed, imprisoned, or are awaiting trial. Alleged leader Mohamed al-Guerbouzi has been convicted in absentia by the Moroccan government for his role in the Casablanca attacks but remains free in exile in the United Kingdom.

Location/Area of Operation

Morocco, Western Europe, Afghanistan, and Canada

External Aid

The GICM is involved heavily in narcotics trafficking in North Africa and Europe to fund their operations. Moroccan security officials believe money from drug trafficking largely financed the 2003 Casablanca attacks. The Madrid attacks were financed mainly by the narcotics trafficking of Moroccan jihadist Jamal Ahmidan.

MUJAHENDIN-E KHALQ ORGANIZATION (MEK)

a.k.a. MKO; Mujahedin-e Khalq; Muslim Iranian Students' Society; National Council of Resistance; National Council of Resistance (NCR); Organization of the People's Holy Warriors of Iran; The National Liberation Army of Iran (NLA); The People's Mujahedin Organization of Iran (PMOI); National Council of Resistance of Iran (NCRI); Sazeman-e Mujahedin-e Khalq-e Iran.

Description

The MEK advocates the violent overthrow of the Iranian regime and was responsible for the assassination of several U.S. military personnel and civilians in the 1970's. MEK leadership and members across the world maintain the capacity and will to commit terrorist acts in Europe, the Middle East, the United State, Canada, and beyond.

The MEK emerged in the 1960s as one of the more violent political movements opposed to the Pahlavi dynasty and its close relationship with the United States. MEK ideology has gone through several iterations and blends elements of Marxism, Islam, and feminism. Following its participation in the 1979 Islamic Revolution, the group rapidly fell out of favor with the Iranian people. The new Iranian government under Supreme Leader Khomeini systematically arrested and targeted many MEK members, causing most MEK leadership to flee to Europe. In 1986, MEK leaders and operatives were evicted from France and provided a safe haven in Iraq by Saddam Hussein. The group has planned and executed terrorist operations against the Iranian regime for nearly three decades from its European and Iraqi bases of operations. Additionally, it has expanded its fundraising base, further developed its paramilitary skills, and aggressively worked to expand its European ranks. In addition to its terrorist credentials, the MEK has also displayed cult-like characteristics. Upon entry into the group, new members are indoctrinated in MEK ideology and revisionist Iranian history. Members are also required to undertake a vow of "eternal divorce" and participate in weekly "ideological cleansings." Additionally, children are reportedly separated from parents at a young age. MEK leader Maryam Rajavi has established a "cult of personality." She claims to emulate the Prophet Muhammad and is viewed by members as the "Iranian President in exile."

Activities

The group's worldwide campaign against the Iranian government uses propaganda and terrorism to achieve its objectives and has been supported by reprehensible regimes, including that of Saddam Hussein. During the 1970s, the MEK assassinated several U.S. military personnel and U.S. civilians working on defense projects in Tehran and supported the violent takeover in 1979 of the U.S. Embassy in Tehran. Despite U.S. efforts, MEK members have never been brought to justice for the group's role in these illegal acts.

In 1981, MEK leadership attempted to overthrow the newly installed Islamic regime; Iranian security forces subsequently initiated a crackdown on the group. The MEK instigated a bombing campaign, including an attack against the head office of the Islamic Republic Party and the Prime Minister's office, which killed some 70 high-ranking Iranian officials, including Chief Justice Ayatollah Mohammad Beheshti, President Mohammad-Ali Rajaei, and Prime Minister Mohammad-Javad Bahonar. These attacks resulted in a popular uprising against the MEK and an expanded Iranian government crackdown which forced MEK leaders to flee to France. For five years, the MEK continued to wage its terrorist campaign from its Paris headquarters. Expelled by France in 1986, MEK leaders turned to Saddam Hussein's regime for basing, financial support, and training. Near the end of the 1980-1988 Iran-Iraq War, Baghdad armed the MEK with heavy military equipment and deployed thousands of MEK fighters in suicidal, mass wave attacks against Iranian forces.

The MEK's relationship with the former Iraqi regime continued through the 1990s. In 1991, the group reportedly assisted in the Iraqi Republican Guard's bloody crackdown on Iraqi Shia and Kurds who rose up against Saddam Hussein's regime; press reports cite MEK leader Maryam Rajavi encouraging MEK members to "take the Kurds under your tanks." In April 1992, the MEK conducted near-simultaneous attacks on Iranian embassies and installations in 13 countries, demonstrating the group's ability to mount large-scale operations overseas. In April 1999, the MEK targeted key Iranian military officers and assassinated the deputy chief of the Iranian Armed Forces General Staff, Brigadier General Ali Sayyaad Shirazi.

In April 2000, the MEK attempted to assassinate the commander of the Nasr Headquarters, Tehran's interagency board responsible for coordinating policies on Iraq. The pace of anti-Iranian operations increased during "Operation Great Bahman" in February 2000, when the group launched a dozen attacks against Iran. One of those attacks included a mortar attack against a major Iranian leadership complex in Tehran that housed the offices of the Supreme Leader and the President. In 2000 and 2001, the MEK was involved in regular mortar attacks and hit-and-run raids against Iranian military and law enforcement personnel, as well as government buildings near the Iran-Iraq border. Also in 2001, the FBI arrested seven Iranians in the United States who funneled $400,000 to an MEK-affiliated organization in the UAE which used the funds to purchase weapons. Following an initial Coalition bombardment of the MEK's facilities in Iraq at the outset of Operation Iraqi Freedom, MEK leadership negotiated a ceasefire with Coalition Forces and voluntarily surrendered their heavy-arms to Coalition control. Since 2003, roughly 3,400 MEK members have been encamped at Ashraf in Iraq, under the supervision of Coalition Forces.

In 2003, French authorities arrested 160 MEK members at operational bases they believed the MEK was using to coordinate financing and planning for terrorist attacks. Upon the arrest of MEK leader Maryam Rajavi, MEK members took to Paris' streets and engaged in self-immolation. French authorities eventually released Rajavi. Although currently in hiding, Rajavi has made appearances via video-satellite to "motivate" MEK-sponsored conferences across the globe.

According to evidence which became available after the fall of Saddam Hussein, the MEK received millions of dollars in Oil-for-Food program subsidies from Saddam Hussein from 1999 through 2003, which supported planning and executing future terrorist attacks. In addition to discovering 13 lists of recipients of such vouchers on which the MEK appeared, evidence linking the MEK to the former Iraqi regime includes lists, as well as video footage of Saddam Hussein handing over suitcases of money to known MEK leaders, and video of MEK operatives receiving training from the Iraqi military.

Strength

Estimates place MEK's worldwide membership in the several thousands, with large pockets in Paris and other major European capitals. In Iraq, roughly 3,400 MEK members are gathered under Coalition supervision at Camp Ashraf, the MEK's main compound north of Baghdad, where they have been designated as "protected persons" under Article 27 of the Fourth Geneva Convention. This status does not affect the group's members outside of Camp Ashraf or the MEK's designation as a Foreign Terrorist Organization. As a condition of the 2003 ceasefire agreement, the MEK relinquished more than 2,000 tanks; armored personnel carriers; and heavy artillery. A significant number of MEK personnel have voluntarily left Ashraf, and an additional several hundred MEK defectors have been voluntarily repatriated to Iran. Many MEK leaders and operatives, however, remain at large, and the number of at-large MEK operatives who received weapons and bomb-making instruction from Saddam Hussein's regime remains a source of significant concern.

Location/Area of Operation

In the 1980s, the MEK's leaders were forced by Iranian security forces to flee to France. Following France's recognition of the Iranian regime in 1986, the group's leadership was forced out of France and took up residence in Iraq. The MEK maintains its main headquarters in Paris and has concentrations of members across Europe, in addition to the large concentration of MEK located at Camp Ashraf in Iraq. The MEK's global support structure remains in place with associates and supporters scattered throughout Europe and North America. Operations target Iranian regime elements across the globe, including in Europe and Iran. MEK's political arm, the NCRI, has a global support network with active lobbying and propaganda efforts in major Western capitals. NCRI also has a well-developed media communications strategy.

External Aid

Before Operation Iraqi Freedom began in 2003; the MEK received all of its military assistance and most of its financial support from Saddam Hussein. The fall of Saddam's regime has led MEK to increasingly rely on front organizations to solicit contributions from expatriate Iranian communities.

NATIONAL LIBERATION ARMY (ELN)

a.k.a. Ejercito de Liberacion Nacional.

Description

The ELN is a Colombian Marxist insurgent group formed in 1965 by urban intellectuals inspired by Fidel Castro and Che Guevara. It is primarily rural-based, although it possesses several urban units. In December 2005, the ELN began preliminary talks with the Colombian government in Cuba, but had not yet agreed to begin a formal peace process.

Activities

ELN conducts kidnapping, hijacking, bombing, and extortion. It has minimal conventional military capability. The group conducts kidnappings for ransom, often targeting foreign employees of large corporations, especially in the petroleum industry. ELN derives some revenue from taxation of the illegal narcotics industry, and its involvement may be increasing. It assaults energy infrastructure and has inflicted major damage on pipelines and the electrical distribution network but has lost much of its capacity to carry out attacks in the past few years.

Strength

Approximately 3,000 armed combatants and an unknown number of active supporters.

Location/Area of Operation

Mostly in rural and mountainous areas of northern, northeastern, and southwestern Colombia, and Venezuelan border regions.

External Aid

Cuba provides some medical care and political consultation.

PALESTINE LIBERATION FRONT (PLF)

a.k.a. PLF-Abu Abbas Faction.

Description

In the late 1970s the Palestine Liberation Front (PLF) splintered from the Popular Front for the Liberation of Palestine-General Command (PFLP-GC), and later split into pro-PLO, pro-Syrian, and pro-Libyan factions. The pro-PLO faction was led by Muhammad Zaydan (a.k.a. Abu Abbas) and was based in Baghdad prior to Operation Iraqi Freedom.

Activites

Abbas's group was responsible for the 1985 attack on the Italian cruise ship Achille Lauro and the murder of U.S. citizen Leon Klinghoffer. In 1993, the PLF officially renounced terrorism when it acknowledged the Oslo accords, although it was suspected of supporting terrorism against Israel by other Palestinian groups into the 1990s. In April 2004, Abu Abbas died of natural causes while in U.S. custody in Iraq. Current leadership and membership of the relatively small PLF appears to be based in Lebanon and the Palestinian territories.

Strength

Unknown

Location/Area of Operation

Based in Iraq from 1990 until 2003, the group currently is based in Lebanon.

External Aid

Unknown

PALESTINE ISLAMIC JIHAD (PIJ)

a.k.a. Islamic Jihad of Palestine; PIJ-Shaqaqi Faction; PIJ-Shallah Faction; Al-Quds Brigades.

Description

Formed by militant Palestinians in the Gaza Strip during the 1970s, Palestine Islamic Jihad (PIJ) is committed to the creation of an Islamic state in all of historic Palestine and the destruction of Israel through attacks against Israeli military and civilian targets.

Activities

PIJ terrorists have conducted numerous attacks, including large-scale suicide bombings against Israeli civilian and military targets. In 2006, the group conducted two suicide bombings and launched numerous homemade rockets from the Gaza Strip into neighboring Israeli towns. PIJ continues to plan and direct attacks against Israelis both inside Israel and in the Palestinian territories. Although U.S. citizens have died in PIJ mounted attacks, the group has not directly targeted U.S. interests.

Strength

Unknown

Location/Area of Operation

Primarily Israel, the West Bank, and the Gaza Strip. The group's central leadership resides in Syria. Other leadership elements reside in Lebanon and official representatives are scattered throughout the Middle East.

External Aid

Receives financial assistance primarily from Iran and Syria provides the group with safe haven.

POPULAR FRONT FOR THE LIBERATION OF PALESTINE (PFLP)

Description

Formerly a part of the PLO, the Marxist-Leninist PFLP was founded by George Habash when it broke away from the Arab Nationalist Movement in 1967. The PFLP does not view the Palestinian struggle as religious, seeing it instead as a broader revolution against Western imperialism.

The group earned a reputation for spectacular international attacks in the 1960s and 1970s, including airline hijackings that killed at least 20 U.S. citizens.

Activites

The PFLP has stepped up its operational activity since the start of the current intifada, highlighted by at least two suicide bombings since 2003, multiple joint operations with other Palestinian terrorist groups, and the assassination of Israeli Tourism Minister Rehavam Ze'evi in 2001, to avenge Israel's killing of the PFLP Secretary General earlier that year. In March 2006, the PFLP's current Secretary General, Ahmed Sa'adat, who had been imprisoned by the Palestinian Authority for his involvement in the Ze'evi assassination, was seized from the Jericho prison compound by Israeli forces and is now awaiting trial.

Strength

Unknown

Location/Area of Operation

Syria, Lebanon, Israel, the West Bank, and the Gaza Strip.

External Aid

Receives safe haven and some logistical assistance from Syria.

POPULAR FRONT FOR THE LIBERATION OF PALESTINE-GENERAL COMMAND (PFLP-GC)

Description

The PFLP-GC split from the PFLP in 1968, claiming it wanted to focus more on fighting and less on politics. Originally, the group was violently opposed to the Arafat-led PLO. Ahmad Jibril, a former captain in the Syrian Army, whose son Jihad was killed by a car bomb in May 2002, has led the PFLP-GC since its founding. The PFLP-GC is closely tied to both Syria and Iran.

Activites

The PFLP-GC carried out dozens of attacks in Europe and the Middle East during the 1970s and 1980s. The organization was known for cross-border terrorist attacks into Israel using unusual means, such as hot-air balloons and motorized hang gliders. The group's primary focus now is on guerrilla operations in southern Lebanon, training members of other Palestinian terrorist groups, and weapons smuggling. The PFLP-GC maintains an armed presence in several refugee camps and military bases throughout Lebanon.

Strength

Several hundred.

Location/Area of Operation

Carried out dozens of attacks in Europe and the Middle East during the 1970s and 1980s. Known for cross-border terrorist attacks into Israel using unusual means, such as hot-air balloons and motorized hang gliders. Primary focus is now on guerrilla operations in southern Lebanon and small-scale attacks in Israel, the West Bank, and the Gaza Strip.

External Aid

Receives logistical and military support from Syria and financial support from Iran.

Al-Qaida

a.k.a. International Front for Fighting Jews and Crusaders; Islamic Army; Islamic Army for the Liberation of Holy Sites; Islamic Salvation Foundation; The Base; The Group for the Preservation of the Holy Sites; The Islamic Army for the Liberation of the Holy Places; The World Islamic Front for Jihad Against Jews and Crusaders; Usama bin Ladin Network; Usama bin Ladin Organization; Qaidat al-Jihad.

Description

Al-Qaida was established by Usama bin Ladin in 1988 with Arabs who fought in Afghanistan against the Soviet

Union. The group helped finance, recruit, transport, and train Sunni Islamic extremists for the Afghan resistance. Al-Qaida's goal is uniting Muslims to fight the United States and its allies, overthrowing regimes it deems "non-Islamic," and expelling Westerners and non-Muslims from Muslim countries. Its ultimate goal is the establishment of a pan-Islamic caliphate throughout the world. Al-Qaida leaders issued a statement in February 1998 under the banner of "The World Islamic Front for Jihad Against the Jews and Crusaders" saying it was the duty of all Muslims to kill U.S. citizens, civilian and military, and their allies everywhere. Al-Qaida merged with al-Jihad (Egyptian Islamic Jihad) in June 2001, renaming itself "Qaidat al-Jihad."

Activities

Even as al-Qaida's top leaders continue to plot and direct terror attacks worldwide, terrorists affiliated with al-Qaida but not necessarily controlled by bin Ladin have increasingly carried out high-profile attacks. Over the past four years, al-Qaida, its affiliates, and those inspired by the group were also involved in anti-U.S. and anti-Coalition attacks in Africa, Europe, the Middle East, Afghanistan, Pakistan, and Iraq, including suicide bombings and vehicle-borne improvised explosive devices.

In 2006, al-Qaida and affiliated organizations continued major efforts to attack the West and its interests. For example, in mid-August, U.K. and U.S. authorities foiled a plot to blow up as many as ten aircraft. Al-Qaida may have been complicit in the plot but the group has made no public statement claiming its involvement. Additionally, al-Qaida in the Arabian Peninsula claimed responsibility for the February 24, 2006, attack on the Abqaiq petroleum processing facility, the largest such facility in the world, in Saudi Arabia. The Salafist Group for Preaching and Combat (GSPC) officially merged with al-Qaida in September 2006, subsequently changed its name to al-Qaida in the Islamic Maghreb (AQIM), and attacked a U.S. contractor bus in December 2006 in greater Algiers, marking its first attack against a U.S. entity.

Bin Ladin's deputy Ayman al-Zawahiri claimed responsibility on behalf of al-Qaida for multiple attacks in 2005 against the London public transportation system. The extent of senior leadership involvement in planning the July 2005 attacks is unclear; however, some suspects in the attacks included homegrown United Kingdom-based extremists who were inspired by al-Qaida.

In 2003 and 2004, Saudi-based al-Qaida operatives and associated extremists launched more than a dozen attacks, killing at least 90 people, including 14 Americans in Saudi Arabia. Al-Qaida may have been connected to the suicide bombers and planners of the November 2003 attacks in Istanbul that targeted two synagogues, the British Consulate, and the HSBC Bank, and resulted in the deaths of more than 60 people. Pakistani President Musharraf blames al-Qaida for two attempts on his life in December 2003.

In October 2002, al-Qaida directed a suicide attack on the French tanker MV Limburg off the coast of Yemen that killed one and injured four. The group also carried out the November 2002 suicide bombing of a hotel in Mombasa, Kenya, which killed 15. Al-Qaida probably provided financing for the October 2002 Bali bombings by Jemaah Islamiya that killed more than 200.

On September 11, 2001, 19 al-Qaida members hijacked and crashed four U.S. commercial jets — two into the World Trade Center in New York City, one into the Pentagon near Washington, DC, and a fourth into a field in Shanksville, Pennsylvania — leaving nearly 3,000 individuals dead or missing. In October 2000, al-Qaida conducted a suicide attack on the USS Cole in the port of Aden, Yemen, with an explosive-laden boat, killing 17 U.S. Navy sailors and injuring 39. Al-Qaida also carried out the August 1998 bombings of the U.S. Embassies in Nairobi and Dar es Salaam killing at least 301 individuals and injuring more than 5,000 others. Al-Qaida and its supporters claim to have shot down U.S. helicopters and killed U.S. servicemen in Somalia in 1993, and to have conducted three bombings that targeted U.S. troops in Aden in December 1992.

Strength

Al-Qaida's organizational strength is difficult to determine in the aftermath of extensive counterterrorist efforts since 9/11. The arrests and deaths of mid-level and senior al-Qaida operatives have disrupted some communication, financial, and facilitation nodes and disrupted some terrorist plots. Additionally, supporters and associates worldwide who are inspired by the group's ideology may be operating without direction from al-Qaida's central leadership; it is impossible to estimate their numbers. Al-Qaida also serves as a focal point of inspiration for a worldwide network that is comprised of many Sunni Islamic extremist groups, including some members of the Gama'at al-Islamiyya, the Islamic Movement of Uzbekistan, the Islamic Jihad Group, Lashkar i Jhangvi, Harakat ul-Mujahedin, Ansar al-Sunnah, the Taliban, Jemaah Islamiya, and the Libyan Islamic Fighting Group.

Location/Area of Operation

Al-Qaida's worldwide networks are augmented by ties to local Sunni extremists. The group was based in Afghanistan until Coalition Forces removed the Taliban from power in late 2001. While the largest concentration of senior al-Qaida members now reside in Pakistan, the network incorporates members of al-Qaida in Iraq and other associates throughout the Middle East, Southeast Asia, Africa, Europe, and Central Asia who continue working to carry out future attacks against U.S. and Western interests.

External Aid

Al-Qaida primarily depends on donations from like-minded supporters and individuals who believe that their money is supporting a humanitarian or other cause. Some funds are diverted from Islamic charitable organizations. Additionally, parts of the organization raise funds through criminal activities; for example, al-Qaida in Iraq raises funds through hostage-taking for ransom, and members in Europe have engaged in credit card fraud. U.S. and international efforts to block al-Qaida funding have hampered the group's ability to raise money.

AL-QAIDAIN IRAQ (AQI)

a.k.a. Al-Qaida Group of Jihad in Iraq; Al-Qaida Group of Jihad in the Land of the Two Rivers;

Al-Qaida in Mesopotamia; Al-Qaida in the Land of the Two Rivers; Al-Qaida of Jihad in Iraq; Al-Qaida of Jihad Organization in the Land of The Two Rivers; Al-Qaida of the Jihad in the Land of the Two Rivers; Al-Tawhid; Jam'at al-Tawhid Wa'al-Jihad; Tanzeem Qaidat al Jihad/Bilad al Raafidaini; Tanzim Qaidat al-Jihad fi Bilad al-Rafidayn; The Monotheism and Jihad Group; The Organization Base of Jihad/Country of the Two Rivers; The Organization Base of Jihad/Mesopotamia; The Organization of al-Jihad's Base in Iraq; The Organization of al-Jihad's Base in the Land of the Two Rivers; The Organization of al-Jihad's Base of Operations in Iraq; The Organization of al-Jihad's Base of Operations in the Land of the Two Rivers; The Organization of Jihad's Base in the Country of the Two Rivers.

Description

In an attempt to unify Sunni jihadists in Iraq, in January 2006, al-Qaida in Iraq (AQI) created the Mujahidin Shura Council (MSC), an umbrella organization meant to encompass the various Sunni jihadist groups in Iraq. AQI claimed its attacks under the MSC until mid-October, when Abu Mus'ab al-Zarqawi's successor, Abu Ayyub al-Masri, took the first step toward al-Qaida's goal of establishing a caliphate in the region by declaring the "Islamic State of Iraq" (ISI), under which AQI now claims its attacks.

On June 7, 2006, AQI leader Abu Mus'ab al-Zarqawi was killed in a U.S. airstrike. Following his death, the MSC announced Abu Hamza al-Muhajir, also known at Abu Ayyub al-Masri, as Zarqawi's successor. Abu Ayyub promptly issued a statement pledging to continue what Zarqawi had started, and AQI has continued its strategy of targeting Coalition Forces and Shi'a civilians in an attempt to foment sectarian strife. Although Coalition and Iraqi security force operations also have cost AQ dozens of lieutenants and high-ranking network members, overall violence in Iraq is at a higher level than it was while Zarqawi was alive.

Activities

In August 2003, Zarqawi's group carried out a major terrorist attack in Iraq when it bombed the Jordanian Embassy in Baghdad, followed 12 days later by a suicide vehicle-borne improvised explosive device (VBIED) attack against the UN Headquarters in Baghdad that killed 23, including the Secretary-General's Special Representative for Iraq, Sergio Vieira de Mello. That same month the group conducted a VBIED attack against Shia worshippers outside the Imam Ali Mosque in al Najaf, killing 85, including the leader of the Supreme Council for the Islamic Revolution in Iraq (SCIRI). The group kept up its attack pace throughout 2003, striking numerous Iraqi, Coalition, and relief agency targets such as the Red Cross. Zarqawi's group conducted VBIED attacks against U.S. military personnel and Iraqi infrastructure throughout 2004, including suicide attacks inside the Green Zone perimeter in Baghdad.

The group successfully penetrated the Green Zone in the October 2004 bombing of a popular cafand market. It also claimed responsibility for the videotaped execution by beheading of Americans Nicholas Berg (May 8, 2004), Jack Armstrong (September 20, 2004), and Jack Hensley (September 21, 2004). AQI was likely involved in other hostage incidents as well. In 2005, AQI largely focused on conducting multiple high-profile, coordinated suicide attacks. AQI claimed numerous attacks primarily aimed against civilians, the Iraqi government, and security forces, such as the coordinated attacks against polling sites during the January elections and the coordinated VBIED attacks outside the Sheraton and Palestine hotels in Baghdad on October 24. The group also continued assassinations against Shia leaders and Shia militia—Jaysh al-Mahdi and Badr Corps.

AQ increased its external operations in 2005 by claiming credit for three attacks: suicide bomber attacks against hotels in Amman on November 9; a rocket attack against

U.S. Navy ships in the port of Aqaba in August, which resulted in limited damage in Jordan and in Eilat, Israel; and the firing of several rockets into Israel from Lebanon in December. In August 2005, an AQI operative was arrested in Turkey while planning an operation targeting Israeli cruise ships. Prior to 2005, AQI planned and conducted limited attacks in Jordan, including the assassination of USAID official Laurence Foley in 2002. In October 2006, AQI declared the ISI would become a platform from which AQI would launch jihad throughout the world. Following the announcement, AQI members marched through cities they considered to be part of their new state as a show of force. AQI attack claims, which the group released under the auspices of the Mujahidin Shura Co.uncil and now the ISI, increased in 2006.

Strength

Precise numbers are unknown, but AQI is the largest terrorist group in Iraq.

Location/Area of Operation

AQI's operations are predominately Iraq-based, but the group maintains an extensive logistical network throughout the Middle East, North Africa, Iran, South Asia, and Europe.

External Aid

AQI probably receives funds from donors in the Middle East and Europe, local sympathizers in Iraq, a variety of businesses and criminal activities, and other international extremists throughout the world. In many cases, AQI's donors are probably motivated by support for terrorism rather than affiliation with any specific terrorist group.

AL-QAIDA IN THE ISLAMIC MAGHREB (AQIM) [FORMERLY SALAFIST GROUP FOR PREACHING AND COMBAT (GSPC)]

a.k.a. Le Groupe Salafiste pour la Predication et le Combat; Salafist Group for Call and Combat.

Description

The Salafist Group for Preaching and Combat (GSPC) officially merged with al-Qaida in September 2006, and subsequently changed its name to al-Qaida in the Islamic Maghreb (AQIM). GSPC members abandoned the Armed Islamic Group (GIA) over disagreements about leadership and tactics, but retained the mission of overthrowing the Algerian Government and installing an Islamic regime. AQIM/GSPC is the most effective and largest armed group inside Algeria. In contrast to the GIA, it has pledged to avoid civilian attacks inside Algeria.

Activities

AQIM/GSPC attacked a U.S. contractor bus in December 2006 in greater Algiers. In Zawahiri's September 11 speech announcing the GSPC's merger with al-Qaida, Zawahiri called on it to be "a bone in the throat of the American and French crusaders" and to sow fear "in the heart of the traitors and apostate sons of France." AQIM/GSPC continues to conduct operations aimed at government and military targets, primarily in rural areas, although civilians are sometimes killed. AQIM/GSPC executed simultaneous attacks on October 30 on two police stations just east of Algiers, killing three civilians, wounding 14 police officers, and causing substantial damage to both facilities. In 2005, the GSPC claimed responsibility for an attack on a remote Mauritanian military outpost, killing 15, while indicating a shift in its strategy toward a more global war beyond Algerian borders.

Police in France, Italy and Spain arrested several Algerians suspected of providing support to AQIM/GSPC, and French officials announced that the AQIM/GSPC had issued an Internet call-to-action against France, declaring France "public enemy number one." The Government of Algeria scored major counterterrorism successes against AQIM/GSPC in 2004, killing AQIM/GSPC leader Nabil Sahraoui and separately taking custody of Abderazak al-Para, who led an AQIM/GSPC faction that held 32 European tourists hostage in 2003.

Strength

Several hundred of fighters with an unknown number of facilitators outside Algeria.

Location/Area of Operation

Algeria, the Sahel, Canada, and Western Europe.

External Aid

Algerian expatriates and AQIM/GSPC members abroad, many residing in Western Europe, provide financial and logistical support. AQIM/GSPC members also engage in criminal activity.

REAL IRA (RIRA)

a.k.a. 32 County Sovereignty Committee; 32 County Sovereignty Movement; Irish Republican Prisoners Welfare Association; Real Irish Republican Army; Real Oglaigh Na Heireann.

Description

Like the Continuity IRA, RIRA did not participate in the September 2005 weapons decommissioning. RIRA was formed in 1997 as the clandestine armed wing of the 32 County Sovereignty Movements, a "political pressure group" dedicated to removing British forces from Northern Ireland and unifying Ireland. RIRA also seeks to disrupt the Northern Ireland peace process. The 32 County Sovereignty Movement opposed Sinn Fein's adoption in September 1997 of the Mitchell principles of democracy and non-violence; it also opposed the amendment in December 1999 of Articles 2 and 3 of the Irish Constitution that laid claim to Northern Ireland. Despite internal rifts and calls by some jailed members, including the group's founder Michael "Mickey" McKevitt, for a ceasefire and disbandment, RIRA has pledged additional violence and continues to conduct attacks.

Activities

Many RIRA members are former Provisional Irish

Republican Army members who left that organization after it renewed its ceasefire in 1997. These members brought a wealth of experience in terrorist tactics and bomb-making to RIRA. Targets have included civilians (most notoriously in the Omagh bombing in August 1998), British security forces, police in Northern Ireland, and local Protestant communities. RIRA's most recent fatal attack was in August 2002 at a London army base, killing a construction worker. The organization wants to improve its intelligence-gathering ability, engineering capacity, and access to weaponry; it also trains members in the use of guns and explosives. RIRA continues to attract new members, and its senior members are committed to launching attacks on security forces. Three suspected RIRA members that engaged in cigarette smuggling were arrested in Spain in 2006.

Strength

The number of activists may have fallen to less than 100. The organization may receive limited support from IRA hardliners and Republican sympathizers dissatisfied with the IRA's continuing ceasefire and with Sinn Fein's involvement in the peace process. Approximately 40 RIRA members are in Irish jails.

Location/Area of Operation

Northern Ireland, Great Britain, and the Irish Republic.

External Aid

Suspected of receiving funds from sympathizers in the United States and of attempting to buy weapons from U.S. gun dealers. RIRA also is reported to have purchased sophisticated weapons from the Balkans.

REVOLUTIONARY ARMED FORCES OF COLOMBIA (FARC)

a.k.a. Fuerzas Armadas Revolucionarias de Colombia.

Description

The FARC is Latin America's oldest, largest, most capable,

and best-equipped insurgency. It began in the early sixties as an outgrowth of the Liberal Party-based peasant self-defense leagues, but took on Marxist ideology, although it only nominally fights in support of Marxist goals today. The FARC is governed by a general secretariat led by long-time leader Manuel Marulanda (a.k.a. "Tirofijo") and six others, including senior military commander Jorge Briceno (a.k.a. "Mono Jojoy"). The FARC is organized along military lines and includes some specialized urban fighting units. A Colombian military offensive targeting FARC fighters in their former safe haven in southern Colombia has experienced some success, with several FARC mid-level leaders killed or captured. France, Spain, and Switzerland formed an international commission in November 2005 to aid the Colombian government and the FARC with humanitarian exchange negotiations, which are currently stalled.

Activities

FARC has carried out bombings, murder, mortar attacks, kidnapping, extortion, and hijacking, as well as guerrilla and conventional military action against Colombian political, military, and economic targets. In February 2003, when a U.S. plane crashed in a FARC-held area, the FARC murdered a U.S. citizen and a Colombian; it continues to hold hostage the three other U.S. citizens that were on the plane. Foreign citizens often are targets of abductions that FARC carries out in pursuit of ransom and political leverage. The FARC has well-documented ties to the full range of narcotics trafficking activities, including taxation, cultivation, and distribution.

Strength

Approximately 15,000 combatants and several thousand more supporters, mostly in rural areas.

Location/Area of Operation

Primarily in Colombia with some activities such as extortion, kidnapping, weapons sourcing, logistics, and R&R

in neighboring countries.

External Aid

Cuba and Venezuela provide some medical care, safe haven, and political consultation. The FARC often uses the Colombia/Venezuela and Colombia/Ecuador border areas for cross-border incursions and Venezuelan and Ecuadorian territory as a safe haven, although the degree of government acquiescence is not clear and seems to vary.

REVOLUTIONARY NUCLEI (RN)

a.k.a. Revolutionary Cells.

Description

Revolutionary Nuclei (RN) emerged from a broad range of anti-establishment and anti-U.S./NATO/EU leftist groups active in Greece between 1995 and 1998. The group is believed to be the successor to or offshoot of Greece's most prolific terrorist group, Revolutionary People's Struggle (ELA), which has not claimed an attack since January 1995. Indeed, RN appeared to fill the void left by ELA, particularly as lesser groups faded from the scene. RN's few communiquàœshow strong similarities in rhetoric, tone, and theme to ELA proclamations. RN has not claimed an attack since November 2000, nor has it announced its disbandment.

Activites

Since it began operations in January 1995; the group has claimed responsibility for some two dozen arson attacks and low-level bombings against a range of U.S., Greek, and other European targets in Greece. In its most infamous and lethal attack to date, the group claimed responsibility for a bomb it detonated at the Intercontinental Hotel in April 1999 that resulted in the death of a Greek woman and injury of a Greek man. RN's modus operandi includes warning calls of impending attacks, attacks targeting property instead of individuals, use of rudimentary timing devices, and strikes during the late evening to early morning hours. RN may have been responsible for two attacks in July 2003 against a U.S. insurance company and a local bank in Athens. RN's last confirmed attacks against U.S. interests in Greece came in November 2000, with two separate bombings against the Athens offices of Citigroup and the studio of a Greek-American sculptor. Greek targets have included judicial and other government office buildings, private vehicles, and the offices of Greek firms involved in NATO-related defense contracts in Greece. Similarly, the group has attacked European interests in Athens.

Strength

Group membership is believed to be small, probably drawing from the Greek militant leftist or anarchist milieu.

Location/Area of Operation

Primary area of operation is in the Athens, Greece metropolitan area.

External Aid

Unknown but believed to be self-sustaining.

REVOLUTIONARY ORGANIZATION 17 NOVEMBER (17N)

a.k.a. Epanastatiki Organosi 17 Noemvri; 17 November.

Description

17 November (17N) is a radical leftist group established in 1975 and named for the student uprising in Greece in November 1973 that protested the ruling military junta. 17N is an anti-Greek establishment, anti-United States, anti-Turkey, and anti-NATO group that seeks the ouster of U.S. bases from Greece, the removal of Turkish military forces from Cyprus, and the severing of Greece's ties to NATO and the European Union (EU).

Activities

Initial attacks were assassinations of senior U.S. officials and Greek public figures. Five U.S. Embassy employees have been murdered since 17N began its terrorist activities in 1975. The group began using bombings in the 1980s. In 1990, 17N expanded its targets to include Turkish diplomats, EU facilities, and foreign firms investing in Greece, and added improvised rocket attacks to its methods. The group supported itself largely through bank robberies. A failed 17N bombing attempt in June 2002 at the port of Piraeus in Athens, coupled with robust detective work, led to the arrest of 19 members, the first 17N operatives ever arrested, including a key leader of the organization. In December 2003, a Greek court convicted 15 members, five of whom were given multiple life terms. Four other alleged members were acquitted for lack of evidence. In December 2005, against the backdrop of a sympathetic press, a group appeals trial opened for the 15 convicted members and two of the previously acquitted members. The appeals trial essentially represents a new trial for the convicts because new evidence and facts can be introduced under Greek law. Moreover, convicted 17N terrorist Nikos Papanastasiou was released from prison in July 2006 on medical grounds. Papanastasiou was the third convicted 17N terrorist to be granted early release from prison for health reasons, following Konstantinos Telios and Pavlos Serifis in 2005.

Strength

Unknown but presumed to be small.

Location/Area of Operation

Athens, Greece.

External Aid

Unknown

REVOLUTIONARY PEOPLE'S LIBERATION PARTY/ FRONT (DHKP/C)

a.k.a. Dev Sol; Dev Sol Armed Revolutionary Units; Dev Sol Silahli Devrimci Birlikleri; Dev Sol SDB; Devrimci Halk Kurtulus Partisi-Cephesi; Devrimci Sol; Revolutionary Left.

Description

This group originally formed in 1978 as Devrimci Sol, or Dev Sol, a splinter faction of Dev Genc (Revolutionary Youth). It was renamed in 1994 after factional infighting. "Party" refers to the group's political activities, while "Front" is a reference to the group's militant operations. The group espouses a Marxist-Leninist ideology and is vehemently anti-U.S., anti-NATO, and anti-Turkish establishment. Its goals are the establishment of a socialist state and the abolition of F-type prisons, which contain one- to three-man prison cells. DHKP/C finances its activities chiefly through donations and extortion.

Activities

Since the late 1980s, the group has targeted primarily current and retired Turkish security and military officials. It began a new campaign against foreign interests in 1990, which included attacks against U.S. military and diplomatic personnel and facilities. To protest perceived U.S. imperialism during the Gulf War, Dev Sol assassinated two U.S. military contractors, wounded an Air Force officer, and bombed more than 20 U.S. and NATO military, commercial, and cultural facilities. In its first significant terrorist act as DHKP/C in 1996, the group assassinated a prominent Turkish businessman and two others. DHKP/C added suicide bombings to its repertoire in 2001, with successful attacks against Turkish police in January and September. Since the end of 2001, DHKP/C has typically used improvised explosive devices against official Turkish targets and soft U.S. targets of opportunity; attacks against U.S. targets beginning in 2003 probably came in response to Operation Iraqi Freedom. Operations and arrests against the group have weakened its capabilities.

Strength

Probably several dozens terrorist operatives inside Turkey, with a large support network throughout Europe.

Location/Area of Operation

Turkey primarily Istanbul, Ankara, Izmir, and Adana and raises funds in Europe.

External Aid

Widely believed to have training facilities or offices in Lebanon and Syria.

SHINING PATH (SL)

a.k.a. Sendero Luminoso; Ejercito Guerrillero Popular (People's Guerrilla Army); Ejercito Popular de Liberacion (People's Liberation Army); Partido Comunista del Peru (Communist Party of Peru); Partido Comunista del Peru en el Sendero Luminoso de Jose Carlos Mariategui (Communist Party of Peru on the Shining Path of Jose Carlos Mariategui); Socorro Popular del Peru (People's Aid of Peru).

Description

Former university professor Abimael Guzman formed SL in Peru in the late 1960s, and his teachings created the foundation of SL's militant Maoist doctrine. In the 1980s, SL became one of the most ruthless terrorist groups in the Western Hemisphere. Approximately 35,000 persons have died since Shining Path took up arms in 1980. The Peruvian government made dramatic gains against SL during the 1990s, but recent SL attacks against Peruvian counter-narcotics police and kidnappings of counternarcotics NGO workers underscore the continuing threat SL poses, as well as the group's increasing ties to narco-trafficking. SL's stated goal is to destroy existing Peruvian institutions and replace them with a communist peasant revolutionary regime. It also opposes any influence by foreign governments. In response to SL's bloody attacks in late 2005, Peruvian authorities have stepped up counter-terrorism efforts against the group. More recently, SL members have attempted to influence the local populace through indoctrination versus violence.

Activities

SL has conducted indiscriminate bombing campaigns,

ambushes, and selective assassinations. Its increased drug ties have raised operating revenue.

Strength

Unknown but estimated to be some 300 armed militants.

Location/Area of Operation

Peru, with most activity in rural areas, specifically the Huallaga Valley, the Ene River, and the Apurimac Valley of central Peru.

External Aid

None

UNITED SELF-DEFENSE FORCES OF COLOMBIA (AUC)

a.k.a. Autodefensas Unidas de Colombia.

Description

The AUC, commonly referred to as the paramilitaries, is an umbrella group formed in April 1997 to organize loosely affiliated illegal paramilitary groups that emerged to retaliate against leftist guerillas fighting the Colombian government and the landed establishment. The AUC increasingly discarded its counter-guerilla activities, electing instead to involve itself in the illegal drug trade. Recently, as the result of a large demobilization process, most of the AUC's centralized military structure has been dismantled, all the top paramilitary chiefs have stepped down, and the majority of the chiefs are being held in a maximum security facility. More than 31,000 paramilitary members demobilized bloc by bloc from 2003 to 2006. Colombia now faces criminal gangs formed by demobilized paramilitaries and other individuals, as well as a few paramilitary groups that refused to disarm. Unlike the AUC, the new criminal groups make little claim to fighting guerrillas and are more clearly criminal enterprises focused primarily on drug trafficking, other lucrative illicit activity, and controlling local politics. They are not part of the AUC.

Activities

Paramilitary operations vary from assassinating suspected insurgent supporters to engaging guerrilla combat units. As much as 70 percent of the paramilitary operational costs are financed with drug-related earnings, with the rest coming from "donations" from sponsors. These groups generally avoid actions against U.S. personnel or interests. Paramilitary operations are reduced as a result of the demobilization of all AUC groups, although some individuals appear to be violating the commitments they made when they demobilized. Colombia's homicide rate is at its lowest level in 18 years, in part because of the ceasefire agreement and demobilization. Other violence indicators such as kidnapping and terror attacks have also decreased significantly.

Strength

The Colombian government has stated that the AUC no longer exists. An estimated 3,000 former members have reengaged in Criminal activities.

Location/Areas of Operation

Paramilitary forces were strongest in northwest Colombia in Antioquia, Cordoba, Sucre, Atlantico, Magdelena, Cesar, La Guajira, and Bolivar Departments, with affiliate groups in the coffee region, Valle del Cauca, and Meta Department.

External Aid

None

5

Other Groups of Concern

OTHER GROUPS OF CONCERN

The following groups of concern have not been designated as Foreign Terrorist Organizations under 8 USC Section 1189, although many have been designated under other U.S. Government counterterrorism authorities.

Al-Badhr Mujahedin (al-Badr)

Al-Ittihad al-Islami (AIAI)

Alex Boncayao Brigade (ABB)

Anti-Imperialist Territorial Nuclei (NTA)

Cambodian Freedom Fighters (CFF)

Communist Party of India (Maoist)

Communist Party of Nepal (Maoist)/United People's Front

Democratic Forces for the Liberation of Rwanda (FDLR)

East Turkistan Islamic Movement (ETIM)

First of October Antifascist Resistance Group (GRAPO)

Harakat ul-Jihad-I-Islami (HUJI)

Harakat ul-Jihad-I-Islami/Bangladesh (HUJI-B)

Hizb-I Islami Gulbuddin (HIG)

Hizbul-Mujahedin (HM)

Irish National Liberation Army (INLA)

Irish Republican Army (IRA)

Islamic Army of Aden (IAA)

Islamic Great East Raiders-Front (IBDA-C)

Islamic International Peacekeeping Brigade (IIPB)

Jamaatul-Mujahedin Bangladesh (JMB)

Jamiat ul-Mujahedin (JUM)

Japanese Red Army (JRA)

Kumpulan Mujahedin Malaysia (KMM)

Lord's Resistance Army (LRA)

Loyalist Volunteer Force (LVF)

Movement for the Emancipation of the Niger Delta (MEND)

New Red Brigades/Communist Combatant Party (BR/PCC)

People Against Gangsterism and Drugs (PAGAD)

Rajah Solaiman Movement (RSM)

Red Hand Defenders (RHD)

Revolutionary Proletarian Initiative Nuclei (NIPR)

Revolutionary Struggle (RS)

Riyadus-Salikhin Reconnaissance and Sabotage Battalion of Chechen Martyrs (RSRSBCM)

Sipah-I-Sahaba/Pakistan (SSP)

Special Purpose Islamic Regiment (SPIR)

Al-Tawhid w'al Jihad (TWJ)

Tenrik Mifaz-E-Shariah Mohammadi (TNSM)

Tunisian Combatant Group (TCG)

Tupac Amaru Revolutionary Movement (MRTA)

Turkish Hizballah

Ulster Defense Association/Ulster Freedom Fighters (UDA/UFF)

Ulster Volunteer Force (UVF)

United Liberation Front of Assam (ULFA)

AL-BADHR MUJAHEDIN (AL-BADR)

Description

The al-Badhr Mujahedin split from Hizbul-Mujahedin (HM) in 1998. It traces its origins to 1971, when a group named al-Badr attacked Bengalis in East Pakistan. The group later operated as part of Gulbuddin Hekmatyar's Hizb-I Islami (HIG) in Afghanistan and, from 1990, as a unit of HM in Kashmir. The group was relatively inactive until 2000. Since then, it has increasingly claimed responsibility for attacks against Indian military targets. Since the late 1990s, al-Badhr leader Bakht Zamin repeatedly has expressed his support for Usama bin Ladin and the Taliban, and in 2002 declared jihad against U.S. forces in Afghanistan.

Activities

The organization has conducted a number of operations against Indian military targets in Jammu and Kashmir. Since late 2001, al-Badhr members have reportedly targeted Coalition Forces in Afghanistan.

Strength

Perhaps several hundred in number.

Location/Area of Operation

Jammu and Kashmir, Pakistan and Afghanistan.

External Aid

Unknown

AL-ITTIHAD AL-ISLAM (AIAI)

Description

AIAI, a Somali extremist group that was formed in the 1980s and reached its peak in the early 1990s, failed to obtain its objective of establishing a Salafist emirate in Somalia and steadily declined following the downfall of the Siad Barre regime in 1991 and Somalia's subsequent collapse into anarchy. AIAI was not internally cohesive, lacked central leadership, and suffered divisions between factions. AIAI was militarily defeated by Ethiopian forces in 1997. In recent years, the existence of a coherent entity operating as AIAI has become difficult to prove. After the downfall of the Somali Council of Islamic Courts in late 2006, AIAI has re-emerged. Former elements of AIAI continue to pursue a variety of agendas ranging from social services and education to insurgency activities in the Ogaden region of eastern Ethiopia. Some sheikhs formerly associated with AIAI espouse a fundamentalist version of Islam, with particular emphasis on a strict adherence to Sharia (Islamic law), a view often at odds with Somalis' emphasis on clan identity. A small group of former AIAI members embrace global jihad and support al-Qaida members in East Africa. 1267 al-Qaida/Taliban/Usama bin Laden Sanctions Committee has listed AIAI for its associations with al-Qaida.

Activities

Individuals formerly associated with AIAI may have been responsible for several kidnappings and murders of relief workers in Somalia and Somaliland since 2003 and in the late 1990s. Prior to its destruction in 1997, factions of AIAI also may have been responsible for a series of bomb attacks in public places in Addis Ababa in 1996 and 1997. Most AIAI factions in recent years have concentrated on broadening their religious base, renewed an emphasis on building businesses, and undertaken "hearts and minds" actions, such as sponsoring orphanages and schools and providing security that uses an Islamic legal structure in the areas where it is active.

Strength

The actual membership strength is unknown.

Location/Area of Operation

Primarily in Somalia, with a presence in the Ogaden region of Ethiopia, Kenya and possibly Djibouti.

External Aid

Receives funds from Middle East financiers and Somali Diaspora communities in Europe, North America and the Arabian Peninsula.

ALEX BONCAYAO BRIGADE (ABB)

Description

The ABB, the breakaway urban hit squad of the Communist Party of the Philippines/New People's Army, was formed in the mid-1980s. The ABB was added to the Terrorist Exclusion List in December 2001.

Activities

Responsible for more than 100 murders, including the murder in 1989 of U.S. Army Col. James Rowe in the Philippines. In March 1997, the group announced it had formed an alliance with another armed group, the Revolutionary Proletarian Army (RPA). In March 2000, the group claimed credit for a rifle grenade attack against the Department of Energy building in Manila and strafed Shell Oil offices in the central Philippines to protest rising oil prices. The group has not been active/conducted attacks in recent years.

Strength

Unknown, but believed to number below 500.

Location/Area of Operation

The largest RPA/ABB groups are on the Philippine islands of Luzon, Negros, and the Visayas.

External Aid

Unknown

ANTI-IMPERIALIST TERRITORIAL NUCLEI FOR THE CONSTRUCTION OF THE COMMUNIST COMBATANT PARTY (NTA-PCC)

a.k.a. Anti-Imperialist Territorial Units

Description

The NTA-PCC is a clandestine leftist extremist group that first appeared in Italy's Friuli region in 1995. It adopted the class struggle ideology of the Red Brigades of the 1970s and 1980s, and a similar logo—an encircled five-point star—for its declarations. It seeks the formation of an "anti-imperialist fighting front" with other Italian leftist terrorist groups, including Revolutionary Proletarian Initiative Nuclei and the New Red Brigades. The group opposes what it perceives as U.S. and NATO imperialism, and condemns Italy's foreign and labor policies. In a leaflet dated January 2002, NTA-PCC identified experts in four Italian government sectors—federalism, privatizations, justice reform, and jobs and pensions—as potential targets.

Activities

To date, NTA-PCC has conducted attacks only against property. During the NATO intervention in Kosovo in 1999, NTA-PCC members threw gasoline bombs at the Venice and Rome headquarters of the then-ruling party, Democrats of the Left. NTA-PCC claimed responsibility for a bomb attack in September 2000 against the Central European Initiative office in Trieste and a bomb attack in August 2001 against the Venice Tribunal building. In January 2002, police thwarted an attempt by four NTA-PCC members to enter the Rivolto military air base. In 2003, NTA-PCC claimed responsibility for the arson attacks against three vehicles belonging to U.S. troops serving at the Ederle and Aviano bases in Italy. There has been no reported activity by the group since the arrest in January 2004 of NTA-PCC's founder and leader.

Strength

Accounts vary from one to approximately 20 members.

Location/Area of Operation

Primarily northeastern Italy and U.S. military installations in northern Italy.

External Aid

None evident.

CAMBODIAN FREEDOM FIGHTERS (CFF)

a.k.a. Cholana; Kangtoap Serei Cheat; Kampouchea.

Description

The Cambodian Freedom Fighters (CFF) emerged in November 1998 in the wake of political violence that saw many influential Cambodian leaders flee and the Cambodian People's Party assume power. With an avowed aim of overthrowing the government, the U.S.-based group is led by a Cambodian-American, a former member of the opposition Sam Rainsy Party. The CFF's membership reportedly includes Cambodian-Americans based in Thailand and the United States, and former soldiers from the Khmer Rouge, Royal Cambodian Armed Forces, and various political factions.

Activities

Alleged CFF leader Chhun Yasith was arrested in June in the United States on charges of conspiracy to kill in a foreign country, conspiracy to damage or destroy property in a foreign country, and engaging in a military expedition against a nation with which the United States is at peace. If convicted, Yasith faces life imprisonment without parole for each of the charges. Meanwhile, a Cambodian court in October dropped charges against five alleged CFF members arrested in April 2004 in connection with a bombing at a ferry, which slightly injured three persons.

In 2003, the Cambodian government arrested seven CFF members who were reportedly planning an unspecified terrorist attack in southwestern Cambodia. Cambodian courts in February and March 2002 prosecuted 38 CFF members suspected of staging an attack in Cambodia in 2000. The courts convicted 19 members, including one U.S. citizen, of "terrorism" and/or "membership in an armed group," and sentenced them to terms of five years to life imprisonment. A

Cambodian court later judged that the three-year sentences of six other members were too light and decided in December 2005 to extend them to 6 to 10 years. The group had claimed responsibility for an attack in late November 2000 on several government installations that killed at least eight persons and wounded more than a dozen. In April 1999, five CFF members also were arrested for plotting to blow up a fuel depot outside Phnom Penh with anti-tank weapons.

Strength

Exact strength is unknown, but totals probably never have exceeded 100 armed fighters.

Location/Area of Operation

Northeastern Cambodia near the Thai border and the United States.

External Aid

U.S.-based leadership collects funds from the Cambodian-American community.

COMMUNIST PARTY OF INDIA (MAOIST)

a.k.a. Maoist Communist Center of India (MCCI) and People's War (PW).

Description

The Indian groups known as the Maoist Communist Center of India and People's War (a.k.a. People's War Group) joined in September 2004 to form the Communist Party of India (Maoist), or CPI (Maoist). The MCCI was originally formed in the early 1970s, while People's War (PW) was founded in 1975. Both groups are referred to as Naxalites, after the West Bengal village where a revolutionary radical Left movement originated in 1967. The new organization continues to employ violence to achieve its goals of peasant revolution, abolition of class hierarchies, and expansion of Maoist-controlled "liberated zones," eventually leading to the creation of an independent "Maoist" state. The CPI (Maoist) reportedly has a significant cadre of women. Important leaders include Ganapati (the PW leader from Andhra Pradesh), Pramod Mishra, Uma Shankar, and P.N.G. (alias Nathuni Mistry, arrested by Jharkhand police in 2002).

Activities

Prior to its consolidation with the PW, the MCCI ran a virtual parallel government in remote areas, where it collected a "tax" from villagers and, in turn, provided infrastructure improvements such as building hospitals, schools, and irrigation projects. It ran a parallel court system wherein allegedly corrupt block development officials and landlords - frequent MCCI targets - were punished by amputation and even death. People's War conducted a low-intensity insurgency that included attempted political assassination, theft of weapons from police stations, kidnapping police officers, assaulting civilians, extorting money from construction firms, and vandalizing the property of multinational corporations. Together the two groups were reportedly responsible for the deaths of up to 170 civilians and police a year. The group conducted two major attacks in 2005. In June, some 500 members attacked a village in Uttar Pradesh, killing several local policemen, destroying buildings, and seizing weapons. In November, an estimated 300 members attacked a prison in Bihar, killing two people, freeing more than 300 inmates, and abducting 30 landowners belonging to a group opposed to the Naxalites.

Strength

Although difficult to assess with any accuracy, media reports and local authorities suggest the CPI's (Maoist) membership may be as high as 31,000, including both hardcore militants and dedicated sympathizers.

Location/Area of Operation

The CPI (Maoist), which is believed to be enlarging the scope of its influence, operates in the Indian states of Andhra

Pradesh, Orissa, Jharkhand, Bihar, Chhattisgarh, and parts of West Bengal. It also has a presence on the Bihar-Nepal border.

External Aid

The CPI (Maoist) has loose links to other Maoist groups in the region, including the Communist Party of Nepal (Maoist), but does not appear dependent on outside sources of support. The MCCI was a founding member of the Coordination Committee of Maoist Parties and Organizations of South Asia (CCOMPOSA).

COMMUNIST PARTY OF NEPAL (MAOIST) (CPN/M)

Description

The Communist Party of Nepal (Maoist) insurgency grew out of the radicalization and fragmentation of left-wing parties following Nepal's transition to democracy in 1990. The United People's Front, a coalition of left-wing parties, participated in the elections of 1991, but the Maoist wing failed to win the required minimum number of votes, leading to its exclusion from voter lists in the elections of 1994 and prompting the group to launch the insurgency in 1996. The CPN/M's ultimate objective is the overthrow of the Nepalese government and the establishment of a Maoist state. On October 31, 2003, the United States designated Nepal's Maoists under E.O. 13224 for terrorist activity.

Activities

The Maoists have used traditional guerrilla warfare tactics and engage in murder, torture, arson, sabotage, extortion, child conscription, kidnapping, bombings, and assassinations to intimidate and coerce the populace. In 2002, Maoists claimed responsibility for assassinating two Nepalese U.S. Embassy guards, citing anti-Maoist spying, and in a press statement threatened foreign embassies, including the U.S. Mission, to deter foreign support for the Nepalese government. Maoists are suspected in the September 2004 bombing at the American Cultural Center in Kathmandu. The attack, which caused no injuries and only minor damage, marked the first time the Maoists had damaged U.S. Government property. The Maoists entered into peace talks with the government in 2001 and 2003, but negotiations failed after a few months. In 2005, the group announced a unilateral ceasefire in September, and entered into an alliance with the seven-party alliance of opposition political parties in November.

Strength

Approximately several thousands full-timer.

Location/Area of Operation

Operations are conducted throughout Nepal. Press reports indicate some Nepalese Maoist leaders reside in India.

External Aid

None

DEMOCRATIC FORCES FOR THE LIBERATION OF RWANDA (FDLR)

a.k.a. Army for the Liberation of Rwanda (ALIR); a.k.a. FAR/Interahamwe.

Description

In 2001, the Democratic Forces for the Liberation of Rwanda (FDLR) supplanted the Army for the Liberation of Rwanda (ALIR), the armed branch of the Party for the Liberation of Rwanda (PALIR). ALIR was formed from the merger of the Armed Forces of Rwanda (FAR), the army of the ethnic Hutu-dominated Rwandan regime that orchestrated the genocide of over 500,000 Tutsis and regime opponents in 1994, and Interahamwe, the civilian militia force that carried out much of the killing.

This occurred after the two groups were forced from Rwanda into the Democratic Republic of the Congo (DRC, then Zaire) that year. Though directly tied to those who organized and carried out the genocide, identified ALIR/ FDLR leaders are not thought to have played a role in the killing. They have worked to build bridges to other opponents of the Kigali regime, including ethnic Tutsis.

Activities

ALIR sought to topple Rwanda's Tutsi-dominated government, reinstitute Hutu domination, and, possibly, complete the genocide. In 1996, a message—allegedly from the ALIR—threatened to kill the U.S. Ambassador to Rwanda and other U.S. citizens. In 1999, ALIR guerrillas critical of U.S.-UK support for the Rwandan regime kidnapped and killed eight foreign tourists, including two U.S. citizens, in a game park on the DRC-Uganda border. Three suspects in the attack are in U.S. custody awaiting trial. In the 1998-2002 Congolese war, the ALIR/FDLR was allied with Kinshasa against the Rwandan invaders. ALIR/FDLR's political wing mainly has sought to topple the Kigali regime via an alliance with Tutsi regime opponents. It established the ADRN Igihango alliance in 2002, but this has not resonated politically in Rwanda. In March 2005, FDLR representatives announced a willingness to cease military actions and return to Rwanda.

FDLR denounced the genocide, committed to a political struggle rather than a military one, and indicated it would voluntarily demobilize and repatriate. No large-scale FDLR repatriation to Rwanda has occurred, however, owing to FDLR concerns about security and the "political space" it would be allowed in Rwanda.

Strength

Exact strength is unknown, but an estimated 8,000 to 10,000 FDLR guerrillas operate in the eastern DRC close to the Rwandan border. In 2003, the United Nations, with Rwandan assistance, repatriated close to 1,500 FDLR combatants from the DRC. A senior FDLR military commander returned to Rwanda in November 2003 and has been working with Kigali to encourage the return of his comrades.

Location/Area of Operation

Mostly in the eastern Democratic Republic of the Congo.

External Aid

The Government of the Democratic Republic of the Congo provided training, arms, and supplies to ALIR forces to combat Rwandan armed forces that invaded the DRC in 1998. Kinshasa halted that support in 2002, though allegations persist of continued support from several local Congolese warlords and militias, including the Mai Mai.

EAST TURKISTAN ISLAMIC MOVEMENT (ETIM)

Description

The East Turkistan Islamic Movement (ETIM) is a small Islamic extremist group linked to al- Qaida and the international jihadist movement. It is the most militant of the ethnic Uighur separatist groups pursuing an independent "Eastern Turkistan," an area that would include Turkey, Kazakhstan, Kyrgyzstan, Uzbekistan, Pakistan, Afghanistan, and Western China's Xinjiang Uighur Autonomous Region. On September 12, 2002, the group was designated under E.O. 13224 for its terrorist activity. ETIM is also listed by the UN 1267 al-Qaida/Taliban/Usama bin Laden Sanctions Committee for its associations with al-Qaida.

Activites

ETIM militants fought alongside al-Qaida and Taliban forces in Afghanistan during Operation Enduring Freedom. In October 2003, Pakistani soldiers killed ETIM leader Hassan Makhsum during raids on al-Qaida-associated compounds in western Pakistan. U.S. and Chinese government information suggests that ETIM is responsible for various terrorist acts inside and outside China. In May 2002, two ETIM members were deported to China from Kyrgyzstan for plotting to attack the U.S. Embassy in Kyrgyzstan as well as other U.S. interests abroad.

Strength

Unknown and only a small minority of ethnic Uighurs support the Xinjiang independence movement or the formation of an independent Eastern Turkistan.

Location/Area of Operation

Afghanistan, China, Kyrgyzstan and Pakistan.

External Aid

ETIM has received training and financial assistance from al-Qaida.

FIRST OF OCTOBER ANTIFASCIST RESISTANCE GROUP (GRAPO); GRUPO DE RESISTENCIA ANTI-FASCISTA PRIMERO DE OCTUBRE

Description

GRAPO was formed in 1975 as the armed wing of the illegal Communist Party of Spain during the Franco era. It advocates the overthrow of the Spanish government and its replacement with a Marxist-Leninist regime. GRAPO is vehemently anti-American, seeks the removal of all U.S. military forces from Spanish territory, and has conducted and attempted several attacks against U.S. targets since 1977. The group issued a communiqué following the September 11, 2001, attacks in the United States, expressing its satisfaction that "symbols of imperialist power" were decimated and affirming that "the war" has only just begun. Spanish authorities believed they had nearly eradicated GRAPO, but a joint Spanish, French, and Italian police operation in October 2005 that resulted in the arrest of two GRAPO members led observers to speculate that the group may be reconstituting itself. GRAPO in a November 2006 internal publication announced that it was trying to find new members and resources but admitted it was having difficulty reorganizing because of sporadic arrests that continued well into 2006. The group was designated under E.O. 13224 in December 2001.

Activities

GRAPO suffered setbacks in 2004, with several members and sympathizers arrested and sentences upheld or handed down in the appellate case for GRAPO militants arrested in

Paris in 2000. Press reports indicate that as of mid-2006, about 30 people connected with the terrorist group were in prison. The group's operations traditionally have been designed to cause material damage and gain publicity rather than inflict casualties, but the terrorists have conducted lethal bombings and close-range assassinations; GRAPO has killed more than 90 persons and injured more than 200 since its formation. GRAPO claimed responsibility for the murder in Zaragoza on 6 February 2006 of a Spanish businesswoman. Members of the group also have been charged with engaging in extortion and for carrying out a series of bank robberies in recent years.

Strength

Fewer than two-dozen activists remain. Police have made periodic large-scale arrests of GRAPO members, crippling the organization and forcing it into lengthy rebuilding periods. In 2002, Spanish and French authorities arrested 22 suspected members, including some of the group's reconstituted leadership. More members have been arrested in the past three years.

Location/Area of Operation

Spain.

External Aid

None.

HARAKAT UL-JIHAD-I-ISLAMI (HUJI)

a.k.a Movement of Islamic Holy War.

Description

HUJI, a Sunni extremist group that follows the Deobandi tradition of Islam, was founded in 1980 in Afghanistan to fight in the jihad against the Soviets. It also is affiliated with the Jamiat Ulema-i-Islam's Fazlur Rehman faction (JUI-F) of the extremist religious party Jamiat Ulema-i-Islam (JUI). The group, led by Qari Saifullah Akhtar and chief commander Amin Rabbani, is made up primarily of Pakistanis and foreign

Islamists who are fighting for the liberation of Jammu and Kashmir and its accession to Pakistan.

Activities

The group has conducted a number of operations against Indian military targets in Jammu and Kashmir. It is linked to the Kashmiri militant group al-Faran that kidnapped five Western tourists in Jammu and Kashmir in July 1995; one was killed in August 1995, and the other four reportedly were killed in December of the same year.

Strength

Exact numbers are unknown, but there may be several hundred members in Kashmir.

Location/Area of Operation

Pakistan and Kashmir. Trained members in Afghanistan until fall of 2001.

External Aid

Specific sources of external aid are unknown.

HARAKAT-UL-JIHAD-I-ISLAMI/BANGLADESH (HUJI-B)

Description

The goal of HUJI-B is to establish Islamic rule in Bangladesh. Bangladeshi veterans of the war against the Soviets in Afghanistan are the group's core membership. HUJI-B has connections to the Pakistani militant groups Harakat ul-Jihad-I-Islami (HUJI) and Harakat ul-Mujahedin (HUM), which advocate similar objectives in Pakistan and Jammu and Kashmir. The leaders of HUJI-B and HUM both signed the February 1998 fatwa sponsored by Usama bin Ladin that declared American civilians to be legitimate targets for attack.

Activities

HUJI-B was accused of stabbing a senior Bangladeshi journalist in November 2000 for making a documentary on the plight of Hindus in Bangladesh. HUJI-B and its detained leader, Mufti Hannan, are suspected in the assassination attempt in July 2000 of Bangladeshi Prime Minister Sheikh Hasina.

Strength

Unknown. Some estimates of HUJI-B cadre strength suggest several thousand members.

Location/Area of Operation

The group operates in Bangladesh.

External Aid

HUJI-B funding comes from a variety of sources. Several international Islamic NGOs, including the South African-based Servants of Suffering Humanity, may have funneled money to Bangladeshi militant groups, including HUJI-B. HUJI-B also can draw funding from militant madrassa leaders and teachers in Bangladesh.

HIZB-I ISLAMI GULBUDDIN (HIG)

Description

Gulbuddin Hikmatyar founded Hizb-I Islami Gul-buddin (HIG) as a faction of the Hizb-I Islami party in 1977, and it was one of the major mujahedin groups in the jihad against the Soviet occupation of Afghanistan. Hikmatyar has long-established links with Usama bin Ladin. In the early 1990s, Hikmatyar ran several terrorist training camps in Afghanistan and was a pioneer in sending mercenary fighters to other Islamic conflicts.

Hikmatyar offered to shelter bin Ladin after the latter fled Sudan in 1996 and has consistently offered public support for him since the 9/11 attacks. Hikmatyar has issued regular statements on the need for Afghans to reject the International community's presence in their country. In 2005, he responded to protests against Danish cartoons of the prophet Mohammad with a new call for the expulsion of international troops from Afghanistan.

Activities

HIG has staged small attacks in its attempt to force the international community to withdraw from Afghanistan, overthrow the Afghan government, and establish an Islamic state. U.S. troops have encountered regular violence in Konar, the area of Afghanistan in which HIG is most active, which has occasionally led to U.S. casualties, and it is likely that HIG is responsible for at least some of this violence.

Strength

Unknown, but possibly could have hundreds of veteran fighters on which to call.

Location/ Area of Operation

Eastern Afghanistan, particularly Konar and Nurestan Provinces, and adjacent areas of Pakistan's tribal areas.

External Aid

Unknown.

HIZBUL-MUJAHEDIN (HM)

Description

Hizbul-Mujahedin (HM) is the largest Kashmiri militant group, and was founded in 1989. It officially supports the liberation of Jammu and Kashmir and its accession to Pakistan, although some members favor independence. The group is the militant wing of Pakistan's largest Islamic political party, the Jamaat-i-Islami, and targets Indian security forces and politicians in Jammu and Kashmir. It reportedly operated in Afghanistan in the mid-1990s and trained with the Afghan Hizb-I Islami Gulbuddin (HIG) in Afghanistan until the Taliban takeover. The group, led by Syed Salahuddin, is composed primarily of ethnic Kashmiris.

Activities

HM has conducted a number of operations against Indian military targets in Jammu and Kashmir. The group also occasionally strikes at civilian targets, but has not engaged in terrorist acts outside India. HM claimed responsibility for numerous attacks within Kashmir in 2006.

Strength

Exact numbers are unknown, but estimates range from several hundred to possibly as many as 1,000 members.

Location/Area of Operation

Jammu, Kashmir, and Pakistan.

External Aid

Specific sources of external aid are unknown.

IRISH NATIONAL LIBERATION ARMY (INLA)

Description

The INLA is a terrorist group formed in 1975 as the military wing of the Irish Republican Socialist Party (IRSP), which split from the Official IRA (OIRA) because of OIRA's ceasefire in 1972. The group's primary aim is to end British rule in Northern Ireland, force British troops out of the province, and unite Ireland's 32 counties into a Marxist-Leninist revolutionary state.

It is responsible for some of the most notorious killings of "The Troubles," including the bombing of a Ballykelly pub that killed 17 people in 1982. Bloody internal feuding has repeatedly torn the INLA. The INLA announced a ceasefire in August 1998 but continues to carry out occasional attacks and punishment beatings.

Activities

The INLA has been active in Belfast and the border areas of Northern Ireland, where it has conducted bombings, assassinations, kidnappings, hijackings, extortion, and robberies. It is also involved in drug trafficking. On occasion, it has provided advance warning to police of its attacks. Targets include the British military, Northern Ireland security forces, and Loyalist paramilitary groups. The INLA did not join the IRA's September 2005 weapons decommissioning, but continues to observe a ceasefire because, in the words of its leadership in 2003, a return to armed struggle is "not a viable option at this time." However, the group continues to recruit members and was responsible for a 2005 arson attack against the home of a local official.

Strength

Unclear, but probably fewer than 50 hardcore activists. Police counterterrorist operations and internal feuding have reduced the group's strength and capabilities.

Location/Area of Operation

Northern Ireland and the Irish Republic. Does not have a significant established presence on the UK mainland.

External Aid

Suspected in the past of receiving funds and arms from sympathizers in the United States.

IRISH REPUBLICAN ARMY (IRA)

a.k.a. Provisional Irish Republican Army (PIRA); the Provos.

Description

Formed in 1969 as the clandestine armed wing of the political movement Sinn Fein, the IRA is devoted both to removing British forces from Northern Ireland and to unifying Ireland. The IRA conducted attacks until its ceasefire in 1997 and agreed to disarm as part of the 1998 Belfast Agreement, which established the basis for peace in Northern Ireland. Dissension within the IRA over support for the Northern Ireland peace process resulted in the formation of two more radical splinter groups: Continuity IRA (CIRA) in 1995 and the Real IRA (RIRA) in 1997. The IRA sometimes referred to as the PIRA to distinguish it from RIRA and CIRA, is organized into small, tightly-knit cells under the leadership of the Army Council.

Activities

Traditional IRA activities have included bombings, assassinations, kidnappings, punishment beatings, extortion, smuggling and robberies. Before the ceasefire in 1997, the group had conducted bombing campaigns on various targets in Northern Ireland and Great Britain, including senior British government officials, civilians, police, and British military targets. In August 2002, three suspected IRA members were arrested in Colombia on charges of helping the Revolutionary Armed Forces of Colombia (FARC) improve its explosives capabilities; the men subsequently escaped from prison and appeared in Ireland in 2005. Irish police have questioned the men but have filed no charges. Colombia has requested their extradition, which is unlikely, since Ireland has no extradition treaty with Colombia.

In July 2005, a spokesperson for the IRA made a statement calling for an end to all forms of IRA illegal activity. This statement was confirmed in September 2005 by the Independent International Commission on Decommissioning's announcement that the IRA had met its commitments to put all arms beyond use. The Independent Monitoring Commission (IMC) also reported that since the September decommissioning the IRA has shown no evidence of training and recruiting terrorists or an intent to return to violence. There have been indications of IRA members using violence in 2006; however, the IMC reports that these incidents were not sanctioned by IRA leadership. The IRA has yet to abandon its extensive criminal activities, which reportedly provide the IRA and the political party Sinn Fein with millions of dollars each year.

Strength

Several hundred members and several thousand sympathizers, despite the defection of some members to RIRA and CIRA.

Local/Area of Operation

Northern Ireland, Irish Republic, Great Britain, and Europe.

External Aid

In the past, the IRA has received aid from a variety of groups and countries, and considerable training and arms from Libya and the PLO. It is suspected of receiving funds, arms, and other terrorist-related materiel from sympathizers in the United States. In addition to the apparent contact with the FARC, similarities in operations suggest the IRA has links to the ETA.

ISLAMIC ARMY OF ADEN (IAA)

a.k.a. Aden-Abyan Islamic Army (AAIA).

Description

The Islamic Army of Aden (IAA) emerged publicly in mid-1998 when the group released a series of communiquàœthat expressed support for Usama bin Ladin and called for the overthrow of the Yemeni government and for operations against U.S. and other Western interests in Yemen. IAA was first designated under E.O. 13224 in September 2001.

Activities

The IAA, a group with established connections to al-Qaida and whose membership includes veteran fighters from the Soviet-Afghan war, in the past has engaged in small-scale operations such as bombings, kidnappings, and small arms attacks to further its agenda. In June 2003, the group reportedly was behind an attack against a medical convoy in the Abyan Governorate. Yemeni authorities responded with a raid on a suspected IAA facility that killed several individuals and captured others, including Khalid al-Nabi al-Yazidi, the group's leader. The IAA's previous involvement in terrorist attacks includes the throwing of a grenade into the British Embassy compound in Sanaa in October 2000. In 2001, Yemeni authorities found an IAA member and three associates responsible for that attack. In December 1998, the group kidnapped 16 British, American, and Australian tourists near Mudiyah in southern Yemen. The group's involvement in a 2003 attack against the medical convoy and reports that its leader was released from prison in October 2003 suggest that the IAA, or at least elements of the group, may remain active. However, Yemeni officials previously have claimed that IAA is operationally defunct, and the group has not claimed any attacks since 2003.

Strength

Not known.

Location/Area of Operation

Operates in the southern governorates of Yemen, primarily Aden and Abyan.

External Aid

Not known.

ISLAMIC GREAT EASTERN RAIDERS-FRONT (IBDA-C)

Description

The Islamic Great Eastern Raiders-Front (IBDA-C) is a Sunni Salafist group that supports Islamic rule in Turkey, is sympathetic to al-Qaida, and believes that Turkey's present secular leadership is "illegal." It has been known to cooperate with various opposition elements in Turkey in attempts to destabilize the country's political structure. The group supports the establishment of a "pure Islamic" state to replace the present "corrupt" Turkish regime that is cooperating with the West. Its primary goal is the establishment of the Federative Islamic State, a goal backed by armed terrorist attacks primarily against civilian targets. It has been active since the mid-1970s.

Activities

IBDA-C has engaged in activities that minimize personal risk, such as bombings, throwing Molotov cocktails, and sabotage. The group has announced its actions and targets in publications to its members, who are free to launch independent attacks. IBDA-C typically has attacked civilian targets, including churches, charities, minority-affiliated targets, television transmitters, newspapers, prosecular journalists, Ataturk statues, taverns, banks, clubs, and tobacco shops. One of IBDA-C's more renowned attacks was the killing of 37 people in a firebomb attack in July 1993 on a hotel in Sivas. In May 2004, Turkish police indicted seven members of the group for the assassination of retired Colonel Ihsan Guven, including the alleged leader of the "Dost" (Friend) sect, and his wife. Turkish police believe that IBDA-C has also claimed responsibility for attacks carried out by other groups in order to elevate its image. Turkish government crackdowns continued into 2006. In a May operation, the government arrested 18 members.

Strength

Unknown.

Location/Area of Operation

Turkey.

External Aid

Unknown

ISLAMIC INTERNATIONAL PEACEKEEPING BRIGADE (IIPB)

Description

The IIPB is a terrorist group affiliated with the Chechen separatist movement demanding a single Islamic state in the North Caucasus. In 1998 Chechen extremist leader Shamil Basayev established the IIPB, consisting of Chechens, Arabs, and other foreign fighters, which he led with Saudi-born mujahedin leader Ibn al-Khattab until the latter's death in March 2002. In July 2006, Basayev himself was killed by Russian forces. The IIPB was one of three groups affiliated with Chechen guerrillas that seized Moscow's Dubrovka Theater and took more than 700 hostages in October 2002. While this group has not been identified by the mujahedin media as conducting attacks since its designation three years ago, those Arab mujahedin still operating in Chechnya now fall under the command of Abu Hafs al-Urduni, who assumed the IIPB leadership in April 2004 after the death of Khattab's successor, Abu al-Walid. IIPB was designated under E.O. 13224 in February 2003 and listed by the UN al-Qaida/Taliban Sanctions Committee for its associations with al-Qaida.

Activities

The IIPB has engaged in terrorist and guerilla operations against Russian forces, pro-Russian Chechen forces, and Chechen non-combatants.

Strength

At its peak, up to 400 fighters, including as many as 100 Arabs and other foreign fighters, but almost certainly has suffered significant attrition.

Location/Area of Operation

Primarily in Russia and adjacent areas of the North Caucasus, particularly in the mountainous south of Chechnya, with major logistical activities in Georgia, Azerbaijan, and Turkey.

External Aid

The IIPB and its Arab leaders appear to be a primary conduit for Islamic funding of the Chechen guerrillas, in part through links to al-Qaida-related financiers on the Arabian Peninsula.

Jamaatul-Mujahedin Bangladesh (JMB)

Description 3

JMB is a Bangladeshi Islamic extremist group dedicated to the use of violence to achieve its objective of a state based on Islamic law. JMB, which emerged in the late 1990s, has been associated with several bombings during the past several years.

The Bangladeshi government banned the group in February 2005.

Activities

On August 17, 2005, JMB claimed responsibility for nearly 500 simultaneous explosions throughout Bangladesh. Subsequent bombings, possibly involving suicide bombers, targeted judges, police, government offices, traditional folk festivals and cultural groups, and local non-governmental organizations. The Bangladeshi government has captured several of the group's most important leaders.

Strength

Estimates range as high as 11,000.

Location/Area of Operation

Bangladesh.

External Aid

JMB probably also receives some support from persons of Bangladeshi origin living in Europe and the Middle East.

JAMIAT UL-MUJAHEDIN (JUM)

Description

The JUM is a small pro-Pakistan militant group formed in Jammu and Kashmir in 1990 that seeks to unite Jammu and Kashmir with Pakistan. Followers are mostly Kashmiris, but the group includes some Pakistanis.

Activities

Has conducted a number of operations against Indian military and political targets in Jammu and Kashmir, including two grenade attacks in 2004.

Strength

Unknown.

Location/Area of Operation

Jammu, Kashmir, and Pakistan.

External Aid

Unknown.

JAPANESE RED ARMY (JRA)

a.k.a. Anti-Imperialist International Brigade (AIIB).

Description

The JRA is an international terrorist group formed around 1970 after breaking away from the Japanese Communist League – Red Army Faction. The JRA's historical goal has been to overthrow the Japanese government and monarchy and to help foment world revolution. The JRA's leader, Fusako Shigenobu, claimed that the forefront of the battle against international imperialism was in Palestine, and in the early 1970s she led her small group to the Middle East. After her arrest in November 2000, Shigenobu announced she intended to pursue her goals using a legitimate political party rather than revolutionary violence, and the group apparently disbanded in April 2001.

Activities

During the 1970s, the JRA carried out a series of attacks around the world, including the 1972 massacre at Lod Airport in Israel, two Japanese airliner hijackings, an attempted takeover of the U.S. Embassy in Kuala Lumpur, and the 1974 seizure of the French Embassy in The Hague, in which the ambassador was among the hostages. During the late 1980s, the JRA began to single out American targets and used car bombs and rockets in attempted attacks on U.S. Embassies in Jakarta, Rome, and Madrid. In April 1988, JRA operative Yu Kikumura was arrested with explosives on the New Jersey Turnpike, apparently planning an attack to coincide with the bombing of a USO club in Naples, a suspected JRA operation that killed five, including a U.S. servicewoman. Kikimura was convicted of the charges and is serving a lengthy prison sentence in the United States. JRA operative Tsutomu Shirosaki, captured in 1996, is also jailed in the United States.

In 2000, Lebanon deported four members it arrested in 1997 to Japan, but granted a fifth operative, Kozo Okamoto, political asylum. Longtime leader Shigenobu was arrested in November 2000 and faced charges of terrorism and passport fraud. In February 2006, Shingenobu was sentenced to 20 years in prison for coordinating the 1974 French embassy siege. Four JRA members remain in North Korea following their involvement in an airline hijacking in 1970; five of their family members returned to Japan in 2004.

Strength

At its peak, the group claimed to have 30 to 40 members.

Location/Area of Operation

Possibly in Asia.

External Aid

Unknown.

KUMPULAN MUJAHEDIN MALAYSIA (KMM)

a.k.a. Kumpulan Militan Malaysia.

Description

Kumpulan Mujahedin Malaysia (KMM) favors the overthrow of the Malaysian government and the creation of an Islamic state comprising Malaysia, Indonesia, and the southern Philippines (and Southern Thailand). Malaysian authorities believe an extremist wing of the KMM has engaged in terrorist acts and has close ties to the regional terrorist organization Jemaah Islamiya (JI). Key JI leaders, including the group's spiritual head, Abu Bakar Bashir, and JI operational leader Hambali, reportedly had great influence over KMM members. The Government of Singapore asserts that a Singaporean JI member assisted the KMM in buying a boat to support jihad activities in Indonesia.

Activities

Malaysia continues to hold a number of KMM members

under the Internal Security Act for activities deemed threatening to Malaysia's national security, including planning to wage jihad, possession of weaponry, bombings, robberies, the murder of a former state assembly member, and planning attacks on foreigners, including U.S. citizens. A number of those detained also are believed to be members of Jemaah Islamiya. Several of the arrested KMM militants reportedly have undergone military training in Afghanistan, and some fought with the Afghan mujahedin during the war against the former Soviet Union. Some members allegedly have ties to Islamic extremist organizations in Indonesia and the Philippines. One alleged KMM member was sentenced to 10 years in prison for unlawful possession of firearms, explosives, and ammunition; eight other alleged members in detention since 2001 were later released in July and November 2004; three others were freed in November 2005. In March 2004, alleged KMM leader Nik Adli Nik Abdul Aziz and other suspected KMM members went on a hunger strike as part of an unsuccessful bid for freedom, but the Malaysian court in September 2004 rejected their applications for a writ of habeas corpus. In September 2005, detention orders for Aziz and eight other alleged KMM members were extended for another two years. The Malaysian government is confident that the arrests of KMM leaders have crippled the organization and rendered it incapable of engaging in militant activities. In May 2004, Malaysian officials denied Thailand's charge that the KMM was involved in the Muslim separatist movement in southern Thailand.

Strength

KMM's current membership is unknown.

Location/Area of Operation

The KMM is reported to have networks in the Malaysian states of Perak, Johor, Kedah, Selangor, Terengganu, and Kelantan. They also operate in Kuala Lumpur. The KMM has ties to radical Indonesian Islamic groups.

External Aid

Largely unknown, probably self-financing.

LORD'S RESISTANCE ARMY (LRA)

Description

The LRA, founded in 1987, succeeded the ethnic Acholi-dominated Holy Spirit Movement and other insurgent groups. LRA leader Joseph Kony has called for the overthrow of the Ugandan government and its replacement with a regime run on the basis of the Ten Commandments. More frequently, however, he has spoken of the liberation and honor of the Acholi people, whom he sees as oppressed by the "foreign" government of Ugandan President Museveni. Kony is the LRA's undisputed leader. He claims to have supernatural powers and to receive messages from spirits, which he uses to formulate the LRA's strategy.

Activities

Since the early 1990s, the LRA has kidnapped some 20,000 Ugandan children, mostly ethnic Acholi, to replenish its ranks. Kony despises Acholi elders for having given up the fight against Museveni and relies on abducted children who can be brutally indoctrinated to fight for the LRA. The LRA kidnaps children and adult civilians to become soldiers, porters, and "wives" for LRA leaders. The LRA prefers to attack camps for internally displaced persons and other civilian targets, avoiding direct engagement with the Ugandan military.

The LRA stepped up its activities from 2002 to 2004 after the Ugandan army, with the Sudanese government's permission, attacked LRA positions inside Sudan. By late 2003, the number of internally displaced persons had doubled to 1.4 million, and the LRA had pushed deep into non-Acholi areas where it had never previously operated. During 2004, a combination of military pressure, offers of amnesty, and several rounds of negotiation markedly degraded LRA capabilities due to death, desertion, and defection of senior commanders.

In October 2005, the International Criminal Court (ICC) issued arrest warrants for Kony and four other top LRA leaders. Since February 2006, the Government of Southern

Sudan has been holding peace talks between the LRA and the Ugandan government.

Strength

Estimated at 500 to 700 fighters.

Location/Area of Operation

Northern Uganda, southern Sudan, and northeast Democratic Republic of the Congo.

External Aid

Although the LRA has been supported by the Government of Sudan in the past, the Sudanese now appear to be cooperating with the Government of Uganda in a campaign to eliminate LRA sanctuaries in Sudan.

LOYALIST VOLUNTEER FORCE (LVF)

Description

An extreme Loyalist group formed in 1996 as a faction of the Ulster Volunteer Force (UVF), the LVF did not emerge publicly until 1997. It is composed largely of UVF hardliners who have sought to prevent a political settlement with Irish nationalists in Northern Ireland by attacking Catholic politicians, civilians, and Protestant politicians who endorse the Northern Ireland peace process. LVF occasionally uses the Red Hand Defenders as a cover name for its actions but has also called for the group's disbandment. In October 2001, the British government ruled the LVF had broken the ceasefire it declared in 1998 after linking the group to the murder of a journalist. According to the Independent International Commission on Decommissioning, the LVF decommissioned a small amount of weapons in December 1998, but it has not repeated this gesture. The LVF was designated under E.O. 13224 in December 2001.

Activities

The group conducts bombings, kidnappings, and close-quarter shooting attacks. It finances its activities with drug money and other criminal activities. LVF attacks have been particularly vicious; the group has murdered numerous Catholic civilians with no political or paramilitary affiliations, including an 18-year-old Catholic girl in July 1997 because she had a Protestant boyfriend. LVF terrorists also have conducted successful attacks against Irish targets in Irish border towns. From 2000 to August 2005, the LVF engaged in a violent feud with other Loyalists, which left several men dead. In October 2005, the group said that it would stand down its "military units," but the Independent Monitoring Commission has no evidence of the LVF disbanding.

Strength

Small, perhaps dozens of active members.

Location/Area of Operation

Northern Ireland and Ireland.

External Aid

None.

NEW RED BRIGADES/COMMUNIST COMBATANT PARTY (BR/PCC)

a.k.a. Brigate Rosse/Partito Comunista Combattente.

Description

This Marxist-Leninist group is a successor to the Red Brigades, active in the 1970s and 1980s. In addition to ideology, both groups share the same symbol, a five-pointed star inside a circle. The group is opposed to Italy's foreign and labor policies and to NATO.

Activities

In 2003, Italian authorities captured at least seven members of the BR/PCC, dealing the terrorist group a severe blow to its operational effectiveness, and the group continued to suffer setbacks in 2005 and 2006, with its leadership in prison, key suspects convicted and sentenced, and additional arrests made. In June 2005, a Rome court sentenced five BR/PCC members to life in prison for the 2002 assassination of Labor Ministry external adviser Marco Biagi. One month later, three of the five also were found guilty of the assassination of Labor Ministry external adviser Massimo D'Antona in 1999, again incurring a life sentence. An additional nine BR/PCC suspects were sentenced to between four and nine years, and some convicted members provided valuable information to Italian authorities, leading to additional arrests. In December 2005, an Italian judge refused to pardon Adriano Sofri, leader of Continuous Struggle (Lotta Continua), a precursor movement to the Red Brigades, whose life sentence was suspended for health reasons. Italian authorities in early December 2006 arrested Fabio Matteini, suspected of trying to recruit new members in an effort to revive the group. The BR/PCC in recent years has financed its activities in part through armed robberies.

Strenth

Fewer than 20.

Location/Area of Operation

Italy.

External Aid

Has obtained weapons from abroad.

PEOPLE AGAINST GANGSTERISM AND DRUGS (PAGAD)

a.k.a. Muslims Against Global Oppression; Muslims Against Illegitimate Leaders.

Description

People Against Gangsterism and Drugs (PAGAD) and its ally Qibla (an Islamic fundamentalist group that favors political Islam and takes an anti-U.S. and anti-Israel stance), view the South African government as a threat to Islamic values. The two groups work to promote a greater political voice for South African Muslims. PAGAD has used front names such as Muslims Against Global Oppression and

Muslims Against Illegitimate Leaders when launching anti-Western protests and campaigns.

Activities

PAGAD formed in November 1995 as a vigilante group in reaction to crime in some neighborhoods of Cape Town. In September 1996, a change in the group's leadership resulted in a change in the group's goal, and it began to support violent jihad to establish an Islamic state. Between 1996 and 2000, PAGAD conducted a total of 189 bomb attacks, including nine bombings in the Western Cape that caused serious injuries. PAGAD's targets included South African authorities, moderate Muslims, synagogues, gay nightclubs, tourist attractions, and Western-associated restaurants. PAGAD is believed to have masterminded the bombing on August 1998 of the Cape Town Planet Hollywood and the 2000 attack on a New York Bagel restaurant in Cape Town. Since 2001, PAGAD's violent activities have been severely curtailed by law enforcement and prosecutorial efforts against leading members of the organization. Qibla leadership has organized demonstrations against visiting U.S. dignitaries and other protests, but the extent of PAGAD's involvement is uncertain.

Strength

Early estimates were several hundred members. Current operational strength is unknown, but probably vastly diminished.

Location/Area of Operation

Operates mainly in the Cape Town area.

External Aid

May have ties to international Islamic extremists.

RAJAH SOLAIMAN MOVEMENT (RSM)

Description

The RSM is a Philippines-based Islamic extremist group comprising Christian converts to Islam, many of whom had embraced extremist Islamic ideology while working in the Middle East. RSM promotes the use of violence and terrorism against Philippine Christians and Westerners with the aim of turning the Philippines into an Islamic state. The group is named after Rajah Solaiman, the last indigenous Muslim ruler of Manila before Spanish rule began in the 16th century.

Activities

The RSM has assisted with the terrorist plots of the Abu Sayyaf Group (ASG) in Manila and other areas in the northern Philippines. It was involved in ASG's bombing of SuperFerry 14 in February 2004, and the February 2005 Valentine's Day bombings, according to Philippine security officials. In 2005 the RSM suffered several major setbacks when in March, Philippine security forces seized more than 1,300 pounds of explosives from an RSM safe house in metropolitan Manila, and in October, Philippine intelligence agents arrested RSM leader Ahmad Santos in Zamboanga City and charged him with plotting to bomb high profile targets, including the U.S. Embassy in Manila. Two months later, Philippine security forces arrested another RSM leader in Zamboanga City. Philippine officials subsequently claimed that debriefing captives helped them thwart an alleged RSM plot to conduct attacks in Manila during the Christmas 2005 holiday season. In late 2006, another RSM leader, Feliciano de los Reyes was arrested.

Strength

The exact number of members in the RSM is unknown, but the group likely has fewer than 50 members.

Location/Area of Operation

The RSM operates throughout the Philippines and maintains a significant presence in metropolitan Manila. Some RSM operatives trained alongside members of the Abu Sayyaf Group and other militants in the southern Philippines.

External Aid

The Abu Sayyaf Group and Jemaah Islamiya have provided training, funds, and operational assistance to the RSM. Some Middle East-based non-governmental organizations and other sympathizers also may provide funds to the RSM.

RED HAND DEFENDERS (RHD)

Description

The RHD is a terrorist group formed in 1998 and composed largely of Protestant hardliners from Loyalist groups observing a ceasefire. RHD seeks to prevent a political settlement with Irish nationalists by attacking Catholic civilian interests in Northern Ireland. In January 2002, the group announced all staff at Catholic schools in Belfast and Catholic postal workers were legitimate targets. Despite calls in February 2002 by the Ulster Defense Association (UDA), Ulster Freedom Fighters (UFF), and Loyalist Volunteer Force (LVF) to announce its disbandment, RHD continued to make threats and issue claims of responsibility. RHD is a cover name often used by elements of the banned UDA and LVF. RHD was designated under E.O. 13224 in December 2001.

Activities

In early 2003, the RHD claimed responsibility for killing two UDA members as a result of what is described as Loyalist internecine warfare. It also claimed responsibility for a bomb that was left in the offices of Republican Sinn Fein in West Belfast, although the device was defused and no one was injured. In recent years, the group has carried out numerous pipe bombings and arson attacks against "soft" civilian targets such as homes, churches, and private businesses. In January 2002, the group bombed the home of a prison official in North Belfast. Twice in 2002 the group claimed responsibility for attacks—the murder of a Catholic postman and a Catholic teenager—that were later claimed by the UDA-UFF, further blurring distinctions between the groups. In 2001, RHD claimed responsibility for killing five persons.

Strength

Up to 20 members, some of whom have experience in terrorist tactics and bombmaking. Police arrested one member in June 2001 for making a hoax bomb threat.

Location/Area of Operation

Northern Ireland.

External Aid

None.

REVOLUTIONARY PROLETARIAN INITIATIVE NUCLEI (NIPR)

Description

The NIPR is a clandestine leftist extremist group that appeared in Rome in 2000. It adopted the logo of the Red Brigades of the 1970s and 1980s, an encircled five point star, for its declarations. NIPR opposes Italy's foreign and labor policies. The group has targeted property interests rather than personnel in its attacks.

Activities

The NIPR has not claimed responsibility for any attacks since an April 2001 bomb attack on a building housing a U.S.-Italian relations association and an international affairs institute in Rome's historic center. The NIPR claimed to have carried out a bombing in May 2000 in Rome at an oversight committee facility for implementation of the law on strikes in public services.

Strength

Fewer than 20 members.

Location/Area of Operation

Mainly in Rome, Milan, Lazio, and Tuscany.

External Aid

None evident.

REVOLUTIONARY STRUGGLE (RS)

Description

RS is a radical leftist group that is anti-Greek establishment and ideologically aligns itself with the Revolutionary Organization 17 November.

Activities

RS is widely regarded as the most dangerous indigenous Greek terrorist group still active and has been linked to attacks against Americans. RS first became known when the group conducted a bombing in 2003 against the courthouse where trials of alleged 17 November members were occurring. In 2004, the group detonated four improvised explosive devices at a police station in Athens. These two attacks were notable for their apparent attempts to target and kill first responders, the first time a Greek terrorist group had used this tactic. RS claimed responsibility for a large explosion in December 2005 in Constitution Square in the center of Athens, apparently targeting the Ministry of National Economy, injuring three and badly damaging the facade of a post office and other buildings. The group claimed responsibility for a bomb explosion in May 2006, near the residence of former Minister of Public Order Giorgos Voulgarakis.

The remotely detonated bomb was placed next to a school along the minister's usual route to work and exploded just minutes before he was due to pass. The explosion wrecked several cars but caused no injuries. RS also claimed responsibility for a rocket-propelled-grenade (RPG) attack against the U.S. Embassy on January 12, 2007. The attack occurred early in the morning when few Embassy personnel were working and there were no injuries, but the RPG damaged a room at the front of the Embassy.

Strength

Likely less than 50 members.

Location/Area of Operation

Athens, Greece.

External Aid

Unknown.

RIYADUS-SALIKHIN RECONNAISSANCE AND SABOTAGE BATTALION OF CHECHEN MARTYRS (RSRSBCM)

Description

Riyadus-Salikhin Reconnaissance and Sabotage Battalion of Chechen Martyrs (RSRSBCM), led by Chechen extremist Shamil Basayev, uses terrorism as part of an effort to secure an independent Muslim state in the North Caucasus. Basayev claimed the group was responsible for the Beslan school hostage crisis of September 2004, which culminated in the deaths of about 330 people; simultaneous suicide bombings aboard two Russian civilian airliners in August 2004; and a third suicide bombing outside a Moscow subway that same month. The group has not mounted a terrorist attack since the Beslan operation. The RSRSBCM, whose name translates into English as "Requirements for Getting into Paradise," was not known to Western observers before October 2002, when it participated in the seizure of the Dubrovka Theater in Moscow. The group was designated under E.O. 13224 in February 2003. The group's viability is in question since its leader Shamil Basayev was killed by Russian forces in July 2006.

Activities

RSRSBCM has primarily engaged in terrorist and guerilla operations against Russian forces, pro-Russian Chechen forces, and Russian and Chechen non-combatants.

Strength

Probably no more than 50 fighters at any given time.

Location/Area of Operation

Primarily Russia.

External Aid

May receive some external assistance from foreign mujahedin.

SIPAH-I-SAHABA/PAKISTAN (SSP)

a.k.a. Millat-I-Islami Pakistan.

Description

The Sipah-I-Sahaba/Pakistan (SSP) is a Sunni sectarian group that follows the Deobandi School. Violently anti-Shia, the SSP emerged in central Punjab in the mid-1980s as a response to the Iranian revolution. Pakistani President Musharraf banned the SSP in January 2002. In August 2002, the SSP renamed itself Millat-i-Islami Pakistan, and Musharraf rebanned the group in November 2003. The SSP also has operated as a political party, winning seats in Pakistan's National Assembly.

Activities

The group's activities range from organizing political rallies calling for Shia to be declared non-Muslims to assassinating prominent Shia leaders. The group was responsible for attacks on Shia worshippers in May 2004, when at least 50 people were killed.

Strength

The SSP may have approximately 3,000 to 6,000 trained activists who carry out various kinds of sectarian activities.

Location/Area of Operation

The SSP has influence in all four provinces of Pakistan. It is considered to be one of the most powerful sectarian groups in the country.

External Aid

The SSP reportedly receives significant funding from Saudi Arabia and wealthy private donors in Pakistan. Funds also are acquired from other sources, including other Sunni extremist groups, madrassas, and contributions by political groups.

SPECIAL PURPOSE ISLAMIC REGIMENT (SPIR)

Description

The SPIR is one of three Chechen-affiliated terrorist groups that furnished personnel to carry out the seizure of the Dubrovka Theater in Moscow in October 2002. The SPIR has had at least seven commanders since it was founded in the late 1990s. Movsar Barayev, who led and was killed during the theater standoff, was the first publicly identified leader. The group continues to conduct guerrilla operations in Chechnya under its current leader, Amir Aslan, whose true identity is not known. SPIR was designated under E.O. 13224 in February 2003. In 2006, SPIR continued to target official Russian targets and Chechen elements it believes to be sympathetic to Russia.

Activities

SPIR has primarily engaged in guerrilla operations against Russian forces and has also been involved in various hostage and ransom operations, including the execution of ethnic Chechens who have cooperated with Russian authorities.

Strength

Probably no more than 100 fighters at any given time.

Location/Area of Operation

Primarily Russia.

External Aid

May receive some external assistance from foreign mujahedin.

AL-TAWHID W'AL JIHAD (TWJ)

a.k.a. Tawhid Islamic Brigades; al-Tawhid Wa al-Jihad; Monotheism and Jihad Organization.

Description

The TWJ is an Egypt-based Islamic extremist group motivated by Cairo's harsh treatment of the Bedouin community and difficult economic conditions in the Sinai. This group is comprised of radicalized Sinai Bedouin, criminals, and smugglers who use their knowledge of the rugged Sinai terrain and their compartmented cell structure to attack Western and Israeli tourist targets.

Activities

The TWJ has conducted bombings and suicide attacks, such as attacks at Taba in October 2004, Sharm ash Shaykh in July 2005, Dhahab in April 2006, and against the Multinational Force and Observers (MFO) in August 2005 and April 2006.

Strength

Unknown. Egyptian security services have killed or captured many high-ranking TWJ members during the past two years.

Location/Area of Operation

Sinai, Gaza.

External Aid

Unknown.

TUNISIAN COMBATANT GROUP (TCG)

a.k.a. Jama'a Combattante Tunisienne.

Description

The Tunisian Combatant Group (TCG), also known as the Jama'a Combattante Tunisienne, seeks to establish an Islamic regime in Tunisia and has targeted U.S. and Western interests. The group is an offshoot of the banned Tunisian Islamist movement, an-Nahda. Founded around 2000 by Tarek Maaroufi and Saifallah Ben Hassine, the TCG has drawn members from the Tunisian diaspora in Europe and elsewhere. It has lost some of its leadership, but may still exist, particularly in Western Europe. Belgian authorities arrested Maaroufi in late 2001 and sentenced him to six years in prison in 2003 for his role in the assassination of anti-Taliban commander Ahmed Shah Massoud two days before 9/11. The TCG was designated under E.O. 13224 in October 2002. Historically, the group has been associated with al-Qaida as well. Members also have ties to other North African extremist groups. The TCG was designated for sanctions under UNSCR 1333 in December 2000.

Activities

Tunisians associated with the TCG are part of the support network of the broader international terrorist movement. According to European press reports, TCG members or affiliates in the past have engaged in trafficking falsified documents and recruiting for terror training camps in Afghanistan. Some TCG associates were suspected of planning an attack against the United States, Algerian, and Tunisian diplomatic missions in Rome in April 2001. Some members reportedly maintain ties to the Algerian Salafist Group for Preaching and Combat.

Strength

Unknown.

Location/Area of Operation

Western Europe and Afghanistan.

External Aid

Unknown.

TUPAC AMARU REVOLUTIONARY MOVEMENT (MRTA)

Description

MRTA is a traditional Marxist-Leninist revolutionary movement formed in 1983 from remnants of the Movement of the Revolutionary Left, a Peruvian insurgent group active in the 1960s. It aims to establish a Marxist regime and to rid Peru of all imperialist elements, primarily U.S. and Japanese influence. Peru's counterterrorist program has diminished the group's ability to conduct terrorist attacks, and the MRTA has suffered from infighting, the imprisonment or deaths of senior leaders, and the loss of leftist support.

Activities

MRTA previously conducted bombings, kidnappings, ambushes, and assassinations, but recent activity has fallen drastically. In December 1996, 14 MRTA members occupied the Japanese Ambassador's residence in Lima and held 72 hostages for more than four months. Peruvian forces stormed the residence in April 1997, rescuing all but one of the remaining hostages and killing all 14 group members, including the remaining leaders. The group has not conducted a significant terrorist operation since and appears more focused on obtaining the release of imprisoned MRTA members, although there are reports of low-level rebuilding efforts.

Strength

Believed to be no more than 100 members, consisting largely of young fighters who lack leadership skills and experience.

Location/Area of Operation

Peru with supporters throughout Latin America and Western Europe and many exiled members live in Bolivia.

External Aid

None

TEHRIK NEFAZ-I-SHARIAT MUHAMMAD (TNSM)

Description

Maulawi Sufi Muhammed (now imprisoned) established TNSM in May 1989 in the former Malakand District of the Northwest Frontier Province (NWFP) of Pakistan with the goal of instituting strict Islamic law in the region because they believe the government failed to institute Sharia law in the NWFP. The group held massive rallies in 1994 and effectively shut down the Malakand District. The uprising ended after the Pakistani government agreed to implement Sharia law in the Malakand District. Islamabad banned the group in 2002 in response to TNSM's deployment of fighters to Afghanistan to fight with the Taliban. Since Sufi Muhammad's arrest in early 2002, the leadership of the group has been in flux. Both Maulawi Faqir Muhammad and Maulawi Fazlullah-Sufi Muhammad's son-in-law-have been mentioned as possible leaders of the group. Faqir Muhammad in November 2006 publicly pledged to continue the jihad in Afghanistan under Taliban leader Mullah Omar.

Activites

TNSM is a party to 2006 peace negotiations with Pakistan. Prior to the peace negotiations, the Pakistani government released nine prisoners associated with TNSM, to include Faqir Muhammad's brother and two senior clerics. On October 28, 2006, TNSM staged an anti-U.S. rally and vowed to continue to support the Taliban but agreed not to shelter foreigners. On October 30, 2006, a madrassa suspected of hosting a terrorist training camp was destroyed in a counterterrorism operation and Pakistani forces killed Maulana Liaqat, the madrassa's director and deputy for the group. At a protest rally following the operation, Faqir Muhammad declared he would continue to wage jihad, but he renewed his pledge to abide by the peace accords and not attack the Pakistani government. Faqir also denied reports that al-Qaida deputy leader Ayman al-Zawahiri was present at the madrassa. Press reports alleged TNSM was responsible for a suicide bombing on November 8 that killed 35 soldiers in Dargai, Pakistan, although the group did not claim responsibility. Pakistan security agencies have reopened investigations on members following this attack. Newspaper announcements requested certain members to appear in court and face charges filed against them under anti-terrorism laws.

Strength

Exact numbers are unknown; however, TNSM has recruited very high numbers of fighters in the past (in the thousands) and has also held demonstrations attended by several thousand people.

Location/Area of Operation

Eastern Afghanistan, Northern Pakistan - particularly Bajaur Agency and Malakand District.

External Aid

TNSM was founded to pursue the implementation of Sharia in the NWFP and stongly supports the Taliban. The group has also been linked to al-Qaida, especially through Faqir Muhammad who has stated that he would welcome Ayman al-Zawahiri and Usama Bin Ladin if they were to come to his area.

TURKISH HIZBALLAH

Description

Turkish Hizballah is a Kurdish Sunni Islamic terrorist organization that arose in the early 1980s in response to the Kurdistan Workers' Party (PKK)'s secularist approach of establishing an independent Kurdistan. Turkish Hizballah spent its first 10 years fighting the PKK, accusing the group of atrocities against Muslims in southeastern Turkey, where Turkish Hizballah seeks to establish an independent Islamic state.

Activities

Beginning in the mid-1990s, Turkish Hizballah, which is unrelated to Lebanese Hizballah, expanded its target base and modus operandi from killing PKK militants to conducting low-level bombings against liquor stores, bordellos, and other establishments the organization considered "anti-Islamic." In January 2000, Turkish security forces killed Huseyin Velioglu, the leader of Turkish Hiz-ballah, in a shootout at a safe house in Istanbul. The incident sparked a year-long series of counterterrorist operations against the group that resulted in the detention of some 2,000 individuals; authorities arrested several hundred of them on criminal charges. At the same time, police recovered nearly 70 bodies of Turkish and Kurdish businessmen and journalists whom Turkish Hizballah had tortured and brutally murdered during the mid-to-late 1990s. The group began targeting official Turkish interests in January 2001, when its operatives assassinated the Diyarbakir police chief in the group's most sophisticated operation to date. Turkish Hizballah has not conducted a major operation since 2001, and probably is focusing at present on recruitment, fundraising, and reorganization.

Strength

Possibly a few hundred members and several thousand supporters.

Location/Area of Operation

Primarily the Diyarbakir region of southeastern Turkey.

External Aid

It is widely believed that Turkey's security apparatus originally backed Turkish Hizballah to help the Turkish government combat the PKK. Alternative views are that the Turkish government ignored Turkish Hizballah activities because its primary targets were PKK members and supporters, or that the government simply had to prioritize scarce resources and was unable to wage war on both groups simultaneously. Allegations of collusion have never been laid to rest, and the Government of Turkey continues to issue denials. Turkish Hizballah also is suspected of having ties with Iran, although there is not sufficient evidence to establish a link.

ULSTER DEFENSE ASSOCIATION/ULSTER FREEDOM FIGHTERS (UDA/UFF)

Description

The Ulster Defense Association (UDA), the largest Loyalist paramilitary group in Northern Ireland, was formed in 1971 as an umbrella organization for Loyalist paramilitary groups such as the Ulster Freedom Fighters (UFF). Today, the UFF constitutes almost the entire UDA membership. The UDA/UFF declared a series of ceasefires between 1994 and 1998. In September 2001, the UDA/UFF's Inner Council withdrew its support for Northern Ireland's Good Friday Agreement. The following month, after a series of murders, bombings, and street violence, the British government ruled the UDA/UFF's ceasefire defunct. The dissolution of the organization's political wing, the Ulster Democratic Party, soon followed. In January 2002, however, the UDA created the Ulster Political Research Group to serve in a similar capacity. In October 2006, a splinter group of the UDA, calling itself Beyond Conflict, publicly announced its mission to assist former UDA members to disengage from the conflict and develop dialogue with local neighborhoods and designated under E.O. 13224 in December 2001.

Activities

The UDA/UFF has evolved into a criminal organization deeply involved in drug trafficking and other moneymaking criminal activities through six largely independent "brigades." It also has been involved in murder, shootings, arson, assaults, and exiling. According to the Independent Monitoring Commission (IMC), "the UDA has the capacity to launch serious, if crude, attacks." Some UDA activities of a sectarian nature directed at the Catholic community are aimed at so-called "soft" targets, and often have taken place at the interface between the Protestant and Catholic communities, especially in Belfast.

Strength

Estimates vary from 2,000 to 5,000 members, with several hundred active in paramilitary operations.

Location/Area of Operation

Northern Ireland.

External Aid

Probably obtains weapons from abroad.

ULSTER VOLUNTEER FORCE (UVF)

Description

The UVF is a Loyalist terrorist group formed in 1966 to oppose liberal reforms in Northern Ireland that members feared would lead to unification of Ireland. The group adopted the name of an earlier organization formed in 1912 to combat Home Rule for Ireland. The UVF's goal is to maintain Northern Ireland's status as part of the United Kingdom; to that end, it has killed some 550 persons since 1966. The UVF and its offshoots have been responsible for some of the most vicious attacks of "The Troubles", including horrific sectarian killings like those perpetrated in the 1970s by the UVF-affiliated "Shankill Butchers." In October 1994, the Combined Loyalist Military Command, which included the UVF, declared a ceasefire, and the UVF's political wing, the Progressive Unionist Party, has played an active role in the peace process. Despite the ceasefire, the organization has been involved in a series of bloody feuds with other Loyalist paramilitary organizations, although the UVF is considering a stand-down similar to that of the Irish Republican Army. The Red Hand Defenders is linked to the UVF.

Activities

The UVF has been active in Belfast and the border areas of Northern Ireland, where it has carried out bombings, assassinations, kidnappings, hijackings, extortion, and robberies. UVF members have been linked to recent racial attacks on minorities; however, the UVF leadership reportedly did not authorize these assaults. On occasion, it has provided advance warning to police of its attacks. Targets include nationalist civilians, Republican paramilitary groups, and, on occasion, rival Loyalist paramilitary groups.

The UVF is a relatively disciplined organization with a centralized command. The Independent Monitoring

Commission has said that UVF members were responsible for the attempted murder in 2006 of Mark Haddock, a former UVF member turned police informant, and main suspect in the 1997 murder of Raymond McCord. Additionally, UVF members are suspected of murdering one individual and attempting to murder another, but the IMC assesses these actions were not sanctioned by UVF leadership.

Strength

Unclear but probably several hundred supporters with a smaller number of hardcore activists. Police counterterrorist operations and internal feuding have reduced the group's strength and capabilities.

Location/Area of Operation

Northern Ireland. Some support on the UK mainland.

External Aid

Suspected in the past of receiving funds and arms from sympathizers overseas.

UNITED LIBERATION FRONT OF ASSAM (ULFA)

Description

Northeast India's most prominent insurgent group, ULFA, an ethnic secessionist organization in the Indian state of Assam, which borders Bangladesh and Bhutan, was founded in 1979 at Rang Ghar, during anti-foreigner agitation organized by the state's powerful students' union. The group's objective is an independent Assam. ULFA enjoyed widespread support in upper Assam in its initial years, especially from 1985 to 1992. ULFA's kidnappings, killings, and extortion led New Delhi to ban the group and start a military offensive against it in 1990, which forced it to go underground.

ULFA began to lose popularity in the late 1990s after it increasingly targeted civilians, including a prominent NGO activist. It lost further support for its anti-Indian stand during the 1999 Kargil conflict. In recent years, the group has been in decline, losing popular support and suffering from aggressive counterinsurgency operations by Indian security forces. The Royal Bhutan Army's attack on ULFA camps in Bhutan in 2003, and the suspension of operations by Bodo tribal insurgent groups in Assam, also contributed to the group's decline. Despite the ban on the group, New Delhi held official talks with ULFA's representative Peace Consultative Group in October 2005, which apparently has had little effect on dampening ULFA's operations against business and government targets in 2006.

Activities

ULFA trains, finances, and equips its cadres for a "liberation struggle", while extortion helps finance military training and weapons purchases. ULFA conducts hit-and-run operations on security forces in Assam, selective assassinations, and explosions in public places. During the 1980s and 1990s, ULFA undertook a series of abductions and murders, particularly of businessmen. In 2000, ULFA assassinated an Assam state minister. In 2003, ULFA killed more than 60 "outsiders" in Assam, mainly residents of the bordering state of Bihar. Some important ULFA functionaries surrendered in Assam, but incidents of violence continue, although of a lesser magnitude than in the past. In 2004, ULFA started targeting civilians and killed some 14 people in August that year.

Strength

ULFA's earlier strength of more than 3,000 dropped following the December 2003 attack on its camps in Bhutan. Total cadre strength now is estimated at several hundred, plus supporters providing safe houses and logistical and intelligence assistance.

Location/Area of Operation

ULFA is active in the state of Assam, and members transit

and periodically conduct operations in parts of the neighboring states of Arunachal Pradesh, Meghalaya, and Nagaland. All ULFA camps in Bhutan are reportedly demolished.

External Aid

ULFA reportedly procures and trades in arms with other Northeast Indian groups.

6

Modus Operandi of International Terrorists Organisations

RELIGION AND TERRORISM

It seems that the opinion of the world has reached a wide accord that the main motive of terrorism is religion. It is widely reported that terrorist action has been theologically justified. In other words, people almost believe that religion gives reason for terror. Therefore, there is a demand that religion is fully responsible of terrorist action. Juergensmeyer, an internationally-respected scholar and analyst on terrorism, agrees as well that one of the main characters of terrorism is —beside the form of violence— being religiously motivated. Moreover, the fact found by Indonesian authorities after the siege Dr. Azahari who is believed as the main actor of terror in Indonesia, also indicates the same. Extreme interpretation on the concept of 'jihâd' in Islam is suspected as theological justification of their violent actions.

Governmental institutions of the United States even believe that theological reason behind violent actions is increasing year by year. In 1980, the American authority identified only one religiously- motivated terrorist organization. The number dramatically increased in 1998 where Albright listed the 30 dangerous groups in the World; more than half is religiously based. RAND-St. Andrews Chronology of International Terrorism even recorded a remarkable development in the next years; 16 of 49 dangerous organization in 1994 became 26 religious groups of 56 dangerous groups have been identified. It is then not surprising if the former State Secretary, Warren Christopher considers that religiously and racistly- motivated terrorist action is the main security challenge after the Cold War.

Interestingly, however, war on terror or killing to fight terrorism declared by President Bush is based as well on the name of God. In his speech in front of US Air troops, President Bush saluted his soldiers, "I'm delighted that I've been invited out here today to salute you, who in my view, are doing the Lord's work." Regardless any other motives, violent and terrorist activities are not dominated only by Muslim. The history records it has been committed almost by all adherents of divined religions. Deadly shooting of 30 Muslims who were praying in al-Quds in 25 February 1994 was perpetrated by Baruch Goldstein, a Zionist-Jews medical doctor. The assassination of John Britton and his bodyguards in Florida was committed by Paul Hill, a conservative Christian.

The killing was even cheerily-welcomed by Christian in America. Moreover, a Christian activist of anti-abortion movement, Eric Robert Rudolph was the perpetrator of the bombing of abortion clinic in Birmingham, Alabama, lesbian bar in Atlanta (Georgia), Atlanta Olympics (1996). Truck and bus explosions in the UK were done by Irish Catholic nationalist. The release of vials of poisonous sarin gas in the Tokyo subway was committed by an adherent of Hindu-Buddhism, Shoko Asahara, and the leader of Aum Shinkrikyo movement. Behind the assassination of Yitzhak Rabin, there was Yigal Amir, a follower of Messianic Zionism movement. The destruction of federal building (1995) was done by Timothy McVeigh, an American Christian militia.

It is almost widely agreed, even though those terrorist actions were not dominated by Muslims, that all these violent and terrorist activities were motivated and justified by religion which conversely has an ultimate goal to share and campaign love and peace among people of the World. Interestingly, only Muslims, according to Lewis, clearly declared that the violent actions are under religion's order, while perpetrators of other religion do not. This was Lewis's answer to a question "why Western media call such crime by Muslim as terror, and does not call the same perpetrators of other religious adherents. In the case of Islam, a devout Muslim, Mark A. Gabriel (a mask name) even says, "Islam is behind terrorism, not Muslims. Muslims are victims. Even the nineteen young people who hijacked the planes and were killed in the crashes-they are victims.

The criminal is Islam." Great scholars of social sciences such as Durkheim, Mauss and Freud, were once perplexed and asked why religion is always joined in these violent actions. Juergensmeyer was also confused, not because bad thing is done by bad people, but by whom who are notabene religious or religiously-good. There must be an explanation, therefore, behind these stories. Because these actions are closely-linked to all religions, the modus operandi is quite different as well. It is possible that background of religious concept and teaching, also influences its various modus operandi.

There is so far, some modus operandi that has been identified; kidnapping, taking hostages and hijacking, armed assassination, bomb blasting, and the most famous suicide bombing or suicide attack. Some other operational modes can be grouped to one the above modus operandi. The concept of self-sacrifice has been long an internal part of war. In the Old Testament, it is reported that a person called Samson killed enemies by sacrificing his self:

And Samson said, "Let me die with the Philistines!" And he bent with all his might so that the house fell on the lords and all the people who were in it. So the dead whom he killed at his death were more than those whom he killed in his life.

In the crusade, a group of Muslim soldiers destroyed one of their vessels, and succeed killed 140 soldiers of their enemy. A Dutch lieutenant, Jan van Speijk, exploded his own vessel at Antwerp port to deny the arrest by the Belgian. In the World War II era, there were a number of suicide cases a kind of struggles. Among the famous, is the case of military suicide mission (kamikaze) of Japan, where a pilot hit his plane of fully explosive materials to a plane of fully soldiers of the Alliance?

Suicide bombing as one of modus operandi of modern terrorist was initially identified in 1972, when the Japanese Red Army (JRA) attacked the hall of Tel-Aviv airport and killed 26 people and injured hundred others. Since then, suicide bombing action is increasing mainly in conflict areas, such as a number of suicide bombings perpetrated by some radical groups in Lebanon in 80s, the explosion of Irâqî's embassy in Beirut (1981) by Islamic Da'wa Party, the bomb blasting of the US embassy by Hizbullah (1983), and the attack of the US and French marine in October 1983. Moreover, the alliance of four groups (Hizbullah, Amal Movement, the Ba'th Party, and Syrian National Party) in Lebanon (1986) has recruited about 50 suicide bombers, including women, to perpetrate suicide bombing in some important places.

The target is not only strategic sites in Lebanon, but also the interests other targeted countries in any place. Besides, the suicide bombing as modus operandi did not only take place in the Middle East region, but also in other regions. Tiger of Tamil group, for example, is suspected to have committed suicide bombing tactics, not less than 240 times since 1987. Among their victim was the Indian Prime Minister, Rajiv Gandhi, who was assassinated by Thenmuli Rajaratnam. In the North Ireland as well since the beginning of 90s, the IRA fighting groups have perpetrated it to fight the soldiers of the United Kingdom. In the same years, the Palestine fighting groups, such as Hamas, Islamic Jihad, and al- Aqsa Martyrs Brigade, have practiced as well the tactic of suicide bombing to fight Israeli troops.

The suicide bombing is getting more popular after the destruction of the World Trade Center (WTC) in New York and Pentagon, Washington DC, on 11 September 2001, which is considered as "the most destructive suicide attacks in history." The tragic attack has killed about not less than 4000 people, including 19 bomb perpetrators. The material and personal loss is uncounted and unpredictable. What is certain is that —after a week— billions of the US dollars dramatically dropped in Free Market. Three months later, exactly on 22 December 2001, it even almost took place again when Richard Reid, tried to blast his/her shoes inside the American Airlines Flight 63.

After the US invasion in Irâq in 2003, suicide attacks have changed to be daily experiment in there, and victims were not only military interests, but also the civil targets which were suspected to support the US and their allies. According to facts recorded, the suicide attacks have taken place in more than 30 countries, such as Afghanistan, Algeria, Argentine, Bangladesh, Chechnya, China, Colombia, Croatia, Egypt, India, Indonesia, Iraq, Israel, Kenya, Kuwait, Lebanon, Morocco, Pakistan, Palestine, Panama, the Philippines, Qatar, Russia, Saudi Arabia, Sri Lanka, Tanzania, Tunisia, Turkey, United Kingdom, Uzbekistan, and USA.

STUDIES ON SUICIDE ATTACKS

The relatively tremendous number of suicide attacks has invited scholars to organize researches and studies on the interesting subject. Links on website and books have been used as media of publication of their scholars' opinion of the subject. The researches and studies vary from the motive, theological reference, up to the ultimate goal of —as they usually consider— the 'sacred' mission. In 1966, Fall already published his studies on Dien Bien Phu, where he focuses his notions on the suicide bombers only while about 30 years later, Swamy published his research on the guerrillas fighter in Sri Lanka. After the famous 9/11, scholars have been more interested to write on the suicide mission. Up to 2005, for example, there have been at least teen publications dedicated to the subject. In this period, Hudson, Bloom, Pape, Gambetta, Scheit and so forth, have published their serious research on various different aspects of suicide attacks.

THE LOGIC OF SUICIDE ATTACKS

When it is blocked and stuck, an extraordinary way usually appears. It could be reckless actions such as suicide attack. The logic of suicide attack is a strategic endeavor to reach a goal while realizing the impossibility of other successful way except the suicide to make pressure. The logic of suicide attack must be taken when natural and ordinary techniques find the way blocked. The main purpose of the suicide attack, according to Robert A. Pape, is "to use the threat of punishment to coerce a target government to change policy, especially to cause democratic states to withdraw forces from territory terrorists' view as their homeland." Terrorists usually reject any alien notions to organize their homeland country believed as their ancestors' inheritance.

They usually have a good and tidy organization as well as strong network system which is uneasy to trace. They usually as well arrange layer organization; they seem as a formal, legal and transparent organization in the surface, but on another layer, they have certain activities that extra carefully work by using cell system, where the lower layer does not know what and whom in the upper layer, but conversely the upper layer clearly understands the lower structure and layer. Therefore, to understand the logic of contemporary terrorism, Harmon has identified some deadly misconception.

First, terrorism is not anymore philosophically defensible, but never moral. Second, the political left and political rights are not anymore the only true enemies, but both are extremes, but not enemies. Third, terrorist acts are not random and mindless, but cold and calculated. Fourth, terrorist are not poor, unemployed, and uneducated, but conversely. Fifth, terrorists are not almost always men, but there are a large number of women terrorists.

FORM OF SUICIDE ATTACKS

Meanwhile, the suicide attack can be generally grouped into three categories:

Firstly, demonstrated terrorism, which is the group who

has a goal to directly win the heart of society. Moreover, one of the purposes of suicide attack is to take attention and support of society, either from the hard liner and the soft one in one hand, and to coerce enemy to follow their instructions and demand, on the other. Extremist or terrorist groups usually have hard and soft targets in their accomplishment of their mission. The former could be armed forces or military, while the latter could be political representatives of unpopular governments. Guerrilla war is of the best choice to destroy the soft target.

There is a shift, however, from targeting the armed forces of a government to its political representatives and even to civilian target. In the case of modern terrorism, they usually have a target a vast number of people watching, not a lot of victim.

Secondly, destructive terrorism which is a more aggressive group. They coerce their will and demand toward enemy with a full pressure, coerce and threat. Doing their action, they selectively choose their real enemy, while other people who do not have any connection to their real enemy are let alive. The Baader-Meinhoft, for example, only points German rich and prosperous people as their main target, as well as some certain Palestine fighting groups who only press certain Israeli groups.

Thirdly, suicide terrorism, which is the most aggressive terrorist groups, as well as the most frightening one. They have no blood and heart to perpetrate destruction, as well as have no care to people mocks toward them. What is the important thing for them is to make full pressure toward their enemy and make them insecure. Their target is usually random and unselective indeed; either "the real opponent" or sympathizers. They become the target entirely.

TACTICS

A suicide attacker generally has a purpose just to make revenge toward a stronger enemy. As the effect of a reality of imbalance of power, there is no possible choice for them except suicide attack. They do not see any feasible solution that will win them, or there is another potential way but it will take an extremely long time and needs more requirements that cannot meet. One of their purpose is to invite people attention; for or against. The wider effect the more successful it is valued. The effect could be unstable market fluctuation, people insecure, and the more widening anxious feeling. The accumulation of negative effect of the suicide attack will then create some discursive solutions within a society, including meeting terrorists' demand.

Their target is not usually addressed to military sites because of certain considerations. They usually address their target to civil sites which directly or indirectly have close connection to the military system and structure, or any other strength. They have no problem with fair facilities and equipment, because they rely very much on their reckless to commit suicide that is unthinkable by common people. They attack by precisely considering the target and time. The IRA, for example, has a slogan "You have to be lucky all the time—we have to be lucky just once". In the Middle East, as well as in the West, meanwhile, they do it in winter where air condition is on and doors and windows are close.

This could lead to more massive explosion. Their skill is usually disseminated from alumni or military deserters, including the technique of bomb installation. In the case of 9/11, a very smart planning and training have been indeed practiced. "... the hijackers spent large sums of money to buy business class seats so that they would be near the front of each plane; the planes chosen were linked to the targets (the two biggest, 767s, with the largest full loads, were targeted at the World Trade Center); the routes flown were those that required most fuel; the date, time and routes of the hijacked planes were deliberately because Tuesday early-morning transcontinental flights have very low passenger numbers with the result that there were few to overpower hijackers armed only with box-cutters; the departure airports were close to the targets, thus producing surprise when the planes went off course and also maximizing the amount of fuel on board; and the timing of the flights was chosen to ensure that the attacks were close together."

Moreover, contemporary terrorists have also sophisticated their mission by using a high grade of high quality of intelligence. They have even infiltrated, according to Gunaratna, Middle Eastern and other governments. Some former police officers and military personnel including European military and at least one US military deserter have served in Al Qaeda. Perpetrators typically wear loose clothe or coat that is bigger than their body so that the bomb installed to their body is unseen. For women perpetrators, they frequently do not find any difficulties since they could hide the bomb inside their loose hijab. Perpetrators habitually wear as well backpack as the case in Bali.

Based on the recording camera, perpetrators will unintentionally show strange and uncommon attitudes, such as clothe model worn, being confused and sweaty, their hand always hold trigger button, being like in a rush while paying extra attention to security in the targeted place. Technical steps of suicide attack frequently have similarities, among them:

Firstly, maximizing the basic concept of the mission. Religious terrorist groups always undergo consolidation and indoctrination to candidates to avoid the presence of doubt in their heart. They should be absolutely sure that what they are going to do is jihad, a sacred mission that will be granted paradise as reward.

Secondly, quarantining the candidates. After being successful in selection, they will directly quarantined in a certain and secret place. During the quarantine, they are barewashed by specialists. It is completely forbidden to make communication to the world, even to their family.

Thirdly, observing the target. To gain a maximum goal, they should monitor the target precisely, including security system, recording camera, skilled dog, detection system, attitude and mobility of people around the target.

Fourth, preattack step. They should master surrounds of the target including seeing any alternatives ways as plan B.

Fifth, last coordination to do the mission. They should be fully sure that there will be no indication to identify perpetrators or the mastermind.

Sixth, tryout that —from the simulation— they can identify any weaknesses.

Seventh, after the tryout, they should take full care to their health and their soul.

Executor is usually not alone. Several people of the group will be around the perpetrator to do anything, including destroying the vehicle of the perpetrator. Eight, post execution. If the perpetrator is arrested or the mission is fail, then the mastermind has been ready with new identity, and tickets to go any secure place. Meanwhile, they usually practice guerilla tactic, moving from an area to another. Everywhere they are in, they really try to win people support, influence them to support terrorist ideology. They create a highly jihad spirit in the community they are in. They often use the language of people to influence the local people, including the use of language and religious reason.

They imagine their struggle as sacred mission that needs support, and conversely they consider the target as evil (tâghût) that has to be destroyed. Muslim terrorist, for example, usually consider their struggle as sacred jihad with entire cost that is also considered as sacred sacrifice (istishhad). Person who dies to fight evil and injustice is considered as shuhâdâ' who do not need to be cleaned and shrouded of unbleached cotton, because they believe that the martyr will directly enter the promised paradise. To support their notion, they quote some pieces of Qur'ânic versed and Hadis that are understood in the framework of their own way of thinking.

PROFILE OF ATTACKER

Person involving in a suicide attack consists of levels. They usually do not know each other. What is certain is that they have locally and internationally intellectual actors, as well as financial funding with a good and tidy management which not uneasy to trace through conventional traces. Moreover, suicide bombers originally come from low level of education, marginalized group in a society, closest family member of victim of their enemy. Nevertheless, these states are not rigid. According to Atran, while pointing out some facts, suicide bombers may conversely come from educated class and established family. This is even the common case nowadays. The perpetrators of 9/11, for example, prove the latter possibility. Therefore, the perpetrators are not only irrational and fanatic groups of economically and educationally low level, but also educated people and financially established. The perpetrators of 9/11 are alumni of great worldly-class universities and from economically established group. One of them is a pilot with annual income 100.000 USD. They even according to Atran's research do not indicate of having symptoms of psychopathology. Strict selection in the recruitment of suicide bombing candidate will not welcome to people with mental disorder, since the mission accomplished is not easy indeed and needs high intelligence. Candidates of hijackers or bomber should have an advance skill well-known as counter-intelligence specialists, as the hijackers of 9/11.

The perpetrators usually have characters as follow:

1. Approximately between 13-47 years-old.
2. Generally not married, and have no children.
3. Generally not married, have no established income, from low level of economy, man or women.
4. It is not necessary that their citizenship is the country of target. Their citizenship could be different, as long as they have the same mission. The perpetrators of the case of 9/11 have various citizenship, albeit they are dominates by Saudis.
5. Some of the perpetrators were sentenced in jail, or being lifetime physically defect by Israeli soldiers.
6. The perpetrators admitted of losing their family members due to Israeli occupation.

MOTIVE AND TARGET OF SUICIDE TERRORISTS

The perpetrators do not only restrict to Islamic jihad groups, but also to other religious adherents and radical groups. Among them is the movement of Liberation Tigers of Tamil Eelam (LTTE), a group recruiting Hindu Tamil groups that affiliate to Marxist/Leninist ideology. LTTE is reported to have perpetrated attacks and suicide bombing 186 times between 1980 and 2001. The group initially struggled for special autonomy in the North region and East Sri Lanka. Perpetrators cannot only be grouped as hardliner or radical group. Among the perpetrator, there are a number of secular groups. In Palestine, suicide attack is not only committed by Hamas and Islamic Jihad (two hardliner groups that recently won the election in Palestine), but also by Fatah, a moderate and secular group.

Meanwhile, the targeted goals of the perpetrators are as follow:

1. To destruct the target with maximum effect, including international attention.
2. International media will cover, then their mission become more popular.
3. Suicide attack is uneasy to be fought since the perpetrator dies, while the perpetrator group has been completely ready to face any possibilities.
4. To attack and suicide bomb is quite simple, and often does not need any cost and energy.
5. In Palestine, family of perpetrators will be guaranteed by the recruiting group.
6. The perpetrator in general was from low level social class and marginalized group. After the suicide bombing, however, their family will be treated as respected family.
7. Considering suicide attack as sacred mission (jihad), their martyrdom is considered shuhadâ' which is believed to enter the promised paradise without any checking.
8. In the promised paradise, they believe to get some privileges such as:
    a. The most honor and eternal place in the paradise.
    b. To have opportunity to see and enjoy the face of God.
    c. To have 72 fairies who will fully serve entire needs.

d. To be granted to allow his 70 close family members to the paradise.

The strength of the religious believes of the perpetrators can be seen from their last will letters to their family, as follow:

1. Hisham Ismâ'îl 'Abd al-Rahmân Hâmid, who committed suicide attack in November 1994 in Nezarim, and killed some Israeli soldiers: "Dear family and friends! I write this will with tears in my eyes and sadness in my heart. I want to tell you that I am leaving and ask for your forgiveness because I decided to see Allah today and this meeting is by all means more important then staying alive on this earth..."
2. Shalâh 'Âbid al-Hâmid Shâkir, who perpetrated suicide bomb in Beit Lid in January 1995, and killed 18 Israel: "I am going to take revenge upon the sons of the monkeys and the pigs-the Zionists infidels and the enemies of humanity. I am going to meet my holy brother Hishâm Hâmid and my distinguished teacher, Hânî al-'Âbid and other Shahids and saints in paradise, Please forgive me" The aforesaid last will statements strongly indicate the strictness of the recruitment and indoctrination that reach their heart, so there will be no sorry for the victim.

THEOLOGY OF SUICIDE ATTACKS

Rather than his various alias names such as Abdul Aziz (real name) or Qudama, he is more well-known as Imam Samudra. He has been sentenced to death on 10 September 2003 after getting arrested on 26 November 2002 as one of Bali bombing (12 October 2002) perpetrators. During in prison he called "istana 'uzlah" (lit. 'uzla palace), he wrote his autobiography and his theological perception on jihad and suicide bombing which is in his term 'bom syahid'. ....

The phenomenon of suicide attack has invited Muslim clerics to issue their legal opinion or fatwâ. Yûsuf al-Qardâwî, one of the most influential Muslim clerics nowadays, for example, allows it only in Palestine, while Nawâf Hayl al-Tikrârî does not only limit it in Palestine. More particular, Ja'far Umar

Thalib, the leader of Indonesian Laskar Jihad, interestingly says that suicide bombing of 9/11 is a bid'a (religious innovation) meaning that it is not allowed.

Imam Samudra likely often quotes the opinion of Sufyân b. 'Uyayna, a prominent Muslim cleric of tâbi'în (second Muslim generation after the sahâba) and one respected teachers and predecessors of Imam al- Syâfi'î, saying that "if you find people having different opinion, completely follow the opinion of mujâhidîn and ahl al-thugûr, because Allah says, "Allah really gives them guidance". "The opinion is quoted in order to free Muslim from various opinions on jihad and suicide bombings. Ahl al-thugûr has been understood as Muslims standing in front lines of jihad.

In order to explain his theological defense, Imam Samudra quotes as well Ibn Nuhâs' opinion in his Mashâri' al-Ashwâq explaining a chapter called inghimâs literarily meaning to enter among enemies. Ibn Nuhâs quotes some heroic stories taking place at the time of sahâba.

- In his al-Musannif, Ibn Abî Shayba tells a riwâya (story), "One of enemi's battalions from the East had arrived. A man of Ansâr welcomed them. He came forward alone and hit the enemy's battalion. He then left the disordered battalion and repeated his action three times. Sa'îd b. Hishâm al-Ansârî told Abû Hurayra the story. Giving his comment, Abû Hurayra recited (a Qur'ânic verse), "there is among people who sacrifice their selves to find the bless of God" (Q.S. al-Baqara [2]: 207)."
- Al-Tirmidhî, Abû Dâwud, al-Hâkim, and Ibn Hibbân reported from Aslam b. Yazîd al-Tujaybî (Abû 'Imrân) saying, "a huge number of Roman troops attacked us when we were in Rome. A relatively fair number of more Muslim troops faced them. Egyptian battalion was under the leadership of 'Uqba b. 'Âmir, while the common troop (al-jumu'a) was led by Fudâla b. 'Ubayd. A Muslim soldier suddenly came forward and hit the Roman barricade. People who saw him screamingly said, "Subhân Allâh, he entered to destruction." Abû Ayyûb

al- Ansâri, however, challenged people scream, and said, "O, Muslims, you have misunderstood the verse that was actually revealed to us, the Ansâr. Allah had won Muslim at the time and the number of Muslim was already huge. Behind the Prophet, we secretly told among others, "our wealth has been and Allah has won Islam. It is much better for us to rehabilitate our wealthy. Allah then revealed the verse, "and spend of your substance in the cause of God, and make not your own hands contribute to (your) destruction" (Q.S. al- Baqara [2]: 195).

- Al-Bayhaqî reported that in a battle to face murtad (sectarian) group that is well-known as Yamama battle, Barrâ' b. Mâlik asked his close friends to throw him passing the barrier of the murtad group, and wearing junna. He completely waged war by killing 10 enemies and getting 80. Commenting the action, none of the sahâba blamed him.

Imam Samudra understood the above stories that suicide attack has been agreed as ijmâ'or convention. He clearly says that jibaku action often called as well as istimât (looking for death) or istishhâd (looking for syahid /martyr) is mashrû'(something divinely ordered). The above stories tell as well that people who acted suicide attack still use weapon to wage war. How about people who acted it without weapon? Imam Samudra then aswers by quoting a Hadis that Mu'âdh once asked the Prophet, "what does people do to make God laugh? The Prophet answered, "Hitting the barricade of enemy without using any covering uniform. Hearing the answer, Mu'adh then took off his uniform, and waged war until getting killed."

Another critical note, however, can be forwarded to Imam Samudra, that suicide attack 'may be divinely allowed' when the martyr is killed by the weapon of enemy, not by his own weapon. Moreover, the above stories clearly indicate that the martyrs were killed by the weapon of enemy. The comment is significant since the contemporary suicide attack would die by his own weapon (read: bom). A famous Hadis tells that, "whoever kills him or her self with a thing; he/she will be tortured by the thing he/she used to kill. The Hadis was reported by Abu Zanad from Thâbit b. Dahhâk r.a., as well as by al-Jamâ'ah in their works, from Abû Qalâbah.

Interestingly, Samudra already has an answer, indeed by the way he usually thinks. He tells again a story of Ghulâm, a young man who struggled for his tawhîd at the time of the Prophet. King of infidels planed to kill him, but always failed. Ghulam said to the King, "you will never kill me unless you follow my instruction." Ghulâm continued, "gather people in a huge court and crucify me on a cross wood. Take my weapon and shoot me after saying bi-ismi Allâh Rabb Ghulâm." The King followed the instruction, and Ghulâm finally died. People who witnessed the event then spontaneously said, biism Allâh Rabb al-Ghulâm literarily meaning "on the name of Allah, God of Ghulâm." What Samudra understands from the story is that Ghulam's instruction to the King to kill him with that way is indeed a suicide act, but – in his own words – "the Syari'a speaks oppositely."

This means – according to Samudra – that the Syari'a allows suicide act, regardless any requirements to act suicide. Moreover, Samudra also quotes a notion from Imâm al-Ghazâlî that "there is no controversy that a Muslim is allowed to attack barricade of enemy, even though he knows that he would be killed." What can be learned from the way Samudra understands on the above stories is that suicide attack is not merely a technically modus operandi as other modus operandi of criminal acts, but – beyond it – it has as well theological references, at least according to his understanding. Therefore, Samudra did not hesitate to commit or to act such suicide as his modus operandi, as well as he never felt sorry for his action that has killed a lot of innocent people.

CASE HANDLINGS OF SUICIDE BOMBING OF TERRORISM IN INDONESIA

In the past decade, the bomb blast cases in Indonesia started in 1999 and have been escalating. However, suicide bombing case in Indonesia started from the Bali Bomb blast case in 2002. In police record, there have been eight suicide bomb blast cases that have been revealed, thirteen suicide bombing perpetrators have been captured. From information of the suspects and evidences obtained, there are the following similarities:

1. The motivation of suicide bombers is to revenge on the death of civilians, women and children in Afghanistan, Iraq and Palestine.
2. They are acting as suicide bombers as it is justified by their religion.
3. They prepare wills to their families, both in the form of letters and electronic recording.
4. They put all citizens of United States and citizens its allies as enemies, and, when met everywhere and anywhere, may be killed and their possessions seized.

This would discuss how police revealed the suicide bombing cases in Indonesia, prevent the suicide bombers, obstacles faced in the implementation, problems faced and some recommendations.

REVELATION OF SUICIDE BOMBING CASES

Bali suicide bomb blast case in 2002 could be revealed in a relatively short time due to the correct processing of crime scene. From the crime scene processing in Legian, Bali, the following facts were found:

1. The main ingredient used for bomb was potassium chloride triggered by some high power explosives such as TNT and RDX.
2. High explosive bomb in front of Sari Club which created a crater of 12 meter square and depth of 65 centimeters was brought using a Mitsubishi vehicle type L-300.
3. Bomb in Paddy's Pub was carried by a person using a vest containing bomb.
4. Suicide bombers in Mitsubishi vehicle were known as coming from Malingping village in Banten, which is more than 1000 kilometers from Bali, and they were identified based on DNA testing of the perpetrators' parents.

Due to police hard work through processing of crime

scene that involved many experts, the owner of Mitsubishi L-300 could be known. Although the ownership of car had changed six times, the last owner of the car could be apprehended, which was AMROZI, in a remote village in Lamongan, East Java. From the interrogation of AMROZI, the network of perpetrators, motivation, fund source and how the bombing in Bali was conducted could be known.

Because of experience and knowledge in revealing the 2002 Bali Bomb blast, other suicide bombing cases using cars as bomb carrier after 2002, could be revealed fast and the perpetrators could be apprehended immediately. The key factor to reveal those bomb blast cases is still the appropriate processing of crime scenes. The JW Marriot bomb blast case (2003) and bomb blast in front of the Embassy of Australia (2004) could be revealed through identification of cars used, type of bombs used and the terrorist network conducting the bombing. Indonesian police is not only able to reveal the bombing perpetrators after the bombing has taken place, but also has been successful in apprehending the suicide bombers ready to conduct their action and preventing them before they activated the bombs they were carrying.

Similarly, the Indonesia police were successful in apprehending candidate perpetrators who were prepared to be suicide bombers who had prepared their wills to their families before they were able to conduct their action. After the terrorists found out that Indonesian police were always successful in revealing suicide car bomb cases, in 2005, the terrorists changed their tactics by using backpack carrying suicide bombers. This was so that the police could not reveal the case since there were no cars used whose owners could be identified. Once again, the police worked hard to conduct crime scene processing on the three bomb blast site in Bali on October 1, 2005. Through crime scene processing, the three perpetrators and the bomb signatures could be revealed.

Since on each of the three crime scenes, parts of heads, arms and legs, as well as maimed torsos were be recovered, police processing the crime scene referred to the suicide Bali bombing case in Paddy's Pub in 2002, in which the suicide bomber suspect left parts of body such as head, arms and legs only. Subsequently, the police tried to reconstruct the three heads as originally as possible, and the reconstruction result was distributed to places suspected as the place of origin of suicide bombers. Once again, through meticulous crime scene processing involving bomb experts from Indonesia, Australia, England, United States, Australia and Japan, the bomb signatures could be identified, such as the container of the bomb, batteries used, detonators, switch system, explosives and materials of the bomb. From the identification of bomb signatures, it could be concluded that those bombs shared similarities with bombs found in Bandung, Cicurug and Leuwiliang, which had the same characteristics of bombs made by DR. AZAHARI. Thus, the search of suspect was focused on DR. AZAHARI's group. At last, through surveillance and analysis of intelligence data, the hiding place of DR. AZAHARI could be found and in the police raid, DR. AZAHARI was shot dead before he could activate his vest bomb. From the revelation of DR. AZAHARI's network, the identities of the three suicide bombers could be revealed from DNA examination of the family members.

HANDLING SUICIDE BOMBERS

The handling of suicide bombing case has been discussed above, in which the processing is dependent on the examination of crime scene, which could lead to the revelation of the identify of suicide bombers and their network. After the network was revealed, analysis on communication of all their activities was conducted through investigation, surveillance, stake out and undercover operation. In the end, some suicide bombers candidates were captured as well as some evidences, such as Abdul Rauf, Andre Oktavia, Andi Hidayat, Junaedi, Urwah, and Apuy.

In the tracking of terrorist network, suicide bombers ready with bombs on their bodies could also be captured. Facing this kind of situation, police must be very careful and must calculate every risk that might occur. Apprehending of JW Marriot Hotel bombing perpetrator, who were TOHIR and ISMAEL, was conducted in Cirebon by waiting for the time when they were unaware, which was during sahur (fasting month breakfast). To eliminate the risk of having the bombs they carried be exploded, the hands of the suspects as the main target were secured and the bombs seized.

The processing was different from the apprehending of bomb perpetrators in front of Australian Embassy, who were ROIS alias IWAN DARMAWAN and SOGHIR. Both suspects in their safe house were lured out of their house with false information to distract their concentration, and the raid team was given specific tasks of securing their hands as well as seizing the bombs from the bodies of the suicide bombers candidates. Not all suicide bombers candidates are ready to conduct suicide, although they have carried the bombs on their bodies. CHOLILY, a house mate of DR. AZAHARI, who became a courier for NOORDIN M TOP, could be captured although he was carrying bombs in his backpack.

When he was apprehended by the police, he showed his backpack containing bombs, but when the police pointed their guns and threatened to shoot his dead, CHOLILY immediately raised his hands and was managed to be apprehended by the police. This is different from the apprehending of DR. AZAHARI, who was an expert in bomb making. During police raid, DR. AZAHARI put a fight by shooting at the police and threw 11 bombs. However, DR. AZAHARI, who had managed to wear the vest bomb died in the raid with two gun shot wounds on his left chest. This condition was different from ARMAN, a room mate of DR. AZAHARI, who died by blowing up himself with vest bomb on his body during the police raid.

OBSTACLES

Although Indonesia is considered to be successful in handling terrorism through law enforcement, there are some obstacles in the implementation. The obstacles among others are the capability of law enforcers, the use of evidences, problems of identification and the use of prepaid cellular phone. Law enforcement officers, investigator, prosecutor and judge, who handle suicide bombing cases, are not specifically prepared for this. What happened is that:

- The handling of terrorism cases with suicide bombers uses the perspective of general crimes
- The handling of secret network uses the perspective of formal organization
- The expertise on terrorist network is minimal
- Willingness to see other terrorism cases and the terrorism data base is lacking, and
- The handling of terrorism cases is assigned to any investigators, prosecutors and judges available.

Therefore, a terrorist defendant who has given testimonials for the prosecution of another defendant could give different testimony on his own prosecution, and this is not known by the law enforcement officers handling the court proceedings. Although there has been extension of evidence used in the Counter Terrorism Law, the minimum use of evidence stipulated in the Criminal Code may not be sufficient to disclose conspiracy or intellectual actors of the terrorism perpetrators. In the investigation process conducted by the police, facts are found that suspects uses many aliases and possessed several identity cards, such as national identity cards, driving licence and passport.

The lack of single identity number system hinders the tracking of terrorist actors and their networks, since it is easy to conduct transactions or activities using forged documents. The use of cellular telephones by the terrorists, who have been very careful in protecting their activities and the identities of themselves and their groups, also hinders the police, because the system of prepaid cellular cards in Indonesia has not obligated the users to give their identities. This makes the investigation hindered since the identities of cellular phone owners known to be communicating among terrorist network are difficult to detect.

Issues

Some of Indonesians only believe what they want to believe and could not accept facts they do not like. The impact is that, there are always biased rumors circulating about the terrorism prevention activities. Such as, the apprehension of terrorist suspects is seen as kidnapping Islamic or mosque activities, the apprehension by the police is because they are being dictated by the United States. They do not want to see the facts that those being apprehended are because they have conducted murders or terrors and so on.

What happened in the Middle East could be inspiration for terrorists to conduct similar activities in Indonesia. For example, bomb blast activities changed into suicide bombings, the bomb targets switched from public places and religious places into western interest, the wills and threat of suicide bombers switched from letters into audio visual electronic recording for propaganda, and so on. From investigation result, some facts are found that in certain society there have been some suicide bombers candidates, both directly recruited by Noordin M Top group as well as those influenced by Osama bin Laden's propaganda. This propaganda could be easily found, both in the form of books as well as electronic data easily accessed from internet.

This means that there may be suicide bombers candidates among us, just waiting for the triggering factors. The suicide bombers have different logics from ordinary people, since death is not a daunting factor for them, but a purpose. The faster they die, the better, since they would be free from all worldly concerns. Most importantly, they would get reward according to the religious belief they practice, and thus, heavy punishment is not a deterrent for them.

RECOMMENDATION

Overcoming suicide bombing problem will not be sufficient by only conducting law enforcement activities. Greater role of the government is necessary to prevent bombings using suicide bombers, with the following means:

- Preventing all activities that may provoke interest on becoming suicide bombers, including involving religious figures that could prevent the interest on becoming suicide bombers;

- Voicing the unfairness of Middle East cases;
- Ulemas should give enlightenment by using religious principles that could straighten the understanding of religious beliefs of all apprehended terrorists, especially for those who have been ready to be suicide bombers.
- Strategic and smart action through international cooperation by publishing books, conducting public debates and disseminating audio visual recordings that are against suicide bombing actions should be conducted as often as possible.

TERRORISM AND ITS IMPACT ON DOING BUSINESS IN ASIA

The reactions of the United States and allied nations' to the terrorist attacks of September the 11th, 2001 have impacted business in Asia through increased costs and compliance. The common costs that have been highlighted are the costs of increased insurance, freight and security costs. However, costs that are often hidden and unquantified by businessmen and women in the region include those relating to the transfer of money, compliance with new laws that are being introduced by the United States, such as the Homeland Security Act of 2001 and the USA PATRIOT Act 2001, and the growing immigration hassles caused by new and perceived threats to the United States and allied nations. This chapter will analyse these issues and suggest some improvements that could ease the process for doing business post September 11th and the compliance regime. The chapter starts with an introduction to the issues and problems.

The 'globalisation' of terrorist groups such as Al Qaeda and their expansion plans in the Asia Pacific region had been neglected by many analysts and the United States until September 2001. The groups such as Jemiah Islamiah (JI), Abu Sayyaf and the Moro Islamic Liberation Front (MILF) have been in existence since the early 70's and have been active in the Asia Pacific region since the early 80's. Their aims are to disrupt trade, overthrow moderate governments, and try to form a triangle of Islamic States in the Asian region. While the United States and associated States knew of their existence they did not see them as a serious threat to their countries.

Prior to September 11th 2001, there were various veterans of the Afghanistan conflict present in the local region and actively recruiting trainees to fight for their causes, including the mujahideen, volunteers who fought the Soviet Union in that conflict. Bin Laden himself was said to have turned his attention to this region to build up his network of fighters who were picked and sent to Afghanistan for training. All of these activities were seen to be domestic in the context of global terrorism and had been ignored by international law enforcement organisations until September 2001. Yet one of the major outcomes of this was that the funds, which were flowing freely for financing of these groups, did not attract the attention of any relevant authority such as the Financial Action Task Force (FATF) or even the United Nations money laundering initiatives.

In fact, it has been argued by US Senators in the recent Joint Hearings on Terrorism before the subcommittee on Asia that much of the funds that were used to finance (and even today continue to finance) these activities were received from charities, sympathetic governments and business organisations that are engaged in business activities in the Asia Pacific region. Thus, one of the greatest challenges facing the global community in its fight against terrorism is the development of effective strategies that can be used to stop funds from reaching the terrorists, especially in the Asian region. Many governments in this region are gaining from the terrorist activities and as such do not have a genuine interest in cutting the free flow of funds to these groups. Moreover, even countries such as Malaysia, Singapore, Indonesia and the Philippines that do have a genuine interest in cutting the free flow of funds to the terrorists, need the support of the entire region and this is not forthcoming.

In January 2002, the Singapore government arrested 32 members of the JI group in Singapore who were alleged to be planning attacks on US interests in Malaysia, Singapore,

Indonesia and the Philippines. Their arrests brought to light the fact that more than 135 JI militants had been travelling through South East Asia while planning these activities, raising questions regarding the ease with which these militants had been travelling through the region both before and after September 11th 2001.

The terrorist attacks of October 2002 in Bali, Indonesia, and August 2003 in Jakarta gave further proof that these activities were being funded actively by various organisations. Recent articles explain in detail how funds from Al Qaeda were channelled to radical groups in the Asian region. The articles assert that not only were Saudi based charities used to channel these funds to Indonesia, but that many front companies and corporate entities have been set up by Al Qaeda in the region. These entities generate revenue, raise capital, and fund radical groups to operate in Indonesia, Thailand and the Philippines. Links by 'mainstream' corporate entities have not been suggested in any of these articles, but the United States original list of banned individuals, companies and charities had many names of individuals and 'mainstream' corporate entities on it. In addition, the very nature of doing business in some countries in the region requires companies to make contributions to charitable and political organisations.

The risk of funds earmarked for major infrastructure projects reaching these organisations or groups cannot be underestimated. Even a very small portion of infrastructure-related funds reaching these organisations would be enough to launch a Marriott or Bali type terrorist activity. One recent documented example of what goes on when major infrastructure projects are being negotiated is provided by a major United States-based power consortium. This consortium is said to have spent between U$18-U$25 billion in payments to consultants and community based organisations including charities in the Asian region when developing relationships with the respective countries.

Some of these funds could easily have been channelled to charities and organisations supporting terrorism and in the current environment, such behaviour would have been heavily scrutinised with the new disclosure related laws and regulations in place to prevent the financing of terrorism. What is odd, however, is that the US since 1967 has had a law strictly forbidding the use of bribes and so on in foreign regions by US citizens, or being condoned by US citizens: yet little has been done to prevent cash flows such as that mentioned above. The existence of hawala (unregulated banking systems) related financing of terrorism has been highlighted but recent estimates put the amount being funded through these systems at less than 5% of funds passing through the entire hawala system.

As an example from South Asia alone, about U$15b-illion dollars is said to be operating in the hawala system. What is important though is to realise that these banking systems almost always seem to serve the terrorist on the ground and their families, and this is one reason why the United States and the United Nations are keen to disrupt the hawala based banking systems.

The question then is how is all or any of this relevant to infrastructure development and productivity? In simplistic terms, all companies operating in the Asia Pacific region now have to comply with the new stringent requirements imposed on them if they want to do business with any of their major trading partners including the United States and many countries of the European Union. The reality of the above situation has resulted in the USA, United Nations and European Union acting fast to try and stop terrorist financing in the region.

While the perceived 'over- reaction' by the USA mainly in creating rigorous disclosure requirements particularly for companies operating in the Asian region may appear harsh, they are understandable, and it is important to recognize the reality of the situation and why these steps could play a crucial role in reducing funding to the radical terrorist organisations in the region.

THE CONTEXT OF THIS STUDY

This chapter is based on a study that was looking into the level of understanding that people in Indonesia, Malaysia, China and Vietnam had in relation to trade liberalisation initiatives in the region. The original study started in early 2001 and was to be completed in December 2002. The part of the study that concentrated on issues to do with understanding the new requirements for doing business post-September 11th 2001: it began in November 2002 and was completed in March 2003. During the course of the original study, it became obvious to the researchers that a major issue facing businessmen and women in the region was the effect of new legislation that was being implemented to curb terrorism, and in particular, legislation and rules introduced by the United States.

The issue was not in relation to the legislation itself but mainly a lack of understanding of what may be required on the part of the local businesses to prevent themselves from being 'blacklisted' by the major trading partners and multilateral agencies. The government of each respective country and financial institution had been publicising the new legislation in relation to financial transactions and rules of scrutiny mainly regarding the need for extreme care in knowing who and what businesses were dealing with. The danger was in being 'involved' with any of the then 300 blacklisted charities, business organisations and individuals on the US list who were operating in this region.

Participants indicated their keen interest to understand how the new rules and regulations would work and what the impact of these new rules would have in their business and day-to-day activities. About 60% of the participants indicated that they already were having problems dealing with their trading partners, especially when they were engaged in major infrastructure related projects that were being funded by firms and agencies overseas. The participants did not know what they would have to do in future and how they could prevent doing business with blacklisted firms and individuals.

The study was based on a methodology known as critical hermeneutics, which uses focus groups to ensure that people from different backgrounds participate in the learning process leading to ownership of the issues in question. This methodology also ensures that effects of cultural differences of the different focus groups are minimised. Two groups from each country participated in the study and each group ranged from six to eight participants. The participants came from various backgrounds including senior government officers, multinational companies and local businesses. Unfortunately there was no gender balance in the ratio of males to females, and each group had only two female participants.

Throughout the process, all participants were assured that their identities would be kept confidential, as numerous concerns were expressed with regards to their identities being made public. This assurance had to be provided at every meeting, and also when private interviews were conducted by the researchers. The groups met twice during the course o the study and had access to the chief researcher at all times during the four months. Private interviews were conducted with the participants after the two meetings to identify any further problems and issues that the participants faced, and wanted to raise. Before the first meeting, a document was circulated to all participants outlining the current status of legislation and rules concerning money laundering, financing of terrorists, rules governing companies that are dealing with defence related tenders in the USA and the new related laws enacted by the United States.

This was to refresh their memory so that they could more easily identify the regulations and laws with which they had faced problems in recent times. The focus groups each had a leader who facilitated the discussion and the main aim was to identify and discuss the obstacles or perceived obstacles faced by the participants in carrying out their business post September 11th 2001. Each group identified the issues and drew up a list that was written up and discussed at the second meeting. It must be pointed out that only the chief researcher was present at all eight focus group meetings.

The groups also discussed how they could improve the way the organisations were operating, based on their experiences relating to the new laws and regulations post September 11th 2001. The group leaders drew up a list of ideas on what could be done to assist the companies and individuals to operate in this new environment, and the issues raised in this list were discussed and further refined. The above project was given the codename Business 911.

DOING BUSINESS IN A POST 9/11 ENVIRONMENT

Issues that were identified by the groups ranged from perceived discrimination through country profiling, religious profiling, and name profiling. The participants felt that having Muslim sounding names for individuals, and Muslim names for businesses have become inappropriate when conducting business in a post 9/11 environment. Other issues are increased insurance, freight and security related costs, through to the effect of doing business under new laws enacted or in some cases the enforcement of old laws since September 11th 2001. The ease with which many of the participants and their associated travelled through the United States, Europe and even Asia had changed considerable. Many countries had introduced visa requirements, furthermore the United States especially was taking no chances and had enforced very tight visa requirements and travel document scrutiny.

INCREASED COSTS

Of particular interest, participants explained, was that in all the cases they did not mind the increased costs in insurance and security; however they did not relish the increases in costs of travel, especially in relation to obtaining the necessary travel documents. The cost of getting a US business visa had increased by up to 147% in one instance, due to the extra documentation that was required, and this was not an isolated example. The increase in costs involved extra certification (in some countries in Asia, lawyers charge up to U$35 to certify the authenticity of one page of a document), while the delayed processing times and the high number of rejections after going through these processes meant cancelled trips. Furthermore, in many instances when the business visas were rejected, no reasons were given and this too irked the participants and their business associates.

Part of the problem is that there are no clear, concise and

well-written instructions for visa applications, and the current set of instructions seems to be controlled by the visa officers located in respective countries. When the participants from the same groups (ie from the same country sample) compared the reasons and problems that they had faced in obtaining US business visas, it became clear that the US officers who were rejecting the applications did not have to provide any reasons and there seemed to be no fixed pattern about the rejected applications. The issue also involved companies that have officers working offshore in the United States as the renewal process for these staff had changed considerably since September 11, 2001.

The results from a recent study, released in June 2004, shows that many United States based businesses which were engaged in exporting goods to Asia have suffered considerable losses due to the delays experienced by their staff in obtaining business visas to the United States and other Western countries. Many of the companies surveyed in this study were multinational companies engaged in infrastructure projects throughout Asia. The study states that the average revenue loss per company was US$ 1,507,560 and the indirect costs averaged US$ 163,383, with medium sized companies suffering the largest revenue loses at US$ 5,075,000. Companies, as well as the governments of the countries involved, must start taking notice of these figures because if it continues unchecked, it will have an impact on their entire economy(s).

The Santangelo study concluded that the impacts of these delays have resulted in postponement of projects, inability to bring consultants and prospective clients to the United States, inability to bring prospective business partners to the United States and unquantifiable damage to the reputation of the companies in the eyes of their business partners. Participants in the Business 911 study indicated that they had made representations through their respective country immigration diplomats to review the business visa application processes as in their opinion, these processes especially for United States business visas had become worse in the past year. Indonesian and Malaysian businesses seemed to be especially affected, as before September 11, 2001, it was not problematic for business visa applicants to get their visas through a very systematic process.

The Chinese and Vietnamese participants in the study commented that it had become just a little more difficult to gain business visas but that the processes were getting better especially for United States business visas. In their opinion, the level of difficulty in getting US business visas had become more difficult immediately after September 2001 but had since improved and become streamlined. These participants also felt that they had better communication with the foreign embassies in their countries since September 2001. This was due to the interest the Chinese and Vietnamese governments were taking to increase the globalisation processes, and to integrate with the World Trade Organisation (WTO) processes since September 2001.

QUESTION OF INSURANCE

Immediately after September 11, 2001, insurance companies started debating on how, where and when to increase insurance premiums. The debate also extended to how the insurance industry had defined risks resulting from terrorism prior to September 11 2001. Governments responded by redefining the government roles in providing insurance for commercial companies from the risks of terrorism. All of this was quick and reactive to a situation that had happened so suddenly that no one agency had had the time to consider these issues prior to the September 2001 terrorist attacks.

In October 2002, members of Al Qaeda committed two terrorist attacks one in Bali and the other in Yemen. Insurance companies that were dealing in marine, cargo and hospitality cover increased their premiums by up to three times in some instances. Indonesia was one of the countries affected by raising insurance premiums, and in some cases insurers were refusing to even consider insuring premises and cargo in Indonesia. The Straits of Malacca, through which an estimated two thirds of all world marine cargo is transported – some 600 ships daily - became categorised as 'extremely high risk' due to piracy and terrorism. This has resulted in increased costs and difficulty in obtaining insurance intended for the 'terrorist, piracy and unforseen risks' category.

In the case of aviation insurance, many of the governments in this regions provided insurance cover for commercial aviation companies that operated from their countries. Airports were also covered by the arrangements that the airport authorities made with the governments of the respective countries in the region. In the case of marine, cargo, hospitality and infrastructure projects, there are no state guarantees when it comes to insurance. This has resulted in businesses having to work through several agents in some instances to obtain the proper insurance since lenders such as banks and financial institutions were not willing to lend to companies that did not have proper insurances for all risks - including terrorism. The United States and other western governments also keep issuing travel warnings and alerts based on their intelligence, and this too has an impact on insurance usually travel insurance.

In these instances, many executives who work in companies that are active in Indonesia and Malaysia have had to cancel their travel plans due to insurance difficulties. Recent studies also indicate that terrorists in the Asian region are most interested in targeting businesses. In 2000 and 2001, terrorists targeted 383 and 397 commercial buildings respectively. Forty- five percent of these were in the Asian region (US State Department, 2003). As such, it is not surprising that insurance companies are hesitant to underwrite companies either operating directly in this region or having associated operations in the region.

The participants in the Business 911 study reflected on what they had to go through as a result of the difficulty of obtaining quality insurance since September 2001. It appeared that in all cases, after gaining expensive guidance from business consultants, the companies were able to obtain insurance for all associated risks. The cost of the insurance had risen due to the multiple agents that these companies had to go through to obtain reasonable quotes. Some of the companies had stuck to their former insurers but at higher premiums. In addition to these problems, all of the companies had to undergo some 'uninsured' periods due to the transformation that the insurance companies were undergoing in terms of deciding what they could and could not insure after September 2001.

The direct and indirect costs associated with the above issues have been quantified to range from US$ 2billion to US$ 12 billion. Recent studies argue that these costs are not accurate and cannot be relied upon. However, what is clear from the Business 911 study is that no one seems to know what the costs are and how to estimate future increases. This is verified by some recent studies on business costs of terrorism in Asia Pacific. Insurance companies, governments and commercial entities are all grappling with this problem with no obvious solution in hand. Infrastructure project managers are also involved in approximating the rising cost of insurance as more terrorists related activities take place in their close proximity.

EFFECT OF NEW AND RENEWED LEGAL IMPEDIMENTS

What many see as new legal impediments such as new Acts, Executive Orders and regulations to doing business post-September 11 2001 is in most instances reinforcement of the earlier laws and regulations. The important change is that all countries are being proactive acting within these rules as the threat of sanctions and other trading embargos are very real since September 11 2001. The following section analyses some of these matters and provides some responses from the participants of the Business 911 study.

United States Executive Orders signed since September 11 201. As discussed previously, participants of the Business 911 study expressed concerns at the lack of understanding that they had with the new rules and regulations that have been introduced since September 2001 especially by the United States. Every participant had heard of the 'blacklist' that had been drawn up by the United States that consisted of companies and individuals that had connections with terrorist organizations and activities. No one knew how to get hold of this list and many had used expensive services of business consultants to assist them in keeping away from this 'blacklist'.

The above 'blacklist' is a compilation of all those 'associated with' designated terrorist groups that was created through the United States Executive Order 13224 signed on the 24h of September 2001. What this executive order did was to expand on previous executive orders to include all terrorist groups not just ones operating out of the Middle East. Under this executive order, the United States can freeze all the U.S. assets of people who are on this list, but more importantly, it provides powers for the United States to prevent anyone dealing with these organizations, and not to have any trade relations with companies that trade in the United States. The United States Treasury Department has the power to prevent access of any company or individual dealing with the 'blacklisted' companies to the United States markets and assets. In broad terms, it may be unlikely that companies other than banks and financial institutions in Asia would be affected by this Order.

Unfortunately, due to all the publicity that was created, especially immediately after September 2001, organizations operating in countries like Indonesia and Malaysia that had similar names to some of the individuals and organizations on the 'blacklist' had to seek costly professional assistance to trade and operate freely. The 'blacklist' is also being constantly being updated, and in some instances names that appeared on the original list that had been removed after complaints by the respective governments and trade organizations returned again to the list. The confusion caused by this constant change had an impact on the post 911-business environment especially in countries that had a predominantly Muslim population. Mainly the cause was the similarity in the names of the people on the US 'blacklist' with organizations and individuals in these countries.

USA PATRIOT ACT AND ITS IMPLICATIONS

The Uniting and Strengthening America by Providing Appropriate Tools Required to Intercept and Obstruct Act 2001 requires all banks that propose to have or already have accounts with any banking institution in the United States to be certified. What this means is that these banks have to provide certification that all the customers that they are dealing with do not have any links with terrorist financing or terrorist organisations. The original intention of this certification was just to get certification confirming that the banks do not do any business with shell banks. Unfortunately, the panic that set in immediately after September 11th 2001 resulted in some countries and banking sectors taking a tougher stand in translating this part of the Act. When this Act was introduced, many banks in Indonesia and Malaysia requested their corporate customers, especially those who had dealings with the United States to complete many forms and administrative procedures before they could operate their accounts in the respective banks.

The USA PATRIOT Act is based on a series of assumptions. The first of these is that offshore banking provides clients with anonymity and this has the potential to be used by individuals and organisations that fund terrorism. Private banking services that have been set up to service illegal gains are also targeted by this Act. Laundering of money and the transfer of funds through the legal and underground banking systems become the main object of this Act. In Asia, these banking systems flourish [and, the underground banking systems are very old institutions (eds.)] and as such both the private and governmental sectors are being requested by the authorities to assist in implementing tighter controls over such activity.

The end result of all these stipulations is additional costs to businesses that are being passed on to the customers and to the funding agencies that provide the funds for infrastructure projects. The USA PATRIOT Act also has clauses in it that make reference to specific industries such as mining, dealers of precious metals, stones and jewels, and technology and scientific research organizations. Several countries in the Asian region are listed as being 'uncooperative' towards preventing money laundering (examples include Indonesia and Philippines) and in not assisting the United States in tackling the money laundering problems. Participants in the Business 911 study indicated hat those of them involved or working with companies dealing in mining, precious stones and metals and imports of any type of chemicals (including cement) had to understand what these rules meant to their business operations.

The USA PATRIOT Act does not make it clear what the rules are for companies that trade in these materials that have close associations with their counterpart companies in the USA. The companies that are in the USA are unsure if they are allowed to do business as usual with the companies in the listed countries and this is causing much confusion, and interrupting business to and from the USA. What the USA PATRIOT does make clear is that dealers in any of the materials discussed above such as precious metals and chemicals must have a set of policies, procedures and controls to prevent money laundering. This includes the employment of a compliance officer and an independent audit function to test these functions.

The larger companies in Indonesia, Malaysia and China are working in close cooperation with the respective governments to try and implement these measures but this is not happening in the small and medium enterprise sector. As a direct result of the USA PATRIOT Act, the United States Treasury has frozen over US$ 550 million around the world and has the cooperation of over one hundred and sixty six countries. The fines for non-compliance are up to US$ one million and criminal charges for bank officers. These fines and officers can be based anywhere in the world and the United States is working towards enhancing the cooperation of the banks and governments where the non-compliers reside. In addition there is always the threat of economic sanctions against countries that do not cooperate or comply.

In addition to this, the USA PATRIOT Act has the capacity to cripple economies through the threat of being 'blacklisted' as a sponsor of 'state terrorism' or a 'non-cooperating' country. This fear is very real in countries like Indonesia, Malaysia, China and the Philippines. What is clear from all of the examples and a review of recent literature is that there are many trade associations, business consultants and government departments in and out of the United States that are providing workshops, creating compliance kits and training programmes for various industries on the USA PATRIOT Act. All of these activities are expensive and in the case of some industries like the banking industry have become compulsory for senior members of the industry to participate in these activities.

Working with countries and organizations in the 'lists' can be extremely dangerous as companies that do so could be prevented from trading with the United States and other Western countries which may be their major trading partners. It is clear from the Business 911 study that the USA PATRIOT Act has certainly created fear of making such mistakes among company executives and investors in Indonesia, Malaysian, Vietnam and China.

THE UNITED STATES CUSTOMS TRADE PARTNERSHIP AGAINST TERRORISM (C-TPAT)

C-TPAT is a good example of the partnership between government and private enterprise. Companies in the United States that comply with C- TPAT (which is a significant undertaking) will be assured of faster and more efficient service when it comes to US Customs clearing. In simple terms, C-TPAT compliance means that the company involved is giving an undertaking to the United States Customs that it knows all of the people with whom the company is doing business, including the importers, manufacturers, brokers, and suppliers. That is everyone in the supply chain up to the time the product reaches the US Customs. The steps required to provide this assurance are very rigorous, and in return the US Customs Service will reduce the number of customs inspections.

The United States Customs and Border Protection (CBP) also have plans to use C-TPAT to prevent terrorists and terrorist weapons from being smuggled into the United States.

The plan includes incorporating foreign manufacturers to comply with C-TPAT and to physically examine containers that depart and arrive from high-risk countries. A separate category of 'high risk cargo' will also be identified and subject to extra checks. Teams of US CBP officers will be located in ports around the world in a 'Container Security Initiative' targeting and inspecting what the United States could term as 'high risk cargo'. Participants in the Business 911 study raised many issues to do with C- TPAT as many of the companies that they are trading with had requested that they provide the information that was required for C-TPAT compliance.

The issue of what the participants saw as unnecessary delays in the inspection process that resulted in extra storage and loss prevention measures was also raised by these participants. In all instances, the participants had to hire business consultants to assist their staff to provide the information required for compliance with C-TPAT. The details essential for C-TPAT compliance required many hours of work and research in the first instance: but the participants felt that after this first exercise, all that they are required to do is to supply the same information. It is unclear as to if this was the intention of C-TPAT when this venture was introduced. The companies that are taking part in C-TPAT cannot be expected to provide all of this information without working in partnership with their business associates in the respective countries from which they import goods and services.

The stringent requirements of C-TPAT to prevent acts of terrorism and to understand the business partners of companies sending goods and services to the United States may be compromised if the necessary checking mechanisms are not done in complete partnership with the foreign manufacturers. The United States Customs needs to work with the companies in the United States as well as educate their counterparts in foreign countries especially in the case of companies that are C-TPAT compliant. The point here is that the partnership between business and government in preventing terrorism and terrorist financing will only work if the business community is serious in its undertakings. Someone has to bear the cost of these strict compliance measures and sharing the costs may provide the best solution to an expensive problem.

SECURITY REQUIREMENTS TO PROTECT MAJOR PROJECTS

One of the new necessities since the terrorist attacks in Bali and New York is the protection of staff and major critical infrastructure projects in the Asian region. As there are frequent terrorism alerts that affect the countries in the region, companies that are willing to be involved in major infrastructure projects must also be prepared to provide the necessary protection for their staff and projects. Recent estimates put this cost of security provision between US$ 12 billion and US$ 18 billion a year for major infrastructure projects worldwide. This includes the cost of securing schools, churches, multinational offices and the personal security of expatriates, which were not needed before the September 2001 terrorist attacks.

The amount of specialised training that staffs that protect critical infrastructures require is unavailable in many countries in Asia unless provided by specialised firms or the government. The participants in the Business 911 study indicated that they had been approached (through intermediaries) by many aid related organizations such as USAID to work in partnership with local security related firms to train local staff to be able to provide skilled critical infrastructure protection. In some cases, this was a primary requirement of securing aid-related funding for infrastructure projects - as the funding bodies are concerned that the expatriate staff involved in these projects will not be otherwise safe.

This is seen as an additional burden as it requires an additional skill set when tendering for these projects. Again there are numerous local and foreign consultants who are willing to provide these services but these consultants have questionable skills in the area of critical infrastructure protection (including protecting of staff). A recent British Broadcasting Corporation report raised the concern of insurance underwriters in providing quotes for companies operating in countries that are high terrorist risk such as Indonesia. The added complication that most of these underwriters are located in London or Frankfurt and have to rely on outdated risk reports that makes this job very difficult.

This is especially true when quoting for infrastructure projects as the knowledge of the project and the exact site of all staff and facilities needs to be correctly input. Add to this the nature and style of security protection offered to the facilities and staff. These issues are fast becoming mandated by both the foreign companies and the insurers, thus causing great problems for companies operating in not only in high risk areas such as Iraq but also in countries that are seen to be at high risk by the United States and their associates.

AVIATION SECURITY REQUIREMENTS

The increased costs of aviation and maritime security since the September 11th 2001 and the Bali attack of 2002 is another major issue faced by business organizations in the Asian region. Unlike some countries such as the United Arab Emirates and Israel where these costs are being borne by the governments, countries such as China, Indonesia, Malaysia and Vietnam are passing on these costs to the customers or the business organizations that use these services. Of greater importance are the stringent requirements that are being imposed by international organizations such as the International Civil Aviation Organisation and the United States Government on how the airport and seaports in these countries must be security compliant to be able to send cargo to any port in the United States.

As discussed above, the United States Customs and Border Protection and the International Maritime Organisation (IMO) are working together with governments across the world to implement the International Ship and Port Facility Security (ISPS) code. The current deadline of July 1 st 2004 to be code compliant is unachievable for many countries in the region and again the issue of what is the role of the private sector in implementing this code is unclear. The shipping companies and the port authorities are all involved as the compliance requirements include the port facilities and the registered fleet of vessels. Security assessments and plans have to be approved by the respective governments and many governments in the Asian region are depending on the privatised port authorities and shipping lines to assist with these processes.

There are questions as to how effectively these plans can and will be implemented and who will bear the costs. In India, for instance, there are considerable concerns about the extra costs as well as the time for compliance. He goes on to say that 200 Indian ships will be covered by the code, and that 70 percent of the ships will have their security plans ready this month. In addition, the 13 major Indian ports, 36 minor ports and 10 shipyards will have to comply. But the biggest difficulty in ISPS Code compliance has been the lack of availability of the required security equipment - such as ship alerts and its software.

The good news, therefore, is that all companies operating in countries such as Indonesia, Malaysia, China and Korea that deal in exports and imports to the United States are working energetically with their governments to implement these regulations. What is complicating this more is that the United States Customs and Border Protection (CBP) and the IMO are now insisting that officers from the IMO and CBP may inspect some of these countries before being approved as code compliant. Initially this function had been left to the discretion of respective governments and port authorities but recent reports suggest that the CBP and IMO might be visiting these ports to approve them.

Infrastructure projects in Asia face renewed pressures ranging from competitive disadvantages through to the question of their lack of basic critical infrastructure and personnel protection due to the new rules and regulations being introduced since September 1st 2001. Countries in the developing world have to balance the new security priorities with increased costs and trade objectives. Aid agencies have to rework their funding for infrastructure projects to get a fair estimate of these renewed costs and pressures. And following on, the business and government community in Asia must take steps to comply with the new measures as otherwise they risk losing their competitive advantage and funding for critical infrastructure projects.

What is clear from the Business 911 and some of the other recent studies on this issue are that the rules are changing fast, and therefore they need to be clearly explained to the business community on a continuous basis. Governments and funding bodies must be clear about this, and do whatever necessary to increase the pace at which the new measures and rules are being explained to the business community. The United States government realises this and is making some efforts towards better training for staff working in their embassies throughout the world. The Internet plays its role also – as noted in the Endnotes citations.

Companies and governments engaged in infrastructure projects have no choice but to embrace these changes positively. The costs have to estimated and calculated, and have to be included in the projects' capitalisation. The new requirements for money transfers and accountability of all financial transactions, especially for major infrastructure projects, may provide the additional benefit of reducing corruption as all monies have to be accounted for more meticulously in this new system. This should result in major cost savings yet on the other hand, these requirements may create more opportunities for corrupt and creative officers. One positive example is seen from the ports in the region: the old 'tea money' for fast clearances has to be done away with, as the new rules make it more stringent for cargo shippers to engage in this practice.

Capacity building and inter-development assistance remain absolutely necessary if the new systems are to be implemented effectively especially in the case of infrastructure projects. Someone has to bear the costs, and the question of who this is has to be decided sooner rather than later. In the meantime, the competitive advantage of doing business is being fast eroded through the new rules and regulations. To maintain competitive advantage with the major trading partners, countries have to implement regulations and codes, and be compliant with the new financial rules - whilst at the same time keeping their overall costs low. The balancing act between the new security regulations and trade is becoming difficult, especially for developing countries. But if these difficulties are not addressed the danger is that these countries, or operators using these counties as a shield, will use whatever means available to them to take shortcuts that could make the whole point of the compliance exercise invalid.

7

Assassination

Assassination is the targeted killing of a public figure. Sometimes for ideological or pol asitical reasons, though some assassinations demonstrate mental instability. Other motivations may be money (contract killing), revenge, or a military operation. The assassination euphemism targeted killing (or extrajudicial punishment/execution) is also used for the government-sanctione d killing of opponents. Assassination may also be used as a form of hyperbole, as in the phrase character assassination, meaning an attempt to impugn another's character, and thus kill, or "assassinate" his reputation and credibility.

The term 'Assassin' derives from the Persian word Hashshashin, a militant Ismaili Persian Muslim sect, active in the Northern parts of Iran (Alamut) from the eighth to the fourteenth centuries. This mystic secret society killed members of the Abbasid and Seljuq élite for political and religious reasons. It is popularly believed that the assassins were under the influence of hashish and opium during their killings or during their indoctrination and that *assassin* derives from *hasishin,* the influence of the drugs. However, this is not true.

At the time of their existence "Hashashins" were people who sold medicine. The region of Alamut was filled with plants rich with natural medicine and many of the residence of that region made a living by selling those plants at Bazaars (Marketplaces) that were called Bazare Hashashin (The medicine market). Due to their advance medicine during that period, they were able to offer free health care to their citizens. Also many people in Iran would travel to the region of Alamut to get cured for unknown illnesses. The earliest known literary use of the term "assassination" is in *The Tragedy of Macbeth* by William Shakespeare (1605).

DEFINITION PROBLEM

The definition of "assassination" varies among sources. *The American Heritage Dictionary* defines "to assassinate" thus:

> *...to murder [a prominent person] by surprise attack, as for political reasons;*

However, the Oxford English Dictionary's definition is:

> *The action of assassinating; the taking the life of any one by treacherous violence, esp. by a hired emissary, or one who has taken upon him to execute the deed.*

There is dispute whether the term assassination should include killings wherein the primary motivation is attracting attention to a political cause, and wherein the victim is of secondary importance (and might be famous, but unrelated to the dispute, or even an unknown). This leads to a number of possible definitions - which may however not all apply in any specific case:

- the killing of someone *by treacherous violence*
- the killing of someone *in the public view* (i.e. someone notable)
- the killing of someone *for political, moral, or ideological reasons*

For the purposes of this article, the third definition predominates, even though the second is often used, and the first would often be found in colloquial use.

Assassination is one of the oldest tools of power politics, dating back at least as far as recorded history. Perhaps the earliest recorded instance is the murder around 586 BC of Gedaliah, described by Jeremiah and lamented by Jews to this day in the Fast of Gedaliah. Philip II of Macedon, the father of Alexander the Great, and Julius Caesar can be noted as famous victims. Emperors of Rome often met their end in this way, as did many of the Shia Imams. The practice was also well-known in ancient China. An example of this is Jing Ke's failed assassination of Qin Shi Huang. The ancient Indian military adviser Chanakya wrote about assassinations in detail in his political treatise *Arthashastra*.

The Old Testament story of Judith illustrates how a woman frees the Israelites by tricking and assassinating Holofernes, the war-lord of the rival Assyrians with whom the Israelites were at war. In the middle Ages, regicide was rare, but with the Renaissance, tyrannicide - or assassination for personal or political reasons - became more common again. The reigns of French kings Henry III and Henry IV, and William the Silent of the Netherlands ended with assassination.

As the world moved into the modern day, the killing of important people began to become more than a tool in power struggles between rulers themselves, and was also used for political symbolism, such as in the propaganda of the deed. In Russia alone, four emperors were assassinated within less than 200 years: Ivan VI, Peter III, Paul I, and Alexander II. In the U.S., four presidents, Abraham Lincoln, James Garfield, William McKinley, and John F. Kennedy died at the hands of assassins, while many other presidents survived attempts on their lives.

In Europe the assassination of Archduke Franz Ferdinand by Serbian nationalist insurgents is blamed for igniting World War I after a succession of minor conflicts, while belligerents on both sides in World War II used operatives specifically trained for assassination. Reinhard Heydrich was killed by Czech partisan killers, and knowledge from decoded transmissions allowed the U.S. to carry out a targeted attack, killing Japanese Admiral Isoroku Yamamoto while he was travelling by airplane. Adolf Hitler, meanwhile, was almost killed by his own officers, and survived various attempts by other persons and organizations.

India's "Father of the Nation", Mohandas K. Gandhi, was

shot to death on January 30, 1948 by Nathuram Godse. In the Philippines, Benigno Aquino, Jr., opposition leader and top critic of Ferdinand Marcos, was shot dead by alleged assassin Rolando Galman as he arrived at Manila International Airport from a three-year exile in the United States, with the death sometimes hailed as the catalyst of the 1986 People Power Revolution that toppled Marcos' 20-year dictatorship.

During the Cold War, there was a dramatic new increase in the number of political assassinations, likely due to the ideological polarization of most of the First and Second worlds, whose adherents were often more than willing to both justify and finance such killings. Liaquat Ali Khan, the first Prime Minister of Pakistan was assassinated by Saad Akbar, a lone assassin in 1951. Conspiracy theorists believe his conflict with certain members of the Pakistani military (Rawalpindi conspiracy) or suppression of Communists and antagonism towards the Soviet Union, were potential reasons for his assassination.

The U.S. Senate Select Committee chaired by Senator Frank Church (the Church Committee) reported in 1975 that it had found "concrete evidence of at least eight plots involving the CIA to assassinate Fidel Castro from 1960 to 1965." Most major powers were not long in repudiating Cold War assassination tactics, though many allege that this was merely a smokescreen for political benefit and that covert and illegal training of assassins continues today, with Russia, Israel, and other nations accused of still regularly engaging in such operations. In 1986, U.S. President Ronald Reagan (who survived an assassination attempt himself) ordered the Operation El Dorado Canyon air raid on Libya in which one of the primary targets was the home residence of Libyan ruler Muammar Gaddafi.

Gaddafi escaped unharmed, however, his adopted daughter Hanna was one of the civilian casualties. In the Philippines, the assassination of Benigno Aquino, Jr. triggered the eventual downfall of the 20-year autocratic rule of President Ferdinand Marcos. Aquino, a former Senator and a leading figure of the political opposition, was assassinated in 1983 at the Manila International Airport (now the Ninoy Aquino International Airport) upon returning home from exile. His death thrust his widow, Corazon Aquino, into the limelight and, ultimately, the presidency following the peaceful 1986 EDSA Revolution.

On December 8, 1980 in New York City former Beatle and Musician John Lennon was assassinated by a deranged fan Mark David Chapman. Nearly 20 years after Lennon's Assassination, former Beatle George Harrison had an assassination attempt on his life. On December 30, 1999 Michael Abram broke into the Harrison's home and stabbed Harrison multiple times, ultimately puncturing his lung. Harrison would soon recover from the attack. On August 17, 1988 President of Pakistan Gen. M. Zia ul Haq died along with his staff and the American Ambassador to Pakistan when his C-130 transport plane exploded in mid-air after taking off from Bahawalpur because of an on-board bomb.

The CIA, KGB and Indian secret service RAW all have been implicated by various conspiracy theorists. Various dictators around the world, such as Saddam Hussein, have also used assassination to remove individual opponents, or to terrorize troublesome population groups. In return, in post-Saddam Iraq, the Shiite-dominated government has used death squads to perform countless extrajudicial executions of radical Sunni Iraqis, with some alleging that the death squads were trained by the U.S. In India, Prime Ministers Indira Gandhi and Rajiv Gandhi (neither of whom were related to Mohandas Gandhi), were assassinated in 1984 and 1991.

The assassinations were linked to separatist movements in Punjab and northern Sri Lanka, respectively. In Israel, Prime Minister Yitzhak Rabin was assassinated on November 4, 1995. Yigal Amir confessed and was convicted of the crime. Many questions were subsequently raised about the actual cause of and rationale for his death. In Lebanon, the assassination of former Prime Minister Rafik Hariri on February 14, 2005, prompted an investigation by the United Nations.

The suggestions in the resulting Mehlis report, that there was Syrian involvement, prompted the Cedar Revolution which drove Syrian troops out of Lebanon. In Pakistan, former prime minister and opposition leader Benazir Bhutto was assassinated in 2007, while in the process of running for re-election. Bhutto's assassination drew unanimous condemnation from the international community.

FURTHER MOTIVATIONS

Assassination for military purposes has long been espoused - Sun Tzu, writing around 500 B.C., argued in favor of using assassination in his book *The Art of War*. Nearly 2000 years later Machiavelli also argued assassination could be useful in his book *The Prince*. In medieval times, an army and even a nation might be based upon and around a particularly strong, canny or charismatic leader, whose loss could paralyze the ability of both to make war. However, in modern warfare a soldier's mindset is generally considered to surround ideals far more than specific leaders, while command structures are more flexible in replacing officer losses.

While the death of a popular or successful leader often has a detrimental effect on morale, the organisational system and the belief in a specific cause is usually strong enough to enable continued warfare. There is also the risk that the target could be replaced by an even more competent leader or that such a killing (or a failed attempt) will "martyr" a leader and support his cause (by showing the moral ruthlessness of the assassins). Faced with particularly brilliant leaders, this possibility has in various instances been risked, such as in the attempts to kill the Athenian Alcibiades during the Peloponnesian War. There are a number of additional examples from World War II which show how assassination was used as a military tool at both tactical and strategic levels:

- The American interception of Admiral Isoroku Yamamoto's airplane during World War II, after his travel route had been decrypted.
- The American perception that Skorzeny's commandos were planning to assassinate Eisenhower during the Battle

of the Bulge played havoc with Eisenhower's personal plans for some time, though it did not affect the battle itself. Skorzeny later denied in an interview with *The New York Times* that he had ever intended to assassinate Eisenhower during Operation Greif and he said that he could prove it.

- There was a planned British commando raid to capture or kill the German General Erwin Rommel (also known as "The Desert Fox").

Use of assassination has continued in more recent conflicts:

- During the Vietnam War, partly in response to Viet Cong assassinations of government leaders, the USA engaged in the Phoenix Program to assassinate Viet Cong leaders and sympathizers, and killed between 6,000 and 41,000 persons, with official 'targets' of 1,800 per month.
- From 1991 till 2006, Russia targeted the top commanders of the separatist groups they were fighting in Chechenya, killing several of them (including Aslan Maskhadov and Shamil Basayev)
- During World War II, underground factions sympathizing with the Allies were known to assassinate rival underground leaders to ensure their chances of governing their nation upon liberation from the Axis, as opposed to their rivals. Naturally, the reason given to the assassin would be that the rival leader was an Axis sympathizer.
- In the Global War on Terrorism, American special operations forces and intelligence agencies employed manhunting operations against key opponents and Al Qaeda terrorist leaders.

AS TOOL OF INSURGENTS

Insurgent groups have often employed assassination as a tool to further their causes. Assassinations provide several functions for such groups, namely the removal of specific enemies and as propaganda tools to focus the attention of media and politics on their cause. The Irish Republican Army guerrillas of 1919–1921 assassinated many RIC Police Intelligence officers during the Irish War of Independence. Michael Collins set up a special unit - the Squad - for this purpose, which had the effect of intimidating many policemen into resigning from the force. The Squad's activities peaked with the assassination of 14 British agents in Dublin on Bloody Sunday in 1920.

This tactic was used again by the Provisional IRA during the Troubles in Northern Ireland (1969-present). Assassination of RUC officers and politicians was one of a number of methods used in the Provisional IRA campaign 1969-1997. The IRA also attempted to assassinate British Prime Minister Margaret Thatcher by bombing the Conservative Party Conference in a Brighton hotel. Loyalist paramilitaries retaliated by killing Catholics at random and assassinating Irish nationalist politicians.

Basque separatists ETA in Spain have assassinated many security and political figures since the late 1960s, notably Luis Carrero Blanco in 1973. Since the early 1990s, they have also targeted academics, journalists and local politicians who publicly disagreed with them, meaning that many needed armed police bodyguards. The Red Brigades in Italy carried out assassinations of political figures, as to a lesser extent, did the Red Army Faction in Germany in the 1970s and 1980s.

Middle Eastern groups, such as the PLO and Hezbollah, have all engaged in assassinations, though the higher intensity of armed conflict in the region compared to western Europe means that many of their actions are either better characterized as guerrilla operations or as random attacks - especially the technique of suicide bombs. In the Vietnam War, assassinations were routinely carried out by communist insurgents against government officials and individual civilians deemed to offend or rival the revolutionary movement. Such attacks, along with widespread military activity by insurgent bands, almost brought the Diem regime to collapse before the US intervention.

For money or Gain

Individually, too, people have often found reasons to

arrange the deaths of others through paid intermediaries. One, who kills with no political motive or group loyalty, only for money, is known as a hitman, or contract killer. Note that by the definition accepted above, while such a killer is not, strictly speaking, an assassin, if the killing is ordered and financed towards a political end, then that killing must rightly be termed an assassination, and the hitman an assassin by extension.

Entire organizations have sometimes specialized in assassination as one of their services, to be gained for the right price. Besides the original hashshashin, the ninja clans of Japan were rumored to perform assassinations, though it can be pointed out that most of what was ever known about the ninja was rumor and hearsay. In the United States, Murder, Inc., an organization partnered to the Mafia, was formed for the sole purpose of performing assassinations for organized crime. In Russia, the *vory* (thieves), Russian organised crime syndicates, are often known to provide assassinations for the right price, as well as engaging in it themselves for their own purposes. A professional hitman is called "cleaner" in Russia; he is used to clean away the target. The Finnish as well as the Swedish underworld uses the word "torpedo" for a contract killer.

TARGETED KILLING

The use of assassinations for political or military reasons by sovereign states is an extremely contentious subject, with opinions ranging from people considering it a legitimate form of defense, especially against non-state actors like terror groups, to people calling targeted killings state terrorism itself. Both those for and against targeted killings are also often faced with accusations of being clearly partisan to one side of the particular struggle discussed.

- **Pro**: Various groups and individuals have supported assassinations such as those undertaken by Israel against opposed terror groups, claiming that the killing of people like Sheikh Ahmed Yassin is justified due to the fact that people like him provide "both religious and political cover" (for terrorist groups to operate), and that the fact that they may not have been physically involved in such crimes does not reduce their role. However, even they sometimes question the tactical prudence of such actions, while arguing that the killings may produce leadership vacuums and disorganise their organisations. They also oppose the use of the term assassination, as it denotes murder, where targeting such leaders is seen as a move in self-defence, and thus killing, but not a crime. Some even argue that targeted killing should be continued for 'retribution and revenge', even though they accept that the killing has little effect on the number and severity of terrorist attacks, or may even increase them in the short and mid-term.

- **Contra**: Criticism of targeted killings focuses on a number of aspects, from being claimed to be against international law to being destabilising to local situations and thus causing more violence, an opinion also held by such intermediaries as Álvaro de Soto, former UN Middle East peace envoy. Criticism often also focuses on the murder of innocent victims of the more heavy-handed or failed targeted killings, in which civilians are often murdered in large numbers, such as the indiscriminate Israeli bombing of Lebanon in 2006 which produced thousands of killed and wounded Lebanese civilians.

Targeted killings are also sometimes called 'extrajudicial punishment', though some states require some form of judicial trial in absentia before such an undertaking.

PSYCHOLOGY

A major study about assassination attempts in the US in the second half of the 20th century came to the conclusion that most prospective assassins spend copious amounts of time planning and preparing for their attempts. Assassinations are thus rarely a case of 'impulsive' action.

However, about 25% of the actual attackers were found

to be delusional, a figure that rose to 60% with 'nearlethal approachers' (people apprehended before reaching their target). This incidentally shows that while mental instability plays a role in many modern-age assassinations, the more delusional attackers are less likely to succeed in their attempt. The report also found that around two thirds of the attackers had previously been arrested for (not necessarily related) offenses, that around 44% had a history of serious depression, and that 39% had a history of substance abuse.

TECHNIQUES

It seems likely that the first assassinations would have been direct and simple: stabbing, strangling or bludgeoning. Substantial planning or coordination would rarely have been involved, as tribal groups were too small, and the connection to the leaders too closes. As civilization took root, however, leaders began to have greater importance, and become more detached from the groups they ruled. This would have brought planning, subterfuge and weapons into successful assassination plans.

The key technique was likely infiltration, with the actual assassination by stabbing, smothering or strangulation. Poisons also started to be used in many forms. Death cap mushrooms and similar plants became a traditional choice of assassins especially if they could not be perceived as poisonous by taste, and the symptoms of the poisoning did not show until after some time. In ancient Rome, paid mobs were sometimes used to beat political enemies to death. With the advent of effective ranged weaponry, and later firearms, the position of an assassination target was more precarious. Bodyguards were no longer enough to hold back determined killers, who no longer needed to directly engage or even subvert the guard to kill the leader in question. Moreover, the engagement of targets at greater distance dramatically increased the chances for an assassin's survival. It is considered that William the Silent of the Netherlands was the first leader assassinated by firearms (July 10, 1584).

Gunpowder and other explosives also allowed the use of

bombs or even greater concentrations of explosives for deeds requiring a larger touch; for an example, the Gunpowder Plot could have 'assassinated' almost a thousand people had it not been foiled. Explosives, especially the car bomb, become far more common in modern history, with grenades and remote-triggered landmines also used, especially in the Middle East and Balkans (the initial attempt on Archduke Franz Ferdinand's life was with a grenade).

With heavy weapons, the rocket propelled grenade (RPG) has became a useful tool given the popularity of armored cars (discussed below), while Israeli forces have pioneered the use of aircraft-mounted missiles for assassination, as well as the innovative use of explosive devices. A sniper with a precision rifle is often used in fictional assassinations. However, there are certain difficulties associated with long-range shooting, including finding a hidden shooting position with a clear line-of-sight, detailed advance knowledge of the intended victim's travel plans, the ability to identify the target at long range, and the ability to score a first-round lethal hit at long range, usually measured in hundreds of meters.

A dedicated sniper rifle is also expensive and hard to acquire, often costing thousands of dollars because of the high level of precision machining and hand-finishing required achieving extreme accuracy. Despite their comparative disadvantages, easy-to-acquire and hard-to-trace handguns are much more commonly used than rifles. Of 74 principal incidents evaluated in a major study about assassination attempts in the US in the second half of the 20th century, 51% were undertaken by a handgun, 30% with a rifle or shotgun, while 15% of the attempts used knives and 8% explosives (usage of multiple weapons/methods was reported in 16% of all cases). In the case of state-sponsored assassination, poisoning offers the greatest level of deniability (the allegations are rarely proven). Georgi Markov, a Bulgarian dissident was assassinated by ricin poisoning. A tiny pellet containing the poison was injected into his leg.

Widespread allegations involving the Bulgarian government and KGB have not led to any legal results. The

CIA has allegedly made several attempts to assassinate Fidel Castro, many of the schemes involving poisoning his milkshakes. A 2006 case in the UK concerned the assassination of Alexander Litvinenko who was given a lethal dose of radioactive polonium-210, possibly passed to him in aerosol form sprayed directly onto his food. Litvinenko, a former KGB agent, had been granted asylum in the UK in 2000 after citing persecution in Russia. Shortly before his death he issued a statement accusing Vladimir Putin, who was the Russian president at the time, of involvement in his assassination. President Putin denies he had any part in Litvinenko's death.

COUNTER-MEASURES

One of the earliest forms of defense against assassins is without doubt the bodyguard. He acts as a shield for the potential target, keeps lookout for potential attackers (sometimes in advance, for example on a planned tour), and is literally supposed to put himself 'in harm's way' - both by his simple presence, forming a barrier in front of the target and by shielding the target during any attack. He is also, if possible, to neutralize an attacker as fast as possible, and thus often carries weapons (where legal or possible).

This bodyguard function was often executed by the leader's most loyal warriors, and was extremely effective throughout most of early human history, leading to attempts by subterfuge, such as poison (which was answered by the food taster). Other notable measures include Shadowing by recruiting similar looking persons to be the apparent figure in public occasions. Examples can be found in Chinese and Japanese history.

Notable examples of bodyguards would include the Roman Praetorian Guard or the Ottoman janissaries - although, in both cases, it should be noted that the protectors often became assassins themselves, exploiting their power to make the head of state a virtual hostage at their whim or eliminating threatening leaders altogether. The fidelity of individual bodyguards is an important question as well, especially for leaders who oversee states with strong ethnic or religious divisions. Failure to realize such divided loyalties leads to assassinations such as that of Indian Prime Minister Indira Gandhi, assassinated by two Sikh bodyguards in 1984.

MODERN STRATEGIES

With the advent of gunpowder, ranged assassination (via bombs or firearms) became possible. One of the first reactions was to simply increase the guard, creating what at times might seem a small army trailing every leader; another was to begin clearing large areas whenever a leader was present, to the point where entire sections of a city might be shut down. As the 20th century dawned, the prevalence of assassins and their capabilities skyrocketed, and so did measures to protect against them. For the first time, armored cars or armored limousines were put into service for safer transport, with modern versions rendering them virtually invulnerable to small arms fire and smaller bombs and mines.

Bulletproof vests also began to be used, though they were of limited utility, restricting movement and leaving the head unprotected - as such they tended to be worn only during high-profile public events if at all. Access to famous persons, too, became more and more restrictive; potential visitors would be forced through numerous different checks before being granted access to the official in question, and as communication became better and information technology more prevalent, it has become all but impossible for a wouldbe killer to get close enough to the personage at work or in private life to effect an attempt on his or her life, especially given the common use of metal and bomb detectors.

Most modern assassinations have been committed either during a public performance or during transport, both because of weaker security and security lapses, such as with US President John F. Kennedy and former Pakistani Prime Minister Benazir Bhutto, or as part of coups d'état where security is either overwhelmed or completely removed, such as with Patrice Lumumba and likely Salvador Allende. The methods used for protection by famous people have sometimes evoked negative reactions by the public, with some resenting the separation from their officials or major figures. One example might be traveling in a car protected by a bubble of clear bulletproof glass, such as the Popemobile of Pope John Paul II (built following an extremist's attempt at his life).

Politicians themselves often resent this need for separation - which has at times caused tragedy when they sent their bodyguards from their side for personal or publicity reasons, as U.S. President William McKinley did during the public reception at which he was assassinated. Other potential targets go into seclusion, and are rarely heard from or seen in public, such as writer Salman Rushdie. A related form of protection is the use of body doubles, a person built similar to the person he is expected to impersonate. These persons are then made up, as well as in some cases altered to look like the target, with the body double then taking the place of the person in high risk situations. Saddam Hussein is known to have used body doubles. According to Joe R. Reeder, a former under secretary for the U.S. Army from 1993–1997 writing in Fox News, Fidel Castro had also used body doubles, though no details were specified.

Bibliography

Adams, James. *The Financing of Terror*, New York: Simon & Schuster, 1986.

Alexander, Yonah and Richard Latter, eds. *Terrorism and the Media: Dilemmas for Government, Journalists & the Public*, Washington, DC: Brassey's, 1990.

Andersan, Sean and Stephen Solan. *Historical Dictionary of Terrorism*, 2nd ed. Lanham, MD: Scarecrow, 2002.

Atkins, Stephen E. *Terrorism;: A Reference Handbook*, Santa Barbara, CA: 1992.

Bell, J. Bower. *Transnational Terror, Washington*, DC: American Enterprise Institute, 1975.

Burton, Anthony. *Urban Terrorism: Theory, Practice, Response*, London: Cooper, 1975.

Chaliand, Gerald. *Terrorism: From Popular Struggle to Media Spectacle*, Atlantic Highlands, NJ: Saqi, 1987.

Comb, Cindy C. *Terrorism in Twenty-First Century*, 2nd ed. Upper Saddle River, NJ: Prentice Hall, 2002.

Crelinsten, Ronald D. and Denis Szabo. *Hostage- Taking*, Lexington, MA: Lexington Book, 1979.

Crenshaw, Martha. *Terrorism, Legitimacy, and Power*, Middletown, CT: Wesleyan University Press, 1983.

Gay, Kathleen. *Encyclopedia of Political Anarchy*, Santa Barbara, CA: ABC-CLIO, 1999.

George, Alexander, ed. *Western State Terrorism*, New York: Routledge, 1991.

Gurr, Ted Robert. *Handbook of Political Conflict: Theory and Research,* New York: Free Press, 1980.

Harmon, Christopher C. *Terrorism Today,* London: Frank Cass, 2002.

Hoffman, Bruce. *Inside Terrorism,* New York: Columbia University Press, 1998.

Jenkins, Brian. *International Terrorism: The Other World War,* Santa Monica, CA: RAND, 1985.

Kushner, Harvey W. ed. *The Future of Terrorism: Violence in the New Millennium,* Thousand Oaks, CA: Sage, 1998.

Laqueur, Walter. *History of Terrorism,* New York: Transaction Publishers, 2001.

Lesser, Ian O. et al. *Countering the New Terrorism,* Santa Monica, CA: RAND, 1999.

Lewis Bernand. *The Political Language of Islam,* Chicago: University of Chicago Press, 1988.

Miller, Abraham H. *Terrorism and Hostage Negotiations,* Boulder, CO: Westview, 1980.

Moss, Robert. *Urban Guerrilla Warfare,* London: International Institute for Strategic Studies, 1971.

Netanyahu, Benzamin. *The Terrorism Reader,* New York: Meridian, 1986.

O'Neill, Bard E. *Insurgency and Terrorism: Inside Modern Revolutionary Warfare,* Washington, DC: Brassey's, 1990.

Peters, Rudolph. *Jihad in Classical and Modern Islam,* Princeton, NJ: Markus Wiener, 1996.

Picard, Robert G. *Media Portrayals of Terrorism: Functions and Meaning of News Coverage,* Ames: Iowa State University Press, 1993.

Pillar, Paul R. and Michael H. Armacost. *Terrorism and U.S. Foreign Policy, Washington,* DC: Brookings Institution, 2001.

Rashid, Ahmed. Jihad: *The Rise of Militant Islam I Central Asia,* New Haven, CT: Yale University Press, 2002.

Rosie, George. *The Dictionary of International Terrorism,* New York: Paragon House, 1987.

Schamis, Geraldo Jorge. *War and Terrorism in International Affairs,* New Brunswick, NJ: Transaction Publishers, 1980.

Segaller, Stephen. *Invisible Armies: Terrorism in the 1990s,* San Diego, CA: Harcourt Brace Jovanovich, 1987.

Sofaer, Abraham D. and Seymour E. Goodman. *The Transnational Dimension of Cyber Crime and Terrorism,* Stanford, CA: Hoover Institution, 2001.

Sonn, Richard D. *Anarchism,* New York: Twayne, 1992.

Stern, Jessia. *The Ultimate Terrorists,* Cambridge, MA: Harvard University Press, 1999.

Tanter, Raymond. *Rogue Regimes: Terrorism and Proliferation,* New York: St. Maytin's, 1998.

Tucker, Jonathan B. *Toxic Terror: Assessing Terrorist Use of Chemical and Biological Weapons,* Cambridge, MA: MIT Press, 2000.

U.S. Department of State, *Patterns of Global Terrorism,* Washington, DC [Annual].

Venzke, Ben N. *First Responder Chem- Bio Handbook,* Alexandria, VA: Tempest, 1998.

Wardlaw, Grant. *Political Terrorism: Theory, Tactics, and Counter-Measures,* New York: Cambridge University Press, 1989.

White, Jonathan R. *Terrorism: An Introduction,* 3rd ed. Belmont, CA: Wadsworth, 2001.

Whittaker, David J. *The Terrorism Reader,* London and New York: Routledge, 2001.

Zinn, Howard. *Terrorism and War,* New York: Seven Stories, 2002.

Index

H

I

J

K

L

M

TERRORIST ORGANISATIONS AND THEIR MODUS OPERANDI

2 Volume Set

Volume 2

Terrorist Organisations and their Modus Operandi

2 Volume Set

Volume 2

Vijay Kumar Verma

MD Publications Pvt Ltd
New Delhi
www.mdppl.com

Published by :

MD Publications Pvt Ltd
"MD House", 11, Darya Ganj,
New Delhi - 110 002
Phone : +91-11-41563325 (Customer Service)
+91-11-41562846 (Editorial)
E-mail (orders): order@mdppl.com
Website: www.mdppl.com

ISBN: 978-81-7533-223-2 (Set of 2 Vols.)
978-81-7533-225-6 (Vol. 2)

Published and Printed by Mr. Pranav Gupta on behalf of **MD Publications Pvt Ltd** at Times Press, New Delhi.

PREFACE

There exist many different definitions of terrorism, but terrorism most commonly includes these elements: Use of unlawful violence or the threat of unlawful violence; Targeting civilians; Non-state actor; Absence of a state of war (specifically conventional warfare), thus excluding war crimes; Designed to coerce, frighten, or "send a message" to the public or a government (thus excluding organized crime performed for personal gain). The organizations have verifiably used or attempted to use terrorist tactics and their description here made purely for study and research purposes.

The new modus operandi was to attack soft targets, including major landmarks and also kill foreign nationals. Soft targets are those that are not subject to special protection that are frequented by the public, which could be local nationals or foreigners and compared to a classical car bomb or suicide attack, this tactic has the advantage for the terrorists of remaining in the news for a much longer time. It has also a much higher psychological value on the population it kills the feeling of security since terrorists can hit anywhere.

There are hundreds of thousands of potential soft targets of terrorists all over the country. It would be just impossible for the government to provide them with physical security. There are various reasons for which terrorists periodically attack soft targets in widely dispersed areas. Firstly, they want to demonstrate their reach. Secondly, they want to discredit the intelligence agencies, the police and other security agencies in the eyes of the people by demonstrating their capability to strike despite the vigilance of these agencies.

Thirdly, they want to make the police and the security agencies over-react in response to their successful strikes. Fourthly, attacks on soft targets are also undertaken in reprisal for perceived wrongs allegedly committed by the government or the police towards the members of the community from which the terrorists have arisen or even towards the terrorists themselves. One cannot totally eliminate attacks on soft targets, but one can reduce them by effective intelligence capability and policing in order to detect and neutralise them.

I am very grateful to Mr. Pranav Gupta, Director of MD Publications Pvt Ltd, New Delhi, for his kind cooperation and support for this book.

Vijay Kumar Verma

Contents

Vol. 2

Vol. 1

8

Suicide Bombers

Suicide terrorism is not a new phenomenon. From the 11th-century Assassins – whose brazen and usually public murders of their rivals invited immediate death to the perpetrators – to Vietcong sympathizers who blew up themselves and U.S. soldiers in Vietnam, many people have proven their willingness to perish while carrying out attacks in pursuit of their political goals? Yet, the "modern" expressions of the suicide terror phenomenon surfaced with the appearance of the first suicide terrorists in Lebanon, more than 20 years ago. Suicide attacks began in Lebanon in 1983 (some say 1981, when a sole suicide attack hit the Iraqi embassy in Beirut), at the instigation of Hizbollah, a Lebanese Shiite terror organization.

Six months after an attack on the U.S. Embassy in Beirut, simultaneous truck bombings killed 241 U.S. Marines and 58 French paratroopers; just four months later, U.S. troops left Lebanon. Five other organizations (most of them not religious) in Lebanon carried out about 50 suicide attacks before this modus operandi was exported to other areas of the world. The use of suicide attacks garnered considerable prestige for the perpetrators and their organizations – particularly in light of the withdrawal of foreign troops from Lebanon, which many attributed to the bombings – and turned the act into a symbol of martyrdom and a source of inspiration for other terror organizations worldwide. What made these actions unprecedented was their scale: driving cars or trucks filled with explosives, an individual (or individuals) could kill scores, if not hundreds, of people. After 1983, many terror groups adapted the concept, giving bombers explosives to carry on their bodies.

The resulting bombings were smaller, though more precise, allowing the bomber to be a "guided human missile." Therefore, modern suicide terror attacks can be defined as violent, politically motivated actions executed knowingly, actively, and with prior intent by individuals who kill themselves while destroying their chosen civilian or military targets. Terrorist groups often choose this tactic because it is available and inexpensive, and the damage caused to the morale of the rival population is grave. A suicide attack, like all other terror attacks in the modern era, is meant to magnify the "power image" of the perpetrating organization.

The Liberation Tigers of Tamil Eelam (LTTE) in Sri Lanka; the Palestinian fundamentalist organizations of Hamas and the Palestinian Islamic Jihad (PIJ) – and later other non-religious groups such as Al Aqsa Martyr Brigades and the Popular Front for the Liberation of Palestine; and the Kurdish PKK in Turkey have adopted and refined suicide attacks as their "strategic weapons" against their adversaries. Under Osama bin Laden's leadership, al Qaeda and its affiliated groups and networks have given a global dimension to what usually appeared to be national, religious, or local conflicts. Bin Laden's fundamentalist Islamic ideology and his grand strategy have spread the suicide terror phenomenon throughout the world.

For bin Laden and his like-minded disciples, suicide terrorism has served as a weapon of defiance and as a symbolic tool to prove the supremacy of the purity of Muslims over the decadence of their rivals. Following the September 11, 2001 attacks, where for the first time an unprecedented number of suicide bombers were used in four simultaneous suicide missions, al Qaeda and others have been leading a global suicide campaign. Through May 2004, al Qaeda and its affiliates had carried out about 80 suicide attacks by about

150 perpetrators. These numbers do not include almost 70 suicide bombers that have operated in Iraq since March 2003 (at least some, if not most, of them belong to the "Global Jihad" movement) and almost the same number of Chechen separatist suicide bombers, who started to operate in 2000.

About 15 percent of suicide bombers have been women. Most of them belonged to the Tamil LTTE or the Turkish PKK; almost two thirds of the PKK's suicide bombers were female. In both of these groups, their charismatic leaders assured the female volunteers that by participating in the suicide campaign, they would support the group cause while proving that they were as brave as their male peers. Until recently, female suicide bombers were unique to the LTTE, PKK, and other non-religious terror organizations, but this trend has changed recently; some religious leaders have sanctified women's participation in such acts under their "loose" interpretation of Islamic tradition. (Ironically, the same men claim "strict" readings of the Koran to justify terrorism.) Thus, the Palestinian Hamas and PIJ as well as Chechen separatists have started utilizing female bombers. Importantly, those organizations have been operating in very conservative and traditional societies where women have not enjoyed equal rights with men.

Terrorist organizations call upon their members to take part in suicide attacks under different banners and slogans. Sometimes it is done on behalf of God and religion, sometimes on behalf of the "nation," and many times as an act of revenge or deterrence against a more powerful adversary. Islamic fundamentalist organizations such as Hamas and the Palestinian Islamic Jihad, al Qaeda, and Hizbollah invoke God and interpret the Koran in a way that fits their political and operational needs. By doing so they justify such a battle against the "infidels" in defense of Islam. Most of these groups also use nationalism in their jargon, usually invoking the redemption of a holy land belonging to the larger Muslim nation from the hands of aggressors.

As all major religions forbid suicide, religiously motivated groups always express the motives of suicide bombers in "altruistic" terms; also, all terror groups, religious or not, wish to project strength. Thus, the personal motives of suicide bombers are often concealed. Research conducted with "failed" suicide bombers throughout the world has shown that such motivations do exist, including personal psychological hardships; despair and uncontrollable eagerness for revenge; and specific goals of personal glory, such as familial honor or even money for the bombers' families. In one notable example, widely reported in the Israeli press, the first female Hamas suicide bomber – a young mother of two – was allegedly having an extramarital affair; killing herself and several Israelis was said to be the only way she could redeem her name.

Many of those who were tempted to take part in these kinds of activities were mobilized – or, perhaps, seduced – by experienced recruiters specializing in this craft. Recruitment has almost exclusively involved encouraging an individual to sacrifice for the alleged well-being of the community, and the use of persuasion and manipulation techniques – but not physical coercion. The Kurdish PKK is the only organization reported to have executed a member who refused to carry out a suicide.

Another alarming aspect of the suicide phenomenon is the utilization of young children as suicide bombers. The participation of boys as young as 10 to 14 in recent suicide campaigns has been mainly overseen by Palestinian terror organizations that wish to take advantage of the boys' unthreatening appearance. This has generated outcry among the children's families and many others. The victorious reputation of suicide terrorism as the ultimate strategic weapon of the poor and the deprived may contribute to its further dispersal around the world in coming years, and more groups and networks may adopt it into their own arsenal. The main threat emanating from this unique modus operandi is a possible combination of lethal tactics such as a mixture of suicide bombing and non-conventional materials. Much like the unprecedented September 11 attacks, an event of this kind could have global implications.

21ST CENTURY ISLAMIC TERRORIST MODEL

When Israel routed a coalition of Arab armies in the 1967 Six-Day War, some in the Arab world realized that they could not defeat the Jewish state in a conventional land war. Palestinian Arabs, however, sought to lead the way in a different type of warfare against Israel. In 1968, Palestinian terrorist groups under the structural umbrella of the Palestine Liberation Organization (PLO) began using a myriad of different terror tactics against Israeli and Jewish targets in and outside the Middle East. These groups ushered in the era of modern terrorism by launching spectacular attacks (e.g. symbolic airline hijackings), which were only made possible by assailants' willingness to sacrifice their lives. With the success of these shocking attacks, the PLO learned that operations using fedayin (self-sacrificers) had utility well beyond their apparent tactical advantages.

The PLO accordingly incorporated self-sacrificing operations into its overall political strategy. The new approach resulted in such romanticized creations as the Black September Organization, which with its horrific massacre of 11 Israeli Olympians at the 1972 Munich Games brought about the contemporary symbiosis between terrorism and the media. Garnering the spotlight of worldwide media attention, the PLO succeeded in arousing international sympathy and support for the Palestinian movement. These early Palestinian groups, however, neither truly harnessed nor exploited the strategic potential of suicide terrorism. Despite sending their fedayin on high-risk operations, which usually projected certain death, Palestinian leadership did not begin to promote laying down one's life intentionally as an end unto itself until years later.

Between the mid-1970s and early-1990s, a number of events affecting the Arab and Islamic worlds drastically changed the political atmosphere in the Middle East. A Sunni-Muslim sahwa (awakening) swept across Arab countries; Grand Ayatollah Ruhollah Khomeini led an Islamic revolution in Iran, overthrowing Shah Mohammed Reza Pahlavi's pro-

Western government; the Soviet Union invaded Afghanistan; sectarian strife ravaged Lebanon in a bloody civil war; the Cold War's end, the first Palestinian intifada (uprising), and the Gulf War all fostered vast political and social change. Accordingly, as identities formed and new viewpoints took effect politically and socially, the manner in which organizations employed violence also fluctuated. As a byproduct of the Iran-Iraq War and Hezballah's guerrilla campaigns in Lebanon against the United States (U.S.), France and Israel, the Shi'a-Muslim world catapulted the concept of the shahid (martyr) to the forefront of militants' imaginations.

By framing the Iran-Iraq War as a "re-enactment" of the historic battle of Karbala in 860 between Hussein the leader of Shi'at Ali (Faction of Ali) and Yazid the Umayyad Caliph, Iran's Supreme Leader Khomeini directly shaped the way Iranian soldiers approached warfare against the advancing Iraqi army. Because the battle in 860 left Hussein dead and thus heralded by Shi'a Muslims as a great Islamic "martyr," Khomeini's framing invoked many Iranians to seek death on the modern battlefield, so they too might reap the benefits of martyrdom as articulated in Shi'a tradition. Indeed, in 1980, amid a fire fight with Iraqi troops, a 13-year old Iranian named Hussein Fahmideh gathered explosives, attached them to himself, charged an Iraqi tank and detonated the explosives—disabling the tank while killing him. Like that of his namesake, Hussein's act of self-sacrifice found widespread praise among Shi'a Muslims. Soon after, the Iranian government plastered his picture on billboards across Tehran; Hussein's martyrdom, like that of the Shi'a patriarch's, inspired countless others.

By 1982, Khomeini harnessed the power of the Shi'a narrative of martyrdom, and began employing "human wave attacks," which regularly consisted of thousands of Iranian youth simultaneously rushing Iraqi positions, oftentimes protected by surrounding minefields. Armed usually with nothing more than clinched fists and a plastic key around their necks, which ensured their post-martyrdom entrance through the gates of paradise, Khomeini's "mine jumpers" helped turn the tide of the war.

With significant success on the battlefields of the Iran-Iraq War, the Iranian Pasdaran, or Revolutionary Guard, sought to export Khomeini's martyrdom strategy to Lebanon.

Engulfed in an overlapping sectarian-divided civil war and Israel-PLO war, Lebanon became the testing ground for suicide-homicide attacks as a tool of guerrilla warfare. In an ultimately successful effort to expel Western peacekeeping forces, the Pasdaran's Lebanese creation, Hezballah, repeatedly attacked U.S. and French targets using suicide-homicide bombers. Hezballah's campaign reached its zenith with the 1983 suicide-homicide attack on the U.S. Marines barracks, which left 241 American servicemen dead, and convinced U.S. President Ronald Reagan to "redeploy" U.S. forces from Lebanon.

Continuing to advance the tactic in its campaigns against the Southern Lebanese Army and Israel Defense Force throughout the 1980s, Hezballah inspired numerous pro-Syrian Lebanese groups to use suicide-homicide bombers. Deeming suicide-homicide attacks "martyrdom operations," the Pasdaran and Hezballah effectively convinced many that the modus operandi held legitimacy, particularly regarding Shi'a tradition. Moreover, by concurrently galvanizing the Lebanese Shi'a population and expelling foreign militaries from Lebanon, Hezballah made the symbolic and strategic utility of suicide-homicide attacks clear to its enemies and other militant organizations alike.

By 1986, Palestinian Islamic Jihad (PIJ) began flirting with the idea of employing "exceptional martyrdom operations" against civilian Israeli targets. In 1989, Hamas similarly accepted the idea of using suicide-homicide attackers; however, not seeing a strategic opportunity to carry out such "martyrdom operations" amid the first Palestinian intifada, PIJ and its Islamist-counterpart Hamas refrained from deploying suicide-homicide attackers. However, as a rebuke to the PLO's participation in negotiations with Israel, Hamas and PIJ carried out eight suicide-homicide attacks in 1993 alone. By the mid-1990s, some Palestinians hoped for the success of the Oslo peace process, but many others put their faith in the continuation of violent resistance, as predominately carried on by Hamas and PIJ's shahids. From 1994 to 2000, the two Palestinian Islamist organizations carried out 25 suicide-homicide bombings against Israeli targets.

As a result of political Islam's return to the forefront of Palestinian politics and the emergence of a complementary culture of martyrdom in Palestinian society, the shahid rose as the Palestinian movement's new icon—in effect replacing the feda'i (self-sacrificer), and making suicide-homicide bombings the operational mode of choice. With the failure of the Oslo peace process, Fatah sought to maintain popularity by joining the Islamist-Palestinian organizations in the suicide-terror industry and established al-Aqsa Martyrs' Brigade.The early 2000s, thus, saw massive waves of suicide-homicide bombers targeting Israeli civilians in the joint terror effort of al-Aqsa intifada. From September 2000 to December 2005, Palestinian organizations successfully carried out 155 suicide-homicide bombings and launched at least 525.

Effectively convincing their own constituencies of the Islamic justifications for suicide-homicide attacks, the Islamist organizations, particularly Hamas, gained widespread support within Palestinian society for carrying such operations. Moreover, by targeting civilians en masse, Palestinian organizations transitioned suicide-homicide attacks from a guerrilla tactic, as previously used on a wide scale first by Hezballah and later by the Liberation Tigers of Tamil Eelam, to a weapon of terror. Additionally, by demonstrating that participation in a "martyrdom operation" marked the fulfillment of a personal goal, the Palestinian shahid/suicide-homicide bomber captivated mass media and sympathetic populations alike, especially in the Arab and Islamic worlds—eventually having effects stretching far beyond the pales of the Israeli-Palestinian conflict.

Today, posters glorifying the latest shahid litter the walls of Palestinian cities, villages and "refugee camps" in the disputed territories of the West Bank, Gaza and East Jerusalem. Everyone from corner shop owners and cab drivers to the 20-something year olds drinking coffee at the local café extol past Palestinian terror leaders such as Chairman Yasser Arafat, Dr. Fathi Shaqaqi, Sheik Ahmad Yassin and Dr. Abdul Aziz al-Rantissi, along with the heinous terrorist acts they spent their days sponsoring. In Bethlehem, children argue in the street over whose turn it is to play the shahid in their casual game of a mock suicide-bomb attack. These sentiments expressed on the Arab streets of the disputed territories represent a popular culture of martyrdom, which has gained and continues to strengthen a stranglehold on Palestinian society.

Identifiable by shahid worship and praise for terrorism, Palestinian society, however, no longer exclusively exhibits this culture of martyrdom. Cities from Jakarta to Baghdad and London have witnessed the fruits of this terror-breeding culture. Similarly, the rapid diffusion of suicide terrorism, geographically and across ideological lines, exemplifies how terror organizations have garnered the strategic utility of employing "martyrdom operations." Furthermore, Palestinian developments in the evolution of suicide-homicide attacks have functioned as alerts of these various strategic components. Moreover, by setting a precedent among Sunni Muslims, and gaining legitimacy for attacking civilians from prominent Islamic authorities within the Sunni world, the Palestinian shahid/suicide-homicide bomber precipitated its own duplication in numerous other conflicts. Thus, to fully appreciate the implications of the Palestinian culture of martyrdom and shahid, one needs to understand the former's social development, the latter's doctrinal roots, and the influence the pair have had on terror campaigns outside the context of the Israeli-Palestinian conflict.

Since the early 1990s, Palestinian terror organizations have drawn from many sources and incrementally refined the process of suicide terrorism. By making the modus operandi socially acceptable and at times even fashionable, Palestinian terror organizations have normalized the deployment of suicide-homicide bombers. In doing so, the progress individuals take from reasoning and justifying to rationalizing and actually committing suicide terrorism has been eerily optimized. Consequently, Palestinian terror organizations have not only developed an extremely successful, if not strategic, weapon for their war with Israel, but also provided Islamist-terror organizations such as those within the global al-Qaeda network with the model 21st Century terrorist, as well as efficient methods to produce such individuals. By mobilizing mass support in the Sunni world and empowering the individual through the concepts of jihad and martyrdom, the shahid, as epitomized by Palestinians during al-Aqsa intifada, secured suicide terrorism's growing organizational partiality, ensured lethality, decreasing targeting discrimination, and frequency in the international arena. Thus, the phenomenon of the Palestinian shahid has become a driving force behind the increasing spread of suicide terrorism worldwide.

SUICIDE TERRORISM AS A FIXTURE OF THE 21ST CENTURY

Through its reemergence as a significant force in the Islamic world, political Islam returned various concepts to the forefront of social discourse and practice, including violent ones like jihad, fard ayn and istishhad. These notions have notably produced violent phenomena such as suicide-homicide bombings, suicidal hijackings and beheadings. While Shi'a-Muslims initially developed the suicide-homicide modus operandi, and some nominally secular organizations have employed such attacks, nearly forty Sunni-Muslim organizations have used suicide-homicide attacks since the Palestinians started doing so in 1993.

Moreover, following the precedents set by Palestinian organizations, Sunni militants and terrorists today carry out the overwhelming majority of suicide-homicide attacks in an increasing number of locations and with a decreasing level of targeting discrimination. That suicide-homicide attacks originated with Shi'a Muslims and currently the Shi'a in Iraq have not resorted to suicide terrorism further demonstrates that the modus operandi has nearly become an exclusively Sunni phenomenon.

Indeed, without Sunni organizations, suicide terrorism would probably arouse minimal international concern. The Palestinians' al-Aqsa intifada would not have had the impact that it did; the wall separating Israel from the disputed territories surely would not stand, and Hamas would not enjoy the popular support that it currently does among Palestinians and other Arabs and Muslims. Al-Qaeda's embassy, USS Cole and 9/11 attacks would not have happened in the manner that they did, if at all. Iraq's reconstruction would not face the severe challenges that it does, as Sunni suicide-terror attacks (e.g. Golden-Dome Mosque attack and Ashura festival attack) have led to major sectarian clashes.

The United Kingdom (UK) would not have faced the horror of British citizens killing themselves in order to murder fellows Britons. Seemingly endless, one could go on with scores of examples, as Sunni organizations have launched numerous attacks in Indonesia, Russia, Egypt, Jordan, Turkey, Morocco, Spain, Tunisia, India, Pakistan, Saudi Arabia, Kuwait, the Philippines, Singapore, Croatia and elsewhere. Disregarding the work of Sunni organizations over the last 15 years, suicide-homicide attacks have struck only in Lebanon, Kuwait, Sri Lanka, India, and Argentina and on the battlefields of the Iran-Iraq War. With an international-Sunni culture of martyrdom shadowing the dispersal of suicide terrorism across the globe, a high likelihood exists that the modus operandi will continue to play a part in Islamist behavior in the foreseeable future. The Palestinian shahid's suicide terror 'MO' has made its mark, and al-Qaeda intends to duplicate it across the globe. Countering suicide terrorism therefore will require well thoughtout strategies that employ a collection of responses that correspond to the varying facilitators and perpetrators of the modus operandi.

9

Terrorist Operation through Internet

The overall picture of terrorism and the methods used by terrorists have greatly changed during the last 10-15 years and especially after the 9/11 attack in the U.S.A. The change has been radical and has occurred, at least partly, simultaneously with rapid development of information technology. In 1998 less than half of all terrorist 30 organizations defined as such by the U.S. State Department had any kind of home pages in the internet. Now all more than 40 organizations defined as terrorist organizations have their web pages. In a study conducted between years 2003 - 2005 more than 4300 different web pages related to terrorist organizations were found.

A modern terrorist organization can easily and effectively operate across borders - no matter, whether the borders are political, geographical or ideological. There is seldom any need for anybody to move physically across these borders. The less physical movement is the less risk to get caught or to leave any clues. Nowadays it is very simple to move money, propaganda or information across the borders simply by pushing a few buttons on a computer keyboard. The same technology that helps the lives of billions of people all around the planet Earth helps at the same time the terrorist organizations.

An 18-year old high school student had entered his school and killed 9 persons by shooting them, including himself. According to the Finnish police, the shooter had left his "testimony" and some videoclips on the Youtube pages in the internet the day before the shooting. He had also used the internet chat groups to express his visions on the world and its state and kept in contact with a youngster in the U.S., who had later been arrested in the U.S. for planning an attack to a school there. Both young men were known to admire the previous school attackers of whom there are plenty of web pages available.

Even though the shooting in Jokela can in no way be described as being a terrorist act, is the fact that if a 18-year old schoolboy can use the internet to promote his "cause", to gather information regarding his future attack, to group with people who share the same opinions and then, finally, get his 15 minutes (or in this case, a lot more) of publicity all over the world in minutes after the horrendous killings had happened surely the terrorist organizations with their skill can do the same and more. And they will.

There is no mutually agreed definition of the word "terrorism" anywhere to be found. The word itself derives from Latin, and it was first used in the aftermath of the French Revolution, when the Jacobines formed "tribunals" which condemned people randomly to death and other punishments not based on any law. Terrorism has many faces: It can be directed against a state or it can be used by states against their opponents or, as in many cases, it can be State-sponsored terrorism. It can be separatist or it can aim for a single aim (animal rights, anti-abortion, etc.). Terrorism can be local or domestic or it can be international, it can be conventional (attacks by weapons, explosives) or it can be nonconventional (use of biological weapons, chemical weapons etc.). Its aim can be socio-revolutionary changes or religious and so on. Shortly, terrorism has so many different and sometimes even opposite goals that it surely can not be defined by its goals.

So the motives, ideological reasons and other reasons of

the terrorists vary greatly so may be terrorism could be defined as some kind of a philosophy. Can terrorism then be defined by its means, the way the acts we call terroristic are performed? Not likely. There are no list or specified requirements; how acts could be classified as terrorist acts just by the way they are performed. One can use a bomb and not perform a terrorist act and at the same time someone can perform a terrorist act by using his or her bare hands.

One definiton comes from the former CIA (Central Intelligence Agency, USA) deputy chief of counter-terrorism, Mr. Paul Pillar, who defines terrorism as containing the following four fundamental elements:

- Terrorism is premeditated and planned. It is never performed in sudden burs of anger or outrage.
- Terrorism is political. The aim of terrorism is to change the prevailing political reality and its aims are not criminal.
- It is targeted against civilians – not soldiers.
- Terrorism is performed by some other group than an army of a state.

Pillar's opinion that terrorism can not be performed by any state army could be challenged by many, including myself after living in the Middle East hotspots for seven years. Probably Pillar's idea is that a state army can be criminal or break the Human Rights Law or International Humanitarian Law but that its actions could not defined as terrorism. If state terrorism is not included, fine. But if state terrorism is included, then surely the troops that perform the terrorist acts ordered by the commanders who may have been ordered by the politicians, are guilty of state terrorism. Somewhat different approach to the definition of terrorism had some international terrorism experts when asked to define it. According to the study, eight most important elements in terrorism included the following:

- Use of violence
- The choosing of victims: symbolistic
- The act is performed by an organization

- The act includes an operative element
- The act has to be preplanned
- Lack of moral restraints
- Politically motivated
- The use of fear and horror

Mikaela Heikkilä raised some interesting questions during her lectures. In the above mentoned definition the international experts named as one of the characteristics of terrorism that a terrorist act should be performed by an organization. Heikkilä asks, if the organization really is needed? In my opinion the answer is a clear "no" the reason being that a single person can perform a terrorist act, if the goals and means qualify - poltically motivated use of violence that causes fear in the public etc. Many experts can't even agree, if some of the terrorist groups are actually organizations in the traditional sense – for example Al Qaeda's name has been used in so many terrorist acts, that it is doubtful if the Al Qaeda "management" has ever even know about these acts before they have occurred. The traditional shape of the organizations has changed since the 1960's and even the 1990's and a very big factor in that are the Internet and its use and possibilities.

Heikkilä also mentioned the term "communicative violence" which can't be found in the expert's list above. The communicative element is of paramount importance, since a terrorist act without publicity has much less influence (if any) than an act, that is widely published in the media. May be in the future some victims can be avoided if the terroristo organizations can get the publicity through the use of Internet without having to resort to violence? If by using the computers a terrorist organization could, for example, paralyze the train system of greater London area, they would for sure get their message through the traditional media without causing as much resistance in the public as by killing randomly innocent people. The next question then is, of course, would this be enough for a terrorist organization? Probably for some it would be and for some not, depending on their final goal.

INTERNET

Internet's first steps were taken in the 1960's but the roots of the modern Internet can be tracked to the 1970's and the Era of Cold War. The Ministry of Defence in the U.S.A wanted to decentralize their computer system in the fear of a nuclear attack by the Soviet Union. Thus a computer network system was created by various academics and researchers. In the network system the computers were physically distanced far away from each other. Because the computers could better be utilized if they could communicate between each other, a net model was created. The network was first opened for commercial use in the 1980's - before that it had been mainly used by various government organs and the academic community.

In the early 1990's the Internet connected approximately 18 000 different networks and it was estimated that the number of Internet users was somewhere around 60 million. In the early years of this millennimum the number of users was estimated be more than one billion and rapidly growing. The latest statistics estimate more than 1.2 billion users or about 19% of the total estimated population in the world. This means, that a huge portion of world's literate population have at least some access to Internet and that they are using it.

There are different definitions describing the Internet. The technical definitions concentrate on the different protocols used in transferring data. Some of them describe the Internet as a network of computer networks, which is linked together by individual computers or computer networks by using certain protocols. Some definitions approach the Internet from more social perspective, where Internet is seen as a group of people who communicate with each other by using computers and computer networks. Internet can also be defined a group of embryos that have an Internet-address - no matter if they are human beings, companies, organizations or chat-groups.

THE USE OF INTERNET FOR TERRORIST PURPOSES

Terrorism has changed. The new millennium faces a new approach by the terrorist organizations, best witnessed by the 9/11 attack. The terrorist organizations themselves have changed, their means have changed and their funding has changed. In the 1970's and even earlier the terrorist organizations' organizational structures were very hierarchical and their decision-making centralized and followed strict patterns. Their organizations consisted of many different levels, each reporting to the next level. The organizations were normally operating in a limited area only and quite often their targets were local and area-dependent.

According to many experts, that era has come to an end. Times have radically changed and so have the terrorist organizations and their methods. A well-known expert, Xavier Raufer, a former agent for the French intelligence services and now a professor and director of a department concentrating on organized crime and terrorism in Paris University, has noted the following 6 changes in the modus operandi of terrorist organizations compared to previous times:

- The organizations are not bound to certain areas or territories or they operate from remote areas which are virtually inaccessible.
- In many cases they lack the support of States, which makes them harder to control and theit actions more unpredictable and incalculable.
- Their nature is more hybrid than before –they can be partly political or religious-fanatics, partly criminal.
- The terrorist organizations can change fast depending "on the course of the dollar".
- Their approach to matters is quite pragmatic. Also their view can be described as Maoist – first we have to learn guerrilla war before we can start the "real" war.
- Their destructive power is massive compared to the organizations from the Cold War Era. The Aum-cult was very close to kill 40 000 people in the Tokyo underground transport system in 1995 – a broken valve in the aerosol can prevented a massive catastrophe from occurring. In the 9/11 attack 15 times more people were killed than in the most destructive terrorist act before year 2000.

The management and giving operational advice and orders has become much easier because of the Internet and the satellite and mobile phones. The command center of any terrorist operation can move - it is no longer bound to a certain address or place. Any operative cell in any country can be reached via anonymous Internet links easily and sometimes without leaving any tracks. The cells thus have become more and more independent and their finding thus more difficult. The many positive facts in the point of view of a terrorist organization include at least the following:

- In many cases the various actors committed to a terrorist act do not know each other at all. Sometimes the meet just prior to the terrorist attack. This reduces the risk of being caught and also the risk of giving information of the other, if caught.
- If one of the terrorists is caught, he or she might be able only to give the interrogators an Internet e-mail address or addresses and a nickname for someone with whom he or she has been in contact with. Needless to say, these pseudonyms can be created in the Internet in seconds and also destroyed and changed in seconds.
- As mentioned, the leadership of the organization can operate virtually from almost anywhere in the world.
- Any single person can make a terrorist attack or an attack that seems to be terrorist in its nature and declare that it was done by or in the name for example, al Qaeda. Al Qaeda leaders can then, after judging whether the attack suits their purposes, declare as their "property". The actual person who committed the act may be has nothing at all to do with al Qaeda and this leads us to the next question again: Can it be said it was the work of al Qaeda, if the person who did the attack and al Qaeda accept mutually that it was an al Qaeda attack, even though they de facto have no links before the attack whatsoever? Again, the Internet gives the possibility to these mushroom "cells" to pop up whenever and wherever and give them all the publicity needed.

- If any single cell or leader is caught, the rest can still be operational.

Internet has thus made the operations of any terrorist organizations easier. Via the Internet it is possible to reach hundreds of millions of potential readers, sympathizers, viewers and listeners virtually anywhere in the matter of split-second. Anyone can join the Internet-community - all you need is the access to a computer, which is linked via telephone lines or other means to the Internet and nowadays you can find a place to use the Internet almost anywhere. The use of Internet is normally quite cheap, compared to "old-fashioned" long distance or country-to-country phone calls. One can easily use the Internet anonymously from an Internet-cafeteria, library or any other such place - one doesn't have to use his or her "own" computer or home to gain the access to the net. Modern mobile phones have also direct access to Internet, making things even easier for the terrorists.

It is easy to create flashy web pages in the Internet, containing pictures, diagrams, videos, music and all of the terrorist organizations, as mentioned earlier, have created their own web pages as mentioned earlier. Controlling the Internet effectively has proven to be very difficult if not impossible. If the webmaster or any other authority decides to close a certain website, as has happened in many instances regarding the terrorist organizations, it is very likely to appear in the matter of hours or day on another website. It has been estimated that there are more than one billion websites which contributes to the difficulty controlling them.

Also the laws in many countries are not suitable for any kind of censorship - in many cases the laws were made before Internet was created. Internet is a cheap, worldwide reliable and easy tool for the purposes of any organizations, including the terrorist organizations.

PSYCHOLOGICAL INFLUENCE

Terrorism tries to affect the decision- making by creating an atmosphere of fear and panic, as noted earlier. According to the American Psychological Association (APA):

Terrorism threatens a society by instilling fear and helplessness in its citizens. It seeks to hold a society or government hostage by fear of destruction and harm. When terrorist acts occur, people generally look for ways to cope with the acute stress and trauma. Terrorism evokes a fundamental fear of helplessness. The violent actions are random, unprovoked, and intentional, and often are targeted at defenseless citizens. Trying to cope with the irrational information that is beyond normal comprehension can set off a chain of psychological events culminating in feelings of fear, helplessness, vulnerability, and grief.

Internet gives the terrorist organizations an excellent tool to achieve exactly what the APA describes as the effects of terrorism. They can easily affect single persons, organizations or communes by sending messages via Internet causing fear, threats and unsecure feelings. The threats can be targeted to certain persons or groups of people. An example from Pakistan gives some idea, how the Internet can be used to achieve the goals of a terrorist organization:

A Pakistani group used the Internet to lure an American journalist, Mr. Daniel Pearls, to meet someone who provided to give him some information he needed in his work as a journalist. Pearls went to meet the person he "met" via the Internet but instead of getting an interview or information, he was kidnapped and killed. A while later the video of his killing was placed on the Internet to cause fear and horror in the public.

It is also easy for the terrorist organizations to create web sites containing false information, for example footages of beheadings that never occurred or stories that never happened. In the chatrooms of the web false information can be spread just as easily as true information – no one is able to control all of the content of the chats.

During the Iraq war the Internet has been used countless time to create fear by showing beheadings of soldiers or civilians or by sen messages from terrorist leaders or even their interviews on videos. The opportunities are countless and the internet also gives the terrorist organizations the possibility to appear even more threatening and dangerous than they really are – in reality, their powers have been greatly exaggarated. Very few people have died as the consequence of their actions, with all due respect to those who have lost their lives in terrorist attacks. Their power is not in their skills to create havoc, but in their skills to manipulate the media and to this the Internet contributes a great deal.

PUBLICITY AND USE OF PROPAGANDA

Earlier the terrorist organizations tried to gain publicity by using the newspapers, radio and television. The success of a terrorist attack was measured often by the coverage it gained in the media. Obviously the attacks that received the most coverage in the media were considered more successful than the ones that were poorly covered or not covered at all – after all, it is useless to attack for example a bus full of civilians, if in the end nobody knows that it happened. So, the terrorists are after spectator ratings, pretty much as the ABC or CNN news but using somewhat different means. Earlier the media was controlled by states (in some cases), media empires or single journalists – effectively, there was a media monopoly.

With the creation of Internet, this monopoly has partly collapsed or, in a way, it has collapsed completely. Today any one can disseminate any kind of information at any time and just about free of charges. Nobody really controls, if the information is false or true – in fact, the third most visited encyclopedia, the Wikipedia, in the Internet, is created by users of Internet – and nobody has controlled, if the information is true or not. This has not gone unnoticed by the terrorist organizations – they gladly advertise their ideologies, publish pictures and film material of their successful or less successful attacks and any other material, they deem useful for their cause.

THE INTERNET- RHETORIC'S OF TERRORIST ORGANIZATIONS

The terrorist organizations´ websites normally use three elements to justify their actions:

- They claim that they have no other possibility than to resort to violence. The violence is seen as justifiable since the enemy is so overwhelmingly strong. On the Internet-pages the organizations seldom advertise the casualties their actions have caused among the civilians. However, the actions of the enemy are often described with words such as "bloodbath", "murder" and "genocide".
- The second element consists of dehumanizing and delegitimizing the enemy. The members of the terrorist organization are portrayed as freedom fighters who are obliged to use violence against an enemy that tries to destroy their people or group from which the terrorists belong. Part of the tactics is to emphasize the "fact" that the use of violence by the group is minimal compared to the use of violence by the enemy. This way the terrorist groups try to transfer the responsibility of their own actions to the enemy.
- The third element is the language used by the terrorists – on their web pages they appear as peace-loving and diplomatic groups searching for a diplomatic solution to their cause. The reality can be totally different, consisting of very violent and horrendous acts against civilians.

Often the organizations mention freedom of speech and the asylum of political prisoners as their goals. These are values that are respected very much in the western democracies and also too many of the supporters of the terrorist organizations. In many cases the freedom of speech would be quite relative, if the organizations were in power - more likely the principle of "one man - one vote - once" would be the outcome, if certain terrorist organizations would gain the power.

TARGET AUDIENCES

The terrorist organizations can, just like anybody else, target their audiences according to their needs at any given time. The media can be immediately be contacted after a successful attack and send them via the Internet any suitable footage and information regarding the incident. The organizations can use their own web sites to publish any material they think is important. Their pages can be linked to other similar pages containing similar material and the material can be sent directly to the enemy or the general public. Some organizations have created special computer games, easily accessible and easily loadable to one's own computer.

Hamas-organization, operating mostly in Gaza and occupied West Bank, have created special websites targeted to children with stories related to the holy war, Jihad. In practice, the target audiences can be the supporters or potential supporters of the organization to whom the ideology is marketed as well as items for sale – books, banners, T-shirts and forthcoming activities, whether legal or illegal.

An important target, may be the most important, is of course the general opinion and in many cases, the general international opinion. The more the terrorist organizations can affect the general opinion in a positive way -for their cause – the more successful they are and the easier it becomes to get funding from various sources. Also, the political success follows the general opinion. The use of Internet can also lead to positive outcomes. A good example is the Zapatista-organization (EZLN) in Mexico, which has, according to Weimann, succeeded in creating positive attitudes towards them by using skillfully the possibilities of the Internet.

The positive use of Internet will be important not only to the terrorist organizations but especially to the terrorist organizations to wings of organizations, who want to change from violence to more traditional politics. Interestingly, most, if not all, terrorist organizations use not only the language of their area but also other languages, English being number one.

FUNDING

Terrorism needs funding and for example Al Qaeda has always been dependent on donations coming from its own sub-organizations, some other NGO's, private donors and others. Often the systems created within the Internet have been used to transfer funds from one country to another.

Also funds are raised in different forums in the Internet, chatrooms and other galleries. In many occasions the mother terrorist organizations have created other organizations which seem to be concentrating on welfare and in many cases they are.

Sometimes nor all the funds raised go to the original target but to the terrorist organization itself. On occasions, Internet inquiries have been analyzed and then the organizations have approached people or companies thought to favor their cause. The IRA collected money for decades quite openly in the U.S., but after the 9/11 attack fund raising for example in the U.S. has been made more difficult. Many accounts have been frozen if there have been some hints that the funding is likely to go to the terrorist organizations.

DATA MINING AND COLLECTING INFORMATION

Preparing a terrorist neither attack nor only requires funding - it requires information of the target and its surroundings as well. It also often requires some special skills in how to use some terrorist's "tools". A lot of this information is readily available from the vast library of more than one billion pages in the Internet. Most of the information in the Internet is useless, but from the remaining mass of data a lot of useful knowledge can easily be accessed through the so called open sources, sources that are open to anybody wanting to utilize them. Donald Rumsfeld told 15.01.2003 that an al Qaeda a handbook was found. In the handbook the terrorist stated, that 80% of the information needed to stage a terrorist attack can be found in the Internet by legal means.

Also found was the structural drawings of a large dam in the U.S. - this information had been obtained legally from the Internet and it was found in the memory of a confiscated al Qaeda computer. Anyone who has used the Internet to search just about anything knows that the problem is not the lack of information but the excessive amount of it. From the net even an inexperienced computer user can find maps, structural drawings of potential targets, addresses, phone numbers, timetables of politicians, photographs from inside potentially interesting targets, photographs of just about anything etc. By using some time, interesting options for a successful terrorist attack can easily be found by combining data from different open sources. Information can also be obtained by attending the various chatrooms and galleries or even by asking directly from companies and organizations – on many occasions even sensible information has been obtained this way.

Dissemination of Information

Internet can be regarded as a vast storage of information containing documents, films clips, photographs, music and anything that can be transformed in binary form. The terrorist organizations not only use this storage to obtain information but also to disseminate information. Dozens of pages can be found on the Internet where one can learn how to build different kind of bombs, how to use weapons or how to get to Iraq and join the war. Famous books on the Internet are for example *The Terrorist's Handbook* and *The Anarchist's Cookbook*".

On the Hamas-organizations's pages could be found already 1996 published Abdul Aziz's *The Mujahedeen Poisons Handbook,* which deals with producing poisonous gases, poisons and other possible materials usage in a terrorist attack, devoting 23 pages for this. Al Qaeda has published on the Internet a huge entity, consisting of several thousand pages named *The Encyclopedia of Jihad* which deals with everything from creating a terrorist cell to performing a terrorist attack.

Recruitment

Money and knowledge is not enough to stage a terrorist attack. The terrorist organizations need people to perform attacks. The organizations not only have their own web sites but they are also active in the exchange of ideas and discussions on different web sites, chatrooms and galleries. If someone in these chats is considered as "interesting" in the eyes of any given terrorist organization, the person may be led carefully to chat rooms where the discussions are may be more radical and if still the opinions of the person match the ones of the organization, he (or she, but seldom) will may be asked to join a prayer on a Friday or to have a meeting in cafeteria for further discussions. This can later lead to anything, including acts of terrorism if the candidate is suitable. Sometimes person interested in terrorism and willing to join, advertise themselves in the Internet. For example Ziyad Khalil, who was studying computer sciences in Missouri Columbia College, U.S.A, started a Hamas-supporting web page in the Internet. After a while, some leaders from al Qaeda started to pay attention to these pages and Khalil, who later started to work for al Qaeda as their logistics officer in the U.S.A. He purchased computers, satellite phones and surveillance equipment for the use of Al Qaeda, which helped the leadership of al Qaeda in their communications between the leaders and lower level cells.

CYBER TERRORISM

Cyber terrorism is normally defined as using the computer networks in a manner which is aimed to make vital organisms or infrastructure of a society defunct (for example government's functions, distribution of energy, traffic etc.) and thus create a situation likely to cause fear and panic. Warnings regarding cyberterrorism have been recorded since early 1990's whereas the other use of Internet by the terrorists has not received much interest – even though using the Internet to everything else than cyber-terrorism seems to be the way the terrorist organizations in real life use the Internet.

Cyberterrorism does not mean the "normal" hackers actions, which are motivated not by terrorist goals but something else. Cyberterrorism is a very tempting possibility for the terrorist organizations – if they could control the vital communications or other relevant factors of a modern society, the impact would be enormous and thus, the publicity. So far there is, however, no proof of a succestful, serious cyberterrorist attack agains any State organs. There has been some "attacks" by sending massive amounts of junk mail to certain e-mail addresses to demonstrate against something or someone, but these can not be classified as "cyberterrorism".

Although this essay is about Internet in the use of terrorists, I devoted just a few lines for this issue, reason being that cyberterrorist acts haven't really been recorded - yet. Future will show if the paths of hackers and terrorists cross and what will be the outcome then.

THE BASIC RIGHTS

Paradoxically the system, that was created for the government to secure its flow of information during a time of crisis and then developed into a great instrument for the promotion of freedom of speech and democracy (maybe the most important since the invention of printing press by Gutenberg), now gives the weapons to the hands of people and organizations, who fight against the democratic values and freedoms of individuals. The governments have some means to control the information in the Internet. In the U.S.A some methods have been created to see, what is actually happening in the vast cyberworld. A system called "Carnivore" (now called the DCS1000) was developed not long ago.

Carnivore can process millions of messages sent via the Internet in seconds and pick up those, which it has been programmed to pick up - maybe by using some keywords related to terrorism or certain persons. Also a method has been developed to break the encrypted messages used by various actors in the Internet. It is called the "Magic Lantern" and its idea is to record any keystrokes on any given computer and analyze them. This means that if my computer is hooked by the Magic Lantern somebody somewhere knows exactly what I am writing, to whom I am sending the message and what my passwords are.

These developments haven't gone unnoticed by various people's rights movements who fear, that the big brother has gained far too much rights to interfere with the fundamental and basic democratic rights of the citizens in the aftermath of the 9/11 incident. The democratic states should be very careful when promoting new laws which affect the freedom of speech, the secrecy of communications and other basic rights.

The fight against terrorism is important, but not at any expense - if the basic democratic values are forgotten, the terrorists have partly reached their goal as the democratic societies would take one step closer to totalitarianism and turn the clock backwards.

CLOSING WORDS

This essay does not concentrate on legal terms or paragraphs. I wrote it mainly to give a brief idea what is happening regarding the Internet and terrorism. I know that many laws regarding terrorism were created in the aftermath of the 9/11 around the world - some of the laws are maybe quite O.K., some are in between and some, one can tell, have been created hastily and are, really, not too good in any aspect. The problem is and will be the definition of terrorism. Our focus is that of a western people and sometimes we might tend to do the same as the terrorists in their propaganda - we demonize our "enemies" and categorize people without any sensible reason. It is quite often "us" and "them". Before there is any real dialogue between various people on planet Earth, the thing called "terrorism" will flourish.

10

Terrorist using Air-Force

THE CONSTRUCTION OF HEZBOLLAH'S AIR-FORCE

It is expected that experts on terrorism would find the evidence of what seems to be the evolution of a military air-force, an interesting perspective, especially when realizing that, to the best of the author's knowledge, there was no evidence that terrorist organizations of the 60's, 70's and 80's had an interest in an air-force platform, mainly due to the huge financial and logistic sources needed to build an effective military air-force. Carlos Marighella, the 'spiritual leader' of modern terrorism, explained in his famous book 'Mini Manual of the Urban Guerrilla that urban guerrillas (authors note: or terrorists) need light weapons, in order to achieve an advantage over the equipped defenders, i.e., mobility vs. stability. Marighella's point of view is based on the assumptions that the urban guerrilla lacks huge financial resources and a logistical infrastructure which are needed for the construction of an air-force.

Moreover: the guerrilla/terrorist fighter cannot adopt the military strategy and platforms as nations have, since the most efficient advantage of the terrorist is mobility, hiding from the 'enemy' by changing locations, minimizing the need of a large, visible military infrastructure, as well as the ability of assimilation among a supporting population. It is clear that hiding a terrorist equipped with a rifle is much easier than hiding an aircraft, not to mention a landing field... So what has changed regarding terrorists' fighting philosophy from the late 1960's to the late 1990's? A few aspects will be discussed, in order to emphasize the understanding that although a terrorist of the 1960's is still the terrorist of the third millennium, the Modus Operandi has changed dramatically, and decision-makers should modify their entire thinking towards modern terrorism.

THE RIFLE HAS BEEN REPLACED BY A ROCKET AND THE HAND-GRENADE BY A FLYING BOMB.

Historically, the idea of using flying-weapons was raised years before the creation of Hezbollah and the terrorist organizations of the 1960's:Johann Most, one of the Mass-Destruction Philosophers predicted the possibility of an aerial terrorism tactic by indiscriminate bombing from the air. When discussing the issue of terrorists and air-infrastructure, it should be emphasized that this article focuses on the implementation of an aerial-weapon platform as an integral means within terrorists' arsenal, and not the simple use of a civilian airplane, by hijacking or sabotaging it, a well-known Middle-East tactic of terrorist organizations, starting with the PFLP(Popular Front for the Liberation of Palestine) headed by Habash and Haddad, Gibril's PFLP-GC (General Command) and closing the list with Al-Qaeda's suicide-mission operation of September 2001.

The possibility of a so-called air-force operated by terrorist groups rises as technological and financial abilities become accessible and when terrorists gain more and more intelligence as to the "enemy's" weaknesses on ground, sea and air. 'Gliders' night': The seeds of an air-force? On November 25, 1987, a flying terrorist, equipped with a motor-glider, managed to cross the Israeli border, taking off from Lebanon (another glider landed in the security strip between Israel and Lebanon and the terrorist was killed by Israeli forces), and due to the size and its low altitude, the glider managed to overcome Israeli radar air control. Six soldiers were killed following this incident. The terrorists were affiliated with Gibril's PFLP-GC, and this incident marks the first incident where terrorists were equipped with aerial means. Since this incident, little attention was given to the possibility of the implementation of aerial-weapons by terrorists. This fact may be the result of several reasons, but some perspectives related to technological and organizational aspects should be emphasized:

1. Historically, terrorists used 'conservative' weaponry, such as pistols, hand grenades, mines, machine guns, light vehicles and rocket launchers. Most of these weapons came from the Soviet Union, and are delivered by supportive Arab countries especially to Palestinian organizations and their supporters, such as the Badder-Meinhof (RAF) group, the IRA and others. These types of weapons were easily transported, easy to hide, and matched the financial ability of the terrorist group. Adopting Marighella's philosophy, light and less-visible means, not to mention many sources of suppliers, have made these weapons highly-favored by terrorists. Certainly, the Russian AK-47 and the RPG-7 was inseparable to almost every terrorist of the 1970's and 1980's.Therefore the fact that a terrorist organization used such an uncommon weapon (glider), did not absorb much attention. The focus was on the AK-47 and not on the flying machine.
2. 'Terrorist Bourgeoisie' or 'terrorist aristocracy': Terrorists modify their tactics and weaponry. Terrorists are in a constant search for the 'weak link' in the enemy's security fence. When they think that they have found such a weak link, then that is the point where they will attack. Since aerial control is normally monitored by technological means, terrorists have learned (even a terrorist group is a learning organization) that technological means suffer some disadvantages. In the case of radar, flying at low-altitude causes difficulty in monitoring the flying machine, and despite the understanding that 'big is good' in the case of gliders or ultralight planes- 'small is better'.
3. Qualification, modernization and Globalization: Terrorists

are everywhere! They grow among a supporting community; they live in Europe, America, Africa and the Middle-East. They learn in universities, gain knowledge in technology, aviation and chemistry. They become intellectual and professional. Therefore accessibility to 'modern' weaponry which demands highly-professional operators becomes more and more relevant when potential terrorists gain more and more knowiedge. Taking for example the IRA, one of whose highly-professional expertise was the use of remote-controlled bombs, using toys which everyone can buy at a toy shop, and converting the remote-controlled lorry toy into a powerful bomb. It is obvious that one cannot control every person who wishes to buy his son a Thanks giving Day present... But globalization has also made use of new weapons more and more accessible: in a world of one-click global shopping, one can buy an electric or gasoline-powered aircraft, some of them weighing a few kilograms, and within 48 hours a delivery agent offers the terrorist-buyer door-to-door service. The ability of converting such flying toys into a flying bomb makes it an alternative for terrorists who wish to escalate their operations, emphasizing that 'if I escalate, it means that I operate' and turning these flying toys into a potential threat.

4. Establishment of a terrorist organization in the political order: Hezbollah is no longer 'another terrorist group': its strategy, infrastructure, massive support by Iran and Syria, well-trained terrorists and its establishment in Lebanon (including representatives in the Lebanese governmental systems), have turned this organization into a new entity: far more established compared to a traditional terrorist group, but less-established compared to a national entity. This fact makes the Hezbollah the dominant factor in Lebanon, and its influence and ability to extend its facilities offers them the opportunity of finding new methods to fight against Israel. The information that the Hezbollah is equipped with surface

to air missiles, aimed at the Israeli surveillance flights over Lebanon demands new thinking as to the new terrorist organization: less moving from one place to another and more entrenching in areas where they become the dominant authority.

5. Glorification causes Imitation: A well known fact is that terrorists try to imitate others' success: Habash did not invent aviation terrorism. He copied this tactic from other places, such as the Cuban-USA saga hijackings of the 1960's.Similar to Habash, The LTTE (Tamil Tigers) leader, Velupillia Prabhakaran admitted that the suicide bomber tactic that the LTTE adopted the first LTTE suicide attack occurred on May 1987 in Sri Lanka) was a result of being inspired by the Lebanese Shia, who committed their first suicide attack in December 1981 against the Iraqi Embassy in Beirut.

Speaking of the LTTE, recent evidence shows that it has managed to acquire an aircraft from East Europe and bring it to Sri Lanka after preparing a landing field. This fact was raised by Bahkutumbi Raman, director of the Institute for Topical Studies in India, following the ICT's conference on counter-terrorism, 2005. Back to the imitation factor, it is clear that a successful operation causes others to imitate the tactic. Taking into account the other element which was highlighted above, one may see that aerial-weaponry may become more and more familiar to terrorists organizations. In the author's thesis, significant attention was given to the potential threat of aerial-weaponry used by terrorists, focusing on either human-operated or UAV (Unmanned Aerial Vehicle) means, which become more and more available.

The use of such flying-means can be adapted to the intelligence aspect but also for the use of loading explosives on a small aircraft (whether conventional explosive or even worse- the use of the aircraft for the purpose of spreading WMD (Weapon of Mass Destruction). Since the use of an aircraft for this purpose demands special modifications, a terrorist organization can start a 'tailormade' production line of flying vehicles while gaining knowledge and experience of converting the vehicles into flying bombs. Turning a cropduster aircraft into a flying bomb demands minor modifications. Such a threat was emphasized by Rabkin (2004), managing Director of the Homeland Security and Justice Issues, following his testimony before the US Senate, claiming that the 11 September terrorists were studying the possible use of crop dusters to spread biological or chemical agents while Al-Qaeda focused on large, commercial aircraft, one may see that terrorists started focusing on other types of aircraft: small or UAV.

According to Israeli officials, some UAV's ('Ultra-Light') were captured in Arafat's headquarters in Ramallah ('The Muqatah') by the Israeli forces during the 'Al Aksa Intifada'. The understanding that a comeback of Bin-Ladin's operation of 2001 is less likely to become possible mainly after strengthening security standards, terrorists will search, inter alia, for aerial weaklink and they have probably found it: the 'holes' in aerial space control. But even if border-control is efficient, it should be emphasized that terrorist organizations are not only crossborder oriented: they can operate even within the state. It is clear that launching a glider from a village in East Jerusalem or from a small air-strip in the Galilee (Northern Israel) is a potential threat that security agencies should take into account. The threat is 'in the air' and attention should be given to how to monitor the purchasing of a gasoline-powered toy aircraft, which can be purchased almost anywhere, especially via the internet. A combination of technological knowledge, financial ability, and day-to-day delivery makes the possibility of the creation of 'mini air force' by terrorist organizations (or individuals) a significant threat.

Over the past forty years, several terrorist groups have emerged, changed policies, and, in many cases, disappeared. Some were primarily suppressed by police and intelligence work, others simply dissolved, and still others persist, but have renounced violence or have ceased to be active. Under what circumstances do terrorists and their organizations bring terror campaigns to an end? What combination of factors brings this about? The conference "Why Do Terrorists Stop?"

brought together specialists on different terrorist groups to look at the data from failed, disbanded, suppressed, and suspended terrorist campaigns from the 1960s through 2006 to analyze causes of defeat and decline in search of lessons that would be useful in fighting currently active terrorists and terrorist organizations.

11

Anti-Terrorism in 2007 and its trends in 2008

ANTI-ISRAELI TERRORISM IN 2007

This study analyzes anti-Israeli terrorism in 2007, an important, continuing influence on the country's political agenda. It includes analyses of the terrorist attack policies and the modus operandi of the various terrorist organizations and networks (Palestinian terrorist organizations, Hezbollah and global jihad). It also analyzes the factors influencing the extent and nature of the terrorism against Israel in 2007 and the trends of the first months of 2008.

TERRORIST ORGANIZATION POLICIES AND MODUS OPERANDI, 2007

i. Rocket and mortar shell fire from the Gaza Strip continued as the Palestinian terrorist organizations' preferred form of attack. In 2007, 896 hits were identified in Israeli territory, compared with 946 in 2006, the year with the largest number. During the past two years there was a substantial increase in rocket fire compared with 2001-2005, the years before the disengagement. The trend continues in 2008. There was also a significant increase in the amount of mortar shell fire, another continuing trend. Rocket and mortar shell fire is relatively less lethal than suicide bombing attacks but has a devastating effect on the daily life and sense of security of the 200,000 residents of the western Negev.

ii. Palestinian suicide bombing terrorism, which was the dominant form of attack during the first years of the current confrontation, has continued declining since the peak of 2002. (There was one such attack in 2007, in the southern city of Eilat, and one so far in 2008, carried out in the southern city of Dimona, compared with four in 2006 and 55 in 2002). That was also manifested by the conspicuous decrease in the number of suicide bombing attacks prevented by the Israeli security forces. In addition, the decrease in number of Israelis killed in suicide bombing attack also continued (three in 2007, compared with 15 in 2006 and 220 in 2002).

iii. Mass-killing attacks and abductions: In 2007 there were sporadic infiltrations into Israeli territory from the Gaza Strip, whose objective was to kill Israeli civilians and soldiers near the border and, should the opportunity present itself, to abduct Israelis. On August 25 such an attack was prevented by the IDF at Netiv Haasara, a village near the Gaza Strip's northern edge. Several attempts to abduct civilians and soldiers in the Gaza Strip, Judea and Samaria were prevented. In 2008, however, there has been an increase in the number of mass-killing attacks, such as Dimona (carried out by suicide bombers), Jerusalem (the shooting attack at the Mercaz Ha'Rav yeshiva), and at border crossings, settlements and military targets near the security fence in Samaria and the Gaza Strip.

iv. In Judea and Samaria there were a number of shooting attacks, two of them fatal. One occurred near Hebron on December 28, 2007, killing two IDF off-duty soldiers on a walking trip. The other was a drive-by shooting which killed an Israeli civilian near the settlement of Kedumim on November 29, 2007. However, many attacks in 2007 were relatively "simple" from an operational point of view, due to the terrorist organizations' operational weaknesses, and consisted of IEDs, stabbings (one fatality) and "cold" attacks (Molotov cocktails and stones.)

v. Hamas and secondly, the Palestinian Islamic Jihad continued as the dominant terrorist organizations. In Lebanon, Hezbollah has avoided attacking Israel since the second Lebanon war in the summer of 2006, focusing instead on rebuilding its military infrastructure. Global jihad networks which have gained a foothold in Lebanon carried out a number of attacks against Israel and UNIFIL. In Judea and Samaria there was no significant global jihad activity against Israel.

Thirteen Israelis were killed in terrorist attacks in 2007, seven civilians and six members of the security forces, continuing the decrease in the number killed in terrorist attacks since the 2002 peak of 453 dead. Two hundred and ninety-one individuals were wounded in terrorist attacks in 2007, most of them members of the security forces. However, in 2008 there has been a significant increase in the number of Israelis killed as a result of the current escalation of the terrorism emanating from the Gaza Strip and the improvement in Hamas's operational capabilities (during the first four months of 2008. 15 Israeli civilians and eight members of the security forces were killed).

In 2007 Hamas accelerated the military buildup of its military-terrorist wing, the Izzedine al-Qassam Brigades , which focuses on terrorist attacks against Israel and defense against the IDF; and of the internal security apparatus (i.e., the Executive Force integrated into the police), Hamas's main arm for internal control, and which supports the Izzedine al-Qassam Brigades. Hamas's military buildup is manifested in a variety of ways: an increase in training (including sending operatives to Iran and Syria), improving its underground tunnel system, acquiring weapons and smuggling them into the Gaza Strip (especially standard rockets and advanced anti-tank missiles) and developing and manufacturing weapons (improving the range and penetration of rockets, manufacturing powerful explosive devices and anti-tank weapons, etc.).

In Lebanon, the military buildup of Hezbollah and the activities global jihad networks were particularly conspicuous.

i. **Hezbollah:** In 2007 Hezbollah continued to avoid attacking Israel, focusing its efforts instead on rehabilitating its military infrastructure and adapting its activities to the new situation created in the south by the second Lebanon war. Particularly conspicuous was the construction of a new rocket arsenal in south Lebanon. With its construction, Hezbollah completed arming itself with the same quantity of rockets it had (20,000) on the eve of the second Lebanon war, and in our assessment, now possesses far more. The rehabilitated arsenal was built with the support of Iran and Syria and is a formidable threat to Israel as far south as Tel Aviv, and even to the southern part of the country.

ii. **The global jihad:** In 2007 global jihad networks worked intensively to strengthen their position in south Lebanon. After the Lebanese government successfully uprooted Fatah al-Islam from the Nahr al-Bared refugee camp in north Lebanon, the Ein al-Hilweh refugee camp near Sidon became the focal point for organization and activity of global jihad-affiliated networks. In 2007 and the beginning of 2008 global jihad groups attacked Israel and UNIFIL a number of times. Two of the more conspicuous attacks were rocket fire targeting Kiryat Shemonah in June 2007 and Shelomi in January 2008. However, their potential for causing damage is much greater.

PALESTINIAN TERRORIST POLICY, ITS SCOPE AND NATURE, 2007

Two important factors influencing Palestinian terrorist policy in 2007 were the Israeli security forces counterterrorist activities and the dramatic developments in the internal Palestinian arena. Both continue to influence Palestinian terrorism in 2008. The successful Israeli security force counterterrorist activities in Judea and Samaria led to a reduction in the number and severity of terrorist attacks. In the Gaza Strip, on the other hand, where there is no permanent Israeli security presence, extensive rocket and mortar shell fire continued. The trends of increasing rocket and mortar shell fire improving their quality rose in 2008. As a result, the number of Israel casualties caused by rocket and mortar shell fire increased.

In Judea and Samaria the security forces maintain counterterrorist activity pressure which includes the detention of wanted terrorists, exposing weapons and killing the terrorist operatives who resisted detention. Successful counterterrorist activities and finishing many sections of the security fence led to a continued decrease in suicide bombing terrorism. In many cases, the operational weakness of the terrorist organizations forced them to make do with relatively "simple" attacks such as shootings, stabbings, laying IEDs, and throwing Molotov cocktails and stones. The Palestinian security forces ' activities, despite their ineffectiveness, also contributed to the difficulties faced by Hamas and the other terrorist organizations in Judea and Samaria.

In the Gaza Strip, which is the focal point of anti-Israeli terrorism, the Israeli security forces increased the level of their counterterrorist activities during the second half of 2007. There were no major operations but rather air strikes and ground activities limited in time were carried out. They included the targeted killings of terrorist operatives; attacks on weapons and ammunitions stores, workshops and weapons-manufacturing lathes; strikes against rocket launching squads; attacks on terrorist bases and offices; the detention of suspected terrorists and the exposure of tunnels dug to smuggle weapons. Although the IDF's activities in the Gaza Strip made it difficult for the terrorist organizations to carry out attacks, they did not stop the rise in the number of rockets fired and did not stop Hamas's military buildup or the improvements in its operational capabilities. Another important factor influencing Palestinian terrorism in 2007 was the dramatic developments in the internal Palestinian arena which occurred concurrently with the continuing peace process, which reached its high point at the Annapolis meeting on November 27. The most important internal Palestinian developments were the schism between Hamas and Fatah, the Hamas military takeover of the Gaza Strip in June, which came after a series of violent incidents, and the brutal oppression on Fatah and the Palestinian Authority security services. Following the takeover, Hamas established a Palestinian entity in the Gaza Strip ("Hamastan") which is in constant confrontation with Abu Mazen's PA.

The dramatic events in the Gaza Strip weakened Abu Mazen's PA, hampering his ability to make effective progress in a peace process with Israel and enabled Hamas to force its agenda on the Palestinians. Its agenda is based on non-recognition of the State of Israel and using terrorism to achieve its aspirations, i.e., the destruction of the State of Israel and the establishment of an Islamic Palestinian state on the ruins. Hamas's Palestinian entity in the Gaza Strip, whose ideology and policies are different from those of the PA headed by Abu Mazen in Judea and Samaria found itself isolated by the international community and even the Arab and Muslim world (with the exception of Syria and Iran , which support it politically, militarily and financially).

The terrorist policy of Hamas, which enjoys unprecedented freedom of action in the Gaza Strip, is influenced by the continual tension between its administrative responsibilities, which force it to respond to the population and to cope with internal and external threats to the Gaza Strip; and its strategic-political and ideological goals, which commit it to maintaining its jihad identity by continually attacking Israel, even when the terrorist attacks clearly harm the Palestinian population in the Gaza Strip. Hamas resolves that fundamental tension by continuing attacks (mainly rocket and mortar shell attacks) while controlling their dosage, keeping them at a level which will not drag Israel into a broad military action in the Gaza Strip. At the same time, inspired by Hezbollah's achievements in Lebanon during the second Lebanon war, it has accelerated the pace of its ongoing military buildup, hoping that will enable it to fight the IDF successfully when the latter enters the Gaza Strip. The buildup is made possible by the Iranian and Syrian support of Hamas (and the other terrorist organizations), partly the result of the Egyptian government's ineffective response, which did not prevent the smuggling of weapons, money and terrorist operatives into the Gaza Strip through Rafah Crossing and the tunnels dug under the Philadelphi Route.

THE UNCONVENTIONAL TERRORISM

The recent interest in the possible use by terrorists of weapons of mass destruction (WMD) has led students of terrorism to reexamine in depth past cases of known or alleged WMD terrorism. One of the major focuses of the new research also involves an effort to answer the question of why not? Why have large and resourceful terrorist organizations refrained from using what appears as a very effective weapon of terror? This looks at the Palestinian terrorist organizations and factions engaged between the 1960s and the 1990s in a fierce struggle against the State of Israel. Looking at all the available information on the small number of cases involving Palestinian use of unconventional weapons, the article tries to explain the outstanding absence of thinking on toxic terrorism in this otherwise very bellicose milieu.

While the Palestinian terrorist organizations rarely appear in the literature on unconventional terrorism, there is one incident that is repeatedly associated with them and is mentioned all over the literature, the 1978 poisoning of Israeli oranges in Western Europe. Even David Rapoport, a leading critic of the WMD terrorism hype, and a careful fact-checker, repeats the story in his most recent article on the subject. Rapoport tells us that, "In 1978 the Palestinian Liberation Organization (PLO) began to poison Israeli oranges in European markets, injuring 12 and seriously damaging the Israeli economy. But then the activity stopped and we don't know why."

The events surrounding the incidents of poisoning of Israeli oranges were indeed reported in the literature on terrorism, but as with other incidents relating to unconventional terrorism, the facts were never investigated in depth and remain unclear to this very day. Ron Purver, who has compiled the most detailed and exhaustive abstract of the literature on chemical and biological (CBW) terrorism until 1995, has included the affair of the poisoning of Israeli oranges among "the successful uses of chemical agents." According to Purver, the contamination by Palestinian terrorists or their sympathizers of Israel's citrus exports to Europe with liquid mercury were reported to have occurred in 1977, 1978, and 1979.

Purver's article summarizes, in fact, all that has become known from these incidents: "Europeans in at least three countries became ill from eating Israeli citrus products - oranges, lemons, and grapefruit - that had been contaminated with mercury, which presumably had been injected under the skins of the citrus products with a syringe. A group identifying itself as the Arab Revolutionary Army - Palestinian Commandos, in a letter to the Dutch government, announced that its goal was 'to sabotage the Israeli economy."

"No one died from the incident and only slightly more than a dozen people were poisoned, but Israel's citrus exports were profoundly affected, with the loss of badly needed foreign exchange." Is this indeed a case of successful use by Palestinian terrorists of chemical agents against Israel, an early preview of WMD economic terrorism? Were Palestinian terror strategists really involved in this sophisticated operation? How unconventional was this unconventional terrorism? And if so effective, why was it stopped?

The sequence of events: On 26 January 1978. Mrs. Maria Berg-Puts bought 3.5 kilos of Jaffa oranges in Maastricht, in the southern Netherlands. The next day she and her four children ate the fruits and felt a bitter taste. Cutting one orange open, the elder son found silver liquid in the flesh of the fruit. After the family doctor sent them to hospital, the authorities moved in, and four of the six remaining oranges were found to have been injected with mercury – one with a large 10-gram dose. All the children involved in the Maastricht incident recovered rapidly without after-effects. On January 27, 1978, a woman found one orange injected with mercury in a shop in Frankfurt, Germany and alerted the authorities. In the same day shoppers in the Dutch city of Heemlen also found oranges injected with mercury. Although they themselves were not affected, the great scare began. The poisoning incidents were not publicized in the European media until January 31, 1978, when Dutch newspapers first broke the story. By that time, the Reuters news agency already knew that an organization calling itself The Arab Revolutionary Army (ARA) had sent letters to 18 European and Middle Eastern governments, including those of Yugoslavia and Romania, threatening to poison Israeli oranges. The Israeli press began reporting the case on February 1, 1978. The publicity given to the first incidents instantly turned the orange poisoning into an affair of grave public anxiety. The European public, the governments concerned, and the Israeli export authorities were greatly alarmed. And due to the centrality of the Jaffa trademark in Europe, Israeli interests seemed to be particularly hard hit.

The hysteria over the poisoning quickly produced a new wave of discoveries of injected oranges, including lemons and grapefruits. However, oranges from countries other than Israel were now added to the contamination list. On February 1, 1978, injected oranges from Spain were discovered in Holland and Germany. The snowball effect was now in full swing. On January 31, 1978, an off-duty policeman in Dortmund, West Germany, became sick after eating a mercury-poisoned Israeli orange. The same day, poisoned oranges were found in Aachen and Frankfurt. On February 1, 1978, peasized amounts of mercury were discovered in Israeli fruit in Darmstadt. Sweden was added to the list on February 2, 1978. Mercury injected into Israeli oranges sold in Sweden was discovered to have caused skin discoloration. Spanish oranges injected with mercury were now discovered in the same Dutch area where contaminated Israeli produce appeared earlier.

A 12-year-old girl was hospitalized in Bremen after eating a poisoned Israeli orange. On February 5, 1978, the first mercury injected oranges reached Belgium and Britain (London). A lemon injected with mercury was found in Heverle the next day. Some cases were now reported in Scandinavia, in the city of Malmo (Sweden) and Copenhagen (Denmark). On February 6, 1978, a woman found a mercury-poisoned Israeli orange in a bag of fruit she had bought in a London store. On February 7, 1978, the Groningen (Dutch) authorities discovered ten contaminated Spanish oranges. On February 13, 1978, Italian health officials banned the sale of grapefruit in Milan and Bergamo after an Israeli-imported grapefruit was found to be poisoned with mercury.

Certain observers were surprised about this, because at the beginning of the poisoning hype, the Italian authorities assured their people that Italy did not import Israeli oranges, and was consequently immune to the plague. The first and main wave of orange poisoning lasted till the middle of February. By February 13, 1978, the number of injected oranges was the following:

- West Germany – 11
- Belgium – 9
- Netherlands – 7
- Great Britain – 3
- Sweden – 2
- Denmark – 1

According to London's the Sunday Times, the entire affair had been blown out of proportion and only 50 oranges contaminated with mercury were found in various cities in Europe. There had, furthermore, been little damage reported. The majority of the infected oranges did not come from Israel, but were exported from Spain, Morocco and Cyprus. Belgium's minister of health declared on February 6, 1978, that three out of four poisoned oranges discovered in his country came from Spain, and only one from Israel. A February 12, 1978 report by an Israeli daily Yedyiot Aharonot listed a total of 21 oranges injected with mercury in Europe, with only six from Israel. The paper counted one orange from Morocco, one from Egypt, and 13 from Spain.

From the middle of February, the number of reported incidents of poisoning decreased significantly: On February 14, 1978, four more cases of contaminated oranges were reported from Hessen, West Germany. Only one of these was reported to have been injected with mercury. In North Rheinland, three cases were discovered. On March 4, 1978, a woman peeling an Israeli orange in Haddington, Scotland, spotted mercury globules. On March 6, two oranges with mercury were found in Sassari, on the island of Sardinia (Italy).

By now it became evident that a significant number of alleged poisoning cases involved hoaxes, some initiated by minors. On January 10, 1978, a 14 year-old English boy was arrested for injecting oranges with thermometer's mercury. A 10-year old boy provoked similar panic in another neighborhood. Swiss authorities reported that an insane person left a poisoned orange in a shop. The European authorities gradually established that the number of hoaxes outnumbered the number of genuine poisoning cases.

Other cases tested suggested false reporting due to panic and fear. Some experts remembered those three years earlier, a similar case of false alarm over poisoned Israeli grapefruits, took place in Italy. Gradually, it became evident that a kind of a "psychosomatic" disease drove an unusual number of people into hospitals, complaining about orange poisoning. Medical tests showed, however, no signs of mercury or any other substance in their stomachs.

The Modus-operandi. The letter associating the poisoning scare with Palestinian terrorism was sent by an anonymous organization that called itself the Arab Revolutionary Army.

Received by several European health ministries, the letter stated that "the oppressed Palestinian workers in the occupied territories have been poisoning the oranges in a widespread campaign" and that all the countries importing Israeli oranges were expected to be flooded with thousands of poisoned oranges. The Israeli authorities discarded this claim at once. Their analysis suggested that the oranges were poisoned either at the Dutch port of Rotterdam or at the Belgian port of Antwerp. From there, poisoned oranges were sent to supermarkets all over northern Europe. According to officials of the Israel Citrus Marketing Board (ICMB) the contaminated oranges found in the Netherlands, arrived in the port of Antwerp on January 18, 1978. Only two contaminated boxes were found, and the mercury used had been injected with a syringe that left clear and visible holes on the fruit's skin.

The injection, according to the ICMB analysis, could only have been done in Europe. The representative of the ICMB in Europe at that period, D.P., confirmed to the authors that there was no possibility to make injections in the fruit without producing their rapid putrefaction and therefore the oranges were for sure poisoned in Europe. West European police investigators supported the Israeli conclusion. They also concluded that the oranges were contaminated in the seaports of Rotterdam and Antwerp, and believed that the sabotage was executed during the transfer from the harbor or in the warehouses.

Another conclusion was reached soon, that many of the reported cases involved local injection of mercury in either the shops themselves or in nearby warehouses. British expert, Dr. Paul Wix, who trained police forensic scientists, assessed that contaminated oranges found at London's Marks and Spencer were injected approximately six days before the contamination was discovered. As the fruit takes three weeks to travel from Israel by boat, he believed that the oranges could not have possibly been contaminated in Israel, and that if they were to be injected in the store, mercury would have spurt all over the floor. Warehouse contamination was the only alternative.

In search of the perpetrators, Several European capitals, including London, received letters from the ARA threatening to poison Israeli agricultural products. The letter sent to Reuters stated that "oppressed Palestinian workers" in the occupied territories were responsible for the act. Most of the letters were sent from the city of Stuttgart in Germany and received between January 27 and mid-February. Phone threats within Germany and from Germany to other countries were also made. The association of the orange poisoning with the

Palestinian struggle against Israel elicited strong denials from the leading Palestinian organizations.

Beirut spokespersons of the Palestinian Liberation Organization (PLO) and the Popular Front for the Liberation of Palestine, (PFLP) insisted that they knew nothing about the ARA. The PLO's press agency denied any involvement in the poisoning, and stressed that the attack involved a provocation intended to "shake the support and confidence won by the PLO among world public opinion" and that "the Palestinian Revolution would not sully its hands by poisoning innocent youngsters." PLO spokesman in London claimed "that the operation is an attempt to discredit the Arabs."

Some newspapers in Holland and Belgium claimed that the Popular Front for the Liberation of Palestine—General Command, an organization headed by pro-Syrian terrorist Ahmed Jibril, took responsibility for the poisonings. No substantial evidence to support this claim had been presented, however, Paul Wilkinson, a leading British terrorism authority, took the ARA seriously. While British police found no trace of the organization, Wilkinson believed that Jibril was involved. The Washington Post reported that the Arab Revolutionary Army first became known in October 1977 when it claimed responsibility for the killing of a United Arab Emirates government minister at Abu Dhabi airport. It was mentioned at the time that the real target was the Syrian foreign minister, Abdel Halim Khaddam, who escaped unhurt.

The adamant Palestinian denials, the failure of the European authorities to identify the ARA and arrest any of the perpetrators, the inability of Israel's intelligence agencies to also identify the individuals or group associated with the orange poisoning, and the growing conviction that most of the discovered cases were hoaxes or expression of panic, seem to support two conclusions: a. no known Palestinian organization was involved; b. the ARA was a fake name made up by a few radical German supporters of the Palestinian struggle, who were involved in the early triggering of the orange poisoning. There is little evidence of additional involvement after the scare wave created its own momentum.

These conclusions are obviously circumstantial. They are reached on the basis of the absence of any clue to the identity of the perpetrators, on the basis of the modus operandi of the Palestinian and European terrorist organizations at the time of the events, and on a textual analysis of the ARA slogans.

Neither the German authorities, who clearly were most involved in the case (because of the many cases of poisoning and the origin of the letter from Germany), nor the Israelis had ever identified the perpetrators. Because of the discovery of the numerous hoaxes involved, the spread of the alleged poisoning to non-Israeli oranges as well as the failure of the attack to claim any real victim, the event was quickly forgotten and did not keep a significant place in the history of Palestinian terrorism. Both the Israelis and Germans had other serious terrorism problems, and their interest in the case had apparently come to an end. Interviews conducted by the authors of this article, as well as efforts to trace the relevant archives have yielded little information.

So who was responsible for the few credible injections of Israeli oranges? Who wrote the ARA letters? Because the threat letters were sent from Stuttgart, and due to the fact that most of the early cases took place in Germany and neighboring Holland, it appears likely that German radical elements, close to Palestinian terrorist organizations, planned and executed this operation with or without consulting their Arab comrades. They probably saw it as an act of solidarity with the Palestinians in a very difficult time. Egypt's President Anwar Sadat had recently returned from a historical peace visit in Jerusalem, and the likelihood of an independent Palestine appeared as uncertain as ever. There existed, in addition, a long tradition of German-Palestinian cooperation, and many German radical activists felt no remorse about direct involvement in Palestinian terrorism. The Marxist-Leninist PFLP was a special favorite of the German extreme left. A textual analysis of the letter renders additional support to the argument that radical Germans could have initiated the orange poisoning. The language of the threatening letter hints to the perpetrators as close to a Palestinian leftist organization, like the PFLP factions or pro-Syrian and pro-Iraqi groups. See for instance the slogans used "Victory to the Arab Struggle for Total Unity against Reaction and Treachery! For a United Socialist Arab State on the Ruins of Zionism!" It reminds one of European neo-Marxist tones and declarations."

Activists or supporters of the German Revolutionary Cells (Revolutionare Zellen - RZ), a small radical underground organization, appear as good candidates for the execution of the scare campaign. In the middle of the 1970s, they were extremely close to the radical Palestinian movements. On July 20, 1978, their members put a bomb in the Frankfurt office of the Israeli company Agrexco, as an expression of solidarity with the Palestinian people. There were no casualties and only material damage to the building. Members of the RZ had been known for their opposition to killing people, at least when operating on German soil. The poisoning campaign, let us recall, did not put the life of anybody in lethal danger.

How "unconventional" was the orange poisoning? It is evident that the substance injected to the Israeli oranges was not lethal. According to the Poison Control Center in New York, whose specialists had studied 18 incidents of people who swallowed solid mercury, none suffered ill effects. Whereas the orange discovered in London's Marks and Spencer shop contained 0.1 grams of mercury, a two-year-old child in New York ate 200 grams without falling ill. A man, who tried to commit suicide by injecting two grams of mercury into his vein, fell ill but survived. The French Center for the Fight against Poisons also stated that the mercury found in the poisoned oranges in Holland and Germany was not dangerous. It determined that an individual could swallow his thermometer's mercury without hurting himself. According to Dr. Hertz, the director of the Center for the Study of Poisonings at the Rambam Hospital in Haifa, mercury in small quantities as found in the oranges is not at all poisonous. Only mercury salts are considered strong poisonous substances. The ARA letter confirms that the real aim of the operation was "not to indiscriminately kill ...[the] population, but to sabotage the Israeli economy." The perpetrators of this campaign were clearly aware, however, of the psychological and political impact of the new chemical modus operandi on civilian population: "The classic fedayin period has come to an end.

We have been patient for long enough and consider all means towards achieving our objective to be legitimate...No more compromises will be made. Those who support the cause of justice must make this clear by ceasing political, economical and military support of the Zionist regime. Those who fail to do so must pay the reckoning." There is, in conclusion, no question that the orange poisoning, as small as it was, sought to elicit fears of unconventional weapons. It certainly accomplished that goal. What appears amazing, however, is how conventional and non-lethal was the substance chosen. If we add to that the short duration and the low intensity of the actual contamination campaign, it is clear that the 1978 orange poisoning was a far cry from present day images of WMD terrorism.

THE 1988 ALLEGED POISONING OF ISRAELI GRAPEFRUITS IN ITALY

In the middle of April 1988, ten years after the poisoning scare in northern Europe, rumors about the poisoning of Israeli Jaffa grapefruits started to spread in Italy. It all begun with an anonymous telephone call informing the Italian Ministry of Finance that grapefruits imported from Israel might have been poisoned. Following the passage of that information to the Ministry of Health, Italian border checkpoints were put on alert. Imported Jaffa grapefruits had to be checked and samples were taken for a thorough analysis. Grapefruit sales were not stopped, however.

The key incident, which finally led to the suspension of all sales, took place in Rome on April 19, 1988. Anonymous phone calls to the leading Roman dailies as well as the authorities named a popular supermarket where poisonous grapefruits had been left. Rome' Sanitary Guard (USL) was immediately dispatched to the place to take samples of the allegedly poisoned fruits. On April 22, 1988, a few additional calls to the Ministry of Health produced a poisoning scare of larger magnitude. The police, the USL, and the Carbinieri were ordered to facilitate the testing of larger samples of Israeli grapefruits from ports, storage places, shops and supermarkets. Six Jaffa grapefruits stained with a blue substance attracted most of the attention. Sales were not officially stopped yet, but large quantities of Israeli oranges could not be marketed.

Instead of concealing the uncertain information from the media, the Lazio Health Bureau, responsible for testing the alleged contamination, was highly cooperative. Reporters and press agencies were briefed about the suspected poisoning, and Italy's television, radio, and newspapers were full of sensational reports. On April 26, 1988, and without waiting for final test results, Lazio's Regional Health Office announced in a crowded press conference that toxin was indeed discovered and that all Jaffa grapefruits had to be taken away from the shelves. The damaging announcement came following the death of guinea pigs tested with the contaminated substance. Dr. Ziantoni, head of the Lazio Health Office, made it unequivocally clear that the fruit was poisoned.

Aware of the great damage to Israeli export and skeptical of the Italian claims, Israel's Ministry of Agriculture decided to send to Rome a highranking specialist. Dr. Israel Adato, a scientist with Israel's Agriculture Ministry, arrived in Rome and went directly to see Ziantoni and his six analysts. The Israeli scientist had a reason to believe that because of the texture of the citrus fruit, the kind of poisoning described in the Italian press was impossible. He was right. Additional tests established that no poison was administered, that the material sprayed was a non-lethal methylene blue, and that the laboratory mice died from the impact of the injections on their stomachs, not from the poison. A short investigation of the Italian authorities resolved beyond doubt that Israeli grapefruits were not poisoned and that the whole scare was caused by a hoax.

On April 27, 1988, all of Italy's political groups raised in Parliament question on what was termed "the very serious story of poisoning of grapefruit in various Italian towns." The Minister of Health, Mr. Donat Cattin, answered detailing all the initiatives taken by his Ministry, and blaming Dr. Ziantoni's warnings for stopping the sale of grapefruit all over Italy. Cattin maintained, however, that Italy's High Health Institute would repeat the analysis of the substance found in Rome, to make sure that there was indeed no toxin. The Health Minister also reported that a left-wing Italian organization, the Organization of Metropolitan Proletariat and Oppressed People (Organizzatione dei Proletari Metropolitani e dei Populi Oppressi) was responsible for the fake operation. Although individual Palestinians residing in Italy may have been involved in the sabotage, no known Palestinian organization in Italy or anywhere else was ever implicated in it.

The 1988 grapefruit poisoning that never was should be seen in a broader context and perspective. The whole psychodrama took place against the background of the Intifada, the Palestinian uprising which broke out in December 1987. Marked in its early stages by intense confrontations between Palestinian women and children and Israeli soldiers, the uprising elicited enormous pro-Palestinian sentiment. The powerful Italian left had long been supportive of the Palestinian cause, but the Intifada uplifted this sentiment to unprecedented heights. The Proletarian Democracy, a small but vocal socialist party, played a special role in this struggle, increasingly becoming its spearhead. However, this time it was not just the left. Pictures of Israeli soldiers beating Palestinian women and children sensitized everybody, including the powerful Vatican. Israel never looked so bad, and the Italian media turned the Palestinian plight into a highly emotional domestic issue.

One way of campaigning against the Jewish State involved attacking the most recognized Israeli symbol in Italy; Jaffa oranges. As of January 1988, there were demands to call off the sale of Jaffas. A large chain of Italian cooperatives,

CO-OP Italia, with many shops in Northern and Central Italy, informed the Verona office of the Israeli Citrus Marketing Board that it was under pressure to stop selling Israeli fruits. Known for its left-wing inclination, the cooperative chain was approached by the local branch of the Proletarian Democracy in Piacenza. Coop officials were reminded of the plight of the Palestinians in the occupied territories, and asked to help by boycotting Israeli products.

When the chain withstood the pressure and continued to sell Jaffa oranges, other incidents ensued, including systematic intimidation by groups of youngsters. Young left-wing activists would enter shops and supermarkets, spray Jaffas with red paint and distribute leaflets calling on customers to boycott Israeli products. Israel was compared to South Africa, with its Apartheid regime, and customers were called upon to punish both "racist" societies. "People sensitive to the values of freedom and democracy are taking initiatives against the racist regime in South Africa and the Israeli government, who instead of solving politically the Palestinian problem is repressing with violence the legitimate rights of the Palestinians...Among our other initiatives, we wish now to add the boycott of South African and Israeli products starting with the famous Jaffa grapefruits.

We shall take action to call the attention of the customers, and we ask you to give up purchasing and selling these products in order not to support economically violent governments till the moment comes when everyone in Palestine and South Africa can live in peace and freedom." Following the increased pressure of the activists of the Proletarian Democracy, the internal committee of Coop Italia demanded that the Management of the chain remove all Jaffa oranges from the stores. In March, a special meeting was convened in Bologna to decide on the issue. However, the demand to remove the grapefruits was defeated again, this time by the argument that Israeli workers who would lose their jobs, not the Israeli government, would pay the price of the boycott.

It was only then, when all other pressures failed to hurt

Israeli oranges that the decision was made to sabotage the sales through spraying methylene blue on a few grapefruits and spreading a rumor about poisoning. Many of the leftist groups that propagated against Israel continued the attack with full force. The anti-Israel press made things worse, with reports from the Intifada, and hostile editorials. On May 23, 1988, two time bombs were placed near the Verona packing store of the Israeli fruits. There were serious fire damages. There could be, thus, no doubt that although unconventional terrorism was not used in this case at all, the fears its alleged presence elicited were quite significant and costly.

THE 1979 PFLP POISONING OF ISRAELI ORANGES IN TEL AVIV

The only confirmed case of serious talk about and concrete preparation for poisoning Israeli products took place in January 1979. The case involved a Gaza Strip terrorist cell belonging to the Popular Front for the Liberation of Palestine. The group was made up of nine members who organized attacks on Israeli targets, interests and products. The cell's commander was 26-year-old Said Hamad Abu Sita, a resident of Rafah, who was previously employed in Israel as a daily worker. The group was geared toward conventional terrorism, and under the instruction of Abu Sita dug a secret bunker to hide him as well as their weapons and explosives.

The first information on the group's intention to poison Israeli oranges reached the authorities in early January. According to an informer close to the ringleader, Abu Sita instructed a few Palestinians working at the Tel Aviv fruit retail market to inject poison to two to three units in every box of oranges. The idea, according to the informer, was to elicit public panic and acute fear. Abu Sita told the informer that the Tel Aviv market was a central distribution venue to the entire country, and that he expected the contaminated oranges to pop up all over Israel. He also talked about future plans to poison Israeli vegetables and water sources. Said Abu Sita was shot and killed by an Israeli military patrol on January 18, 1979, at approximately 8:30 PM. Apprehended for an ordinary security check in the Dir Al Balah area, he refused to stop and tried to escape.

Weapons and documents found on his body left no doubt about his identity and intentions. A letter he was carrying on his body confirmed that under his command, a member of the group injected mercury and Agarin to Israeli Shamuti oranges. The letter also mentioned that similar operation by another group member was scheduled to take place between January 15 and 19. The documents disclosed further that the Israelis discovered a few contaminated oranges, but did not find the perpetrator of the operation. The killing of Abu Sita and the discovery of the letter led to the arrest of all the eight remaining members of the cell. Their investigation revealed their past and future planned operations.

One member of the cell, Mahamud Halabi, admitted that he knew of Abu Sita's plans to poison Israeli fruits, vegetables, and water. Halabi personally obtained for his commander mercury and injectors in a Gaza pharmacy. According to his testimony, he watched him warming the mercury and pumping it to an injector. It is of interest that on January 23, 1979, several European capitals received letters from the ARA (believed to be the Arab Revolutionary Army) threatening to poison Israeli agricultural products destined for all European Community (EEC) countries. The letters resembled the letters received in the UK a year previously, followed by the contamination of several Israeli oranges with mercury.

The letter to the Dutch government, which was shown to journalists, claimed that the contamination would be on a greater scale and would use more lethal substances. In spite of the similarity with the beginning of the 1978 incidents and the use of the ARA name, nothing happened in any of the threatened countries. The fact that the Abu Sita cell used mercury to poison oranges and at the same period there was a threat to poison oranges in Europe by the same method, could perhaps imply that his organization, the PFLP, either was somehow involved in the 1978 incidents in Germany and Holland or that they have learned something from those events and tried to copy them.

POISONING THREATS IN THE 1980S

The vast majority of the thousands of Palestinian terrorist acts since the 1960s involved the use or the credible threat of use of conventional weapons. Only rarely had the screens of Israel's security services monitored threats of use of unconventional weapons. The following is a list of rumors, confirmed and unconfirmed reports about a possible use of poisons against Israeli targets brought to the attention of the Israeli authorities by various informers in the course of the 1980s. The recorded threats had never been checked, nor ever acted upon.

1. September 12, 1985. Information on a discussion about poisoning the food of cabinet minister Ariel Sharon. PFLP-GC (Ahmad Jibril's organization) sympathizer working in a Tel Aviv restaurant, expressed willingness to poison Sharon's food if provided with the right toxin.
2. October 4, 1985. An anonymous letter informs Israeli security officer in New York City of an Arab plan to poison the food of Israelis in two NY restaurants, in Manhattan and Queens.
3. January 28, 1986. A security officer at Ben Gurion Airport is told by an informer of a plan to smuggle to Israel poisonous pills. The potential smuggler is a Palestinian criminal involved in illegal drug trafficking, who also wishes to make a contribution to the national struggle. The pills are to be dissolved in water in hospitals and public places, with the purpose of creating a large scale panic.
4. June 4, 1986. Activists of the PFLP-Abu l'Abas faction discuss the possibility of a large scale poisoning of Israeli targets. The plan is to pour several glasses of Polidol (a chemical fertilizer usually sprayed in vineyards), to containers of drinking water placed on the roofs of Israeli houses. It was also suggested to pour Polidol to the water sources of chicken coops, as well as to try and inject it to bread loaves at Israeli supermarkets. The whole idea is to create panic in Israel: "it is better to destroy the economy

of a whole family, than to kill one member of that family."

5. September 14, 1986. A terrorist cell is discovered in Beit Furik, in the Gaza Strip. They plan several conventional terrorist attacks, but also talk about using chemical substances for poisoning purposes.
6. October 17, 1986. A member of Force 17 (one of Fatah's terrorist units) is reported to have expressed an interest in poisoning ponds of fish nurseries near Haifa. It is unclear whether the fishponds are the target or the Israeli buyers expected to eat the poisoned fish.
7. June 25, 1987. The Abu Musa split faction of Fatah intends to poison the food in an Israeli restaurant.
8. July 28, 1987. Reliable information refers to a possible use of cyanide against the drinking water of Jewish settlements in the West Bank. The report details the idea of making a whole in a water pipe and injecting the poison.
9. August 21, 1987. Warning of a plan to poison the water reservoirs of several West Bank Jewish settlements by Fatah – Revolutionary Command (the Abu Nidal) organization, which allegedly had successfully developed a liquid poison that cannot be detected in routine tests.
10. October 25, 1987. A Palestinian working in a Tel Aviv restaurant serving the city's Engineering School expresses an interest in poisoning the food.
11. December 4, 1987. Information about a group of Palestinian youngsters discussing the possibility of poisoning the drinking water of Elon Moreh, an Israeli settlement in the Nablus area. The idea is to make a hole in the settlement's water pipe and inject unspecified toxin.

ATTITUDES OF FORMER PALESTINIAN TERRORISTS

It has already been shown above that the Palestinian record of using unconventional terrorism is very poor. Why is it so? What is the attitude of Palestinian terrorists to the use of weapons of mass destruction? In a recent series of twenty-five indepth interviews about terrorist decision-making conducted in Israeli jails and in territories currently belonging to the Palestinian Authority, a question on the use of unconventional terrorism has been added. Here are some of the answers.

The most common response to the question has been something like "we have never given it any thought." Several interviewees who expanded on the same theme maintained, in addition, that they did not really need that kind of stuff, and that had it been up to them they would have loved to posses as sophisticated conventional arms as the Israelis. "As an underground organization we never needed anything more than light automatic weapons and grenades. I would like to have good equipment, like the Israeli soldiers, including special binoculars and sniper rifles."

Although it is theoretically possible to question the great surprise of the respondents when asked about unconventional weapons, for who could make sure they were telling the truth, there seems to be little reason to question their sincerity. None of the 25 interviewees, who happened to represent different Palestinian and Lebanese organizations, was known to have ever used poisons or chemicals, and all of them responded more or less in the same vain. Moreover, those who had the WMD idea crossing their minds before did not try to conceal it,

"As for weapons of mass destruction or unconventional weapons, the truth is that all I ever wanted was a Kalashnikov rifle. Unconventional weapons were never a realistic option. But sometimes, the thought did cross my mind that it could help in this war. In my view, if the fanatics had the option of unconventional weapons, they would use it."

What most of the interviews make clear is that the reason the use of weapons of mass destruction is dismissed has nothing to do with morality or hesitation to kill a large number of civilians? Had they been ordered to use it, they would have willingly done so without any moral qualms. "As for unconventional weapons and weapons of mass destruction, we never gave it any thought during the armed struggle, but morally, I don't see any problem using such weapons. Had I been able to get them, I would have gladly used them precisely because the effect would have been that many times greater. I would not have had any problem with 200,000 casualties." "I would like us to have any kind of weapons that can inflict damage on the enemy. Anything that can advance our cause."

Surprised by the unexpected WMD question, most of the interviewees responded without a serious consideration of the operational problems involved. Only few were really scared. "As for us having conventional or unconventional weapons, I personally made do with a pistol. But would like our organization to have arms that could wipe out a village or a neighborhood. Atomic and chemical weapons and things like that though, frighten me. I would worry about their impact and the consequences of using them."

The interviews with these rank and file Palestinian terrorists confirm what we know from other sources (i.e., that the option of using weapons of mass destruction was never discussed in the operational levels of Palestinian terrorism). Most of the interviewees heard of this terror option for the first time during the interview. Almost all of them addressed the question as a science fiction issue.

The above cases of Palestinian use, potential use, consideration of use and disinterest in using chemical and biological weapons, exhaust all the available information. We have; nevertheless, reason to believe that we do not yet posses the full story of the Palestinian interest in unconventional terrorism, and that additional evidence may come to light in the future. We were particularly unable to talk about this subject to the top echelons of Fatah, the major PLO organization. However, the information we obtained and our general understanding of the history, politics, and modus operandi of the various PLO organizations allow at the minimum several interim conclusions:

a. There is no evidence of any past strategic interest in the use of unconventional terrorism among the PLO's top leadership. In the PLO top leadership, we include the historical heads and decision-makers of the major Palestinian organizations such as Yassir Arafat, Abu Jihad, Abu-Iyad, George Habash, Wadi Haddad, Naif Hawatme, Ahmed Jibril, the outsider Abu Nidal, and colleagues and officers directly under their command. By strategic interest, we mean intentions or plans to devastate the enemy, win a major battle, or change the balance of power through the use of unconventional means (chemical, biological, nuclear, radiological). None of the cases presented above involved any strategic thinking.

b. There is no evidence of any past tactical WMD interest among the PLO's top leadership. By tactical interests, we mean an intention to inflict on the enemy a heavy though temporary blow with relatively short-range consequences. This judgment is based on the absence of any evidence of top echelon involvement in the cases discussed above. We have reason to believe that an involvement of top PLO decision-makers in any of these cases would have either left traces of evidence or led to more significant consequences. The amateurish and sloppy nature of the rumors and minor cases presented in this paper cast serious doubt on any potential involvement of the leaders of the PLO. However, it is probable that the leaders of the organizations new post-factum about the failed attempts.

c. The 1978 orange poisoning in Europe, the 1979 effort by the local PFLP Gaza group to contaminate Israeli oranges in Tel Aviv, the 1988 effort by pro-Palestinian groups in Italy to instill fear of grapefruit poisoning, and the occasional rumors in the 1980s regarding poisoning Jewish targets in Israel proper and in the occupied territories, suggest some Palestinian awareness of the psychological impact of toxic terror. It is, however, almost totally clear that the interest in these operations was local, rudimentary, and extremely superficial. It is, in fact, amazing, how little and inefficient the Palestinian WMD effort to devastate Israeli economy ever was. This total failure suggests that a WMD campaign against Israel had never been launched and that most of what happened represents a combination of angry wishful thinking and local desperation.

It should be stressed, however, that a number of radical Palestinian terrorist organizations had no moral constraints to engage in mass casualty terrorism against Israel: they have perpetrated or tried to perpetrate in the 1970s and 1980s many attacks with sophisticated barometer or time bombs against air planes, mainly of Israeli and Western countries: Swissair, Austrian Airlines, TWA, Pan Am (in Honolulu, and not at Lockerbie) which took the life of more than a hundred innocent civilians could have had many more casualties.

Fortunately, many attacks were foiled by the security services or by sheer luck and thus saved many other lives. But why had the Palestinian leaders, caught since the early 1960s in a deadly struggle with Israel, shown so little interest in the use of weapons of mass destruction? Why is it that they apparently had been so ice cold to both the strategic and tactical advantages of chemical and biological weapons? It is our conclusion that the most important reason stems from the absence of any real Palestinian need to use unconventional weapons against Israel. Since the 1965 resumption of anti-Israel Palestinian terrorism, the function of these operations was never to defeat or destroy the Jewish State. Not a single Palestinian strategist ever believed that a total Palestinian victory over the Israelis was possible in the foreseeable future. Moreover, none of them was eager to provoke a massive Israeli retaliation against the Palestinians living under Israeli occupation. The major objectives of Palestinian terrorism had been to get other Arab nations fight Israel for them, put the Palestinian case on the world's agenda, obtain legitimacy inside the Arab world and within the community of nations, reinforce the Palestinians' national identity and convince them that through armed struggle they had a collective hope, and force the Israelis at least to share the land with them if not to throw them away.

These objectives had been obtained by a limited armed struggle. They furthermore called for the forging and framing of a positive image of Palestinian freedom fighters. The very use of terror was by itself occasionally damaging to the Palestinian cause, and the use of "dirty" and "illegitimate" weapons could harm even more their strategic international goals and bring about a devastating Israeli reaction. The case was explained to Rand terrorism specialist, Bruce Hoffman, in very simple terms. "Many times people came and proposed these things (BW or CW attacks) to us. But we always turned them down. First, we were going to be an army and wanted to fight like an army; Fatah's goal was to defeat or destroy the Israeli army. Second, we knew that the Israelis had these same types of weapons and would not hesitate to use them against us. That is why we never used them."

Moreover, since their 1965 military rise, PLO and other Palestinian organizations had never suffered from a shortage of conventional weapons. Soon after 1967, they became the darlings of both the Arab world and the communist block, with plenty of military supplies at hand. In addition, they benefited in the 1970s from the oil-related economic boom in the Arab world. The deepening vacuum in Lebanon, increased dramatically since the mid-1970s, enabled them to form in that ravaged country a mini-state with plenty of resources and military arsenals. Consequently, there never existed a real Palestinian need to substitute unconventional for conventional weapons. It is not surprising that the only place where Palestinian fighters had occasionally fanaticized about using chemical weapons were the occupied territories. For it was under heavy Israeli pressure that Palestinian terrorists found themselves occasionally helpless, weaponless, and bitterly vengeful.

The fact, however, that none of the plans for a tactical use of poisons and chemicals ever reached operational level teaches us that even in the occupied territories there was no shortage of conventional weapons. This also explains the WMD ignorance of the interviewed terrorists. Neither the Palestinian leaders nor their field activists had ever felt the need to turn to unconventional weapons. More recently, the radical Islamist Palestinian organizations, Hamas and Palestinian Islamic Jihad

(PIJ) have used in the 1990s, quite successfully it should be remarked, the suicide bombing attacks as their main strategic weapon against Israel, achieving even the temporary interruption of the peace process between Israel and the Palestinian Authority. It seems that these extremist organizations were also aware of the operational difficulties and the political and existential dangers of the use of unconventional weapons.

The experience (or its lack thereof) of the Palestinian terrorist organizations with unconventional terrorism is instructive. It shows that terrorist organizations in need of public sympathy and legitimacy (most terrorist organizations are!) are highly unlikely to use weapons of mass destruction. We should add to this rationale the obvious fear of justifiable massive retaliation to this "dirty" terrorism, which would fatally and physically endanger the very constituency they pretend to represent. There is also the important element of the enormous difficulties in the production, control and mainly the operational dissemination of the chemical, biological or nuclear materials.

The conclusion of the 2002 article by Prof. Sprinzak and me was that terrorist organizations in need of public sympathy and legitimacy are highly unlikely to use weapons of mass destruction. The fear of massive retaliation against the very constituency they pretend to represent also excluded, at least theoretically, the probability of the use of chemical, biological or radiological weapons or agents by Palestinian groups against Israeli targets. There is also the important element of the enormous difficulties in the production, control and mainly the operational dissemination of the chemical, biological or nuclear materials. This conclusion was valid for the period covered in the original article. In June 1999, an Israeli daily claimed that Muhammad Abu-Tayr, a Hamas military commander being held in Jerusalem, revealed a plan to poison Israeli water sources. Ibrahim Ghawshah, the Hamas spokesman, immediately denied any such plan by the movement and claimed that Israeli allegations in this connection are aimed at associating Hamas with terrorism, as it has always done in the past.

It appears that things changed since two major events: the opening of the violent al-Aqsa intifada by the Palestinians in September 2000 as a result of the failure of the Camp David negotiations, and the al-Qaeda terrorist attacks against the United States on September 11, 2001.

DETERRING TERRORIST ORGANIZATIONS

The concepts used in modern theories of deterrence tend to focus on the relationship between states, and on the high end of potential conflict. For example, confrontation between regular armies or nuclear conflict between states. These theories naturally overshadowed traditional descriptions of coercion – deterrence and compellence–which have existed since time immemorial for deterrence relations between states as well as between states and non-state (insurgents, guerillas, terrorists). The relationship between a state (Israel) and non-state terrorist organizations is, by nature, asymmetric. This asymmetry makes doctrines of deterrence, which were formulated for relationships between states unsuitable solutions for many cases. The asymmetry however differs from case to case.

The degree of state-like attributes of the organization, or the links between such an organization and a state with state-type interests has a significant influence on strategies that can be implemented to coerce that organization. The terms that have been used in this study are: Deterrence – the prevention from action by fear of the consequences; a state of mind brought about by the existence of a credible threat of unacceptable counteraction. Deterrence will be defined here as: a situation in which the deterring party (A) presents to the object of the desired deterred party (B) a threat of harm to B's interests if B takes a certain action (C) that is perceived as harmful to the interests of A and beneficial to those of B. This harm will either neutralize C (deterrence by denial) or prevent it from achieving its goal, or (2) make any benefit from C not worth the damage incurred in retaliation by A on B (deterrence by punishment).

Compellence (or "coercive diplomacy") – the threat of

force or the demonstration of limited force to convince an adversary to desist from actions that it is already involved in. Compellence will be defined here as a situation in which the compelling party (A) presents to the party of compellence (B) a threat or actual causing of harm to B's interests if B does not desist from (D), an action which serves B's interests and contradicts A's interests. This harm may be based on (1) neutralization of the benefits of D for B (disruption), leaving B to suffer only the disadvantage of the action or, (2) a punishment for D that makes any benefit from D not worth the damage incurred by the retaliation of A on B. In addition to these definitions, we will use the following definitions, which focus on the channels of transmitting the deterrent message: Direct deterrence or compellence - based on threat or implementation of direct action by the deterring party (A) towards the target of deterrence (B).

This may be through: preemptive action, disruption (e.g. deterrence by denial) or retaliation (deterrence by punishment). Indirect deterrence or compellence - based on threat or implementation of actions of the deterring party (A) directed at a third party (E) which is closely linked to the target of deterrence (B). Such a third party may be: (1) the population associated with B, (2) the host state (when dealing with non-state actors associated with a certain territory under a state regime) or association of states in which B operates, (3) external actors with which B has mutual interests and therefore have influence over B (occasionally, a "patron state" when dealing with non-state actors). The objective of such an action is that: (1) harm caused to E will disrupt B's activities and inhibit B's operational activity, either directly or by causing E to exert pressure on B to refrain from its actions against A.

This study will also distinguish between strategic and tactical deterrence. Israel has succeeded in maintaining strategic deterrence vis-à-vis neighboring states through both high-end conventional capabilities on the ground, in the air, and through an assumption by those neighbors of an Israeli non-conventional capability. Deterrence of terrorist organizations however has been based – when it existed – mainly on tactical deterrence through day-to-day actions, which add up to an ever-shifting perception of the object of deterrence. This inconsistency of targets for deterrence creates great difficulty for Israel's freedom of action and ability to implement a coherent deterrent doctrine. Ultimately, deterrence is a matter of mutual perceptions.

These are laden with cultural and psychological overtones and passed through overlapping prisms of history, culture, language, ideological axioms, modes of transmission and reception of information on the "other". Other important influences include: the psyche of the leadership of the party to be deterred, identification of the decision makers with the interests which are threatened, and the dynamics of threat assessment within that leadership. All of these must be assessed in order to arrive at a proper discussion of deterrence.

THE CULTURE AND LEADERSHIP

While the understanding that even strategic deterrence has to be "tailored" to the adversary has become more accepted in Western defense circles, it is more critical to gain understanding regarding the cases involving non-state organizations. The existence of sources of authority – religious, ideological or political – of the non-state actors, which can be influenced by Israeli actions, is also a potential channel for deterrence, though it has been difficult to exploit. All the organizations in this study are ideologically motivated – either by a secular nationalist ideology (Fatah), or an Islamic – Sunni (Hamas), or Shiite (Hizballah) worldview. The role of religious authorities is much greater in the two latter organizations than that of the secular ideological authorities for Fatah. In the case of Hamas, there are those who claim that deterrence towards the spiritual authorities of the organization in Saudi Arabia and Egypt would have an effect on the leadership.

The mechanism of a "source of emulation" (*marja' taqlid*) in Shiite Islam however, holds much more potential for influencing the behavior of a Shiite organization such as Hizballah. This has been evident in the way that the organization has responded to criticism by senior Lebanese Shiite clerics after the last war. Those clerics see themselves as a moral compass for their communities and feel responsible for the "maslaha" (public interest) of their flock. The religious nature of the object of deterrence also has a significant influence on the ability to deter. While one may not be able to know how sincere religious beliefs are, the social acceptability - and consequent social pressures - of the Islamic interpretation impedes compliance with deterrent pressures. Military deterrence is based on proving to "the Muslims" that certain actions, which are sanctioned or even obliged by Islam, are counter-productive to their collective interests. The emergence of a "thanatophile" ideology of jihad with wide social currency confounds such military theories of deterrence.

If an act of jihad is, by definition, an act of faith in Allah, by fighting a weaker or equal enemy, then the Muslim is relying on his own strength and not on Allah; by entering the fray against all odds, the *mujahid* is proving his utter faith in Allah and will be rewarded accordingly. Ideological tenets of the non-state actors, which supersede pragmatic political interests, are a central force in resisting deterrent signals. The content of the ideology also affects the efficacy of deterrence. In organizations, which have the destruction of Israel and martyrdom as fundamental tenets of their ideology, "capitulation" to deterrence is more difficult for them to swallow. Even if the leadership understands the prices and the need to be deterred, it stands before a much more difficult task of explaining its actions to its followers and its spiritual leaders compared to a leadership which is not dedicated to such principles.

A central factor in the way a party reads deterrent signals of an adversary is the type of leadership that exists in that party, and the way that the leadership receives and processes information. Some salient questions that arise in this context are:

1. What type of sensors does the leadership possess and who controls them?

2. How is information transmitted into the leadership and handled there?
3. What biases and personal inclinations affect the reading of signals and images?

The three cases analyzed in this study have in common a strong reliance on monitoring of the Israeli media and the domestic Israeli debate as a basis for their assessments of Israel's intentions and resolve to carry them out. While Hizballah - and to a lesser degree, Hamas - is privy to the composite intelligence of a state (Iran) which can complement the overt sources, this type of intelligence does not seem to have had a great influence on their assessments regarding acts of deterrence implemented by Israel. The personal inclination of two of the leaders analyzed - Arafat and Nasrallah - was to rely on their own intuition and sources of intelligence. It would seem that efforts to infuse deterrent messages through sophisticated disinformation campaigns would be difficult when leaders are using such paradigms. Once a message of deterrence has been transmitted, the three cases have shown the importance of the paradigm, which exists in each organization for command and control in regards to the success of the message.

A unified line of command between the leadership and the terrorist forces, and between them to the patron states facilitates deterrence. Once the leadership has been convinced that a deterrent signal should be taken into account, and it has dealt with all the other obstacles (ideological justification, spiritual leadership, and patron states); if it lacks a unified command and control, the conviction to accept the signal of deterrence may lose its relevance. This has been the case with Fatah. Hamas, on the other hand has shown a relative discipline once a decision was made to refrain from attacks. This can be explained by the relative control of the "external" leadership over the main terrorist weapon.

This issue raises an additional one; decapitation of key leaders has frequently been a two-edged sword; while it has raised the price for the surviving leaders, it has frequently disrupted their line of command and complicated the implementation of decisions that derive from the success of deterrence. Individualist or collective decision-making processes in the leaderships of the non-state organizations have an obvious influence on the absorption of deterrent signals. The studies of the three organizations show that there are fundamental differences in their decision-making processes.

Whereas Fatah was almost totally controlled by Yasser Arafat until the period before his death, and since then is almost devoid of any effective decision-making process; Hamas is based on a collective leadership, in which each member of the political bureau has different interests that can be influenced. While Hizballah is formally based on such a collective leadership, it has become more and more governed by the personal leadership of the Secretary General, Hasan Nasrallah. A general observation of this study is that the more "pluralist" the decision making process of a group is within the leadership (as opposed to a chaotic line of command and control), the greater the options for effective deterrence is.

THE POWER OF WEAKNESS

The Palestinian side and Hizballah have benefiled from what is called in Israeli deterrence parlance, "the power of the weak". This is the relative power that the weaker side maintains vis-à-vis the stronger party. It can be based on one or a combination of three strategies:

a. By finding a defense against the tactics that are central to that advantage or; b. By creating circumstances that prevent the enemy from using those capabilities that give it the advantage.

Creating an internal situation in the target society that renders acquiescence to pressure or to deterrent threats virtually impossible. Arafat's policy of controlled chaos in the West Bank and Gaza eventually created a multipolar terrorist space in the West Bank and especially in Gaza with no one "address". While Arafat was at the helm, he could conceivably have used his personal influence and financial perks to rein in the various groups. Since his demise, there is no individual person in the PA with enough succulent carrots and hard enough sticks to influence the plethora of warlords who have taken over the Palestinian scene. The situation has been likened by one senior Israeli intelligence officer to deterrence of organized crime as opposed to small non-organized criminals. The former is much easier, once a clear picture of the "godfather's" interests is drawn. In the case of the latter, there is no way to develop a comprehensive policy of deterrence that would apply to hundreds of autonomous warlords.

Posing counter-threats that occupy the superior power and narrow it's for maneuver. The counter-threat in the Palestinian case was terrorism against the Israeli civilian community. The very fact that the Israeli defense community and public debated whether or not it was wise to continue in the targeted killings and whether they created more terrorism (for revenge), showed that this counter- threat was effective. As the Israeli system found solutions for terrorism within the borders of Israel (the security barrier, reducing the number of Palestinians allowed to work in Israel), the Palestinians adopted new methods to create a counter-threat (the Qassam rockets), based on the model that was successfully used by Hizballah.

The ramifications of the "power of the weak" are, in any case, an erosion of the ability of the stronger party to pose a credible deterrent. In the Israeli case vis-à-vis both the Palestinians and Hizballah, the main source of the "power of the weak" is Israel's commitment to international norms and conventions. Both the Palestinians and Hizballah have succeeded in taking advantage of this factor. Thus, Israel is constrained from using indiscriminate firepower in the vicinity of civilians; is forced to restrict military operations when there are large-scale collateral casualties among civilians; and cannot use prisoners of war as a bargaining chip by keeping them incommunicado (hiding whether they are even dead or alive) as their adversaries do.

THE IMAGE OF ISRAEL

A primary source of deterrence is the image of the

deterring entity in the eyes of the target. This image can be "imported" from the intelligence of the patron state, or it can be independently built through an intelligence collection process within the organization. The case of Hizballah integrates both modes of imaging of Israel, with the organization accepting assessments of the IRGC, but also collecting current intelligence. Hamas and Fatah, on the other hand, enjoy an intimacy with Israel which allows it to draw a much more accurate image of Israeli intentions. There is no doubt that the role of psychological warfare and information warfare is critical to the depiction of this image.

In all the cases analyzed there is evidence that the leaders of the organizations developed an image of Israel's resolve (or lack of resolve) from the input of the Israeli media. The Israeli experience towards these organizations has shown the limitations of a democratic society with a free press, and a culture of open political debate. When the deterring body is an autocratic state, it has a relatively high control over the image it projects to its friends and enemies. In neither case however do the projected image (that of a confused democratic society which lacks steadfastness and determination or of a undeterred regime) necessarily reflect the truth. In any case, Israel has made no strategic attempt to manipulate the image that was projected to these organizations.

Furthermore, it may be assumed that even were such an attempt made it would not have been able to overcome the open culture of the Israeli media. Some participants in this study pointed out that in the past; the Israeli radio in Arabic (and Persian) was much more effective as it did not attempt to endear the State of Israel on its Arab audience. Images formed from open sources notwithstanding, Israel's policy towards terrorist attacks by these organizations has also fed the image of "negative deterrence". In the cases presented above it is clear that Israel's restraint, whatever its justified reasons, has created an image that encourages the organizations to continue their terrorist attacks. Occasional attempts to restore deterrence (for example - the bombing of Lebanese infrastructure in order to pressure Hizballah in February 2000) tended to be short-lived and were not followed up.

The public debate within Israel to any actions directed at the population or host state tends to feed the image that Israel cannot persevere with such a policy. Israeli analysts of the Israeli-Palestinian crisis have placed the blame for the lack of deterrence against Palestinian terror (to some degree or another), on the image of the constraints of Israeli democracy, and the modus operandi of its governments (all governments) in making decisions. Thus, it has been claimed that Israel's restraint in the first Gulf War, while it could be explained rationally to the Israeli public (who accepted it) as deriving from the fact that the US was operating in Iraq and the added value of an Israeli attack was minor; had a psychological effect on the Palestinians that Israel could be attacked without it retaliating and that political circumstances could preclude Israel from retaliating.

It has been claimed that in Middle Eastern societies, a person or group who does not extract revenge for wrongs perpetrated, loses all status and becomes a target for further attacks. Here, the fact that restraint was based on Israel's clear *raison d'état* does not mitigate the psychological result. Other examples have been found in rational statements made by Israeli leaders that "there is no military solution" but only a "political solution" to terrorism. These statements were perceived as excusing the leadership from taking full advantage of the military capabilities that it had at its disposal. The willingness of Israel to negotiate under fire was also perceived as a weakening factor in Israel's deterrence credibility. Finally, Israeli attempts to satisfy the international community regarding its rules of engagement and its desire to present itself as an open society, have all been viewed by the Palestinians as representing constraints that prevent Israel from bringing its obvious military superiority into play.

An important component of the deterrent image is the image of "intelligence dominance" – the perception of Israel as an intelligence superpower with the ability to target the leaders of the other side at will, and to eliminate them. This image has been occasionally reinforced by successes in targeted killings of senior figures, but it has also been impaired by failure in attempts to kill others. It is noteworthy that a central component in Israel's deterrent image, in all cases, has been the perception of US backing for Israeli counter-terrorism policies.

This perception has become stronger since September 11, and was reinforced during the last Lebanon war. It is noteworthy that there is no evidence that the image of the US imbroglio in Iraq, which ostensibly has diminished American deterrence (at least vis- à-vis Iran), and the failure of the US to capture bin Laden, have not diminished the perception of American backing for Israel as a component of Israeli deterrence. On the other side of the coin, strengthening of Israeli deterrence is often interpreted as enhancing American deterrence vis-à-vis the Muslim world. This is particularly true in the case of the Lebanese war, which was portrayed in the Muslim world - and among various Islamic non-state actors - as a proxy war between the US and Iran or even as a "promo" for a future American attack on Iran.

INTER-RELATIONSHIP OF THEATRES

Any Israeli attempt to deter the Palestinians or Hizballah must take both groups into account, regardless of the individual target. The Intifada broke out in September 2000 on the heels of what was perceived as an Israeli defeat at the hands of Hizballah in Lebanon (the Israeli withdrawal). Similarly, Hizballah's attempts to challenge Israel's deterrence have been, in many cases, linked to escalation on the Palestinian front and Hizballah's assessment that Israel would refrain from acting on two fronts simultaneously. The deterrent effect of Israeli actions against states and non-state actors (e.g. Palestinian vs. Lebanese) has been mixed. Israel's reaction to the killing of six soldiers on the border of Gaza, and the abduction of one other soldier in July 2006 was not anticipated by Hamas and seemed to indicate a new policy - or at least a new mindset - of the new Israeli government.

Nevertheless, Hizballah did not draw an analogy from this event to a possibly similarly severe Israeli reaction to such an action on the northern front. This may have been due to an assessment that its own deterrence towards Israel (long-range rockets) was more potent than that of Hamas (short-range Qassam rockets). On the other hand, since the war in Lebanon there has been a sharp decrease in attempts to launch Qassam rockets by Hamas. While this can be attributed in part to IDF disruptive operations, it seems that the Israeli reaction in the North coupled with the impression of an American carte blanche to Israel; enhanced Israel's deterrent image in the eyes of Hamas, and caused the terrorist group to adopt a more circumspect attitude. This enhanced deterrent image seems to have been behind the willingness of Hamas to negotiate over the abducted soldier.

MODES OF DETERRENCE

An almost universally accepted axiom in Israel's defense and security community is that there is no way to "deter" the individual suicide bomber (or even the individual terrorist who is putting his life at high risk). Nor is there a way to deter the terrorist organization, which has no "public assets" that it could lose as a result of the deterring party's reactions. In addition, the Israeli security community is well aware of the fact that success for a terrorist organization is measured quite differently than the success of the attacked state; one successful attack out of tens or even hundreds of disrupted plans is a total success for the terrorist organization, whereas for the state, it is seen as a total failure. Nevertheless, Israel has directed a de facto strategy for deterring terrorist organizations. This strategy was built on four main pillars: direct military deterrence to bring its leadership to decide to lower its profile; threatening the institutionalized assets of the "host" (the PA, Lebanon); deterrence towards the host population; and indirect deterrence via the patron (Syria).

DIRECT INTERVENTION

The first pillar - direct military intervention and disruption - has been the core of Israel's de facto deterrence of Hizballah and Palestinian organizations. Israeli disruptive actions against the Palestinian organizations - particularly targeted killings of top-level activists – have had a temporary deterrent effect. The most salient example has been the series of targeted killings that Israel implemented in 2003. During that period, every activist at any level had to take into account that his movements may result in his death. This eventually brought the leadership to a de facto moratorium on suicide attacks. This period also gave birth to the discussion of a *hudna* (ceasefire). Such deterrence is almost always "tactical" and not strategic. The paradigm of strategic deterrence in which one state can cause damage to another on the strategic level is almost never applicable towards terrorist organizations. Nevertheless, tactical threats towards terrorist organizations can result in temporary deterrence.

The conclusions that arise from this analysis are:

1. Tactical deterrence towards terrorist organizations usually derives from real actions (as opposed to declarations and signaling which comprise the bulk of the deterrent image in strategic deterrence); the terrorist organization knows that an attack of one type or another has resulted in a certain level of retaliation and it has to take that into account.
2. Declarations that are not fulfilled create "negative deterrence". Such a case is rare in a paradigm of strategic deterrence between states (and certainly in nuclear deterrence). In attempts to deter terrorism though, they are a daily phenomenon.
3. Tactical deterrence begins to erode the moment it is fielded. If it is not replenished from time to time by actions, it loses its efficacy. This, of course, differs from paradigms of strategic deterrence which are based on a much more stable perception of the other side's capabilities and the conditions under which they may act.
4. Tactical deterrence is frequently nearly indiscernible from "operational considerations". The goal of the terrorist leader is to carry out the attack or attacks. If he receives signs of high alert from the warring side that may thwart his efforts, he may freeze the operation until such a time that the alert goes down. This, it is claimed, is not an

expression of deterrence but a purely tactical consideration.

5. Tactical deterrence is based on execution of a threat as opposed to the core definition of deterrence which is, as noted above, the threat of punishment. It has been claimed that as in other areas, "familiarity breeds contempt"; a threat of punishment of unknown proportions looms much darker than a punishment which is meted out on a regular basis.
6. Deterrence via "Host States"

The second pillar of this strategy aims at bringing pressure of the "host" state (or quasi-state in the case of the PA) to bear on the terrorist organization. The affinity and dependence of the non-state actor on its relationship with existing states (Lebanon) or (the Palestinian Authority) can be important channels for deterring the terrorist actors. This has been demonstrated in the case of Fatah, when pressure on the material interests of the Palestinian Authority brought about occasional restraint of Fatah elements in the field. This is also true in the aftermath of the second Lebanon war, in which the dependence of Hizballah on a modus vivendi with the Lebanese state allowed the state to impose restraints on the guerilla group. The efficacy of this strategy largely depends on the community of interests between the host and the organization that is the ultimate target of deterrence. The greater the identification between the two, or the closer a non-state actor gets to being a state, the more susceptible it is to deterrence. Fatah, for example, evolved into states, gathered interests and assets, and hence became vulnerable to deterrence methods. In the cases analyzed above, it is clear that effective and credible threats to the hosts (Lebanon or the PA) had the potential of deterring the terrorist organizations from actions that would. Israel did not succeed however in generating such deterrence. Both hosts benefited from their weakness; Israel (and the West) had a political interest in the continuing functioning of the PA and Lebanon so as not to have even greater chaos at its doorstep, or in the case of the PA, to have to take over its civil functions and reoccupy the West Bank and Gaza. This restrained any Israeli response that could conceivably bring about a collapse of those entities. Another channel, which Israel has attempted to exploit for indirect deterrence on host and patron states, has been the international community.

While inclusion of the organizations themselves in lists of terrorist organizations has not perturbed these countries a great deal, the prospects of international sanctions have always been considered a potential deterrent. Such sanctions have been implemented against the PA, Afghanistan under the Taliban, Syria and Iran. However, without total commitment of the international community it is doubtful that such measures will A terrorist organization can "evolve" into a host state and internalize the considerations and constraints of the state, including its view of the cost-benefit analysis of continuing to be involved in terrorism. This is clearly evident in the case of the Palestinian Authority, and conceivably in the future in the case of Lebanon, where Hizballah may take complete power. However, in most cases of Arab and Islamic organizations, any trend towards institutionalization of a terrorist organization induces a split in those organizations, with the splinter groups rejecting any moderation of positions.

DETERRENCE VIA THE POPULACE

The third pillar was also attempted extensively in the confrontations between Israel and Palestinian terrorism and with Hizballah in Lebanon. A major component of Israeli deterrence towards the Palestinian organizations - and to a lesser extent Hizballah - has been the attempt to deter the populace from providing support to them. This has been met with only modest success. Israeli pamphlets distributed over Gaza and South Lebanon could not warn the populace of levels of retribution that Israel, as a state committed to the Geneva Conventions, could not implement. Israel has tried to deter terrorists through the host populaces both in the Palestinian and the Lebanese context. However, this policy also did not yield any real success in either theatre. Obviously, the ability of a democratic state to take full advantage of this element is curtailed by its international commitments to the laws of war and human rights, not to mention its status as an occupier (when such a case applies).

The failure of these attempts may have been due, inter alia, to the fact that Israel's political and humanitarian constraints precluded development of a credible threat. Proposals for indirect deterrence of Palestinian organizations have been raised. One such proposal was to present a "price table" for launching of Qassam missiles from Gaza by linking the Israeli early warning system for short range rockets (codenamed "Red Dawn" - *Shahar Adom* - it was changed to Tzeva Adom) to the Gaza electric grid in Israel, so that every launching of a rocket would turn off the electricity in Gaza for one hour.

The "automatic" blackouts would, according to this proposal, bring about public pressure on Hamas to refrain from launching rockets at certain hours. This proposal was never seriously discussed. The role of propaganda and Psyop is pivotal for deterrence through a host population. In discussions with senior Israeli security officials, it has been claimed that Israel's attempts to project an image of openness and free press (lacking in the Arab countries) in Arabic language broadcasts has been counter-productive, and Israel's goal of deterrence would be better served by amplifying the threatening image of Israel in case of an attack.

DETERRENCE VIA THE PATRON STATE

The fourth pillar is indirect deterrence via the patron state. This was the basis of Israel's strategy of deterrence against terrorism in the early days of the State. Reprisals were launched against the states (Egypt, Jordan, and Lebanon) in a manner that was intended to bring them to rein in the terrorists. Questions that influence this pillar are: Is the proxy group (the terrorist non-state organization) so controlled by or identified with the patron (host internationally legitimate State) that the efficacy of threatening the direct interests of the proxy is diminished and deterrence can be achieved only by direct threats to the interests of the patron? On the other hand, are the interests of the proxy important enough to the patron to justify being deterred so as not to impinge upon these interests? This pillar is closely linked to the second.

The stronger the dependence on the patron is, the less influential the host state may be. In many cases, the non-state terrorist organization adopts the strategic interests and narrative of its patron. This was true in the past in the cases of Palestinian organizations that acted as total proxies of Arab states (al-Sa'iqa as the Palestinian organization of the Syrian Ba'ath; the Arab Liberation Front which represented the Iraqi Ba'ath), and it is true today in the relationship between Hizballah and Iran. Another mode of relationship is that of the Syrian relationship with both Hizballah and Hamas - Syria remains a facilitator and political supporter, but does not intimately involve itself with the ideology and planning of the organizations.

Attempts to deter patron states must also take into account all the factors of leadership, modes of collecting signals, the ways in which they process them and feeding them to their decision makers, and the decision making process itself in those states. Ultimately, though they are contingent upon the existence of levers of deterrence of the deterring party towards those patron states. When such levers exist, the transfer of deterrence from the patron state to the non-state proxy does not have to be a complicated decision-making process. However, in practice, Israeli options for deterring Iran and Syria have been limited. The ability to deter Iran has been almost non-existent due to the absence of a common border, and Iran's deterrence towards Israel - the option of international terrorism against soft Israeli and Jewish targets abroad. At the same time, deterrence towards Syria has been impaired by the fact that Syria and its proxies knew that Israel had no interest in risking a fullfledged war with Syria over acts of terror.

The deterrence relationship between Israel and Syria is built on preventing Syria from initiating a war against Israel. Any attempt to prevent Syria from supporting terrorism (closing offices of terrorist organizations, etc.) entails compellence. Any attempt to pressure Syria to prevent its proxies from performing terrorist attacks would call for allocating part of the "punishment" reserved for acts of war by Syria for acts of terrorism. This course was never employed by Israeli governments. Along with the process of terrorist organizations becoming proxies of Arab or other states, a reverse process can also be identified. The freedom of action that Afghanistan under the Taliban accorded al-Qa'ida reflected both the failure of the Taliban to internalize their "statehood", and a total identification of the Taliban with the al-Qa'ida narrative to the point that they were willing to risk the consequences of this identification.

There are signs that Syria under Bashar al-Asad is undergoing a similar process in relation to Hizballah; Bashar's public statements have become more and more identical to those of Nasrallah, and seem to reflect an adoption of the Hizballah-Iran narrative. This should raise the question whether Syria will necessarily react to deterrence "as Syria" per se, or might behave with less caution out of its identification with Hizballah. An important lesson from the history of Israeli-Hizballah interaction is the difficulty for an open democracy to neutralize domestic debate and changes of government from impinging on the deterrent image it attempts to project to a terrorist adversary. This dilemma places an onus on the Israeli political and military leadership to bolster the deterrent message with unambiguous messages and actions.

Nevertheless, Israel has achieved temporary and fragile deterrence vis-à-vis the Hizballah and the Palestinians over the years. There is no doubt that period of relative quiet derived from concern not to provoke an Israeli reaction to a terrorist attack that would neutralize any benefit from such an attack. This occasional tactical deterrence was achieved not by the threat of force, but by actual application of force inducing fear that the force would be reapplied and even increased. Deterrence of this type is difficult to distinguish from disruption and many Israeli security experts would categorize it as "operational considerations" that dictate when and where to perform acts of terrorism, as opposed to deterrence that deals with whether or not to do it.

In the course of this study, a number of senior Israelis were interviewed on questions regarding whether or not Israel had developed a comprehensive doctrine of deterrence towards terrorist organizations, and whether there had been conscious and coordinated efforts to project a certain deterrent image. The conclusion from these interviews and from the objective case studies presented above is that no comprehensive military-political-economic doctrine for deterring terrorist organizations was ever adopted by Israel, either at military and security levels or at the government level. This was partially due to the sense of existential conflict with terrorist entities, which are sworn to the ultimate destruction of Israel and are motivated by religious and not political motivation or by an uncompromising nationalist agenda.

The conventional wisdom in Israel has been that such organizations cannot be effectively deterred, but should be fought until extirpated. Consequently, the politically sensitive aspect of dealing with terrorism in Israel precluded any official doctrine of deterrence, as that would have implied acceptance of the assumption that those organizations cannot be eradicated. Some former officials pointed out that the predominance of the military and security sectors in counter-terrorism hindered the development of such an integrated policy. Nevertheless, almost all the Israeli experts and decision makers who were interviewed for this study saw the main obstacle in deterring non-state actors in the absence of a wide array of vulnerable interests that could be threatened, in contrast to the interests of a state.

Hence, the more such an organization took on itself attributes and interests of a state, the more susceptible it became to deterrence. Israel has succeeded from time to time in achieving deterrence that was limited in time and place. This was achieved, unlike in the case of classic deterrence, not by threat of force, but by show of force. The deterrence did take effect immediately after Israel proved its willingness to use force and subsequently began wearing off shortly afterwards. The conclusion therefore is that deterrence against terrorist organizations can rarely be based on an image of the deterring state's capability (after all, the terrorist organization is, by definition, struggling against a much stronger adversary), but on actual use of that capability. Furthermore it is necessary from time to time, to refresh the awareness of the terrorist leadership that the state will indeed employ such capabilities. To paraphrase a well-known expression of classic deterrence, the state that attempts to deter terrorism must "speak loudly and periodically use a big stick".

12

The Collective Action of Terrorist Groups

In the past decade, a surge in the public awareness of terrorist activity has instigated a number of policies designed at the prevention and deterrence of terrorism. In response, public choice scholars have provided analyses of the constitutions of terrorist groups and critically examined government efforts through an economic framework. In "Extremism, Suicide Terror and Authoritarianism," Ronald Wintrobe explores modern terrorist groups in the context of conventional collective action theory. The analysis is primarily concerned with explaining the formation of terrorist groups and the reasons why terrorist groups adopt extreme methodology. Similarly, in "Terrorism, Interest-group Politics, and Public Policy", Roger Congleton examines the nature of healthy political games and then examines the costs of those games as a constant in order to diagnose terrorist groups as deviations from the typical interest group model in need of a different policy response.

"Extremism, Suicide Terror and Authoritarianism"

Wintrobe posits that the actions of terrorist groups are similar to any interest group that employs the use of rent seeking; they are rational actors working for the recognition of their political goals. According to Wintrobe, terrorist groups are differentiated by the methods they choose to adopt, specifically extremist and inherently risky behavior. Extremist methods are demonstrated by groups with indivisible goals which result from the inability to separate intermediate goals from ultimate goals. For example, the goal of Islamic Fundamentalism to establish complete Islamic theocracy within a state is seemingly indivisible with the intermediate goal of removing all secular and foreign influence. In this situation, the payoff from adopting extreme methods is very high compared to employing moderate methods, which lead to partial recognition of indivisible goals and disproportionately low utility. While extreme methods entail an inherent risk of failure, they also present the prospect of completely satisfying the ultimate goal of a group, and utility maximization. Therefore, the likelihood that a group will participate in extreme behavior is positively related to the ratio of utility resulting from extreme methods compared with moderate methods.

THE FREE-RIDER PROBLEM AND SELECTIVE INCENTIVES

In the recruitment of constituents, terrorist groups confront a common problem within collective action: the free-rider effect. When terrorists achieve their goals, the result is public good beneficial for anyone that shares the same ideology. Potential constituents are likely to free-ride because participation comes at a cost and the benefit is freely available. To combat the free-rider problem, interest groups offer selective incentives that offset the costs of participation. Wintrobe argues that solidarity or social cohesion is the primary incentive to join a terrorist group. The production possibilities boundary for a potential constituent illustrates a tradeoff between individual autonomy and solidarity. Based on individual preferences, utility can conceivably be maximized by a movement away from autonomy toward solidarity. In addition, as a group's ability to provide solidarity increases, the production of solidarity bows outward and the utility derived from a movement toward solidarity increases. By effectively offering solidarity, terrorist groups can persuade individuals to trade their beliefs for the more cohesive goals of the group.

"Terrorism, Interest-group Politics, and Public Policy"

As public choice scholars have long recognized, in traditional politicking, interest groups employ a variety of means to gain rents for particular groups of citizens and that these efforts result in deadweight losses. Roger Congleton attempts to minimize the inefficiencies created by terrorist groups by advocating a clearer understanding of the actual costs incurred.

COMPETITIVE GAMES AND SOCIAL GAIN

The first building block of his analysis rests on a distinction between types of competitive games. Some games depend upon the relative position of the players involved, consequently generating high deadweight losses from wasted resources. Alternatively, games that value absolute effort, such as competitive sports, often produce value is "generally larger in the aggregate than the value of all the resources invested by those participating in the debate". In political debates, these positive gains include the dissemination of information to the electorate. However, if the quality of information is poor, political debate can equate to deceiving the electorate by means of rhetoric instead of argument. Congleton assesses the quality of the political message conveyed through terrorism and concludes that "the threatened disruptive acts are largely independent of the 'policy argument' being communicated", thus a poor medium.

CRIMINAL DEVIATIONS FROM THE INTEREST GROUP MODEL

From the cost side, Congleton explains that terrorist organizations do conform to the typical model insofar as their activities generate all the normal costs associated with interest groups: rent-seeking costs, externalities, and policy mistakes provoked by lobbying pressures. However, they also generate a fourth category of costs of such great magnitude as to warrant treating them as criminal organizations. The most evident additional cost is the "actuality of destructive activities", which invariably has a multiplied effect beyond the actual site of an attack. The multiplier includes disrupted business patterns, policy reactions, increased preventative measures, and psychological harm from both present loss and the anticipation of future harms.

POLICY RESPONSE AND INCENTIVES

Dealing with deterrence, Congleton emphasizes the need for cost-effective policies structured around incentives. Specifically, he urges consideration of "the differences in the degree to which people respond to changes in expected punishment". He suggests that demand for terrorism becomes increasingly inelastic relative to the place of an individual within the terrorist organization. Thus, he argues that incentives ought to be focused at the junior levels within terrorist groups because the marginal costs of deterrence are significantly lower.

Furthermore, he asserts that the policy appropriate to terrorism must be proportional to the gravity of the expected harm times the probability of that harm. Congleton warns against the sort of reactionary policy fraught with inefficiencies that might arise as a result of the pressures created by terrorist acts. His data suggest that the rate of increase in terrorism has been vastly outmatched by the increase in preventative spending and that this response needs to be curtailed.

CLASSIFICATION AS INTEREST GROUPS

Wintrobe and Congleton's initial classification of terrorist groups is nearly identical. Terrorist groups are a form of collective action that have similar goals and face the same problems as ordinary interest groups. Terrorist groups employ the use of rent-seeking behavior to wield excessive influence in the realm of political competition, seeking recognition of their policy goals. While the two authors both stress the essential role of violent and destructive behavior, their analysis of terrorist group formation and differentiation from other interest groups reveals differences. Ultimately, their contrasting points of emphasis lead the authors to make divergent policy suggestions.

FORMATION

According to Congleton, the entire point of terrorism is

using violent means to bring about government sanctioned policy change. Individual terrorist group constituents have an inclination toward extreme behavior and are willing to join a group if the probability that they achieve their goals is high. In Congleton's view, terrorist groups offer participation in a successful mission as a selective incentive to their potential constituent base. However, the fact that governments rarely give in to the pressure of terrorists seems to imply a very low success rate, and raises questions about the possibility of recruitment based on the selective incentive of success.

Wintrobe, on the other hand emphasizes group solidarity as the primary incentive to join terrorist groups. While types of social pressure are incentives in ordinary interest group formation, Wintrobe's version of solidarity is exclusive to those that hold extreme beliefs. In contrast to Congleton's analysis of formation, Wintrobe's explanation is independent of the overall success of a group, and more accurately reflects an attempt by the interest group to combat the free-rider problem. Both authors fail to address the significance of material incentives - food, shelter and family support - that terrorist groups offer in the recruitment process.

DIFFERENTIATION BETWEEN TERRORIST AND NON-TERRORIST INTEREST GROUPS

The manner in which Congleton and Wintrobe differentiate between terrorist groups and ordinary interest groups is divergent, but not mutually exclusive. Congleton focuses on the costs incurred on society by terrorist groups in comparison with other interest groups. Congleton explains that all interest groups impose costs due to their participation in wasteful rent-seeking contests and by encouraging policy production that does not benefit the overall efficiency of society. In addition to these costs, terrorist groups impose direct, destructive costs on society, in addition to a number of indirect impacts. The indirect impacts of terrorism include the reduction of potential economic output and losses associated with the risk of future terrorism. In contrast,

Wintrobe explains the difference of terrorist groups based on the nature of their goals and their adoption of extreme methodology. Unlike the proponents of tax reform or gun rights that receive satisfaction from the accomplishment of intermediate goals, terrorist groups are only satisfied with the accomplishment of their ultimate goals.

As a result of the high payoff, terrorist groups are much more likely to participate in risky behavior. The imposition of costs on society does not play a role in Wintrobe's classification, but reference to such costs is implicit in the adoption of extreme methodology.

POLICY EXTENSION

Congleton and Wintrobe converge at a fundamental level in their assessment of extremism as the modus operandi for terrorist leaders. However, in terms of policy, Congleton focuses on the usefulness of the criminal justice model for terrorism, while Wintrobe attempts to understand the divergence of terrorist groups from interest groups in order to understand what sorts of incentives would minimize the incidence of terror.

PROPORTIONATE RESPONSE

Congleton focuses primarily on encouraging appropriate levels of response to terrorism, based on the probability of attacks. He notes that the very nature of terrorism tends to evoke disproportionate responses from the government that are often wasteful, and suggests a simple criterion. "A particular terrorist attack should not trigger policy changes unless the attack reveals new and important information about the likelihood of future attacks".

This information-sensitive response curtails reactionary spending, and keeps deterrence where marginal benefit equals marginal cost. Furthermore, Congleton argues that policy ought to begin with the continued improvement of the internal police system. He cites the 9/11 hijackings as evidence of a time where the simple precaution of locked bay doors might have prevented mass destruction.

SOLIDARITY AND INCENTIVES

On the other hand, Wintrobe looks to unbundle terrorist groups as a means of disrupting their activity, arguing that "extremists in position adopt extremist methods when there is an indivisibility which characterizes the relationship between the intermediate goal of the group and its ultimate goal". He focuses on the idea of solidarity within a terrorist organization as the primary motivator for the commitment of the individual member. Thus, his policy suggestions revolve around means of discouraging terrorists from seeking solidarity within the bosom of the terrorist group and around means of disassociating their immediate goals from the extreme.

Accordingly, Wintrobe's policy recommendations also champion sociopolitical systems that can offer solidarity and hope to disrupt the association of the group's intermediate and ultimate goals. Authoritarian regimes generally do not attempt to provide solidarity, and are consequently notorious for the production of terrorist groups. Democratic reforms, however, offer solidarity through political freedoms and the provision of public goods.

His specific policy has followed two general avenues, those of carrot and stick. The carrot method places greater emphasis on the solidarity sought by terrorists, seeking to encourage the healthy acquisition of that solidarity in other, more pacific areas.

The stick method applies force to discourage participation. However, Wintrobe accurately notes that if the desire for solidarity is great, the application of 'the stick' will likely inflame the psychological benefit derived from solidarity and could increase commitment. The optimal solution, particularly when information is scarce, applies both carrot and stick.

CONCLUSION

Wintrobe and Congleton show that terrorism requires a response governed by cost-conscious spending and an appropriate understanding of terrorists as extreme versions of traditional political interest groups. While they approach terrorist groups with the same initial framework, as their analyses progress, their points of emphasis diverge. Ultimately this leads to different policy suggestions aimed at the effective deterrence of terrorism.

13

Strategic Assessment of Terrorism

FIVE YEARS ON, PROGRESS IS MIXED

SIGNIFICANT ACHIEVEMENTS

Five years after 9/11, the international community's conflict with transnational terrorists continues. Cooperative international efforts have produced genuine security improvements—particularly in securing borders and transportation, enhancing document security, disrupting terrorist financing, and restricting the movement of terrorists. The international community has also achieved significant success in dismantling terrorist organizations and disrupting their leadership. This has contributed to reduced terrorist operational capabilities and the detention or death of numerous key terrorist leaders.

Working with allies and partners across the world, through coordination and information sharing, we have created a less permissive operating environment for terrorists, keeping leaders on the move or in hiding, and degrading their ability to plan and mount attacks. Canada, Australia, the United Kingdom, Saudi Arabia, Turkey, Pakistan, Afghanistan, and many other partners played major roles in this success, recognizing that international terrorism represents a threat to the whole international community.

Through the Regional Strategic Initiative, the State Department is working with ambassadors and interagency representatives in key terrorist theaters of operation to assess the threat and devise collaborative strategies, action plans, and policy recommendations. We have made progress in organizing regional responses to terrorists who operate in ungoverned spaces or across national borders. This initiative has produced better intragovernmental coordination among United States government agencies, greater cooperation with and between regional partners, and improved strategic planning and prioritization, allowing us to use all tools of statecraft to establish long-term measures to marginalize terrorists.

CONTINUING CHALLENGES

Despite this undeniable progress, major challenges remain. Several states continue to sponsor terrorism. Iran remains the most significant state sponsor of terrorism and continues to threaten its neighbors and destabilize Iraq by providing weapons, training, advice, and funding to select Iraqi Shia militants. Syria, both directly and in coordination with Hizballah, has attempted to undermine the elected Government of Lebanon and roll back progress toward democratization in the Middle East. Syria also supports some Iraqi Baathists and militants and has continued to allow foreign fighters and terrorists to transit through its borders into Iraq.

International intervention in Iraq has brought measurable benefits. It has removed an abusive totalitarian regime with a history of sponsoring and supporting regional terrorism and has allowed a new democratic political process to emerge. It also, however, has been used by terrorists as a rallying cry for radicalization and extremist activity that has contributed to instability in neighboring countries.

Afghanistan remains threatened by Taliban insurgents and religious extremists, some of whom are linked to al-Qaida (AQ) and to sponsors outside the country. In Afghanistan public support for the government remains high, national institutions are getting stronger and the majority of Afghans believe they are better off than under the Taliban. But to defeat the resurgent threat, the international community must deliver promised assistance and work with Afghans to build counterinsurgency capabilities, ensure legitimate and effective governance, and counter the surge in narcotics cultivation.

The Israeli/Palestinian conflict remains a source of terrorist motivation. The holding of free elections in the Palestinian Territories was a welcome sign of democratization, but HAMAS' subsequent refusal to disavow terrorism or accept Israel's internationally-accepted right to exist undermined the election's impact. Terrorist activity emanating from the Palestinian Territories remains a key destabilizing factor and a cause for concern.

The summer war in Lebanon between Israel and Hizballah was a prime example of how Hizballah's continued efforts to manipulate persisting grievances along the Israeli/Lebanese border can quickly escalate into open warfare. The conflict did force the international community again to demand Hizballah's complete disarmament, in UN Security Council Resolution (UNSCR) 1701, and generated a renewed international commitment to support a peaceful, stable, multisectarian democracy in Lebanon. Even so, Hizballah, a designated foreign terrorist organization, in combination with state sponsors of terrorism Iran and Syria, continues to undermine the elected Government of Lebanon and remains a serious security threat in the Middle East.

AQ and its affiliates have adapted to our success in disrupting their operational capability by focusing more attention and resources on their propaganda and misinformation efforts. They exploit and interpret the actions of numerous local, pseudo-independent actors, using them to mobilize supporters and sympathizers, intimidate opponents and influence international opinion. Terrorists consider information operations to be a principal part of their effort. The international community has yet to muster a coordinated and effectively resourced counter to extremist propaganda.

Overall, AQ and its loose confederation of affiliated movements remain the most immediate national security threat to the United States and a significant security challenge to the international community.

KEY AL-QAIDA TRENDS

Single terrorist events, like the Askariya mosque bombing in Samarra, Iraq on February 22, 2006, which provoked widespread sectarian violence and changed the character of the war in Iraq, can become triggers for broader conflict or templates for copycat attacks. Because terrorism is fundamentally political, the political significance of major events is vital in determining meaningful responses. Thus, the trends presented in this section are interpretive - they provide qualitative insight to complement the statistical detail.

TRANSITION FROM "EXPEDITIONARY" TO "GUERRILLA" TERRORISM

Early AQ terrorist attacks were largely expeditionary. The organization selected and trained terrorists in one country, then clandestinely inserted a team into the target country to attack a preplanned objective. The 1998 U.S. embassy bombings in Nairobi and Dar es-Salaam, the 2000 attack on the USS Cole, and the 9/11 attacks were examples of this. Improved international border security, transportation security and document control have made this type of attack more difficult. Clandestine insertion across borders is harder, reconnaissance is more risky, and international movement of funds and equipment is more likely to be detected.

Thus we have seen a trend toward guerrilla terrorism, where the organization seeks to grow the team close to its target, using target country nationals. Through intermediaries, web-based propaganda, and subversion of immigrant expatriate populations, terrorists inspire local cells to carry out attacks which they then exploit for propaganda purposes. This circumvents the need to insert a team across borders or clandestinely transfer funds and materiel. The 2004 Madrid bombing, the London attacks of July 2005, and the thwarted

August 2006 attempt to attack passenger jets operating from British airports include elements of this approach.

Both expeditionary and guerrilla approaches co-exist, alongside true "home-grown" terrorism involving local cells acting spontaneously rather than being than consciously inspired by transnational terrorists. Rather than adopting a single modus operandi, AQ and its affiliated movements continue to be highly adaptive, quickly evolving new methods in response to countermeasures.

TERRORIST PROPAGANDA WARFARE

As identified in the 2005 Country Reports, the international community's success in disrupting terrorist leadership and operational capacity led AQ to focus greater efforts on misinformation and anti-Western propaganda. This trend accelerated this year, with AQ cynically exploiting the grievances of local groups and attempting to portray itself as the vanguard of a global movement. AQ still retains some operational capability and the intent to mount large-scale spectacular attacks, including on the United States and other high-profile Western targets. Overall, however, AQ's current approach focuses on propaganda warfare - using a combination of terrorist attacks, insurgency, media broadcasts, Internet-based propaganda, and subversion to undermine confidence and unity in Western populations and generate the false perception of a powerful worldwide movement.

THE TERRORIST "CONVEYOR BELT"

Radicalization of immigrant populations, youth and alienated minorities in Europe, the Middle East, and Africa continued. It became increasingly clear, however, that such radicalization does not occur by accident, or because such populations are innately prone to extremism. Rather, there was increasing evidence of terrorists and extremists manipulating the grievances of alienated youth or immigrant populations and then cynically exploiting those grievances to subvert legitimate authority and create unrest.

Terrorists seek to manipulate grievances represent a "conveyor belt" through which terrorists seek to convert alienated or aggrieved populations, convert them to extremist viewpoints, and turn them, by stages, into sympathizers, supporters, and ultimately, members of terrorist networks. In some regions, this includes efforts by AQ and other terrorists to exploit insurgency and communal conflict as radicalization and recruitment tools, especially using the Internet to convey their message.

Countering such efforts demands that we treat immigrant and youth populations not as a source of threat to be defended against, but as a target of enemy subversion to be protected and supported. It also requires community leaders to take responsibility for the actions of members within their communities and act to counteract extremist subversion.

A NEW KIND OF ENEMY

AL-QAIDA AS A GLOBAL INSURGENCY

The surface events mentioned above highlight a deeper trend: the transformation of international terrorism from the traditional forms that Congress intended to address when it established the annual Country Reports series into a broader, multifarious approach to transnational non-state warfare that now resembles a form of global insurgency. We have entered a new era of conflict that may demand new paradigms and different responses from those of previous eras.

AQ and its core leadership group represent a global action network that seeks to aggregate and exploit the effects of widely dispersed, semi-independent actors. It openly describes itself as a transnational guerrilla movement and applies classic insurgent strategies at the global level. AQ applies terrorism, but also subversion, propaganda, and open warfare, and it seeks weapons of mass destruction in order to inflict the maximum possible damage on its opponents. It links and exploits a wider, more nebulous community of regional, national, and local actors who share some of its objectives, but also pursue their own local agendas. Finally, it works through regional and cross-border safe havens that facilitate its actions while hampering government responses.

DISAGGREGATING THE THREAT

To the extent that AQ succeeds in aggregating this broader constellation of extremist actors, it can begin to pursue more frequent and geographically extensive terror attacks. Therefore, we must act to disaggregate the threat, through international cooperation, counterpropaganda, counter subversion, counterinsurgency, and traditional counterterrorism.

Disaggregation breaks the links in the chain that exploit ordinary people's grievances and manipulates them into becoming terrorists. It seeks to provide those who are already radicalized with a way out and to create pathways for alienated groups to redress their legitimate grievances without joining the terrorist network. Disaggregation denies AQ its primary objective of achieving leadership over extremist movements worldwide and unifying them into a single movement. It does not remove the threat but helps reduce it to less dangerous local components, which can be dealt with by individual governments and communities working together.

TRUSTED NETWORKS

Such cooperation requires the creation of trusted networks to displace and marginalize extremist networks. While killing and capturing key terrorist actors is fundamental in combating terrorism, it can have detrimental effects. These actions do not eliminate the threat and, if mishandled, can be actively counterproductive. Instead, we must seek to build trusted networks of governments, private citizens and organizations, multilateral institutions, and business organizations that work collaboratively to defeat the threat from violent extremism.

Such networks, over time, help wean at-risk populations away from subversive manipulation by terrorists and create mechanisms to address people's needs and grievances, thus marginalizing terrorists. Youth organizations, educational networks, business partnerships, women's empowerment, and local development initiatives can all play a role, with government as a supportive partner.

LEADERS, SAFE HAVENS, UNDERLYING CONDITIONS

To make such active measures effective, the three strategic components of the terrorist threat that must be neutralized are leaders, safe havens, and underlying conditions. Leaders provide a motivating, mobilizing, and organizing function and act as symbolic figureheads. Safe havens, which are often in ungoverned or under-governed spaces, provide a secure environment for training, planning, financial and operational support; and a base for mounting attacks. They may be physical or virtual in nature. In addition, underlying conditions provide the fuel, in the form of grievances and conflicts that power the processes of radicalization.

Treating this new era of conflict as a form of global insurgency implies that counterinsurgency methods are fundamental in combating the new form of transnational terrorism. These methods include firstly, a focus on protecting and securing the population; and secondly, politically and physically marginalizing the insurgents, winning the support and cooperation of at-risk populations by targeted political and development measures, and conducting precise intelligence-led special operations to eliminate critical enemy elements with minimal collateral damage.

INTEGRATING ALL ELEMENTS OF NATIONAL POWER

All elements of national power including diplomatic, military, economic, and intelligence, must be integrated and applied in a coordinated whole-of-government fashion. The intellectual and psychological dimensions of the threat are at least as important as its physical dimension, so countermeasures must be adequately coordinated and resourced. Thus, the military component of national power plays only a supporting role in this effort; the primary focus is on non-military influence.

Because the enemy is a non-state actor who thrives among disaffected populations, private sector efforts are at least as important as government activity. Citizen diplomacy, cultural activity, person-to-person contact, economic cooperation and development, and the application of media and academic resources are key components of our response to the threat. Motivating, mobilizing, and supporting such privately led activities are key leadership tasks in the new environment.

COMMITMENT - THE KEY TO SUCCESS

Experience since 9/11 has shown that the key success factor in confronting violent extremism is the commitment by governments to work with each other, with the international community, with private sector organizations, and with their citizens and immigrant populations.

Where governments cooperate, build trusted networks, seek active informed support from their people, provide responsive, effective and legitimate governance, and engage closely with the international community, the threat from terrorism has been significantly reduced. Where governments have lacked commitment in working with their neighbors and engaging the support of their people, terrorism and the instability and conflict that terrorists exploit remain key sources of threat.

SUMMARY

This chapter sets the scene for the detailed analysis that follows. In reviewing events since 9/11, it is clear that progress has been mixed. Significant achievements in border security, information sharing, transportation security, financial controls, and the killing or capture of numerous terrorist leaders have reduced the threat. But the threat still remains, and state sponsorship, the terrorist response to intervention in Iraq, improved terrorist propaganda capabilities, the pursuit of nuclear weapons by state sponsors of terrorism, and terrorist exploitation of grievances represent ongoing challenges. Recent trends include the emergence of "guerrilla" terrorism in parallel with traditional "expeditionary" approaches, improved AQ propaganda warfare capacity, and emerging evidence of terrorist "conveyor belt" that seeks to deliberately manipulate and exploit grievances in at-risk populations.

A deeper trend is the shift in the nature of terrorism, from traditional international terrorism of the late 20th century into a new form of transnational non-state warfare that resembles a form of global insurgency. This represents a new era of warfare, and countering this threat demands the application of counterinsurgency techniques that focus on protecting, securing, and winning the support of at-risk populations, in addition to targeting violent extremist networks and individual terrorists.

Trusted networks of private and government organizations and individuals, and the application of integrated civil-military measures across all elements of national power are keys to this approach. Terrorist leaders, safe havens, and the underlying conditions that terrorists exploit are the principal strategic targets that we must address. The key success factor that has emerged so far is commitment by governments to work with the international community, their own populations, and at-risk immigrant or youth populations, to counter the threat collaboratively.

14

Efforts to Counter Terrorism

ASEAN EFFORTS

ASEAN Leaders, at their 7th Summit on 5 November 2001 in Brunei Darussalam, adopted the 2001 ASEAN Declaration on Joint Action to Counter Terrorism. The ASEAN Leaders viewed terrorism as a profound threat to international peace and security and "a direct challenge to the attainment of peace, progress and prosperity of ASEAN and the realization of ASEAN Vision 2020". They expressed commitment to combat terrorism in accordance with the Charter of the United Nations, other international laws and relevant UN resolutions. They also underlined that "cooperative efforts in this regard should consider joint practical counter-terrorism measures in line with specific circumstances in the region and in each member country".

They also identified specific measures for ASEAN to implement the Declaration, namely:

- Review and strengthen national mechanisms to combat terrorism;
- Call for the early signing/ratification of or accession to all relevant anti-terrorist conventions including the International Convention for the Suppression of the Financing of Terrorism;
- Deepen cooperation among ASEAN's frontline law

enforcement agencies in combating terrorism and sharing "best practices";

- Study relevant international conventions on terrorism with the view to integrating them with ASEAN mechanisms on combating international terrorism;
- Enhance information/intelligence exchange to facilitate the flow of information, in particular, on terrorists and terrorist organisations, their movement and funding, and any other information needed to protect lives, property and the security of all modes of travel;
- Strengthen existing cooperation and coordination between the ASEAN Ministerial Meeting on Transnational Crime (AMMTC) and other relevant ASEAN bodies in countering, preventing and suppressing all forms of terrorist acts. Particular attention would be paid to finding ways to combat terrorist organisations, support infrastructure and funding and bringing the perpetrators to justice;
- Develop regional capacity building programmes to enhance existing capabilities of ASEAN member countries to investigate, detect, monitor and report on terrorist acts;
- Discuss and explore practical ideas and initiatives to increase ASEAN's role in and involvement with the international community including extraregional partners within existing frameworks such as the ASEAN + 3, the ASEAN Dialogue Partners and the ASEAN Regional Forum (ARF), to make the fight against terrorism a truly regional and global endeavour;
- Strengthen cooperation at the bilateral, regional and international levels in combating terrorism in a comprehensive manner and affirm that at the international level the United Nations should play a major role in this regard.
- The specific measures outlined in the Declaration have been incorporated in the Terrorism component of the Work Programme to Implement the ASEAN Plan of Action to Combat Transnational Crime adopted in May

2002. The Work Programme is based along 6 strategic thrust namely:

- Tnformation exchange;
- Cooperation in legal matters;
- Cooperation in law enforcement matters;
- Institutional capacity building;
- Training; and
- Extra-regional cooperation.

ASEAN is also carrying out training programmes and projects in counter terrorism in 2003, including on psychological operation/psychological warfare courses for law enforcement authorities and on intelligence procuring. Courses on bomb/explosive detection, post-blast investigation, airport security and passport/document security and inspection are also planned. In addition, ASEAN focal points on counter-terrorism have also been established.

STAGE A:

Several ASEAN Member Countries have already become the party to some of the 12 international conventions and protocols relating to terrorism. In the Work Programme, ASEAN Member Countries are also urged towards an early signing or ratification of or accession to all relevant anti-terrorist conventions including the International Convention for the Suppression of the Financing of Terrorism.

As part of the Terrorism Component of the ASEAN Work Programme, ASEAN Member Countries are now working toward the establishment of a regional database for disseminating information on respective national laws, regulations, bilateral and multilateral treaties or agreements of respective countries. The Terrorism Component, in addressing the issue of prevention and suppression of terrorist financing, calls for the enhancement of information or intelligence exchange to facilitate the flow of information, in particular, on terrorists and terrorist organizations, their movement and funding, and any other information needed to protect lives, property and the security of all modes of travel.

STAGE B:

The Annual Conference of ASEAN Chiefs of Police (ASEANAPOL) held in May 2002, called for a joint cooperation among the ASEANAPOL members in fighting terrorism. ASEAN Chief of Police are committed to developing capacity-building initiatives to ensure that each ASEANAPOL member has the capacity to effectively monitor, share information on and combat all forms of terrorist activities. They also agreed to enhance cooperation among law enforcement agencies through the sharing of experiences on counter-terrorism and the exchange of information on suspected terrorists, organizations and their modus operandi.

In addition, ASEAN immigration authorities have committed to assist and to coordinate with the other ASEAN law enforcement authorities to prevent the movement of terrorists or cross-border terrorism by working toward the establishment of intelligence units in their respective agencies on the issues of trafficking in persons, human smuggling and terrorism. They have also set up an ASEAN focal point directory for ASEAN immigration authorities to exchange information.

STAGE C:

In May 2002, Indonesia, Malaysia and the Philippines signed the Agreement on Information Exchange and Establishment of Communication Procedures to cooperate among them to combat transnational crime, including terrorism. Thailand and Cambodia have also acceded to the Agreement. ASEAN senior officials are also looking at the possibility of a regional convention to combat terrorism. In addition, several Member Countries within ASEAN are looking at a regional Mutual Legal Assistance Agreement.

In terms of information exchange, the Work Programme has put in place a comprehensive information exchange mechanism to facilitate sharing of information and analysis of critical intelligence information such as "modus operandi" and offences involving terrorist activities. ASEAN is taking a comprehensive and coordinated approach in tackling the various areas of transnational crimes that have links to terrorism as the Work Programme also has components on trafficking in small arms, illegal drug trafficking and money laundering.

In January 2003, ASEAN police and law enforcement officials agreed that each ASEAN Member Country shall establish an anti-terrorism task force to strengthen cooperation on counter-terrorism and to collaborate with the affected ASEAN member country following a terrorist attack. Such assistance requested can be in the form of, but not limited to identifying, pursuing and apprehending suspects, examination of witness (es), searching and seizing evidence, evacuating and treating of victims, forensic and crime laboratory.

In terms of cooperation at the international and regional levels, ASEAN and China, in November 2002, issued a Joint Declaration of ASEAN and China on Cooperation in the Field of Non-Traditional Security Issues where counter-terrorism has been included as one of the priorities for ASEAN-China cooperation. ASEAN is cooperating with China, Japan and the Republic of Korea under the ASEAN+3 process of East Asia cooperation to address the threats of terrorism and transnational crimes.

The ASEAN Ministers on Transnational Crime will start holding joint consultations with their counterparts from China, Japan and the Republic of Korea (the AMMTC+3) in Thailand this year. At the 9th ministerial meeting of the ASEAN Regional Forum (ARF) in Bandar Seri Begawan on 30 July 2002, the ARF Statement on Measures against Terrorist Financing was adopted. The ARF participating states and organization (the EU) agreed on concrete steps that included: freezing terrorist assets, implementation of international standards, cooperation on exchange of information and outreach, and technical assistance.

The 9th ARF also agreed to establish the intersessional meeting on counter-terrorism and transnational crimes (ISM-CT/TC), which will be co-chaired in the 2002-2003 year by

Malaysia and the U.S.A. Malaysia plans to convene the first meeting of the ISM-CT/TC in Sabah in March 2003. ASEAN and the U.S.A. signed the Joint Declaration for Cooperation to Combat International Terrorism during the 35th AMM/PMC in Bandar Seri Begawan on 1 August 2002. One of the objectives of the cooperation is to prevent, disrupt and combat international terrorism through the exchange and flow of information, intelligence and capacity-building assistance.

ASEAN and the E.U. issued the Joint Declaration on Cooperation to Combat Terrorism at the end of the 14th ASEAN-EU Ministerial Meeting in Brussels on 28 January 2003. The Joint Declaration reiterated the commitment of the two sides to work together and contribute to the global efforts to stamp out terrorism. In addition, some ASEAN member countries have entered into bilateral cooperation arrangements with other countries outside the ASEAN region to enhance their capability in counter-terrorism. Malaysia and the U.S.A., for example, have established the Regional Counter-terrorism Center in November 2002 in Kuala Lumpur. Indonesia and Australia have formed the joint task force to investigate the Bali terrorist bomb blasts.

RAMALLAH

Ramallah is located on a major crossroads in the West Bank, with a commanding view of its surroundings, ensuring a continuity of population from the city of Jerusalem northwards. The Ramallah area is composed of two main sectors: the lower city of Ramallah and the city of el-Bira (a separate municipality) to the east. South of the city is the el-'Amari refugee camp and to its north is the town of Bir Zeit (known for its university, the largest on the West Bank), and the Jalazoun refugee camp.

Ramallah is one of the two major Palestinian seats of power. The central Palestinian governing institutions are located within Ramallah, including: offices of the Legislative Council, the executive branch and a large number of Palestinian West Bank security forces' headquarters. Ramallah is a relatively modern city with Jerusalem-style high-rise buildings. In the past, Ramallah constituted a tourism and entertainment center. The Ramallah district contains 220,000 residents. Of these some 57,000 are located in the cities of Ramallah and el-Bira.

Arafat, until recently, had divided his time between Gaza and Ramallah, due to the presence of central governing institutions presence in both cities. Ramallah Prison (al-Mukata'a) was established by the British in order to detain revolutionaries. Jordan used it as a military base. Israel used it as a prison for arresting Palestinian activists. This prison is considered the principal site for detaining security prisoners from all the districts of the West Bank. It is also considered important because the Presidential helicopter lands in it when the President arrives in the West Bank. The Presidential guard surrounds the area whenever the President is in Ramallah.

After the coming of the Palestinian Authority, the prison was transformed into a security compound that was divided into different sections to accommodate the different security services. General Intelligence is responsible for security matters and arresting political activists from opposition groups. Military Intelligence is responsible for security prisoners (collaborators with Israel). National Security is responsible for protecting the city of Ramallah by setting up checkpoints in the streets. Military Collaboration specializes in coordination with Israel.

RAMALLAH AXIS OF TERRORISM

Since the beginning of the current conflict, Ramallah has stood out as a major center of terrorist activity against Israeli civilians and security personnel. According to Israeli authorities, the terrorist infrastructure in the city, and at times in the entire West Bank, are dependant on senior Fatah leadership and senior commanders of the Palestinian security apparatus. Since the death of Raed Karmi on January 14, 2002, the city has been characterized as the capital of Palestinian terrorism, from which many terrorist attacks have emanated.

Among those we may count the suicide attack in Tel Aviv's Sea Food Market restaurant, the terrorist infiltration of 'Ayn 'Arik, and the attack on civilians and IDF soldiers at the British Police roadblock.

PALESTINIAN SECURITY FORCES

Due to the fact that Ramallah constituted an administrative and governmental center, the Palestinian Authority security forces established their headquarters in the city. The National Security headqarters is located in Ramallah's Mukt'ah as are the headquarters of Force-17, Preventive Security and Civil Police. The Palestinian security forces, and especially Force-17, have played to varying extents, an active role in major terrorist attacks against Israeli civilians and IDF troops perpetrated within in the Ramallah area, in Jerusalem and elsewhere in Israel. The mutual relationship existing between the Fatah in Ramallah and members of the security forces (often on a personal basis, due to the fact many security force personnel were originally from the Fatah) has blurred the distinction between the Palestinian security forces and the Fatah. The former participate actively in terror operations, either as individuals or on an organizational level (e.g. Force-17).

TERRORIST ORGANIZATIONS

The Israeli government has singled out the Fatah, headed by Arafat as the major terrorist organization operating out of Ramallah. Marwan Barghouti, Secretary General of the Fatah, who is also head of the Tanzim, serves directly under him. Many senior Fatah leaders have established themselves in Ramallah. Fatah is accused of being responsible for a long list of deadly terrorist attacks (suicide operations, shooting attacks, kidnappings and bombings) which took the lives of many dozens of Israelis, though given the multiple linkages and affiliations between the various Palestinian factions, direct causation is as of yet still uncertain. Following the death of local Tanzim leader Raed Karmi on January 14, 2002, terrorist organizations have changed their modus operandi from shooting attacks on roads to suicide bombings in Israeli cities, and terrorist attacks against IDF checkpoints.

Other terrorist organizations operate from the city, among them the Hamas which had carried out the major suicide bombings in Jerusalem (e.g. the Sbarro pizzeria bombing, a Jerusalem pedestrian mall double-suicide bombing and the Cafe Moment attack which claimed the lives of 11 Israelis). Israel has accused terrorist operatives of enjoying the protection of the security forces who do not stop the activities in the city. Even though Ramallah is not the primary site of Hamas activity on the West Bank, Ramallah does constitute a "relay station" for suicide attacks in Jerusalem.

An additional terrorist organization that operates in and from the city is the Popular Front for the Liberation of Palestine. This organization, even though it is relatively small, has chosen Ramallah as the main focal point for its military and political operations. The leadership of the terrorist organization within the territories is situated in Ramallah. It has carried out a large number of spectacular attacks which have claimed the lives of many victims. Among these: the bombings in the Ariel hotel and the Karnei Shalom mall, and the assassination of the late Minister of Tourism Rechavam Ze'evy, whose murderers departed from and returned to Ramallah. The organization now specializes in suicide bombings. The remaining Palestinian terrorist organizations, such as the Islamic Jihad, maintain "representatives" in Ramallah. They reportedly cooperate together and with the official security forces of the Palestinian Authority.

ARAFAT'S BURIAL

Arafat Spent his final three years confined to his Ramallah headquarters, only leaving when he fell seriously ill and was flown to France for treatment. Palestinians filed past the burial site of Yasser Arafat on Saturday 13 November 2004, a day after he was laid to rest in an emotional funeral in his compound in the West Bank city of Ramallah. The Palestinian leader was laid to rest amid chaotic scenes, as thousands of mourners mobbed his coffin as it was carried on its final journey. Earlier, there was a funeral ceremony in Cairo, where foreign dignitaries paid their respects to the man who for decades was a symbol of the Palestinian resistance. Palestinian officials announced they expected to hold elections by January 9th to choose a successor.

Within hours after Mr. Arafat's funeral in Ramallah on Friday, President Bush and British Prime Minister Tony Blair called for reinvigorating efforts to establish a democratic Palestinian state and peace between Israelis and Palestinians. The mood at Yasser Arafat's Muqata compound was calm and composed. Palestinians still filed past his marble coffin to lay wreaths, flowers and olive branches and to say prayers. But gone was the raw emotion that characterized his funeral a day earlier when tens of thousands of mourners swarmed in and around the compound to say goodbye to their leader of 40 years as he was laid to rest.

While Friday had been dedicated to remembering the Palestinian leader, the talk Saturday turned toward the future. Palestinian law calls for elections within 60 days to choose a successor to Mr. Arafat as president of the Palestinian Authority. Palestinians officials said they expected to hold the vote within that timeframe. Some called on the international community to help by pressuring Israel into pulling back from the Palestinian territories to allow a proper election to take place.

15

Change of Modus Operandi Terrorism Online

TERRORISM IN CYBERSPACE

Cyber terrorism is a part of information warfare and is a generic term that involves a number of hostile activities towards society with political, religious, ideological and/or ethnical aims. The purpose of an action is to disturb, distort, manipulate or destroy an opponent's critical information and communication infrastructure, SCADA. Cyber terrorism is comprised of different types of means and methods such as computer network operations (CNO), electronic warfare (EW) and psychological operations (PsyOps). More or less daily cyber attacks occur today: hacking, distribution of viruses, trojans and worms, password thefts etc. By using functionality providing denial of services (DOS) and spamming, it is possible to overload and saturate an opponent's servers in order to delay or interrupt communication. Qualified hackers outside an organisation or planted within it could perform industrial espionage.

Companies, authorities and individuals are exposed to exploitation and penetration campaigns. There are numerous examples of fraud attempts against important public systems such as bank accounts and information stored in databases. In some cases, the activities are quite harmless, in others considerably more serious and costly for the target. Incidents have been reported from Sweden and abroad where cyber terrorists may be the originators. For law enforcement authorities it is difficult to clarify the people and organisations behind an attack. Hence, it is not always possible to identify either the aggressor or the real purpose behind it.

The Internet makes it possible to act anonymously provided that the cyber antagonists have proper skills and knowledge of how to avoid digital tracing and computer forensics. The consequences so far, in terms of dead and wounded, have been very limited compared to the effect of traditional terrorism. However, a directed and qualified cyber attack against critical information systems could have great effects on society and could be lethal depending on what system is being attacked. To gain public trust it is essential for authorities to deal effectively with the situation in an upcoming cyber crisis.

Even if the cyber attack fails due to effective prevention techniques such as IDS and others, it is important to realise that the aggressor may have collected valuable knowledge and information. Every attack, if it succeeds or not, exposes the target groups vulnerability, for instance what type of protection mechanisms and methods that are used by the defender. This is vital information in a any future operation. Hence, a cyber attack can be regarded as asymmetric in the sense that the target groups do not get any information about the aggressors own vulnerabilities or constraints. Evidence shows that, over a period of time terrorists and other hostile actors develop methods and strategies for conducting electronic and digital attacks on a larger scale. Especially dangerous and lethal will be the case when insurgents learn to use EW more frequently for instance against air traffic systems and GPS.

The costs for carrying out such operations are quite low but the effects would be massive. Collin estimates that the number of cyber attacks will increase over a period of time. That implies that ordinary analysis models, used for monitoring traditional terrorist activities, have to be adjusted to the new information warfare threats, such as cyber terrorism. Therefore the methods have to be adapted to changes in insurgents' logic and modus operandi as well as attack patterns in the cyber arena, their usage of advanced IW- weapons, technological knowledge and organisational structures et cetera.

ACTORS AND ANTAGONIST IN CYBER SPACE

There is a discrepancy between actors and antagonists. Actors are individuals, groups and organisations that have the ability to conduct malicious activities but lack motives for doing so. Antagonists on the other hand, are groups that have the motives, resources and willingness to conduct operations of different kinds against specific targets. Over a period of time an actor could transform to an antagonist and vice versa. The choice of organisational structure depends on objectives and goals, resources and the historical backgrounds of the insurgents. In order to fulfil a certain task the antagonist could be organised in a wide range of structures from hierarchical ones to adhoc-networks.

The first could be an intelligence organisation, the latter a terrorist cell acting more ore less autonomously depending on intention. Al-Qaeda, for instance, have a centralised command that decides overall goals but acts in a distributed and autonomous way at lower levels with a high degree of freedom of actions for the cell members. Some examples of different types of antagonists in the cyber arena are script kiddies, crackers, hackers, hacktivists, cyber terrorists and insiders. Some decisive factors in determining whether an individual becomes a cyber terrorist in a specific situation are: personal motivation, risk acceptance, current personal circumstances, IT-skills, and ethical/moral limitations and restrictions.

When planning an attack there is also some kind of economical and personal risk evaluation of whether the operation will succeed or not in relation to the potential cost of conducting the operation. The term 'cyber terrorist' can be divided into "pure" cyber terrorists and "traditional" terrorists using Internet for coordination of (physical) activities. The boundary between them is not sharp and tends to blur. Contrary to traditional terrorists the "pure" cyber terrorists wants to act anonymously on the Internet as well as to hide the real intention behind an info logical attack as long as possible. The Internet is both the tool and enabler of cyber attacks. For an insurgent, the nature of terrorism online is quite safe, beneficial and hard to detect compared to that of traditional terrorist action.

The numbers of identified cyber attempts with a lethal outcome are low, so far. But cyber terrorists have tried to attack critical infrastructure with a varying degrees of success. An insider could act as a cyber terrorist. This type of antagonist is by definition placed within an organisation. Such persons could act independently, without any support from outside. Driving forces for this category of individuals is discontent with the current situation and a feeling of unfair treatment from management and/or by co-workers. Redundancy processes and organisational cut backs could provoke the behaviour as well as economical benefits. Insiders, for instance individuals that hold terrorist sympathies in combination with good IT-skills, could also be planted in an organisation.

The purpose and goal is to steal vital information, to put malware into control functions or to open up for future attacks. Such individuals apply for work in high tech companies, research agencies and public authorities etc. that are responsible for critical infrastructure. The consequences of insider activity can be serious.

RESOURCES AND MEANS

The combination of resources together with motives, driving forces and current security situation, defines and steers possible antagonistic approaches. Compared to single individuals (stand alone) and smaller groups, Intelligence agencies for instance could supply and house large resources.

Resources may vary over time and comprise personal, economical and logistical resources as well as knowledge in and access to (IT and EW) weapons and networks. Some examples of cyber weapons are logical bombs, worms, viruses and trojans. Electronic warfare weapons could be used for monitoring and jamming mobile communication and navigation system GPS. By directed microwave pulses (EMP), electronic components could be destroyed.

As mentioned, there is a relation between cost and risk. The probability for an insurgent to conduct a qualified cyber attack depends on calculated costs and the risk of detection by digital tracking methods. The Internet can in many cases provide manuals and instructions on how to either design IW tools or ways to purchase them. For instance it is possible to buy cheap EW-equipment for monitoring and jamming communication systems for a few hundred dollars. Sketches and blueprints are to some extent available on the Net. Compared to the Cold War era, sensitive information is no longer exclusively restricted to the intelligence and military sector but could be available to many people provided that they have the right knowledge and skills to find the information. The barriers against antagonistic operations are likely to decrease over time due to continuing price-reductions in combination with easier access to information on techniques and procedures. It is possible, with small means, to affect critical infrastructure on a large scale, if the motives and willingness are right.

TARGETS, EFFECTS AND CONSEQUENCES

In general, the cyber antagonist wants to act at a large distance from the target (if he or she is not an insider). The apparatus for doing so is quite simple and cheap. To carry out a malicious cyber operation it is enough to have an advanced computer and effective network connected to it. EW weapons may require more sophisticated equipment depending on purpose of the action.

In order to hide the intention of an operation and to avoid digital tracking, an antagonist could use closed peer-to-peer networks and bittorrent-techniques for communication and information exchange. High level security could be achieved between members of a terrorist cell by using acceptance control and continuous approval. Ad-hoc networks are preferred in the sense that the network activates only when necessary and shuts down after the information exchange processes are finished.

By using modern network techniques it is also possible to gain information about objects to attack, to discuss suitable methods and to coordinate people and resources in time and space. The exchange process of sending and receiving important messages can be hidden in information files and on web sites e.g. stegonography. Especially useful for this purpose, are sensitive web sites for instance those that contain pornographic material which can be used to hide information. It makes it hard for counter insurgents to find them.

Available target for attack depends on the purposes and resources of the insurgent. Information about interesting objects could be downloaded from the Internet describing placing of the target, what design and construction it has as well as methods to jam, intercept or to destroy the object. The target could be symbolic, an individual or an organisation but could also be a part of a critical SCADA system such as banking transactions, transmission links, traffic control systems and power networks et cetera. Nunes argues that there are three effects that may occur through information warfare and they are:

- Physical effects: physical destruction of information structure with the consequences that an operation cannot be fulfilled in a proper way because the information services could not be used fully (DOS-attacks). A number of weapons and techniques could be used to knock out electronics; some of them are non-lethal EW weapons such as EMP and RF
- Syntax effects: the purpose is to attack the logic of the information system by delaying information and/or by developing "unpredictable" behaviours in information

through, for instance, the introduction of viruses and trojans, and other hacking activities which include IT-weapons (CNO).

- Semantic effects: to destroy the trust in the system and information by manipulation, change of information and deception which may be harmful for the decision making process.

One conclusion is that there are a wide range of possible targets to attack and the effects and consequences regarding death-rates etc, vary. Regardless of whether the object is a symbol, physical infrastructure, an organisation or an individual, the antagonist may in some cases wish to achieve political-ideological-religious aims by his actions. In these cases the insurgent wants to draw attention and to show to the public that the government and other authorities have failed to provide safety for the citizens.

A feeling of distrust may arise in ordinary people who may feel that the systems or the persons responsible for administrating them can't be trusted. In other cases the insurgents don't want to be detected at all depending on their mission. That case is perhaps the most feared situation of all for authorities working with counter insurgency in the cyber arena.

CHANGE OF CYBER TERRORISM MODUS OPERANDI

Cyber terrorism is a development of traditional terrorism in a new arena using other means but with the same political and ideological aims. The advantages for cyber antagonists are the fact that modern society is heavily dependent on computer networks especially the Internet. The development of cyber terrorism can also be related to misjudgement by western intelligence authorities. To some extent have they failed to understand the insurgents' resources, willingness and motives?

Cyber terrorists are very keen to find information that will help them to map critical infrastructures. Directed attacks against databases are a growing problem in order to collect sensitive information about specific targets, their structure and the level of information security. Another area of concern is the ongoing attempts to plant corrupt information into sensitive databases such as air traffic control systems, nuclear power systems and the pharmaceutical industry. These activities are well planned with clear purposes and goals for the operation as well as desired effects and consequences. The cyber terrorist focuses mainly on civilian targets. Compared to military objects civilian targets are more vulnerable and less protected. Moreover, from an effect perspective the consequences for society will be bigger and it will probably also result in more media attention.

A trend since 2004 is both the change of target picture and modus operandi. The actors have gone from using quite simple working methods to being very rational and sophisticated with great accuracy in their actions. Historically, the cyber antagonists have based their methods on "fishing with a large net" in order to get viable information of any kind. Today their approaches have changed. If they want specific information they are using smaller and more granulated fishnets and only try to catch the fish they are after. Hence, the key questions are: what types of methods are being used by the insurgents and for what purpose? This chapter describes the development of this new professionalism exemplified by al-Qaeda and other terrorist groups such as al-Mujahedin and their usage of modern information technology techniques and procedures for ideological and political purposes.

THE AL-QAEDA EXAMPLE

In the early stages of the battle against terrorism, the western intelligence authorities' misjudged al-Qaeda strives to become an actor in the cyber arena. For a period of time some "experts" on terrorism thought that the organisation was more or less based on a bunch of misled individuals that lived under simple conditions in the Torabora-mountains in Afghanistan. Moreover, they were thought to lack overall strategies and goals others than traditional terrorism as well as the competence to use modern ICT techniques.

The problem with such narrow description is that it doesn't consider either the educational elite that is the basis and inner circle of the organisation nor the leadership and organisational structure. The terror group is built on decentralised networks with relatively autonomous cells spread over a large number of countries in all continents. There is no direct contact between the cells and top management acting as a central command. The development of an overall ideology, description of main objectives and initiator of attacks are defined by the top level. The autonomous groups plan and conduct operations by themselves.

A possible strategy and way of working in the preparation process for a cyber operation is the following:

Within strategic management so called "dispatchers" coordinate the information gathering process looking for suitable targets to be attacked. The reasons for using dispatchers are, except for the coordination process, to reduce own vulnerabilities and to limit the cyber terror networks knowledge of its own size and channels. If the counter insurgency authorities discover the network the damage will be limited. A member of a cyber network doesn't necessarily have to have any ideological or political sympathies. Moreover, people at lower levels do not always know that they are a part of an operation. Instead they are used as useful idiots for the inner circle's higher intents and purposes.

Through the dispatchers the top management level tries to attend actively on as many "bulletin boards" as possible on the Internet that discuss information assurance, cracking and hacking techniques etc. The purpose is to create channels and to make contacts with hacker- and cracker communities on the Web. By using faked usernames and identities they can act anonymously and pretend to be "legal" members of the community. When a membership is established they try to get sensitive information from the bulletin boards by adding questions and "thoughts", for instance regarding types of security problems a target system or network may have. The questions is said to describe problems that the (fake) member can't solve by him self.

By using a method built on pieces of a puzzle, where questions are added in small portions to a number of bulletin boards, they can gather relevant information piece by piece. Over time a clear picture of the selected target system and its vulnerabilities is produced. Based on that information the critical infrastructure will be reviewed together with methods for making penetration attacks. This information is appropriated without displaying either the full purpose of the operation or those behind the questions.

Consequently, the task for the dispatchers is to co-ordinate and to synchronize contact people towards the hacker and cracker communities. Dispatchers may also organise the requested information and deliver it to the dispatchers contact at top level management. In 2005 the London police found in a raid e-mail correspondence between the Islamic organisation *al-Muhajirun* highest ranking leader Omar Bakri Mohammed and well known al-Qaeda sympathizers.

The documents included the following content:

"In a matter of time, you will see attacks on the stock market. I would not be surprised if tomorrow, I hear of a big economic collapse because of somebody attacking the main technical systems in big companies."

According to Hamid Mir, editor at the newspaper Ausaf, Usama biń-Laden said following:

> *" that hundreds of young men have pledged to him that they were ready to die and that hundreds of Muslims scientists were with him and who would use their knowledge in chemistry, biology and ranging from computer to electronics against infidels".*

Moreover, Bin-Laden is said to be given instructions to his sympathizers similar to "it is very important to attack the American economy because of the fact that US military strength is based on the economy". The above mentioned quotations and statements describe quite well the capability of the al-Qaeda's inner circle to judge what type of technological competence is required for conducting cyber attacks.

Recruitment

In comparison to the strategies and methods used by traditional terrorists in recruiting and converting young stray persons of Muslim background to become suicide bombers, the logic of cyber terrorism differs somewhat as does the work to develop competence and recruit the right people. The vein of the terrorists is based on a good and continuous supply of sympathizers. There are several methods for recruiting self-sacrificing individuals. Common ways are articles, using local preachers, audio-videos and cds describing the "cause". Other more intricate ones are recruitment sites on the Web. The websites describe the history of the organisation and overall goals of the struggle. These websites are often linked to other sites that could be of interest to a dedicated person and encourage enlistment.

The people they want to recruit for cyber actions are very skilled, often with higher education from universities. They understand the western culture and some of them are born in Europe and USA with full citizenship. Contrary to traditional terrorist, they are not potential suicide bombers. The terror groups also use web pages that make it possible to donate funds for deserving purposes or operations that will be conducted.

The e-mail correspondence and recruitment sites show that al-Qaeda and other insurgent organisations have moved from traditional terrorist activities into the cyber arena. The impression is that the opponent is well qualified with good ability to take action. The members have high education, good training and the organisation thus has access to competent individuals with knowledge of information technology.

OTHER EXAMPLES OF CYBER TERRORISM

Another type of insurgent in the cyber arena is the terror

group al-Mujahedin. The organization is, compared to al-Qaeda, based and sponsored by a single country in the Middle East. In March 2007 an Islamic recruiting site was found with a directed request to the viewers to join a special pact called "Hilf al-Muhajaidin". The reader was informed that, in order to be enlisted, he or she must accept leadership of Muhajaidin brigades. The purpose, in translation from Arabic, was to "conduct cyber warfare, to solemnly offer obedience to its leaders in all situations, not to question the leadership as well as not to hesitate to conduct attacks towards goals that violate or could harm Islam and Muslims".

The request shows clearly that new forms of terrorism appear to be addressed solely to well educated persons and not to suicide bombers in a traditional sense. Furthermore, the supporters of the organisation perceive themselves as devoted soldiers closely united by a pact in order to execute an ideological mission. Today there are at least six prominent hacker groupings that represent Muhajaidin with their own websites. Except for recruitment, the websites are used as communication links between other groupings that are involved in the electronic jihad. Some examples of information that is co-ordinated from the websites are: IP- addresses to the target that will be attacked as well as the type of information that will be transmitted and to whom.

To avoid any discovery attempts from counter insurgency authorities, those responsible for the websites encourage and teach the supporters how to behave anonymously on the Internet. During March 2007 an Islamic forum carried out a survey on the Internet directed to its Muslim "hacktivist brothers". The questions addressed to the respondents were to point out without any order of precedence the most important targets for an electronic jihad attack. The answers show that the hacktivists prioritize websites associated with Western financial systems, homepages connected to CIA/FBI as well as servers used by the military. Only some weeks after the proposal on the forum, a list of IP-addresses to key western military institutions was published on one of the Islamic hacker grouping websites.

Simultaneously, another group declared in a web message that the group under the code name "the Electronic Guantanamo Raid" had well defined plans including dates to conduct cyber attacks against US banking systems. At the last moment the operation was cancelled due to a warning to the banks. The web message clarified also that: " the panic shown by the intense media attention, points out that it is important for us to attack sensitive web pages".

The messenger added following: "if we attack websites serving financial exchange and banks, and we makes them inaccessible for days or only for couple of hours, that will render multi million damages". "By that we proclaim to all members of this forum to focus on that type of websites. We invite all other Muslims that have the possibility to take part in the Islamic intifada, to attack website connected to American bank and financial system".

Furthermore, a suggestion was presented describing methods for the electronic jihads to conduct denial of service attacks, viruses etc, with the aim of shutting down vital nodes to create financial chaos. From a counter insurgency perspective, information on whether the jihadists have been successful or not in their intentions is vague and unclear. The information shown on jihad websites is limited with two exceptions. The first example is from October 2006. In a message on an Islamic website a direct link was shown connected to surveillance system at Anchorage airport. There was also a link to an administrative system that gave the "surfer" access to the airport security cameras.

If this was an authentic penetration campaign, it indicates that Islamic hackers have pretty good computer capabilities due to the fact that the systems were guarded by intense security arrangements. The second example is from 2005 when the 22 year old Londoner Younis Tsouli, better known as Irahbi 007, was taken into custody by the British police. In his short but vigorous existence as cyber terrorist he managed the hacker manuals of the Mujahedin members. Irhabi also penetrated American university servers and used them for loading up files with jihad related contents. Terrorism in the cyber arena is a growing problem. In order to reduce danger to the open society from online threats as well as to act proactively, it is important to gain knowledge and to develop strategies and tactics for counter-action. The methods must be adapted to the change of insurgent logic and modus operandi. A fruitful method may be the actor-target-effect chain together with other procedures. Moreover, the threat from cyber terrorism will be a challenging task to deal with for the law enforcement agencies around the globe. Cooperation between authorities and organisations is therefore a necessity.

COUNTER-TERRORISM

Counter-terrorism refers to the practices, tactics, techniques, and strategies that governments, militaries, police departments and corporations adopt in response to terrorist threats and/or acts, both real and imputed. The tactic of terrorism is available to insurgents and governments. Not all insurgents use terror as a tactic, and some choose not to use it because other tactics work better for them in a particular context. Individuals, such as Timothy McVeigh, may also engage in terrorist acts such as the Oklahoma City bombing.

If the terrorism is part of a broader insurgency, counter-terrorism may also form a part of a counter-insurgency doctrine, but political, economic, and other measures may focus more on the insurgency than the specific acts of terror. Foreign internal defense (FID) is a term used by several countries for programs either to suppress insurgency, or reduce the conditions under which insurgency could develop. Counter-terrorism includes both the detection of potential acts and the response to related events.

Anti-terrorism vs Counter-terrorism

The concept of anti-terrorism emerges from a thorough examining of the concept of terrorism as well as an attempt to understand and articulate what constitutes terrorism in Western terms. It must be remembered that in military contexts, terrorism is a tactic, not an ideology. Terrorism may be a tactic in a war between nation-states, in a civil war, or in an insurgency.

Counter-terrorism refers to offensive strategies intended to prevent a belligerent, in a broader conflict, from successfully using the tactic of terrorism. The U.S. military definition, compatible with the definitions used by NATO and many other militaries, is "Operations that include the offensive measures taken to prevent, deter, preempt, and respond to terrorism." In other words, counter-terrorism is a set of techniques for denying an opponent the use terrorism-based tactics, just as counter-air is a set of techniques for denying the opponent the use of attack aircraft.

Anti-terrorism is defensive, intended to reduce the chance of an attack using terrorist tactics at specific points, or to reduce the vulnerability of possible targets to such tactics. "Defensive measures used to reduce the vulnerability of individuals and property to terrorist acts, to include limited response and containment by local military and civilian forces." To continue the analogy between air and terrorist capability, offensive counter-air missions attack the airfields of the opponent, while defensive counter-air uses antiaircraft missiles to protect a point on one's own territory. The ongoing Israeli-Palestinian conflict, Sri Lankan Civil War, and Colombian Civil War are examples of conflicts where terrorism is present, along with other tactics, so that a participant uses counter and anti-terrorism to limit the opponent's use of terror tactics.

PLANNING FOR DETECTING AND NEUTRALIZING POTENTIAL TERRORIST ACTS

Building a counter-terrorism plan involves all segments of a society or many government agencies. In dealing with foreign terrorists, the lead responsibility is usually at the national level. Because propaganda and indoctrination lie at the core of terrorism, understanding their profile and functions increases the ability to counter terrorism more effectively. Most counter-terrorism strategies involve an increase in standard police and domestic intelligence. The central activities are traditional: interception of communications, and the tracing of persons. New technology has, however, expanded the range of military and law enforcement operations. Domestic intelligence is often directed at specific groups, defined on the basis of origin or religion, which is a source of political controversy. Mass surveillance of an entire population raises objections on civil liberties grounds.

To select the effective action when terrorism appears to be more of an isolated event, the appropriate government organizations need to understand the source, motivation, methods of preparation, and tactics of terrorist groups. Good intelligence is at the heart of such preparation, as well as political and social understanding of any grievances that might be solved. Ideally, one gets information from inside the group, a very difficult challenge for HUMINT because operational terrorist cells are often small, with all members known to one another, perhaps even related. Counter-intelligence is a great challenge with the security of cell-based systems, since the ideal, but nearly impossible, goal is to obtain a clandestine source within the cell. Financial tracking can play a role, as can communications intercept, but both of these approaches need to be balanced against legitimate expectations of privacy.

TERRORISM AND HUMAN RIGHTS

One of the primary difficulties of implementing effective counter-terrorist measures is the waning of civil liberties and individual privacy that such measures often entail, both for citizens of, and for those detained by states attempting to combat terror. At times, measures designed to tighten security have been seen as abuses of power or even violations of human rights. Examples of these problems can include prolonged, incommunicado detention without judicial review; risk of subjecting to torture during the transfer, return and extradition of people between or within countries; and the adoption of security measures that restrain the rights or freedoms of citizens and breach principles of non-discrimination. Examples include:

- In November 2003 Malaysia passed new counter-terrorism

laws that were widely criticized by local human rights groups for being vague and overbroad. Critics claim that the laws put the basic rights of free expression, association, and assembly at risk. Malaysia persisted in holding around 100 alleged militants without trial, including five Malaysian students detained for alleged terrorist activity while studying in Karachi, Pakistan.

- In November 2003 a Canadian-Syrian national, Maher Arar, alleged publicly that he had been tortured in a Syrian prison after being handed over to the Syrian authorities by U.S.
- In December 2003 Colombia's congress approved legislation that would give the military the power to arrest, tap telephones and carry out searches without warrants or any previous judicial order.
- Images of torture and ill-treatment of detainees in US custody in Iraq and other locations have jeopardized the legitimacy of the US war on terrorism and brought on international scrutiny.
- Hundreds of foreign nationals remain in prolonged indefinite detention without charge or trial in Guantánamo Bay, despite international and US constitutional standards outlawing such practices.
- Hundreds of people suspected of connections with the Taliban or al Qa'eda remain in long-term arbitrary detention in Pakistan or in US-controlled centres in Afghanistan.
- China has used the "war on terror" to justify its repression policies in the predominantly Muslim Xinjiang Uighur Autonomous Region to stifle Uighur identity.
- In Morocco, Saudi Arabia, Tunisia, Yemen and other countries, scores of people have been arrested and arbitrarily detained in connection with suspected terrorist acts or links to opposition armed groups.
- Until 2005 eleven men remained in high security detention in the UK under the Anti-Terrorism, Crime and Security Act 2001.

Many would argue that such violations exacerbate rather than counter the terrorist threat. Human rights advocates argue for the crucial role of human rights protection as an intrinsic part to fight against terrorism. This suggests, as proponents of human security have long argued, that respecting human rights may indeed help us to incur security. Amnesty International included a section on confronting terrorism in the recommendations in the Madrid Agenda arising from the Madrid Summit on Democracy and Terrorism:

> "Democratic principles and values are essential tools in the fight against terrorism. Any successful strategy for dealing with terrorism requires terrorists to be isolated. Consequently, the preference must be to treat terrorism as criminal acts to be handled through existing systems of law enforcement and with full respect for human rights and the rule of law. We recommend: (1) taking effective measures to make impunity impossible either for acts of terrorism or for the abuse of human rights in counter-terrorism measures. (2) the incorporation of human rights laws in all anti-terrorism programmes and policies of national governments as well as international bodies."

While international efforts to combat terrorism have focused on the need to enhance cooperation between states, proponents of human rights (as well as human security) have suggested that more effort needs to be given to the effective inclusion of human rights protection as a crucial element in that cooperation. They argue that international human rights obligations do not stop at borders and a failure to respect human rights in one state may undermine its effectiveness in the international effort to cooperate to combat terrorism.

Preemptive Neutralization

Some countries see preemptive attacks as a legitimate strategy. This includes capturing, killing, or disabling suspected terrorists before they can mount an attack. Israel, the United States, and Russia have taken this approach, while Western European states generally do not. Another major method of preemptive neutralization is interrogation of known or suspected terrorists to obtain information about specific plots, targets, the identity of other terrorists, and whether the interrogation subjects him as guilty of terrorist involvement.

Sometimes more extreme methods are used to increase suggestibility, such as sleep deprivation or drugs. Such methods may lead captives to offer false information in an attempt to stop the treatment, or due to the confusion brought on by it. These methods are not available to European powers because in 1978 the European Court of Human Rights ruled in the Ireland v. United Kingdom case that such methods amounted to a practice of inhuman and degrading treatment, and that such practices were in breach of the European Convention on Human Rights Article 3 (art. 3).

Non-military Preventive Actions

The human security paradigm outlines a non-military approach which aims to address the enduring underlying inequalities which fuel terrorist activity. Causal factors need to be delineated and measures implemented which allow equal access to resources and sustainability for all people. Such activities empower citizens providing 'freedom from fear' and 'freedom from want'.

This can take many forms including the provision of clean drinking water, education, and vaccination programs, provision of food and shelter and protection from violence, military or otherwise. Successful human security campaigns have been characterised by the participation of a diverse group of actors including governments, NGOs, and citizens. Foreign internal defense programs provide outside expert assistance to a threatened government. FID can involve both non-military and military aspects of counter-terrorism.

MILITARY INTERVENTION

Terrorism has often been used to justify military intervention in countries where terrorists are said to be based.

That was the main stated justification for the U.S. invasion of Afghanistan. It was also a stated justification for the second Russian invasion of Chechnya. History has shown that military intervention has rarely been successful in stopping or preventing terrorism. Although military action can disrupt a terrorist group's operations temporarily, it rarely ends the threat. Provoking repression is actually a key goal of terrorism, as most of the time it increases the popularity of the terrorist cause as well as furthers the motivation for continuing terrorism.

Most probably such a strategy against terrorism is not successful and cannot be as the structural causes of terrorism are not addressed: Relative deprivation that leads to frustration, aggressive foreign policy that leads to 'hate', and psychosocial effects of globalization (as well as other causes) are not solved. Thus repression by the military in itself (particularly if it is not accompanied by other measures) usually leads to short term victories, but tend to be unsuccessful in the long run (e.g. the French's doctrine described in Roger Trinquier's book *Modern War* used in Indochina and Algeria). However, new methods (see the new *Counter-insurgency* Field Manual) such as those taken in Iraq have yet to be seen as beneficial or ineffectual.

PLANNING FOR RESPONSE TO TERRORISM

Police, fire, and emergency medical response organizations have obvious roles. Local firefighters and emergency medical personnel (often called "first responders") have plans for mitigating the effects of terrorist attacks, although police may deal with threats of such attacks. Whatever the target of terrorists, there are multiple ways of hardening the targets to prevent the terrorists from hitting their mark, or reducing the damage of attacks. One method is to place Jersey barrier or other sturdy obstacles outside tall or politically sensitive buildings to prevent car and truck bombing.

Aircraft cockpits are kept locked during flights, and have reinforced doors, which only the pilots in the cabin are capable of opening. English train stations removed their waste bins in response to the Provisional IRA threat, as convenient locations for depositing bombs. Scottish stations removed theirs after the 7th of July bombing of London as a precautionary measure. The Massachusetts Bay Transportation Authority purchased bomb-resistant barriers after the September 11 terrorist attacks.

A more sophisticated target-hardening approach must consider industrial and other critical industrial infrastructure that could be attacked. Terrorists need not import chemical weapons if they can cause a major industrial accident such as the Bhopal disaster or the Halifax explosion. Industrial chemicals in manufacturing, shipping, and storage need greater protection, and some efforts are in progress. To put this risk into perspective, the first major lethal chemical attack in WWI used 160 tons of chlorine. Industrial shipments of chlorine widely used in water purification and the chemical industry, travel in 90 or 55 ton tank cars.

To give one more example, the North American electrical grid has already demonstrated, in the Northeast Blackout of 2003, its vulnerability to natural disasters coupled with inadequate, possibly insecure, SCADA (supervisory control and data acquisition) networks. Part of the vulnerability is due to deregulation leading to much more interconnection in a grid designed for only occasional power-selling between utilities. A very few terrorists, attacking key power facilities when one or more engineers have infiltrated the power control centers, could wreak havoc.

Equipping likely targets with containers (i.e., bags) of pig lard has been utilized to discourage attacks by Islamist suicide bombers. The technique was apparently used on a limited scale by British authorities in the 1940s. The approach stems from the idea that Muslims perpetrating the attack would not want to be "soiled" by the lard in the moment prior to dying. The idea has been suggested more recently as a deterrent to suicide bombings in Israel. However, the actual effectiveness of this tactic is probably limited as it is possible that a sympathetic Islamic scholar could issue a fatwa proclaiming that a suicide bomber would not be polluted by the swine products.

Command and Control

In North America and other continents, for a threatened or completed terrorist attack, the Incident Command System (ICS) is apt to be invoked to control the various services that may need to be involved in the response. ICS has varied levels of escalation, such as might be needed for multiple incidents in a given area (e.g., the 2005 bombings in London or the 2004 Madrid train bombings, or all the way to a National Response Plan invocation if national-level resources are needed. National response, for example, might be needed for a nuclear, biological, radiological, or large chemical attack.

Damage Mitigation

Fire departments, perhaps supplemented by public works agencies, utility providers (e.g., gas, water, electricity), and heavy construction contractors, are most apt to deal with the physical consequences of an attack.

Local Security

Again under an incident command model, local police can isolate the incident area, reducing confusion, and specialized police units can conduct tactical operations against terrorists, often using specialized counter-terrorist tactical units. Bringing in such units will normally involve civil or military authority beyond the local level.

Medical Services

Emergency medical services will bring the more seriously affected victims to hospitals, which will need to have mass casualty and triage plans in place. Public health agencies, from local to national level, may be designated to deal with identification, and sometimes mitigation, of possible biological attacks, and sometimes chemical or radiologic contamination.

Counter-terrorism Tactical Units

Today, many countries have special units designated to handle terrorist threats. Besides various security agencies, there are elite tactical units, also known as special mission units, whose role is to directly engage terrorists and prevent terrorist attacks. Such units perform both in preventive actions, hostage rescue and responding to ongoing attacks. Countries of all sizes can have highly trained counter-terrorist teams. Tactics, techniques and procedures for manhunting are under constant development.

Most of these measures deal with terrorist attacks that affect an area, or threaten to do so. It is far harder to deal with assassination, or even reprisals on individuals, due to the short (if any) warning time and the quick exfiltration of the assassins. Of course, if the assassination is done by a suicide bomber, exfiltration becomes moot.

These units are specially trained in tactics and are very well equipped for CQB with emphasis on stealth and performing the mission with minimal casualties. The units include takeover force (assault teams), snipers, EOD experts, dog handlers and intelligence officers. The majority of counter-terrorism operations at the tactical level, are conducted by state, federal and national law enforcement agencies or intelligence agencies. In some countries, the military may be called in as a last resort. Obviously, for countries whose military are legally permitted to conduct police operations, this is a non-issue, and such counter-terrorism operations are conducted by their military.

MILITARY COUNTER-TERRORIST ORGANIZATIONS BY COUNTRY

Given the nature of operational counter-terrorism tasks national military organisations do not generally have dedicated units whose sole responsibility is the prosecution of these tasks. Instead the counter-terrorism function is an element of the role, allowing flexibility in their employment, with operations being undertaken in the domestic or international context. In some cases the legal framework within which they operate prohibits military units conducting operations in the domestic arena; United States Department of Defense policy, based on the Posse Comitatus Act, forbids domestic counter-terrorism operations by the US military.

Units allocated some operational counter-terrorism task are frequently Special Forces or similar assets. In cases where military organisations do operate in the domestic context some form of formal handover from the law enforcement community is regularly required, to ensure adherence to the legislative framework and limitations such as the Iranian Embassy Siege, the British police formally turned responsibility over to the Special Air Service when the situation went beyond police capabilities.

16

CIA and the Terrorist Organisation

The CIA itself a ruthless, terrorist organisation inspires terrorism in response. In some cases, notably the CIA and al Qaeda, the relationship between the CIA and terrorism is symbiotic. The CIA has perpetrated an "American Holocaust", the deaths of some 6 million people from its inception to the year 1987. As long as the CIA Exists, the US will never be safe from terrorism. CIA operations follow the same recurring script. First, American business interests abroad are threatened by a popular or democratically elected leader. The people support their leader because he intends to conduct land reform, strengthen unions, redistribute wealth, nationalize foreign-owned industry, and regulate business to protect workers, consumers and the environment. So, on behalf of American business, and often with their help, the CIA mobilizes the opposition. First it identifies right-wing groups within the country (usually the military), and offers them a deal: "We'll put you in power if you maintain a favorable business climate for us." The Agency then hires, trains and works with them to overthrow the existing government (usually a democracy).

Pakistan is a case in point. Since 9/11, the Bush administration has been propping up Musharraf's military regime with $3.6 billion in economic aid from the US and a

US-sponsored consortium, not to mention $900 million in military aid and the postponement of overdue debt repayments totaling $13.5 billion. But now the administration is debating whether Musharraf has become too dependent on Islamic extremist political parties in Pakistan to further US interests, and whether he should be pressured to permit the return of two exiled former prime ministers, Benazir Bhutto and Nawaz Sharif, who have formed an electoral alliance to challenge him in presidential elections scheduled for next year.

The late Benazir Bhutto revealed the truth before she was brutally gunned down in the streets of Karachi: US policy causes world terrorism. She died before she could tell the rest of the story.

When the United States aligns with dictatorships and totalitarian regimes, it compromises the basic democratic principles of its foundation — namely, life, liberty and justice for all. Dictatorships such as Musharraf's suppress individual rights and freedoms and empower the most extreme elements of society. Oppressed citizens, unable to represent themselves through other means, often turn to extremism and religious fundamentalism.

A favorite CIA tactic is the CIA "front". The May 12 terrorist attacks on the al Hamra, Jadawal and Vinnell compounds in the Saudi Arabian capital, Riyadh, which killed more than 90 people, were not merely assaults on "symbols" of the imperialist West. The bombers were also intent on weakening the rule of Saudi royal family. While the timing of the bombings in Saudi Arabia and in other countries - just hours before US Secretary of State Colin Powell arrived in Saudi Arabia - suggested a coordinated assault on US targets, the bombings in Riyadh were targeted at key props of the reactionary regime. All three Saudi Arabian targets were associated with Saudi Arabia's role as a US client state: residential compounds housing mainly expatriates working in the country, the offices of the Vinnell Corporation and the residences of its employees. Vinnell, founded in California in 1931, first gained a foothold in Saudi Arabia in 1975.

An article by Matt Gaul in the June 1998 Loyola of Los Angeles Law Review, revealed that it was the culmination of a close relationship between the corporation, the US military and Washington's intelligence agencies. This relationship stretched back to the end of World War II, when the US government used the company to ship supplies to the China's counter-revolutionary party, the Kuomintang. During the 1950s and '60s, Vinnell constructed US military airfields in Japan, Okinawa, Taiwan, Thailand and southern Vietnam. According to Gaul, it was during this period that Albert Vinnell, the corporation's founder, "offered his staff's services to the [CIA], and several CIA agents used employment with Vinnell as cover for operations in Africa and the Middle East".

It uses every trick in the book: propaganda, stuffed ballot boxes, purchased elections, extortion, blackmail, sexual intrigue, false stories about opponents in the local media, infiltration and disruption of opposing political parties, kidnapping, beating, torture, intimidation, economic sabotage, death squads and even assassination. These efforts culminate in a military coup, which installs a right-wing dictator. The CIA trains the dictator's security apparatus to crack down on the traditional enemies of big business, using interrogation, torture and murder. The victims are said to be "communists," but almost always they are just peasants, liberals, moderates, labor union leaders, political opponents and advocates of free speech and democracy. Widespread human rights abuses follow.

The CIA uses all those methods to install dictators like Musharraf, whom it most certainly trained. The CIA is ruthless in its ongoing efforts to eliminate with torture and murder, if necessary, all opposition to the interests of American imperialists. Saddam Hussein was among the dictators propped up by the US, the CIA specifically. Saddam ran afoul of Bush Sr by opposing efforts by the Bush regime to keep the price of oil high. The tran script of US Ambassador April Glaspie's interview with Hussein on the eve of his invasion of Kuwait proves conclusively that Hussein had been set up by the master spy —George Bush Sr. The CIAs allegiance to the US oil industry is overt and is most certainly at the very heart of well-founded suspicions about the CIA, Texas oil barons, and JFK. Dealy Plaza is said to have been the nexus of all three! The origins of Bush's war in Iraq may be found in the Arab Oil embargo of the 1970s.

Three decades ago, in the throes of the energy crisis, Washington's hawks conceived of a strategy for US control of the Persian Gulf's oil. Now, with the same strategists firmly in control of the White House, the Bush administration is playing out their script for global dominance. In the geopolitical vision driving current US policy toward Iraq, the key to national security is global hegemony – dominance over any and all potential rivals. To that end, the United States must not only be able to project its military forces anywhere, at any time. It must also control key resources, chief among them oil – and especially Gulf oil. JFK promised to "smash the CIA into a thousand pieces".

Bill Clinton, on the 50th anniversary of "the company", defended it with an absurdity that one might have expected from the GOP! Americans, Clinton said, don't know or understand what the CIA does and should, therefore, lay off! Our not knowing what the CIA is up to is precisely the problem. Bill Clinton is as dead wrong on this issue as Barack Obama is dead wrong about Ronald Reagan. Both positions are premised upon the idea that the American people are stupid and those that are not ought to be! The fact is: the CIA is out of control and they will continue to get away with it as long as the American people are either ignorant, kept in the dark, or both! Because the CIA is unaccountable and remains a cancerous source of unchecked corruption and most certainly the inspiration for generations of American hating terrorists who will fight back in kind! Much has been written about the CIA's operations, by insiders and outsiders.

One insider who has chronicled what he witnessed in the CIA is Ralph McGehee. He worked for the CIA from 1952 until 1977 and now writes about intelligence matters, notably the book *Deadly Deceits* – My 25 years in the CIA (New York: Sheridan Square Press, 1983). He has compiled a computer data base on CIA activities. Persons interested may write to him at: 422 Arkansas Ave., Herndon, VA 22070.

Here are some excerpts of what he has written:

> "...it is essential to provide background on the scope and nature of its worldwide operations. Between 1961 and 1975 the Agency conducted 900 major or sensitive operations, and thousands of lesser covert actions. The majority of its operations were propaganda, election or paramilitary. Countries of major concern, such as Indonesia in the early 1960s, were usually subjected to the CIA's most concerted attention. Critics of the CIA have aptly described the mainstays of such attention: "discrediting political groups... by forged documents that may be attributed to them. . . ," faking "communist weapon shipments," capturing communist documents and then inserting forgeries prepared by the Agency's Technical Services Division.

Much of the rest of the world knows the truth about the CIA; Americans are kept in the dark. The media dare not tell the truth about the CIA and the Bush administration, in particular, is complicit. Rare media outlets that dare tell the truth are demonized. "Liberal" activist Steve Kangas, for example, turned up dead just outside the office of Richard Mellon Scaife, the multibillionaire about whom it is no stretch to say he coordinated and bankrolled the "vast right wing conspiracy" to impeach, remove and, in other ways, smear Bill Clinton. As more documents are declassified and the hidden history is made painfully clear, the CIA's predictable response is compared to the Medieval Church's oppressive response to the Scientific Revolution. Indeed, there are many things about the CIAs relationship to the world around it that are medieval: intolerance, fear, repression, secrecy and torture. Initially, the CIA would merely harass American writers but foreign writers were tortured and/or murdered. With the death of Steve Kangas, one wonders if the CIA now operates against the domestic media. What's next? An inquisition? The CIA, whose very is name is enough to inspire generations of "terrorists", has outlived its usefulness. The time has come to abolish the CIA – to smash it into a thousand pieces! Its leadership should be dismissed and investigated. Where there is probable cause, CIA members should be investigated and tried for crimes against humanity.

DEVELOPMENT RESEARCH GROUP

Security is a paramount development issue – for two reasons. First, insecurity, whether due to crime, war, or the violation of economic and noneconomic rights, creates and perpetuates poverty traps: it is both a cause of and is caused by economic underdevelopment. And second, the poorest are most vulnerable to the hazards of insecurity. For example, civil war directly affects or threatens to affect 1.1 billion poor people. One of every five people in Sub-Saharan Africa is directly affected by civil wars. The devastation of war afflicts women, children and uneducated men most heavily; groups that even in non-conflict situations have the greatest incidence of persistent poverty. Our understanding of insecurity has expanded and changed dramatically in the last five years, particularly for crime, terrorism, and civil war. For example, in contrast to the conventional wisdom, which had emphasized the role of social cleavages as a primary cause of conflict and crime, recent research has underlined the role of economic motivations? Research has also revealed that crime and civil war are persistent phenomena: one of the best predictors of future conflict is past conflict; one of the best predictors of future crime rates is past crime rates.

Crime and conflict require sustained policy attention. As our understanding of conflict increases with better data on political violence, crime and terrorism, questions on the intensity and type of conflict come to the fore. Development is surely related to other pressing and related security issues that accompany failed and fragile states: terrorism, drug and human trafficking. The security of personal, property and contract rights is well-known prerequisite of economic growth. Although this is clear, the policy prescriptions are often complex. For instance, does conflict resolution entail tradeoffs between current objectives (stopping the violence) and future objectives (sustaining peace and encouraging development)? Or regarding drug trafficking does the policy of prohibition and criminalization lead to even worse problems for developing countries? We need a better understanding, however, of how governments provide security in all forms to their citizens.

Two World Bank Research Projects on civil war have examined the role of "greed and grievance" in motivating civil conflict. Results from the first research project found a significant economic incentive for conflict: in countries where the cost of rebellion is low, civil war is most likely, suggesting that stagnant growth and pervasive poverty reduce the reservation wages of potential soldiers and rebels. Also, reliance on commodity exports, particularly oil, is significantly related to conflict. Presumably this is because commodity exports can be a ready source of cash for combatant groups, *they* are less sensitive to the depredations of war, and the rights to them are often associated with control of the government. Diasporas can also be a potential source of finance for combatants, decreasing the cost of conflict. Delving deeper, recent research suggests that ethnic polarization and identity, when associated with large horizontal inequalities, can contribute to conflict.

Regional factors and past experience contribute significantly to the likelihood of future civil conflict. Vulnerability to civil wars is persistent and often dependent upon neighbor fragility. Economic, social and political conditions that make civil war more likely in some countries are not generally resolved and may be exacerbated by conflict. Also, instability in neighboring states and international efforts to forcefully establish a political regime can actually be destabilizing. In fact, elections and democratic progress can actually reduce the likelihood of peace and stability, as they can serve as catalysts for civil conflict. Finally, evidence suggests that demobilization, reintegration, and security sector reform must be carefully managed and timed to avoid conflict relapse.

Outside interventions can mitigate the risk of civil war. Ongoing research confirms our initial findings that countries benefit from external intervention and suggest how that intervention should be structured. The policy lessons from this research include:

- Aid flows must be sensitive to the absorptive capacity of post-conflict countries and require an integrated approach. The Bank has responded to this challenge in several ways. The Fragile States Unit (formerly Low Income Countries under Stress, LICUS) initiative has developed new tools for post-conflict financing including pre-arrears clearance grants, a post-conflict IDA window and multidonor trust funds. The Conflict Prevention and Reconstruction Unit has taken a leading role in mainstreaming conflict analysis and designing aid programs for post-conflict countries.
- There is still room for progress in aid effectiveness in post-conflict. Aid often rushes in to post-conflict countries and then falls dramatically after only two or three years, creating volatility and vacuums in government budgeting when these governments are the most vulnerable. Aid guaranteed for longer periods and with less dramatic phaseouts can be more effective. Also, worries about "Dutch disease" and post-conflict inflation are often unfounded, suggesting that monetary controls on government spending of aid to avoid inflation are unwarranted. In fact, research suggests that aid can assist in monetary reconstruction and stability.
- Post-conflict assistance must include institution-building efforts that improve government capacity to make credible commitments. This can be important for both the effective provision of public goods and social services and to guarantee that rebel demobilization and integration into new national armies is successful. The ending of civil wars, especially ethnic wars, may require more explicit commitments by politically mandated international and regional bodies, including military presence for peace-keeping.
- Sustained economic growth can dramatically reduce the risk of conflict. To promote this growth, donors can assist countries at risk in diversifying away from dependence on primary commodities and toward labor-intensive,

processed and manufactured goods. The international community can also contribute to this growth by promoting transparency in relations with fragile states with respect to mineral resources and the nature and composition of aid.

Terrorism is as old as war, but it was only with the attacks of September 2001 in New York and Washington, March 2004 in Madrid, and July 2005 in London that it became a central concern of many governments in the rich countries of the West. This concern prompted policy makers to focus on the potential links to development of both terrorism and the response to terrorism, quickly revealing important lacunae in the literature. To what extent is terrorism related to development? If development is a determinant of terrorism, what are the relative weights of the economic, political and social aspects of development? And what is the development impact of different responses to terrorism?

The forthcoming book *Terrorism, Economic Development, and Political Openness,* a Bank research effort funded by the President's Contingency Fund, addresses these crucial questions, synthesizing what we know about the development links with terrorism - and pointing out what we do not. Four principal conclusions emerge from the volume. Among recent terrorist acts, the 9/11 attacks had the largest economic consequences. But even they were fleeting and leading to a small drop (in percentage terms) in national income ($90 billion over a period in which the US economy generated $10 trillion worth of goods and services).

Growth dropped briefly but quickly returned to its pre-attack path. Poor countries are also frequent targets of terrorist activity. The available evidence indicates that the costs of terrorism are much greater in small, poor countries. Why the difference between large rich and small poor countries? The reasons are intuitive: large, diversified economies are better able to shift resources to less affected sectors. Moreover, rich countries tend to have well-functioning policy institutions that can respond to shocks adroitly and with ample information. It is analytically useful to separate source countries of international terrorism from target countries. The evidence indicates that source countries tend to be poor, politically oppressive, and weakly linked with the rest of the world. Target countries, on the other hand, tend to enjoy economic success and be more democratic and politically open.

Although these results are intuitive in view of recent terrorist attacks in rich countries, they emerge from estimates based on thousands of terrorist episodes recorded in the data. It is also useful to separate aggregate (national or regional) characteristics from household and individual characteristics related to terrorist agents. The evidence indicates that terrorists are driven not by personal poverty, but by the political and economic climate of the countries from which they come. Why should the social environment be more important than individual income? Why are terrorist organizations more common in countries with difficult political climates? The answer may lay in the challenges of constructing a terrorist organization. Even though terrorism is not a purely ideological phenomenon, terrorist organizations depend on ideologically-motivated, educated recruits. Close monitoring by terrorist leaders of their "employees" is not possible. Ideological commitment and education helps solve part of this contracting problem.

The incremental increases in US government expenditures that can be traced to 9/11 amount to $19-$26 billion per year, most of which has gone to domestic security, or $69-96 billion if the military operations in Afghanistan and Iraq are included. Of these expenditures, only $2-4 billion represent incremental annual spending on development assistance. Moreover, the evidence does not suggest that wealthy countries have increased assistance to offset the costs of terrorism for the poor countries that have been victimized by terror. The structure and modus operandi of terrorist organizations vary considerably. They depend on the quality of government institutions, their degree of popular support, the sources and magnitude of funding they receive, and their degree of internal cohesion.

This observation underscores the need for a specifically designed tactical response to fight terrorist organizations.

This tactical approach —focused on the incentives of the marginal actor and the structural weaknesses of the terrorist organization— is likely to be the most successful in the short run. In the long run, however, terrorist organizations would keep reappearing and in different shapes unless their fundamental causes are removed. This is where a development response becomes relevant.

With crime an endemic and growing feature of many developing countries and a significant hurdle to poverty reduction in middle-income and fast-growing poor countries, a large research project on crime uncovered important new insights. Even controlling for illicit drug activity, and cultural and demographic characteristics of countries, economic factors appear to drive homicides and especially robberies. Income inequality and slow economic growth significantly increase the rates of violent crime. In contrast, controlling for these other features of countries, education has no significant impact on violent crime.

We know that crime discourages economic activity—firm expenditures on security exceed 15 percent of their variable costs in some countries. Research has also shown that crime is persistent, even in countries that mitigate its economic causes. Research has tested the arguments that social capital of various kinds can reduce crime. One kind of social capital—individuals' trust of others in their community—was found to reduce crime, controlling for the natural possibility that crime itself should reduce social capital.

Terrorism Engender Common Crime

Research has shown that the incidence of homicides and robberies is the highest and has grown the fastest in countries affected by civil war or terrorism. Common violent crime is often a legacy of these large-scale social ills. The interdependence of all manifestations of conflict is an important issue to be studied in the future. The effectiveness of prohibition and drug criminalization in actually reducing consumption and production of drugs is limited. Although the benefits of prohibition are apparently low across countries, the unintended costs of prohibition seem to be borne disproportionately by developing countries that traditionally grow crops associated with the production of drugs.

These costs range from the loss of wealth of poor farmers involved in the cultivation of these crops to the increased institutional instability caused by criminal organizations that distribute drugs. The recent research on crime does not undercut the importance of effective law enforcement in fighting crime. It emphasizes, however, the key role of social and economic factors. Where public policy allows inequality and low growth to persist, or where it encourages the breakdown of trust in communities, crime will proliferate and crime-fighting policies that rely on law enforcement will be both more expensive and less likely to succeed.

FUTURE RESEARCH ON PEACE AND DEVELOPMENT

Fragile and post-conflict states have special needs in poverty reduction, because they must balance sustainable development while avoiding conflict. As the Bank redoubles efforts to keep these countries on target for the Millennium Development Goals ongoing research will shed light on these important questions. While all developing countries, by definition, face the challenge of poverty reduction, fragile and post-conflict states face the dual challenges of poverty reduction while avoiding relapses or downward spirals into the conflict trap.

Ongoing research in this area focuses on the dual challenge faced by fragile and post-conflict states: How to balance poverty reduction while mitigating risks of civil conflict and violence in three important areas: Political governance and democratization, peace building through peace agreements and power sharing, and effective macro-economic policy for fragile and post-conflict states. Following on successes with a recent conference in Khartoum on "Management of Post-Conflict Transition: The Challenges of

Institutional Reform in Sudan," this project will bring together policymakers from developing countries and distinguished researchers in the areas described above. By bringing researchers and country policymakers together we have found that the resulting research papers are better informed by the needs of practitioners and that the policymakers benefit from the buy-in associated with early involvement in the research process. Case studies exploring the results of the research papers in the context of policymakers' specific country experiences will further increase participation and ownership for countries involved.

17

Evolution of Terrorism Risk Modelling

ROOTS OF TERRORISM MODELLING

As with natural perils, the insurance of international terrorism risks has a long history, predating any attempt at formal risk analysis. In the absence of computational tools, risk management has traditionally relied upon the experience and judgement of specialist political risk underwriters, who have often proven effective and skilful in circumstances where mainstream underwriters have declined to offer terrorism coverage. For certain individual terrorism risks, specialist underwriters might seek the advice of law enforcement or military personnel, proficient at surveying site security. For a regional portfolio, premiums might be set higher for locations historically attacked or threatened by terrorists, and maximum aggregate loss exposure would be carefully monitored and capped, but the overall risk assessment procedure would remain essentially qualitative.

To anticipate rare acts of terrorism, beyond the experience of even the most seasoned underwriter, the judgement of external terrorism experts might be invoked. Terrorism risk management would still be largely qualitative, with underwriting being supported by the greater knowledge and perception of terrorism experts as to the intent and capability of the terrorists. For organizations, such as the IRA, whose acts of terror were politically restrained, this qualitative risk management approach might suffice, but for Al Qaeda, whose threats of violence acknowledge no such political or moral restraint, a more formal analytical methodology is demanded. This methodology has evolved rapidly since 9/11, in response to US insurance industry concerns about the viability of terrorism underwriting, and subsequently the passage of TRIA, the Terrorism Risk Insurance Act.

TRIA applies to foreign terrorism, of which there was little before 9/11, but does not cover domestic terrorism. However, the insurance loss burden from US domestic terrorism has been sufficiently low as to be effectively absorbed within the losses from criminal acts of violence and vandalism, which many home-grown terrorist acts resemble. Attacks on vivisection laboratories, mink farms, hamburger restaurants, ski resorts, sports utility vehicles etc. might be committed under the banner of the Animal or Earth Liberation Front, but nonetheless are crimes by another name. Right-wing militias have hatched more grandiose attack plans by which to rein back perceived government erosion of individual freedom, but such anti-government sentiment diminished after the Oklahoma bombing. Furthermore, left-wing terrorism has never recovered its motivation or state support since the fall of the Berlin wall. As a result, US domestic terrorism may still be treated as a residual background loss burden, geographically distributed broadly across the USA. But whereas US domestic terrorism risk can be managed conveniently at an aggregate loss level, the much more severe threat from Al Qaeda and associated Islamic militants requires scenario-specific modeling.

DETERMINISTIC SCENARIO LOSS MODELING

Coincident with the shock of the 9/11 Al Qaeda attack itself was the shock realization that an enormous aggregate insurance exposure, across many lines of business, was concentrated around a single location. Whatever the terrorist threat may be, insurers need to understand and control their exposure accumulations. Accordingly, GIS software tools are being licensed which allow insurers to map their exposures, and to evaluate loss potential within designated spatial footprints. These losses may vary significantly from one footprint to another, so worthwhile insight is gained by compiling a loss-footprint table. Ranking these losses by severity leads inexorably to the critical actuarial issue of estimating probable maximum loss. In earthquake insurance, a deterministic approach may be taken to estimate Probable Maximum Loss (PML) using the following three-step procedure: identify the fault posing the greatest threat to the portfolio; assign the maximum credible earthquake to the fault; calculate the portfolio loss assuming this sized event occurs on this fault.

For terrorism insurance, this kind of deterministic PML approach may also be attempted, assuming that a maximum credible size of weapon is deployed at the spot where it would cause the worst portfolio loss. This deterministic approach largely removes the human behavioral component from PML estimation, since it assumes pessimistically that the terrorist will have the upper hand in his conflict with counter-terrorism forces, and be allowed the weapon and target of his choosing. This conservative assumption reduces PML estimation to a series of problems in the domain of the engineering, physical, chemical and biological sciences: evaluating the blast effect of a bomb detonation; the extent of fire from a fuel tanker explosion; the radiation fallout from a radiological dispersal device; the spread of contagion from a smallpox outbreak etc. These problems may still be technically complex and challenging, but at least the core mathematical models for blast analysis; conflagration; atmospheric dispersion, pollution transport, epidemiology, etc. are well established.

The models are founded on standard scientific principles, and the model results have some validation against observational or surrogate data. But, as with the vulnerability of individual buildings against earthquake or windstorm loading, lack of detailed information about a building's protection against a terrorist attack limits the resolution of site-specific loss estimation. Another limiting factor for workers' compensation and other casualty risks is the temporal variation in the size of population within the area under terrorist attack. Generic assumptions may be made for this, as for supply chain bottlenecks which may indirectly affect business interruption. The uncertainty in scenario loss modeling is one reason why, as with natural hazards, a deterministic terrorism PML approach can only be partially satisfactory. Another cogent reason is that the probability of extreme loss is not addressed.

Detonation of a nuclear device, or the sabotage of a nuclear plant, might lead to massive losses, but these hypothetical contingencies should not dominate terrorism PML evaluation, since these are very unlikely, even if conceivable, scenarios. PML is best inferred from the tail of a loss exceedance probability distribution, which can only be constructed through a probabilistic terrorism risk model. Assignment of probabilities to the terrorist attack scenarios is a task which has an intrinsic human behavioral dimension, and so requires a new set of mathematical modeling tools, and makes greater recourse to the elicitation of expert judgement than for natural hazards.

THE USE OF EXPERT JUDGEMENT

Prior to the Earth Science revolution of plate tectonics in the 1960's, earthquake risk assessment was predominantly judgement-based. There were historical catalogs on past earthquakes, but no adequate theory by which seismic phenomena might be properly understood. Even into the 1980's, professional seismologists, who monitored earthquakes, were sceptical of the objectivity of practical engineering seismic hazard analysis. But with the increasing power of computation and theoretical developments, earthquake modeling has become more quantitative, and less subjective. In principle, not just terrorism or earthquakes but any technical risk issue may be resolved simplistically just by direct interrogation of experts. One might ask US space-flight engineers the probability of a shuttle disaster, or UK railway workers the probability of a rail crash.

Answers can be readily obtained through such direct use of expert judgement, but we have known since at least the Challenger disaster of 1986, that this is not a very reliable approach: an underlying structural event model is needed. It is hard to avoid a fair measure of expert judgement in terrorism risk assessment, but minimizing subjectivity is the key to the scientific evolution of terrorism risk modeling. Where expert judgement is elicited, the most informed terrorism experts should be sought: those in the prime of their careers, engrossed regularly in advising and receiving intelligence from governments and leading news agencies. Since Al Qaeda operates in almost a hundred countries across the globe, the use of international experts is crucial. These experts should have active contact with terrorists and a current appreciation of their modus operandi.

Because each expert is privy to his own sources of intelligence often gained verbally from debriefings, and has his own security clearances, there is no common database of information upon which all experts can form their judgements. If there were a common literature, as in the sciences, relevant publications could be distributed to all experts, whose opinions might then be elicited on an individual basis. But the world of intelligence is opposite to that of science: the most crucial information is often the most confidential. Accordingly, expert judgement is well elicited through decision conferences, at which intelligence and other confidential information can be pooled and opinions shared.

QUANTITATIVE TOOLS FOR TERRORISM RISK MODELLING

The most rigorous attitude to any risk model development spurns the excessive use of expert judgement, and terrorism risk is no exception. The use of expert judgement can be minimized through exploring and developing mathematical models and simulations of the underlying causative processes, which can then be parametrized from observational data. In the following sections, a review is given of mathematical concepts which have already found their way into advanced terrorism risk modeling, and an outline is given of additional ideas which currently are being researched.

MODEL FOR THE OCCURRENCE OF TERRORIST ATTACKS

Randomness plays a significant part in any human conflict. This is reflected in Bismarck's perceptive comment that when you draw the sword, you roll the dice. But there are causal factors as well, which shape the conflict landscape, including the temporal pattern of successful attacks. In constructing a stochastic model of terrorist attacks, these non-random factors need to be taken into account through invoking an appropriate methodological paradigm, such as cybernetics. Magnus Ranstorp, director of the renowned Center for the Study of Terrorism and Political Violence at St. Andrews University, has referred to Al Qaeda operatives as parasites on globalization. In common with other prey-predator situations, the conflict between the forces of terrorism and counter-terrorism may be represented using the principles of cybernetics. In particular, the time development of the Al Qaeda conflict is a stochastic process which may be described by a controlled Markov chain model.

At any moment in time, the predator (i.e. Al Qaeda) is in some specific state of attack preparedness, whilst the prey (i.e. USA) is in some corresponding state of defense preparedness. In a democracy, there are rigorous checks and balances imposed on the law enforcement and security services. Accordingly, the counter-terrorism response has to be commensurate with the terrorism threat: draconian measures (e.g. detention without trial) are only tolerable when the threat level is high. Democracies are prevented constitutionally from mounting an unlimited war on terrorism. A Markov chain is defined by the series of states that Al Qaeda occupies, and makes transitions to and from. This is a controlled Markov chain because, whatever state Al Qaeda occupies, the police and security forces counter the prevailing threat with actions which aim to control terrorism. These actions are commensurate with the threat, and hence are a function of the Al Qaeda state. Because of these controlling counter-actions, the process of attack occurrence is not Poissonian, as is generally assumed for natural hazards. In mathematical terms, these counter-actions are termed the 'Markov feedback policy'.

The Markovian concept of a system state is well suited to the fluctuating dynamics of the terrorism conflict, with the need for periodic updating of the threat situation. System states are distinguished from one another in respect of significant differences in the terrorists' organization, attack capability, and modus operandi. In some substantive degree, the threat parameters vary from one state to another. In increasing threat order, the alternative states of the terrorist network range from destabilization, to facility at launching conventional attacks, to capability of attempting attacks using weapons of mass destruction. The term 'macroterrorism' has been coined to describe a spectacular act of terrorism, (which may be a multiple strike at several locations), which causes more than $1 billion of loss, or 500 deaths. Minor 'potboiler' terrorist acts, such as house bombing, may occur haphazardly, but the occurrence of spectacular macroterrorism events does not satisfy the prerequisites of a Poisson process.

Once a terrorist's message has been delivered successfully across the media through a spectacular macro-terrorism event, perhaps after a series of failures, a publicity reminder may not be needed for a while. On the counter-terrorism side, following an act of macroterrorism, security and border controls are inevitably strengthened and extra government funding made available for improving protection.

Civil liberties may be temporarily curtailed as suspects are detained without trial, and the human rights pleas of asylum seekers and refugees may be denied. Examples of more brutal terrorism suppression methods are to be found from previous conflicts. Scandalously, in response to an IRA bombing outrage at Enniskillen in 1987, the British security services even colluded in the murder of a Catholic human rights lawyer in an attempt to control support for republican violence.

ADAPTIVE LEARNING OF ATTACK MODES

Avoid strength, and attack weakness', a saying of the legendary military strategist Sun Tzu, is a fundamental precept for the terrorist conduct of asymmetric warfare against a much more powerful adversary. For Al Qaeda, this may be expressed in the succinct language of physical science as: follow the path of least resistance. The notion that this principle may guide the probability distribution of certain human actions was originally developed by Zipf in his quantitative sociological studies, and may be considered in the context of attack mode preferences. One of the main signposts on the path of least resistance is adaptive learning. Al Qaeda is eager to learn from past terrorist experience – the successes and failures of attacks perpetrated by its own network, and by other terrorists around the world.

Al Qaeda would tend to 'copycat' methods which either have proven to be successful, or are perceived to have the potential to be successful. If an attack mode has demonstrated effectiveness, or has the promise of being effective, it is likely to be an attack option. Statistical learning models may be more relevant than pure frequency models in quantifying attack mode likelihood. The basic arsenal for terrorists contains a range of conventional weapons: improvised explosive and incendiary devices, and standard military weapons such as automatic rifles, grenades, mortars, and surface-to-air missiles. Sticking with off-the-shelf or tried-and- tested weapons might seem to be the easiest strategy, but further variety in attack modes is necessary from time to time as it keeps counter-terrorism forces guessing.

This necessity leads to the invention of unconventional attack modes: industrial, infrastructure and agricultural sabotage, hijacked jets, helicopters and ships, bomb-laden boats and planes, chemical-biological-radiological-nuclear (CBRN) weapons, cyberspace hacking, food and drink contamination etc.. The process of terrorist attack mode selection can be simulated as follows. At any given time, there is a small probability that a new terrorist attack mode will be chosen, and a complementary probability that one of the existing attack modes will be chosen. In keeping with the principle of adaptive (copycat) learning, the relative likelihood that a specific existing attack mode will be preferred may be assumed to be an increasing function of the amount of its previous usage. The more often an attack mode has been used, the more likely it is to be reused in another terrorist operation. This usage growth pattern is common to a number of sociological contexts, where this type of stochastic growth modeling has proved instructive. An outcome of this simulation is insight into the empirical probability distribution of attack mode preferences: some of the key modes dominate the distribution, with a long tail of other ancillary attack modes.

THE SELECTION OF TARGETS

There is an earthquake engineering adage that an earthquake will expose the weakest link in a building. But if a number of structures are randomly distributed in a region, the pattern of seismicity does not alter so that the weakest structure is most likely to be shaken. Yet, with a terrorist threat to a number of prize targets, the most vulnerable may have the highest probability of being attacked. This effect may be recognized explicitly using the mathematical theory of conflict, i.e. game theory, which is a collection of tools designed to help understand the interaction of decision-makers.

The two fundamental precepts underlying game theory are that the protagonists are rational and intelligent in strategic reasoning. These are justifiable for macroterrorism. As a weaker force confronting a nation state with far greater military and economic resources, a terrorist organization needs to have a smart strategy to survive and launch spectacular attacks: terrorists poor in strategic reasoning fade rapidly into oblivion. Indeed, Dr. George Habash, cofounder of the Popular Front for the Liberation of Palestine, referred to terrorism as a thinking man's game. Like Dr. Habash, Dr. Ayman Al-Zawahiri, the Al Qaeda chief strategist, was an eminent doctor before turning to terrorism, and noted for his brilliance. In applying game theory to terrorism, it is important to leave behind popular notions of rationality, and to return to the formal mathematical definition of rational behavior, namely that actions are taken in accordance with a specific preference relation.

There is no requirement that a terrorist's preference relation should involve economic advantage or financial gain. Much of the purpose of terrorism is psychological: inspiring the global Jihad; whipping up malicious joy at seeing the USA suffering loss; and terrorising the general public. Nor is it necessary that a terrorist's preference relation conform to those of society at large. Game theory is not restricted to any one cultural or religious perspective. In particular, we should not be surprised if a terrorist who prefers the company of ladies in Paradise to men on Earth takes action along the path to martyrdom. For the faithful, martyrdom is a rational choice: everyone has to die, so why not die on the path of God? The test of any mathematical risk model is its explanatory and predictive capability. Game theory predicts that, as prime targets are hardened, rational terrorists will tend to substitute lesser softer targets.

This prediction is essentially equivalent to the statement made by the CIA director, George Tenet, in his prophetic unclassified but unheeded testimony of February 7, 2001, (prior to 9/11): 'as security is increased around government and military facilities, terrorists are seeking out softer targets that provide opportunities for mass casualties.' In the language of terrorism experts, this is called target substitution. A year after the destruction of the World Trade Center, the Bali bombing provided another tragic confirmation of this game theory prediction.

A bomb left at the US consulate perimeter fence was too distant at 100 meters to cause any damage, but a bomb-laden truck could park immediately outside a nightclub and kill hundreds. Explicit admission of this soft target strategy has since come from Khalid Sheikh Mohammed, the Al Qaeda chief of military operations, who was arrested in March 2003. Further validation of the terrorism target prioritization model is provided by analysis of the IRA campaign in Ulster and England, and the GIA campaign in France. The success of this game theory model illustrates the future potential for quantitative terrorism model development.

DEVELOPMENTS IN TERRORISM SIMULATION

The simplest approach to modeling a conflict is by considering the interplay between two opposing force blocks. This is the approach described above, with the terrorist organization opposing the counter-terrorism organization. But extra insight into the dynamics of a terrorist network can be gained by looking inside: analysing the social network of interconnections between network nodes, which correspond to individual terrorists. The French magistrate, Jean-Louis Bruguière, has aptly likened Al Qaeda to a virus. In order to survive, a virus must mutate faster than its environment changes.

Similarly, the Al Qaeda network has shown flexibility in adapting to survive counter- terrorism action. This adaptation process can be simulated by evolving the social network according to a set of basic rules. Nodes communicate with one another to exchange information, financial and logistical resources, subject to the risk that any communication might be detected by security services. Local cells are autonomous to a substantial degree, and recruit attack team members and carry out target reconnaissance. Spectacular attacks are planned, but the larger and more ambitious that an attack becomes, the higher the chance of it being compromised by one of the attack team. If any node is removed from the network, there is a chance that any node connected to it might also be named and removed. Thus, the more hierarchichal the network, the greater is the chance of destabilization through the arrest of senior leaders.

Through repeated computational network simulation following these rules, an ensemble of different network evolutions can be generated, the contrasting patterns of network structure can be studied, and the relative likelihood of different network configurations can be gauged. From analysis of these simulations, cell statistics and the network capability to launch major multiple attacks can be assessed probabilistically. Such network analysis has to cope with the problem of missing data. As in the war on terrorism, massive amounts of uncertainty and dearth of data plague decision-makers on the military battlefield. Where should we attack? When should we attack? What weapons should we use? These are some of the critical questions facing military leaders. In this parallel warfare context, battle decisions might just be left to the judgement of generals, rather as terrorism insurance decisions might be left to the judgement of underwriters. Creditably, instead of an air of technical resignation pervading the Pentagon, massive investments of resources are being made to provide quantitative decision-support tools for the military.

Sophisticated methods of combat modeling are being developed which incorporate all manner of extraneous factors that impact upon the decision-making processes of battlefield commanders. This wargaming has been substantially advanced through a variety of quantitative means: mathematical equations, also large-scale simulations, and distillations (i.e. relatively simple simulations that capture the salient features of the situation, without trying to model all the details). Similar bottom-up combat modeling initiatives are being explored for the war on terrorism. One of the purposes of the analysis is to identify emergent dynamic behavior, such as might arise if there were a concentration of terrorist resources in a particular threat mode, as defined by choice of weaponry, target and mode of attack delivery.

The terrorism threat from Islamic militants may well be the defining conflict of the 21st century. Already, wars in Afghanistan and Iraq have been waged by the USA in retaliatory response to this perceived threat. In his seminal treatise, 'Paradise and Power', Robert Kagan has elucidated starkly the different parts that America and Europe play in the new world order which is unfolding. Kagan explains this using a metaphor from the Wild West. In dealing with rogue muslim states, the world's superpower is prepared to play the role of the sheriff, even while weaker European nations play the role of saloon-keepers doing business as usual. The price of such Middle Eastern intervention by USA is likely to include increasing hostility amongst Muslims around the world.

Given that Islamic extremists form the apex of a pyramid of global Muslim discontent, the need for US insurance against foreign terrorism seems assured for decades to come. The maneuver warfare techniques used by the US military for decision-making, and successfully exercised in the Iraq war, are being made more elaborate, complex and computationally intensive. Progress is being made to introduce these techniques into terrorism risk assessment. The insurance industry plays a key part in the war on terrorism, not least by devising risk-based methods to assist Homeland Security in the allocation of finite resources for civil protection, and the Office of Management and Budget in the cost-benefit analysis of federal security legislation. With such diverse and important commercial and government applications, the methods for quantifying terrorism risk will continue to evolve with increasing mathematical and computational sophistication, in the same way that the methods for quantifying windstorm and earthquake risk have systematically advanced over the past decade since the devastation caused by Hurricane Andrew and the Northridge earthquake.

18

Al-Qaeda's Catastrophic Terrorist Warfare

The aim of this chapter is to provoke consideration of a new way to conceptualize al-Qaeda's intentions and plans to conduct catastrophic warfare against the United States, its allies, and other threatened nations around the world. In response to the horrific attacks of 11 September 2001, follow-on attacks in Southeast Asia and the Middle East, and several thwarted plots in Europe, anticipating and preventing future attacks by al-Qaeda and its affiliated terrorist groupings have become first-order national security priorities for many of the world's intelligence and law enforcement communities. Such analysis is also required in the nongovernmental, open-source communities as well. Although it is difficult to predict the likelihood of every major attack by a group such as al-Qaeda, because terrorist groups have the advantage of striking at a time and location of their choosing, there already exists a wealth of diagnostically predictive indicators pointing to the next waves of catastrophic attacks by a group such as al-Qaeda and its network of terrorist allies.

This chapter outlines seven predictive attack indicators to forecast catastrophic terrorism. Political leaders, policy planners, and military, intelligence, and law enforcement operators at all levels will greatly improve their capabilities to respond to the terrorist challenge if they operationalize these predictive indicators against al-Qaeda's historic and potential strategies, tactics, and targeting. Such "red-teaming" of a terrorist group's warfare potential is similar to the way military commanders play adversary forces (the "red teams") against their own forces (the "blue teams"). Building a robust predictive capability to anticipate and preemptively prevent attacks by groups such as al-Qaeda now is more important than ever because of their determination to inflict catastrophic damage upon their adversaries.

As demonstrated by the suicide attacks against Australian and British tourists in Bali, Indonesia; Israeli tourists in Mombassa, Kenya (where an additional 250 Israeli lives could have been lost had the Arkia airliner been hit by the shoulder-fired rocket); and the large residential complex in Riyadh, Saudi Arabia, housing American and other foreign families; as well as a suicide attack by two British al-Qaeda operatives on a popular seaside bar in Tel Aviv; al-Qaeda is as determined as ever to demonstrate its viability as the world's most lethal terrorist group. The catastrophic attacks of 11 September and the follow-on poisonous anthrax letter campaign (which reportedly was not carried out by al-Qaeda) have ushered in a new terrorist warfare paradigm in which attacks against the United States and its allies have vastly escalated in the lethality of their weaponry and targeting.

The threshold from "conventional" low-impact terrorist warfare has been crossed, as demonstrated by the horrific attacks against the World Trade Center and news reports about interest in acquiring or actual experimentation by al-Qaeda in chemical, biological, radiological and nuclear devices and weapons—however crude and low tech. As a consequence of these factors, the new means of terrorist attacks we are likely to face will involve not only such weapons of mass destruction and disruption but conventional means to attack critical infrastructural targets such as nuclear and chemical plants, agricultural nodes such as livestock feeding centers, and the heart of the American and world economy—such as the New York Stock Exchange—with catastrophic human and economic consequences. Usama bin Laden's al-Qaeda terrorist network and its satellite affiliates are the most likely groups to carry out such catastrophic attacks because of their intent—a virulent hatred of their adversaries—capability, and resources.

As the top leaders, members of sleeper and active cells, and other operatives of al-Qaeda and its allies are being arrested or killed in their former centers of gravity in Afghanistan, Pakistan, and other parts of the world (reportedly, some 3,000 operatives, forming one-third to one-half of the group's upper and lower echelons, have been eliminated as active terrorists), there still undoubtedly remain hundreds of new leaders, operatives, and sleeper cells armed with target folders for the next waves of catastrophic terrorist operations. The U.S.-led overthrow of al-Qaeda's Taliban allies in Afghanistan and Saddam Hussein's regime in Iraq, as well as holding Taliban and al-Qaeda operatives in detention centers such as Guantanamo Bay, cumulatively are likely to serve as major triggers for their remaining operatives to seek catastrophic revenge on behalf of their fallen, retreating, or arrested comrades. To forecast the next waves of likely catastrophic terrorist attacks, this analysis uses a methodology based on seven predictive attack indicators, generated from al-Qaeda's mindset, modus operandi, and target selection based on its training handbook (available on the Department of Justice website); public statements by bin Laden and his associates that have been broadcast on television news programs; and the extensive media reporting of the group's previous failed attacks and plots (as outlined in captured documents), which often serve as blueprints for its future targeting. To anticipate, preempt, and deter future catastrophic attacks, the following methodology employing seven predictive attack indicators can be operationalized to forecast the next waves of al-Qaeda terrorist operations, as outlined in the following threat matrix.

Al-Qaeda and its allies have carried out numerous successful attacks since the early 1990s; however, they also have experienced quite a few significant failed attacks. In other cases, some plots have never been executed. Synthesizing the lessons learned from a group's successful attacks, failed attacks, and plots can generate insight into its future intentions and capabilities. Plots, for example, can be uncovered by covertly penetrating a group, capturing its documents, or interrogating its apprehended operatives. In the case of al-Qaeda, much insight into its warfare proclivity can be gained by examining its training manual, which spells out missions that include destroying a nation's foreign embassies, critical infrastructure nodes (such as vital economic sectors and bridges), and even places of amusement (because they are considered sinful).

Underlying the first predictive indicator are some of the following historical observables and actions:

- The February 1993 bombing of the World Trade Center towers. This attack resulted in extensive property damage and some loss of life but failed to bring down the towers. The bombing was intended to be accompanied by the bombing of several other targets in New York City, such as the Empire State Building, the Holland Tunnel, and United Nations headquarters.
- In December 1994, an al-Qaeda affiliate, the Algerian Armed Islamic Group, hijacked an Air France Airbus with 171 passengers aboard, intending to plunge it into the Eiffel Tower. None of the hijackers could fly the aircraft to its intended target, so, instead, the plane landed in Marseilles, where French police stormed it.
- In the mid-1990s, Ramzi Yousef, the mastermind of the 1993 World Trade Center bombing, while in the Philippines, plotted to blow up 11 U.S. airliners and, in a separate plot, fly planes filled with explosives into the CIA headquarters in Langley, VA, and nuclear facilities elsewhere in the United States.
- In December 1999, an al-Qaeda affiliate was involved in a foiled plot to bomb Los Angeles International Airport. At the same time, al-Qaeda operatives were foiled by Jordanian security authorities in their attempt to blow up tourist sites in Jordan, and internal hurdles prevented them from bombing the *U.S.S. Sullivans* in the Yemeni port of Aden.
- On 8 September 2001, two al-Qaeda operatives pretending to be journalist's assassinated Northern Alliance

commander General Ahmed Shah Masoud at his Afghanistan base by detonating a bomb concealed in their video camera.

- The airplane that ultimately crashed into the Pentagon during the 11 September hijackings reportedly also targeted the U.S. Capitol and the White House. The fourth airplane, which crashed in a Pennsylvania field, reportedly was unable to crash into the U.S. Capitol or the White House, or, in another published although unconfirmed scenario was en route to crash into a nuclear facility.
- Al-Qaeda operatives had planned to hijack airplanes in Britain and crash them into the Houses of Parliament and London's Tower Bridge.

Operationalizing attack indicator #1 yields this forecasting assessment: the 11 September bombing of the World Trade Center signifies that when al-Qaeda fails in its initial mission (in this case, the abortive 1993 attack), it is likely to return—whatever length of time is required to prepare for the next mission—to complete that objective. It can be surmised, therefore, that al-Qaeda operatives are likely to persist in their objective of attacking the following that are part of their target folder (all information is entirely speculative): the Holland Tunnel, the Empire State Building, United Nations headquarters, the Eiffel Tower, the CIA headquarters, the U.S. Capitol, the White House, and nuclear power facilities. In addition, Disney World amusement parks are likely targets.

In Britain, the Houses of Parliament and the Tower Bridge, which reportedly were contemplated by al-Qaeda as part of their 11 September worldwide attack repertoire, are still likely to remain at the top of al-Qaeda ranking of trophy targets. In addition, the September 2001 assassination of General Masoud by operatives in disguise and several attempts since then to assassinate members of the current Afghan leadership portend continuous efforts by al-Qaeda operatives and their allies to assassinate leaders of their adversaries. Of particular concern are likely efforts by these terrorist operatives to carry out their assassination attempts in disguise or to use operatives who do not fit regular profile attributes in order to evade possible detection.

A TERRORIST GROUP'S MODUS OPERANDI/TACTICS

Al-Qaeda's modus operandi, as demonstrated by the 11 September attacks and outlined in its training manual, involves meticulous planning, training, and precisely timed simultaneous execution. Such warfare capability is attained through extensive training and operational and tactical innovations. Based on its modus operandi, publicly announced intentions, and previous actions, al-Qaeda's future attacks will likely involve some of the following tactics:

> Truck bomb attacks on the ground or using aerial or maritime delivery means, such as miniature submarines or shipborne containers, to transport chemical, biological, radiological, or nuclear devices to a targeted site.

Driving a truck loaded with a hazardous-material explosive against a prominent target, such as a tunnel, bridge, or busy downtown area.Detonating a radioactive dispersal device (a "dirty" bomb) near a nuclear power facility or a major financial center, such as the New York Stock Exchange.

The simultaneous suicide bombing attacks of 11 September portend that the next phase will likely involve even more catastrophic assaults, with each successive plot employing highly innovative and deadlier weapons and devices to inflict maximum casualties and physical damage. Current news reporting is filled with discussions of possible chemical, biological, radiological, or nuclear attacks by al-Qaeda operatives. Such speculation is not without foundation.

Bin Laden's Afghan training camps taught skills for using weapons of mass destruction—such as feeding poison gas through the air vents of office buildings. Other reports claimed that bin Laden's operatives tried to obtain uranium from the former Soviet republics but instead were given low-grade reactor fuel and radioactive garbage. Also possible, in this catastrophic scenario, are attacks that would use conventional or unconventional explosives against a nuclear power plant or chemical facility.

A chemical attack could be carried out by a crop-dusting plane spraying sections of a city. One of al-Qaeda's operatives who were involved in the 11 September attacks reportedly had in his possession a manual for operating crop-dusting equipment, so such an attack should not be discounted. Another worst-case scenario might involve al-Qaeda operatives crashing a truck into the New York Stock Exchange building (which reportedly has inadequate perimeter defenses) to detonate a dirty bomb mixed with conventional and radioactive materials.

Such an attack would render the stock exchange and its immediate surroundings inactive for weeks, setting off temporary worldwide economic turmoil—although this might be offset by the backup computer data storage systems located elsewhere. The London Stock Exchange, which has already been contemplated as a target by al-Qaeda, represents another likely trophy target, also with potentially devastating economic consequences worldwide.

Based on al-Qaeda's intention to inflict maximum economic damage, another worst-case scenario involves a biological agent attack against a U.S. agricultural sector, which would produce an impact similar to that of the foot-and-mouth outbreak that devastated British agriculture. Such an attack would also severely impact the U.S. and worldwide commodities trading market. Similarly, a terrorist-induced outbreak of severe acute respiratory syndrome would devastate a region's tourism or export industries.

State sponsors are crucial to terrorist groups engaging in catastrophic warfare because the resources of a state can be helpful in so many ways. Afghanistan's Taliban rulers provided bin Laden and al-Qaeda with a safe haven. Saddam's regime in Iraq, until its overthrow, may have provided the group with some degree of support because of the convergence of their objectives, particularly in taking revenge against the United States. According to press reports, terrorists have been trained at Iraqi camps in chemical and biological warfare and in flying commercial aircraft. Press reports also indicated that an al-Qaeda operative, Muhammad Ataf, met an Iraqi intelligence official in Prague several times.

Iran now is reported to provide al-Qaeda with logistical and other forms of support, including collaboration with Iran's terrorist proxy, the Lebanese Hizballah. Although there may be few apparent smoking guns, it is reasonable to assume that al-Qaeda is interested in obtaining the support of Iran's radical clerical leaders in mounting its catastrophic warfare against their common adversaries. Such state support would provide al-Qaeda with access to certain types of weapons of mass destruction that would be difficult for the group to obtain on its own.

THE GEOGRAPHIC FACTOR

The geographic factor is a crucial predictive indicator because it pinpoints a group's operational center of gravity and logistical capability to reach, conduct surveillance of, and attack its adversary. Al Qaeda is the umbrella organization of an international network of like-minded groups with hundreds of cells around the world. These groups operate as planets in al-Qaeda's solar system, which makes them highly dangerous because they already possess the infrastructure to carry out terrorist attacks in any part of the world, as demonstrated by their capability to carry out attacks with relative ease in dispersed countries such the Philippines, Pakistan, Kuwait, Saudi Arabia, Tunisia, Morocco, and Kenya, with reported sleeper cells in Western countries such as Britain, Spain, and the United States.

Already, al-Qaeda operatives have carried out or attempted to carry out attacks against American targets in these countries, including a thwarted attempt by an al-Qaeda cell to attack American and British warships in the Strait of Gibraltar. Moreover, al-Qaeda has expanded its geographic target folder to include Israel, as demonstrated by its successful attack in Kenya against Israeli tourists and the near-miss attack against the Israeli airliner. In fact, in May 2003, two British nationals allegedly affiliated with al-Qaeda traveled to Israel to carry out a suicide bombing of a popular bar in Tel Aviv. Based on this predictive indicator, potential regions to be targeted by al-Qaeda are likely to range from the United States to foreign lands, especially those where the United States maintains facilities that represent significant trophy targets, such as military bases or symbols of America's economy—a fast food restaurant chain, a hotel chain, a cruise liner, or car dealerships.

HISTORICAL DATES OF PARTICULAR SIGNIFICANCE TO TERRORIST GROUPS

Terrorist groups, particularly religious groups, place a high premium on historical dates that are significant to their religion or their religioethnic community. Other types of historical dates, such as politically or militarily traumatic events, are also significant. 11 September may have been especially significant because the conspirators who carried out the 1998 African embassy bombings were to be sentenced the following day for their crimes. During that period, the conspirators were in a holding cell at a courthouse in downtown Manhattan near the World Trade Center, which fact may have propelled the terrorists to attack on the preceding day.

A spectrum of triggers propels terrorist groups to hasten the timing of terrorist attacks, usually resulting from sudden developments, such as a severe military setback. For example, al-Qaeda's conspiracy for the 11 September attacks began some two years prior to the attacks, but 12 September may have served as a trigger for the attacks to occur on the previous day. New and devastating al-Qaeda attacks are likely to be triggered in response to its recent military defeats, particularly in Afghanistan, the detention of their captured operatives in centers at Guantanamo Bay and other areas, the overthrow of their previous state sponsors in Afghanistan and Iraq, and other factors.

The 11 September attacks and follow-on operations are part of al-Qaeda's asymmetric warfare against the United States and its allies, in which small, fanatically dedicated teams are employed to inflict maximum psychological and physical damage on their much more powerful adversaries. Terrorist attacks by groups such as al-Qaeda are intended to be catastrophic in terms of human and physical damage in order to punish and send a strong political message to the targeted adversary and to the group's constituents that the group is a world-class destroyer and political force to be reckoned with. In response, the United States, Britain, and their allies have greatly upgraded their intelligence, situational awareness, and defensive, preemptive, and deterrence postures.

Failing to anticipate the 11 September horrific attacks represented more than a failure of intelligence—it was a failure of imagination. Previously, such attacks were viewed as too grandiose and farfetched to be taken serious by intelligence and law enforcement authorities. Now these attacks, the attacks that have been thwarted, and other plots are perceived as likely blueprints for future catastrophic terrorist operations against the United States and its allies. Security and risk assessment professionals must always adopt proactive measures to anticipate, defend against, and preempt new types of terrorist threats. Moreover, one should not expect past trends to necessarily reveal future attack patterns because terrorists, especially al-Qaeda planners, always seek to exploit new vulnerabilities and new and innovative modes of warfare in order to evade detection and inflict maximum damage.

Therefore, to avert catastrophic attacks that previously were considered beyond the imagination of those responsible for security, we need to begin thinking like the terrorist enemy—always anticipating and preparing to counteract new types of attacks and targeting potentialities. Continuous red-teaming is required, using outside-the-box threat and risk assessments and the most advanced (yet user-friendly) computerized predictive analytic tool kits. Such red-teaming must focus on multidimensional, not unidimensional, baskets of potential threats. Above all, emphasis must be placed on intelligence tracking of suspected terrorist networks, cells, and operatives; detection; and, above all, preemption during the earliest possible preattack incubatory phases.

MODUS OPERANDI OF OSAMA BIN LADEN

Al-Qaeda is clearly weaker than it was at the formal commencement of the war on terrorism, on October 7, 2001. It has been deprived of operational bases and training camps in Afghanistan. Its command-and-control capabilities have been disrupted. Its headquarters have been destroyed. Its leaders and fighters have been forcibly dispersed, and they are now consumed as much by providing for their own security as by planning and executing attacks. Communication and coordination among the disparate parts of al Qaeda's global network are more inconvenient—if not necessarily less effective—than ever before. These setbacks have forced al Qaeda to alter its targeting patterns.

Displaced and harried, its operatives must now rely on local groups to carry out their plans and, as a result, have focused on "softer," more accessible targets, in places as diverse as Tunisia, Pakistan, Jordan, Indonesia, Kuwait, the Philippines, Yemen, and Kenya. These have included German, Australian, and Israeli tourists; French engineers and a French oil tanker; and such long-standing targets as U.S. diplomats and servicemen. But not everything has changed, of course; al Qaeda remains a powerful threat. The organization has continued to use suicide bombing, both at sea and on land, and commercial aviation remains a focus—as was made clear in December of 2001, when the shoe bomber Richard Reid attempted to blow up an American Airlines plane en route from Paris to Miami, and then eleven months later, when a group in Kenya with links to al Qaeda tried to shoot down an Israeli charter flight using a hand-held surface-to-air missile.

Al Qaeda has, in fact, proved to be remarkably nimble and adaptive—and the group's strength derives precisely from its flexibility. The loss of Afghanistan may thus, in the long run, have little effect on al Qaeda's ability to harm us. Some of al Qaeda's biggest plots—among them Ramzi Yousef's 1993 bombing of the World Trade Center, and his subsequent failed plot to bomb twelve U.S. commercial aircraft over the Pacific—predate the group's strong presence in Afghanistan, which for al Qaeda was important mainly as a base from which to prosecute a conventional civil war against the late Ahmad Shah Massoud's Northern Alliance. This conflict required arms dumps, training camps, staging areas, and networks of forward and rear headquarters—but none of these specific facilities are necessary to an ongoing international terrorism campaign.

Al Qaeda's core leadership is still alive and at large—perhaps only a third of its leaders are now dead or captured. Moreover, the two most important figures in al Qaeda, Osama bin Laden and Ayman al-Zawahiri, are both widely believed to be alive. Its activities are therefore probably still centralized, and controlled by top leaders, to some degree. Pakistan, for example, remains crucially important in al Qaeda operations today, serving as something of a clearing house for operatives and wouldbe recruits on both the individual and the group level. The process may be less organized and more fractured than it was in Afghanistan, but the looseness of control is not necessarily a liability.

Al Qaeda can still fill its mid-level operational command positions—perhaps in part because of the vast reservoir of fighters and operatives (some 70,000) that the group trained during the 1990s, in camps in Sudan, Yemen, and Afghanistan. But what makes al Qaeda strong is its continuing ability to recruit and mobilize fighters, supporters, and sympathizers worldwide. Osama bin Laden is perhaps best viewed as a terrorist CEO. He has essentially applied the techniques of business administration and modern management, which he learned both at university and in his family's construction business, to the running of a transnational terrorist organization.

In the 1990s he did what the executives of transnational companies did throughout much of the industrialized world—namely, design and implement a flexible new organizational framework and strategy incorporating multiple levels and both top-down and bottom-up approaches. In his top-down mode bin Laden has defined specific goals, issued orders, and ensured that they are carried out. This is generally the way al Qaeda organizes its "spectaculars": high-visibility, usually high-casualty operations such as the September 11 attacks, the bombing of the *USS Cole*, and the East Africa embassy bombings. But he has also operated as a venture capitalist, soliciting ideas from below, encouraging creative approaches, and funding proposals he finds promising. Unlike many other terrorist organizations, therefore, al Qaeda has no single modus operandi—and it is all the more formidable as a result.

At least four al Qaeda levels of operation can be identified.

1. Professional cadres. This is the most dedicated element of al Qaeda: the people entrusted with the spectaculars. These teams are carefully selected, provided with very specific instructions, and generously funded (during the days preceding the September 11 attacks, for example, Mohammed Atta and his confederates were sending surplus money back to their paymasters in the United Arab Emirates and elsewhere).
2. Trained amateurs. An exemplar of this category is Ahmed Ressam, who was arrested in December of 1999, at Port Angeles, Washington, shortly after entering the United States from Canada with explosive materials in the trunk of his car. Ressam had some background in terrorism, having belonged to Algeria's Armed Islamic Group. After being recruited into al Qaeda he was given a modicum of basic training in Afghanistan. Unlike the professional cadres, however, Ressam was given only open-ended instructions before being dispatched to North America—he and the members of the terrorist cell to which he had been assigned in Afghanistan had themselves decided to attack an airport or foreign consulate in the United States. He received $12,000 in seed money and was expected to raise the rest of his operational funds through petty thievery—by swiping money, credit cards, passports, traveler's checks, and computers from tourists, for example. He was told to recruit members for his terrorist cell from among the Muslim expatriate communities in

Canada. Ressam, of course, panicked when he was confronted by a U.S. Customs agent immediately upon entering the United States—a demonstration that he lacked the resolve and presence of mind characteristic of the professional cadres. Nevertheless, as ill-prepared and as inept as the trained amateurs may be (Richard Reid is another example), their ability to succeed once, and thereby to inflict pain and destruction, should not be dismissed.

3. Local walkins. These are groups of Islamic radicals who come up with terrorist-attack ideas on their own and then attempt to obtain funding from al Qaeda. One example is the group of Islamic radicals in Jordan who, observing that American and Israeli tourists often stayed at the Radisson in Amman, proposed to attack the hotel on the eve of the millennium. (They received funding from al Qaeda, but were arrested before they could execute their plan.) Another is the cell of Islamic militants who were arrested in Milan in April of 2001, after wiretaps revealed plans to attack American targets in Italy. A more disquieting example, however, is the group of Islamic radicals —associated with but not formally a part of al Qaeda—who plotted to attack the American and Israeli embassies and the British and Australian high commissions in Singapore, along with a subway stop used by U.S. sailors taking shore leave in that city. The Singapore plotters, who were arrested before they could carry out their intentions, spent at least four years planning their attacks, conducting the kind of detailed and meticulous reconnaissance—including extensive videotaping, with detailed voice-over discussions of potential targets—that is emblematic of al Qaeda spectaculars.
4. Like-minded guerrillas and terrorists. This level embraces existing insurgent or terrorist groups that have benefited over the years from either bin Laden's largesse or his spiritual guidance; that have received al Qaeda training in Afghanistan or elsewhere; or that the organization has provided with arms, materiel, and other assistance in order to further the cause of global *jihad*. Among the

recipients of this "revolutionary philanthropy" have been insurgent forces in Uzbekistan, Indonesia, Chechnya, the Philippines, Bosnia, and Kashmir. Such philanthropy is designed not only to harness the energy of geographically scattered, disparate movements but also to ensure that al Qaeda operatives can, in turn, call on these local groups for logistical services and manpower.

Underpinning all of this is bin Laden's vision—a self-perpetuating mythology that he has crafted carefully and communicates skillfully. His message is simple: The United States is a hegemonic power, opposing change and propping up Israel and corrupt and reprobate regimes that would not exist but for American backing. But the United States cannot bear the pain or the losses inflicted by terrorist attacks—as became clear when it withdrew from Lebanon after the 1983 bombing of the U.S. Marine barracks, and again when it withdrew from Somalia following the deaths of eighteen U.S. Army Rangers and Delta Force commandos, in 1993. In bin Laden's view, terrorism against the United States—and allied Western countries—therefore works.

Despite the destruction of the Taliban and the liberation of Afghanistan during this first phase of the war against terrorism, bin Laden very probably still clings to that assessment. In his view, the United States is now more than ever committed to preserving the status quo (in the guise of "global stability") and ensuring the longevity of morally bankrupt regimes in Egypt, Saudi Arabia, the Persian Gulf, Pakistan, Uzbekistan, and elsewhere. He reasons that the defeat of the Taliban was accomplished mostly by the Northern Alliance, not by the United States. Despite overwhelming evidence to the contrary, bin Laden and his followers probably still regard the United States as a "paper tiger" (a favorite phrase of his) that can be toppled if al Qaeda survives the current onslaught in Afghanistan and elsewhere —which it almost certainly can. For bin Laden and al Qaeda, as for guerrillas and terrorists everywhere, not losing is winning.

The operations of al Qaeda have had a seismic effect on

the United States and the entire world; bin Laden is one of few people alive who can claim to have fundamentally changed the course of history. And the epic battle that he has launched is not over yet: the multiyear planning period of all previous al Qaeda spectaculars suggests that some monumental new operation may have been set in motion before September 11. Now, because of the destruction of the Taliban and because of what al Qaeda sees as America's global "war on Islam," the organization's sense of commitment and purpose is surely greater than ever.

19

Threat Proliferation

IN LATIN AMERICA

Venezuelan President Hugo Chavez has risen once again, in Argentina, to organize and lead mob demonstrators against what he touts as U.S. imperialism. This as President George W. Bush visited neighboring Uruguay in March, during a five-nation tour of Latin America. Although regularly ignoring Chavez's antics, Bush said rather assertively, "I don't think America gets enough credit for trying to help improve people's lives." The Latin America tour, Bush's longest in Latin America of his presidency, included the development and completion of an agreement with Brazil for ethanol as a leading alternative to oil. Argentina has also expressed interest in an ethanol agreement with the U.S.

Chavez, on an Argentine turf podium, replied "Gringo go home" and called the ethanol idea "a crazy thing – off the wall." The U.S. and Brazil will, under agreement, share technology to enhance ethanol production and push its development in other Latin American countries and the Caribbean. U.S. aid to Latin America last year doubled, to US$1.6 billion, whereas Chavez has spent vast sums from oil revenue on purchases of weapons from Russia. Bush contrasted the Venezuelan President's rhetoric by saying that ethanol production in this hemisphere can bring us all out of "dependence on oil and you're dependent upon people to work the land."

Regional South American polls have shown noticeably low numbers for Chavez. Colombia, a grateful recipient of U.S. aid to battle drugs, guerrillas and paramilitary insurgents, greeted Bush with a military honor guard and red carpet. President Alvaro Uribe's administration has fared well in strengthening Colombia's homeland security. Uribe enjoys a 65 percent approval rating in Colombia. President Bush praised Uribe's positive efforts to bring human rights violators to justice in Latin America. Too, both discussed "Plan Colombia II," a US$43 billion six-year plan to continue the fight against drug organizers and guerrillas.

The potential threat of terrorist organization and movement throughout the region is high. Some terrorism experts refuse to categorize terrorists under one heading, citing Hezbollah and Hamas as more complex organizations than al-Qaeda, involved in politics and social welfare networks and elections. Still, the commonality of these three terrorist organizations is an intense hatred for Israel and the United States. In South America, the triborder confluence of Argentina, Brazil and Paraguay boasts a large melting pot of Middle Eastern ethnicity. Moreover, Hamas, Hezbollah and al-Qaeda extremists are all represented in the region.

And Hezbollah has already left its murderous mark on South American soil. In 1992 they bombed the Israeli Embassy in Buenos Aires, killing 29 persons. In 1994 they struck again, killing 95 people at the Argentine Jewish Cultural Center. As a result, and due to extremists present in the tri-border region, Israel's Mossad intelligence agency has a large contingent in Argentina. It is clear that Hezbollah, Hamas and al-Qaeda have similar, even mutual, agendas regardless of their own identities and mindset. Consequently, they are a unified ideology of hatred and murder in the global terrorism arena. More specifically, terrorist acts are their stratagem and modus operandi by virtue of their extremist mindsets. The terrorist has many faces, with each led by their respective organization's mission or jihad. Some elements operate overtly political, as others are the muscle or brawn on the ground. Their agendas, ego and influence may often collide, but the networks and cells can and do cooperate, with Shi'a and Sunni joining together to accomplish common goals.

A global terrorist threat is a potential smorgasbord of organized criminals and/or merchants of death and destruction, aligned however so slightly to exert power, influence or control over targeted adversaries. Hezbollah currently has a military mission to defend Lebanon from possible Israeli advances into its territory. Too, they are state sponsored by Syria and Iran, which raises the "nuclear card" temperature in the scheme of things. In Latin America the terrorism threat has to be assessed from the standpoint of a training and launching or deployment base of operations. As well, drug revenue, weapons, intricate knowledge of county-border distinctions and protocols for entry, smuggling routes and related homeland defense agendas or deficiencies fuel sinister ideas.

U.S. Senator Arlen Specter (Republican, Pennsylvania) has recently suggested taking away some of the FBI's authority under the USA Patriot Act, and he suggested the Act should be rewritten. This is in response to alleged "overextensions" by agents in investigating terrorist links within the United States. However everyone in the Americas must recognize that the potential for the strengthening of terrorist cells and their heinous acts, in this hemisphere, is real and fluid.

NATION AT WAR

We assess that Al Qaeda and other terrorist groups will continue to plan to attack this country and its interests abroad. Their modus operandi is to continue to have multiple attack plans in the works simultaneously and to have Al Qaeda cells in place to conduct them. We know that the terrorists have considered attacks in the U.S. against high-profile government or private facilities, famous landmarks and U.S. infrastructure nodes such as airports, bridges, harbors and dams. High-profile events such as the Olympics or last week's Super Bowl also fit the terrorists' interests in striking another blow within the United States that would command worldwide media attention.

Al Qaeda also has plans to strike against U.S. and allied interests in Europe, the Middle East, Africa and Southeast Asia. American diplomatic and military installations are at high risk, especially in East Africa, Israel, Saudi Arabia and Turkey. Operations against U.S. targets could be launched by Al Qaeda cells already in place in major cities in Europe and the Middle East. Al Qaeda can also exploit its presence or connections to other groups in such countries as Somalia, Yemen, Indonesia and the Philippines.

Although the Sept. 11 attacks suggest that Al Qaeda and other terrorists will continue to use conventional weapons, one of our highest concerns is their stated readiness to attempt unconventional attacks against us. As early as 1998, bin Laden publicly declared that acquiring unconventional weapons was a religious duty. Terrorist groups worldwide have ready access to information on chemical, biological and even nuclear weapons via the Internet, and we know that Al Qaeda was working to acquire some of the most dangerous chemical agents and toxins.

Documents recovered from Al Qaeda facilities in Afghanistan show that bin Laden was pursuing a sophisticated biological weapons research program. We also believe that bin Laden was seeking to acquire or develop a nuclear device. Al Qaeda may be pursuing a radioactive dispersal device, what some call a dirty bomb. Alternatively, Al Qaeda or other terrorist groups might also try to launch conventional attacks against the chemical or nuclear industrial infrastructure of the United States to cause widespread toxic or radiological damage. The terrorist threat goes well beyond Al Qaeda. The situation in the Middle East continues to fuel terrorism and anti-U.S. sentiment worldwide. Groups like the Palestinian Islamic Jihad and Hamas have escalated their violence against Israel, and the intifada has rejuvenated once-dormant groups like the Popular Front for the Liberation of Palestine. If these groups feel that U.S. actions are threatening their existence, they may begin targeting Americans directly, as Hezbollah's terrorist wing already does.

We're also watching states like Iran and Iraq that continue to support terrorist groups. Iran continues to provide support, including arms transfers, to the Palestinian rejection groups and Hezbollah. Tehran also has failed to move decisively against Al Qaeda members who have relocated to Iran from Afghanistan. Iraq has a long history of supporting terrorists, including giving sanctuary to Abu Nidal. The war on terrorism, has dealt severe blows to Al Qaeda and its leadership. The group has been denied its safe haven and strategic command center in Afghanistan. Drawing on both our own assets and increased cooperation from allies around the world, we are uncovering terrorist plans and breaking up their cells. These efforts have yielded the arrest of nearly 1,000 Al Qaeda operatives in over 60 countries and have disrupted terrorist operations and potential terrorist attacks.

Al Qaeda has not yet been destroyed. It and other like-minded groups remain willing and able to strike at us. Al Qaeda's leaders, still at large, are working to reconstitute the organization and resume its terrorist operations. We must eradicate these organizations by denying them their sources of financing, eliminating their ability to hijack charitable organizations for their terrorist purposes. We must be prepared for a long war and we must not falter.

We have already seen in Afghanistan and elsewhere that domestic unrest and conflict in weak states is one of the factors that create an environment conducive to terrorism. More importantly, demographic trends tell us that the world's poorest and most politically unstable regions, which include parts of the Middle East and sub-Saharan Africa, will have the largest youth populations in the world over the next two decades and beyond. Most of these countries will lack the economic institutions or the resources to effectively integrate these youth into their societies. Islam itself is neither an enemy nor a threat to the United States. But the increasing anger toward the West and toward governments friendly to us among Islamic extremists and their sympathizers clearly is a threat to us.

GREEK TERRORIST ORGANIZATION

It may not be as well known as Islamic Jihad in the Middle East or the Irish Republican Army, but the Greek terrorist organization known as November 17 has been around committing terrorist acts in Greece since 1975. November 17 is known as the most feared group in Greece and is also one of the most deadly in all of Europe. The signal birth of this group came on December 23, 1975 when Richard Welch, the United States Central Intelligence Agency station chief in Athens was shot and killed by three men as he returned from a party. Welch was killed by a .45-caliber pistol that became the trademark of the terrorist group. The number of murdered victims that can be attributed to November 17 would be considered small. Only 20 since 1975. Their victims include three other American officials and one person who worked for Americans. Two Diplomats from Turkey and 13 Greeks.

Through the years the terrorist group has also been responsible for about 35 attacks, mostly bombings and missile attacks, on Greek tax offices and multinational corporations. But the one thing that distinguishes the November 17 terrorist organization from any other terrorist organization is – in over twenty years – not one single member of this group has ever been arrested. The identities of any November 17 members remain unknown to Greek, American and European police and intelligence agencies. No other terrorist group can make that same claim.

One Greek politician, who was one of the few to ever survive a November 17 attack, said, "From then until now, Greece is the only country where it has been impossible to not only smoke out terrorism, but even to make a single substantial strike against it." Why has November 17 been able to remain untouched? German authorities were able to destroy the Red Army Faction. France wiped out a terrorist group that was known as Action Direct. In 1987, Italy was able to bring an end to the Red Brigades. In other nations in Europe – Irish separatists, Basque Separatists in Spain, and Corsican separatists in France have had members arrested.

In Greece, it's an altogether different story. The group has several known M.O's. Authorities can tell that the people who make bombs for the organization were apparently trained in the Middle East during the early 1970's.

Greek authorities will not directly comment on terrorism issues. But counter-terrorism experts from other countries believe that the group has between 10- 25 members. It believed to be very small and and thus able to maintain its secrecy and security. The origin of the group is still somewhat vague, but it is believed that its founders were part of resistance group that was formed during the 1967-75 military dictatorship in Greece. It is also believed that Greek Socialist Premier Andreas Papendreou may have played some hand in its beginnings. After democracy returned to Greece in 1975, it is believed that many of the original members went their own way. Papendreou, who has been seriously ill for a long time, is believed to know the identities of some of the members of the group, but it is expected that he will take those names to his grave. It is said that the name of the group comes from the day in 1973 when the Greek military sent tanks and soldiers to squash a student uprising at Athens Polytechnic University.

The ideology of November 17 leans toward Marxist-Leninism. They are known to be anti-European Union, anti-NATO and anti-American. The United States was picked as a target because it supported the former Greek military dictatorship.They are extremely nationalistic and have recently called for an armed uprising against the middle and upper classes in Greece. Essentially, to cause fear in the population – a common terrorist's tactic. One counter-terrorism expert said that November 17 is unique in that it appears not to lead any political movement. They don't call for a separate state for any one particular ethnic group as do many other terrorist organizations in places like Spain, France or India.

But since the Cold War ended a few years ago, it caused an ideological problem for November 17. The group is now shifting targets. The group's last known attack was made in

May of 1995 when it fired two anti-tank rockets at a Greek television network building. The television network was called a capitalist tool. There were no injuries in the attack. It was announced by Greek authorities in mid-December that they plan to spend about $30 million to overhaul their anti-terrorism services. But one counter-terrorism expert said that he didn't think that money alone will be able to stop November 17. He said, "We just hope they make a mistake one day."

CONTEMPORARY ARMENIAN TERRORISM

The ongoing discussion on an internationally agreed definition of terrorism embodies a special interest to Turkey, which is targeted by violent groups. This is not, however, a new phenomenon as a costly campaign of terrorism against the Turkish officials, citizens and institutions inside or outside Turkey was in operation by certain Armenian groups nearly since 18th century. During those troubled years, an argument was echoed by the Armenian side that these activities should not to be called "terrorism" but simply "a just war" further justified by the alleged "Armenian genocide by Turks" in 1915.

First published in 1986, even the title of Professor Günther's this study indicates that although it was placated "just" by the Armenians, they were no doubt acts of terrorism. On the presumption that the title indicates, it rather gives a comprehensive account of acts and their reasoning and nature. The Introduction is a special section which gives not only a general description of the characteristics of terrorism but also a background to the Armenian terrorism. It is noted that the acts were perpetrated not only against Turkish elements abroad but also inside Turkey. In this wide spectrum, those who were doing business or cooperating with Turkey were targeted. The acts were in a large scale and mostly justified by what happened in 1915. The study accordingly gives an account of history of the "Armenian issue" that still dwells on.

The Turks and the Armenians are said to be widely divided on the reasons for the emergence of the Armenian issue and its persistence. The author seems to suffice with giving a smooth listing of the events that took place until and during the World War I. He notes strikingly that "Since they were the weaker party, the Hunchaks and the Dashnaks, in a manner similar to what the Armenian terrorist are attempting to do today, began deliberately using terror against the Turks to incite Turkish reprisals and massacres". It should be added that the author gives a fairly sufficient account of "deportation and massacres"in the World War I in the light of first accounts of ambassadors and historians. In any account, the author emphasizes that there was no "premeditated genocide" of Armenians by the Turks although many Armenians perished as a result of war conditions and negligence.

The study then takes on the beginnings of the current Armenian terrorism by starting with the name "Nemesis" which is described as a secret Dashnak network and said to be responsible for killing many former Ottoman officials in exile in 1920s. In those years, the reasons behind the terror campaign also started to emerge and were mostly linked to feelings of revenge leading to a widespread support especially among the Armenian community. The very recent wave of Armenian terrorism was said to have started on 27 January 1973 with killing of the Turkish council general and vice council in New York. As soon as these events started to take place so did the names of ASALA and then JCAGARA. The author accordingly devotes separate sections to reviewing of these notorious terrorist organizations.

ASALA (Armenian Secret Army for the Liberation of Armenia) was subjected to a comprehensive analysis of origins and nature and found clearly responsible for assassinating many Turkish diplomats or their immediate family. The statements were that ASALA was doing more than it was despite splits inside ASALA. JCAG-ARA (Justice Commandos of the Armenian Genocide, Armenian Revolutionary Army) is linked to Dashnaks and dated back to 1890. The review also emphasizes the divergences between ASALA and JCAG-ARA. Having noted that a simple account of terrorist acts might be misleading, Professor Gunter analyses in detail the modus operandi of these organizations trying particularly to reflect the scale and the effects.

The period of 1978-80 was the peak of Armenian terrorism, 30 Turkish diplomats or their immediate family members are said to have been killed in the years 1973 to 1984. The Armenian terrorism is described as having a large scale taking place in four different continents. More importantly, the study analyses the financial support behind the Armenian terrorism pointing particularly to the donations from the Armenian community in various countries and even to the drag-trafficking. The personal characteristics of those who have taken part in the acts are also reflected. As to the transnational support for the Armenian terrorism, he points to the link between ASALA and the similar groups in the western European countries and the sympathy for Armenians among the western countries giving credit to the belief among the Turks that a campaign of terror to weaken Turkey was planned and supported by outsiders.

The study goes one step further and examines the link between the Armenian terrorism and particular States such as Lebanon, Palestinian, the Soviets, the United States, France and Cyprus. On the other hand, Greece, Syria and Iran are termed as those indirectly supporting the Armenian terrorism against their "historic enemy". In all these events, were there any "Turkish counter terror and harassment"? This is a highly controversial issue as indicated by the author with a question mark after the title "Turkish counter terror and harassment?" The allegations seem basically stem from the statements of the Turkish officials including the then President Kenan Evren to the effect that Turkey would seek to punish those who had taken part in terrorist acts against Turkey and the Turks. For the reasons that the author contemplates on, there was simply no Turkish counter terror against the Armenians or Armenian terrorists.

However, whether or not there was a Turkish harassment against the Armenians and especially those living in Turkey seems to be a more important issue. The allegation is raised by the Armenians that "The Turkish Government today harasses, persecutes and terrorizes its few (c. 60,000) remaining

Armenian citizens". It is argued that Armenian monuments and other remaining are destroyed in many forms or the Armenian names are forcefully changed in Turkey. Professor Gunter emphasizes the statements of many Armenians living in Turkey that the outsiders distort the real situation of the Armenian origin citizens of Turkey. In his synthesis, he says that although the Turkish treatment of the minorities have not always been at an ideal level, there were reasons since the late Ottoman years for this and these reasons were mostly unrelated to an idea of premeditated government policy.

It is rather that Turkey today restores and cleans up the important Armenian sites in eastern Anatolia especially to protect them and facilitate the visits. The author concludes as to the Armenian terrorism with an impressive expression that "It is obvious that the Armenian terrorists are a deadly, secretive and important manifestation of contemporary international terrorism". But, more than that, it is possible to see in the Conclusion the factors on which the Armenian terrorism against Turkey was based. All come to a point that Armenians associate themselves with the eastern Anatolia. But the author concludes as to this point that at this late date the Armenians have absolutely no international legal or even moral claim to eastern Anatolia. However, as a stateless people who suffered a wrong that has never been rectified and since they are a party to contemporary terrorist movement against Turkey, it behooves us to search for a possible solution to the current impasse.

It certainly reflects on the current situation between Turkey and the Armenians although the current Armenian stance against Turkey does not comprise violence or terrorism but an intensive political and sometimes legal campaign to secure the approval of the so-called "Armenian genocide". In this context, a sentence of dissatisfaction to the remarks of Professor Gunter should be added. The comments in the Conclusion unnecessarily concentrate on the treatment of the Armenians by the Ottomans and on the alleged "Armenian genocide". This should not distort the fact that nothing can be a justification for resorting to terrorism as a way of pursuing a goal. Moreover, as author emphasizes, what happened during the World War I and in 1915 was not, in any account, premeditated but rather happened for some other reasons that should be perceived as mostly related to the natural components of a war situation.

CODIFYING THE UNCONVENTIONAL

The Swiss government's January 2003 roundtable to discuss the Geneva Conventions and 1977 Protocols in light of the so-called war on terrorism is now the talk among experts in international humanitarian law. To some academics and NGOs, the discussions provide a long-overdue opportunity to consider updating the Conventions and Protocols – to tailor them for a war they were never designed to address. In that sense, a new round of codification would be as important a response to terrorism as was the ICRC's diplomatic conference of the 1970s a response to anti-colonial wars and internal conflicts. Although governments and other experts should ensure that the employment of coercion against terrorists is regulated according to some normative framework, I believe that most claims for a major reform of international humanitarian law are premised on a variety of misconceptions of that law. As a result, any intergovernmental process is not likely to lead to any significant new norms nor, I believe, should it.

A common assumption in favor of updating the law of war is that the existing corpus of international humanitarian law is ill-equipped to address uses of force by and against terrorist groups. While the laws of war provide detailed rules for interstate conflicts, conflicts between states and liberation movements, and conflicts between states and well organized insurgencies, they do not provide any guidance to those fighting in wars between states and terrorist movements. It is, of course, undeniable that the Conventions and Protocols only cover what they cover. If one side in the conflict does not meet the definitions provided in Common Article 2 of the Geneva Conventions, Article 1(4) of Protocol I, and Article 1 of Protocol II, the Conventions and Protocols qua treaties simply do not govern the conflict.

But international humanitarian law has a sizeable "place-holder" for all other conflicts - one that Protocol I explicitly recognizes: "the principles of international law derived from established custom, from the principles of humanity and from the dictates of public conscience." These terms are no mere rhetoric. At a minimum, their content includes: (a) the principle of distinction, i.e., that combatants must distinguish between other combatants and civilians, and that combatants must neither deliberately target nor indiscriminately or disproportionately harm civilians; (b) the status of hors de combat, under which combatants not taking part in hostilities shall be treated humanely; (c) limitations on methods of combat to those that do not cause unnecessary suffering. These basic notions are admittedly vague around the margins. But states have made clear that they recognize such obligations in all conflicts. Thus, while at first denying, and later limiting, the application of the Geneva Conventions to its operations against Afghanistan and Al Qaeda, the United States and its allies have repeatedly stated their acceptance of basic principles of humanitarian law.

Indeed, the full scope of customary international humanitarian law is far more detailed than these basic principles. If asked, most states would point to numerous provisions of Hague and Geneva Law as still binding on this conflict, even though it does not meet the definition of armed conflict in those instruments. For instance, the ban on killing someone in the course of a bona fide surrender, as well as the possibility to shoot those engaging in perfidy by faking surrender (with some gray areas as to how the bona fides of the surrender is determined), would seem well accepted.

This is not to suggest that every scenario in the "war on terrorism" is addressed by customary international law. That, after all, is why states draft treaties. Ambiguities over the definition of combatant, the meaning of hostilities (and the end of them), and other problems will remain beyond the scope of existing customary international law simply because customary law has not had time to develop regarding certain aspects of these new conflicts. The question, however, is whether those ambiguities can and should be resolved through a new round of codification, or whether other methods are open to decisionmakers.

The burden needs to be on those calling for revision to demonstrate exactly what needs to be improved. Are they asserting that, under current law, combatants are underprotected, as when members of so-called terrorist groups are taken prisoner and not granted POW status; or that they are overprotected, as when the U.S. army targets and kills an Al Qaeda leader in Yemen and claims this action is a legitimate engagement in an armed conflict? Are civilians currently underprotected, as when they are killed in collapsing buildings; or are they said to be overprotected, because many members of terrorist cells, e.g., those organizing or financing activities, never wear uniforms or ever show arms? Even now, while the United States denies the applicability of the POW provisions of Geneva Convention III to Taliban detainees (almost certainly unjustified under that Convention) or Al Qaeda detainees (far more convincing under extant law), the ICRC is able to monitor their conditions at a number of detention facilities.

More likely, the harms arise from the prospect that states, such as the United States, may be claiming the right to kill terrorists (as the U.S. defines them) anywhere or detain them indefinitely. This is a significant expansion of the notion of armed conflict, and eats away at much of the traditional ways of addressing transnational crime, e.g., through extradition and trial. But if that is the case, those inside and outside of governments should focus on those narrow issues, rather than assume that international humanitarian law has little to say about such conflicts.

One of the hallmarks of IHL since Henri Dunant has been the need to protect victims of armed conflict regardless of its cause or the blameworthiness of the sides under the law governing recourse to force (*jus ad bellum*). Today, the Conventions and Protocols apply equally to entities acting unlawfully - in violation of the UN Charter's ban on the use of force — and those acting lawfully — in selfdefense, under UN authority, or in opposition to colonial domination (or even against an unjust regime, although international law tends to be rather agnostic on this issue). Without such a clear distinction, combatants would argue that the justness of their cause allows for all sorts of indignities against combatants and civilians, clearly defeating the whole enterprise of IHL. With regard to terrorism, the argument would be that the question of who is right and who is wrong in the decisions by certain states and non-state groups to use violence against each other should not detract from the need to regulate that conflict in a humanitarian manner.

The *jus in bello/jus ad bellum* distinction is thus premised on the idea — based on fundamental principles of humanity — that all combatants and civilians deserve protections regardless of the merits of their side. In addition, international actors may well have other reasons for granting both sides protection. They may understand the difficulty of knowing (or at least reaching a consensus among states) in certain conflicts which side has violated *jus ad bellum* by initiating the war; in these cases, it is better to grant both sides protection.

But the reality is not a clearcut as this distinction suggests. First, the inclusion of wars of liberation in Protocol I's coverage stemmed from the sense among many governments that certain struggles against colonial or alien domination were legitimate; and even Protocol II's protections recognize that insurgent groups might be engaging a legitimate activity. Second, even for wars that are illegal, i.e., clear aggression under the UN Charter, states seem to have found these not so obnoxious to merit denying even the offenders humanitarian protections. States quietly accept that wars still happen; that aggression still occurs; and that they might, after all, even be aggressors themselves one day. They are not willing to say that the aggressor is so evil - that his goal is so beyond the pale of civilized conduct — that he forfeits all protections for his troops and his civilians.

But what happens when we have non-state actors whose

goal is simply to kill innocent people and terrorize a population? While not all groups labeled as terrorist by states have this goal - many use attacks on civilians as a means to gain control of specific territory (e.g., the IRA or Palestinian groups) – there seems to be no such goal for Al Qaeda. It has no leaders in waiting to take over the United States or the United Kingdom. It claims to want those states to change their foreign policies on various issues, but there is also evidence that it is simply the way of life practiced in these states that it finds a threat.

In these situations, can and should governments make the leap of faith that such conflict against organized states deserves regulation by detailed protections of international humanitarian law? When the goal of a group is so beyond acceptable conduct it finds no defenders among governments, extending the protections of international humanitarian law to such conflicts serves a legitimating function. Equally significant, key governments likely have the same fear, and are unlikely to engage in a process that they will regard as tarnishing IHL. Another mantra of international humanitarian law is that, unlike much international law, the targets of its norms deserve protection even if they themselves violate them. Thus, traditional norms of treaty interpretation that permit a state to suspend its obligations in the event of a material breach by the other side do not apply in many key situations.

At a minimum, reprisals - i.e., otherwise unlawful acts taken in response to prior unlawful acts – against POWs, civilians, and wounded, sick, and shipwrecked combatants are explicitly prohibited by Geneva Convention III (article 13), Geneva Convention IV (article 33), and Protocol I (articles 20 and 51(6)). Some might call for the abolition of all reprisals based on the underlying purposes of IHL. Another form of non-reciprocity appears in Protocol I's requirement (article 44(2)) that combatants do not lose their status even if they violate most norms of IHL in the course of their operations. Under this non-reciprocity model, the violations of IHL by various terrorist groups should not be an excuse for denying them certain protections. But non-reciprocity is not and should not be all-encompassing.

First, current IHL does not preclude reprisals during combat against combatants that might violate IHL. Second, even the bans on reprisals in Protocol I have their detractors, such as the United Kingdom, which issued a reservation to that treaty allowing for the possibility of measured reprisals against civilians if the opposing party itself engaged in serious, deliberate attacks on civilians. Lastly, the granting of protections in Protocol I was, in fact, part of a reciprocal bargain, not simply extending protections to guerrilla groups as a gesture of goodwill, but creating obligations for those movements as well. Thus Protocol I denies combatant status to guerrilla groups that do not follow certain requirements regarding open carrying of arms.

The nature of terrorist organizations - whose modus operandi typically includes targeting of civilians (although it is not limited to that) - pushes the need for non-reciprocity even further. One side is determined from the outset to carry out a struggle regardless of even the most fundamental principles of humanity. If these acts are not simply an aberration but its principal way of operation, why should its members be afforded anything more than treatment consistent with those basic notions of humanity? (Some will suggest that they do not even deserve that treatment, of course.) States will not and should not tolerate a legal regime whereby only one set of combatants' benefits from the protections of IHL.

This solution is not a recipe for a free-for-all in the war against terrorism. As noted, basic principles of humanity still apply and are accepted by governments. They would mean, for example, that terrorists cannot be tortured upon capture and that their families cannot be targeted. But to suggest that the IHL's non-reciprocal approach to protections requires granting them a vast array of other protections, such as the combatant's privilege (against prosecution) or POW status, is unwarranted. One argument made for the revision of the Conventions and Protocols is that they reflect an outdated notion of what constitute armed conflict and those participating in it. Thus, Al Qaeda's actions against the United States - whether against civilians or military personnel, whether within the United States or abroad - are clearly a form of armed conflict; and the U.S. actions in fighting, capturing, and killing Al Qaeda forces - whether in Afghanistan, Pakistan, Yemen, or elsewhere - are equally armed conflict.

The argument is not that customary law does not offer some protections, but that the Conventions and Protocols, which on their face govern only three sets of conflicts (state vs. state, state vs. national liberation movement, and state vs. organized insurgency), need to respond to the changing nature of armed conflict. This apparent need for updating seems bolstered by the very use of the war paradigm by states engaging with Al Qaeda. Thus, the United States and its allies have used the rhetoric of armed conflict to respond to the attacks of September 11. U.S. officials refer to their operations as the "war" on terrorism; and the United States has invoked its rights under *jus ad bellum* - Article 51 of the United Nations Charter - in attacking Afghanistan and Al Qaeda targets and personnel around the world. The U.S. relies on this characterization to avoid treating Al Qaeda as simply a criminal organization that can be targeted only through traditional law enforcement activities, e.g., police investigations, extradition requests, and civilian trials with full due process. Advocates for change say that the U.S. is trying to have it both ways - asserting various rights under *jus ad bellum* while denying the applicability of key aspects of *jus in bello*.

It seems unquestionable that the United States and others are engaged in an armed conflict with Al Qaeda. But the subsidiary concepts of combat operations and combatants that permeate Hague and Geneva Law are not and should not be infinitely elastic. Part of the core of international humanitarian law is the creation of physical and temporal space in which it is perfectly legal for certain categories of people to kill each other: that space is combat and those people are combatants. The combatant's privilege means that combatants (at least in international conflicts) may not be punished for lawful combat operations, though, of course, they can be punished for war crimes. The notions of armed conflict, combat, and combatant have changed since the days of the Hague Conventions, as Protocol I makes especially clear; today, the problems of determining whether the unconventional nature of some armed forces' garb (like the Taliban) serves to deny them combatant status are well known.

Yet, even with the expansion of the notion of armed conflict to cover acts by national liberation movements in Protocol I, there remain the ideas of the military engagement and the military attack. For instance, under Protocol I, if a fighter does not carry his arms openly during the engagements as well as during the deployment before an attack while visible to the adversary, he is not a lawful combatant (entitled, for example, to POW status). This compromise (though opposed by the United States) preserves the idea of combat operations and the special nature of the combatant, who must distinguish himself from the civilian population in combat and the time leading up to it. The ban on perfidy also reinforces this idea. To expand the laws of wars to apply to any situation where an organization (or conceivably an individual) initiates force is to blur the distinction between cases where the law allows individuals to kill each other and those where the law prohibits it.

Under such a view, every attack on a military installation, even if undertaken without any separation from the civilian population (indeed, this is the modus operandi of many terrorist operatives) is per se a combat operation and those who carry it out combatants. The result is to turn every act of violence into an act of war, and all those who commit it into lawful combatants who enjoy the combatant's privilege. It infinitely expands the protected zone in time and space. Where does one draw the line between Al Qaeda attacks and those of the mafia or simply an insane person? For the combatant's privilege to remain, as it should, a hallmark of international humanitarian law, it must be confined to a highly limited set of circumstances. States will not and should not agree to extend it to any individual or group that chooses to attack a military target.

PRIORITIES FOR NORMATIVE DEVELOPMENT

Of course, as noted, the United States government conceives of the struggle against Al Qaeda as a war, and it wants to expand the geographical zone of legitimate combat significantly - to cover, for instance, the killing by remotely piloted vehicle of a suspected Al Qaeda leader in Yemen. The United States also wants to expand the notion of combat temporally. It refuses to talk about an end to the hostilities, partly to justify the indefinite detention without trial of Al Qaeda and Taliban personnel.

These two expansions of the notions of armed conflict, combat, and combatant - geographical and temporal - are the most vexing questions for IHL today. On the geographical plane, it is hard to accept the U.S. position that treats Al Qaeda operatives around the world as legitimate targets for wartime killing while rejecting the idea that Al Qaeda operatives are acting as lawful combatants when they kill U.S. soldiers anywhere in the world. The U.S. squares the circle by relying on the notion of the "illegal combatant," something that IHL already accepts in terms of spies, mercenaries, and guerrillas who do not meet the special requirements of carrying arms openly. This allows a state to kill them but afford them no protections. But is there no limit to how and where someone becomes such an illegal combatant?

The simplest solution is to say that the armed conflict paradigm does not apply at all - that Al Qaeda's members are criminals and that the United States should use law enforcement techniques to try and punish them, just like European states are rounding up suspected members of Al Qaeda cells. Human rights law, which governs peacetime law enforcement, still recognizes significant discretion for police acting in genuine selfdefense, while protecting criminals from arbitrary killing by the state. The question is whether this attitude will suffice in a world where Al Qaeda can gain access to weapons of mass destruction. If states treat the campaign against Al Qaeda as an armed conflict, then they need to do so in a way that does not entail a wholesale change in the notion of combat. The conflict with Al Qaeda needs to have boundaries beyond which the special privileges that the law of war gives to combatants do not apply.

As for the temporal question, namely the U.S. willingness to tolerate indefinite detention of Al Qaeda fighters, it is clearly unsustainable in the long term. (As noted, their position on the Taliban seems to be a misreading of the Conventions.) Humanitarian and human rights law make clear those individuals - whether lawful combatants, civilians, or others – cannot be held indefinitely without trial. But rather than recognizing some form of combatant status for Al Qaeda and then trying to determine at what point hostilities cease (so that they would have to be released), another possibility is available. They should enjoy protections consistent at a minimum with basic principles of humanity. Beyond that, states might apply the list of minimal protections found in Article 75 of Protocol I to any captured terrorist. This list currently applies to anyone in the control of a party to an interstate conflict who does not enjoy better treatment under other parts of the Convention and Protocol.

These include the basic human right to a trial for suspected crimes. In summary, as a predictive matter, it seems exceedingly unlikely that states will agree to a significant revision or augmentation of the laws of war to address the sorts of unconventional threats posed by transnational groups such as Al Qaeda. To date, only a very small part of those activities that some states refer to as terrorism - guerrilla warfare as part of a legitimate war of national liberation - has come under the protection of international humanitarian treaties. The remainder of unconventional activity is still subject to baseline principles of humanity, and states see little reason to grant more.

Protocol I was expanded to cover liberation movements because a group of states - those in the developing world - insisted upon such protections. Al Qaeda and other groups have no such vocal constituency, however, as much as some states may support them sub silencio. If, for some reason, enough states were to find the absence of treaty law in the war on terrorism an unacceptable gap, a Protocol III is likely to be far more limited than Protocol II turned out to be. Indeed, I suspect it will do nothing beyond recognizing the most basic principles of humanity. As a normative matter, any codification that goes beyond the obvious principles of humanity is at best premature. The legitimization function accomplished through codification sends a signal to these unconventional fighters that their tactics are acceptable – that they are lawful combatants, even if they consider their great victories to be crashing a plane into a commercial building or incapacitating a major city via germ or chemical weapons.

The immediate threat to public order around the world from groups whose mission is to create civilian casualties – who themselves reject the most basic principles of the law of war – argues against enveloping their activities in a set of detailed law of war norms. Any such process will do little to protect the victims of such acts, as those people are already illegitimate targets under international criminal law, humanitarian law, and human rights law. So it seems to benefit only one side in the conflict. Whatever protections those fighting colonial domination may have deserved, Al Qaeda and its allies fall into a completely different category. Clearly, states do need to figure out some limits to armed conflict as a geographic and temporal matter, and academic and governmental discussion of such issues can help elaborate whether the existing norms work or need some further elaboration. But beyond that, as long as those fighting terrorism respect the basic principles of humanity in that struggle, international humanitarian law ought to live with something close to the status quo.

ANTI-ISRAELI TERRORISM, 2006

This study examines and analyzes the terrorism directed against Israel, which continued during 2006 as a central factor influencing the agenda of the State of Israel. It examines the activities of the Palestinian terrorist organizations, Hezbollah and the global jihad, and compares their modus operandi with previous years. It also deals with the support given by Iran and Syria to the terrorist organizations operating against Israel as well as other factors influencing the extent and nature of anti-Israeli terrorism.

During 2006 the number of terrorist attacks carried out by the Palestinian terrorist organizations constantly continued to decline, especially suicide bombing attacks , despite the fact that motivation to carry out such attacks has been increasing. The decline in the number of suicide bombing attacks is a result of many factors, the most prominent of which are the successful counterterrorist activities of the Israeli security forces and Hamas's policy of restraint, which because of political considerations, kept them from focusing their efforts on such attacks.

During 2006 abductions and rocket fire replaced suicide bombing terrorism as the dominant factor of the campaign against Israel. Abductions and rocket fire are less lethal than suicide bombing attacks, but their consequences have long-term strategic influences on the internal Israeli arena, on the Lebanese arena and on the entire Middle East, and those influences will continue to make themselves felt in Israel through 2007. In 2006 events focused on two separate abductions of IDF soldiers. The most significant, which took place at Zar'it on the Lebanese border, was carried out by Hezbollah according to a modus operandi familiar from past attacks. Israel's uncompromising response caught Hezbollah by surprise and led to the 33-day second Lebanon war.

The war temporarily overshadowed the Palestinian terrorist campaign and forced Israel to transfer its attention and efforts to the northern border. The other abduction, carried out by Hamas in collaboration with two other terrorist organizations, also escalated the confrontation and resulted in forceful IDF actions in the Gaza Strip for the first time since the disengagement of August 2005. The second Lebanon war enabled Hezbollah, for the first time, to use its massive arsenal of advanced weapons (provided by Iran and Syria) against both Israel's civilian population and the IDF. Especially menacing with respect to offensive capabilities were the massive volleys of rocket fire directed at civilian population centers in Israel on every single day of the fighting, a total of approximately 4,000 rockets which hit targets as far south as Hadera. Defensively, Hezbollah's advanced anti-tank missiles were effective against Israeli ground forces in south Lebanon, as was the attack of a Chinese-made C-802 rocket fired at an Israeli Navy ship. During the war the IDF succeeded in destroying some of Hezbollah's long-range rockets, caused extensive damage to the organization's military infrastructure and created a new situation in south Lebanon. The manifestations of that new situation were the transfer of three Lebanese army brigades to the south, the upgrading of the UNIFIL forces and pushing Hezbollah posts further back from the border. Nevertheless, Hezbollah continues to foster the myth that it was "victorious" in the war, based on its success to activate its rocket arsenal throughout the war and the Israeli failures, both in the way the army was put into action and on the home front. That has made it necessary for Israel to rethink and reorganize its military and political systems, based on the lessons of the war (a process which is still in progress). Hezbollah as well began, with the aid and support of Iran and Syria, reconstructing its damaged operational capabilities.

Hezbollah's rocket and missile capabilities in the second Lebanon war served as a model for the Palestinian terrorist organizations, which make every effort to acquire advanced weapons, especially long-range rockets and anti-tank missiles. That is part of the buildup project currently being undertaken in the Gaza Strip, especially by Hamas, and which accelerated after the disengagement and Hamas's rise to power. As part of the project, during the past year Hamas and the other terrorist organizations have organized themselves in a quasi-military fashion, with both offensive and defensive elements. One aspect was a new military framework was established this year under the aegis of the Hamas government's interior ministry, called the Executive Force.

In addition, there have been massive amounts of weapons

smuggled into the Gaza Strip mainly through a system of tunnels dug along the wide-open Philadephi route, including 122 mm Grad rockets and Konkurs second-generation anti-tank missiles. Massive amounts of homemade weapons have been manufactured, including rockets, anti-tank weapons and explosive devices; terrorist-operatives have received extensive training both in the Gaza Strip and abroad (Lebanon, Syria, Iran); and an enormous number of underground bunkers and tunnels have been built for both offensive and defensive purposes. So far, the post-disengagement efforts of the terrorist organizations to copy the buildup process (including the ability to fire mortars and rockets) in Judea and Samaria have failed, principally because of Israel's counterterrorist activities. However, despite the blows inflicted on the terrorists in Judea and Samaria, they continue to try to dispatch suicide bombers to carry out attacks in Israel. The Fatah and PIJ infrastructures in Nablus and Jenin, which are directed by external headquarters, continue as foci of terrorist activities in Judea and Samaria even though in 2006 their operational capabilities were inferior to those of former years.

COMPARISON BETWEEN 2006 AND THE PREVIOUS YEARS

Since September 2000 the Palestinians terrorist organizations have waged an unremitting terrorist campaign against Israel (called by the Palestinians "the second intifada" or "the Al-Aqsa intifada"). During the campaign, which has been unprecedented in both extent and force since the beginning of the Israeli-Palestinian confrontation, terrorism has spiraled up and down and from time to time the terrorist organizations have made significant changes in their methods. The peak of the terrorist campaign was during 2001-2002, and since then number and deadliness of the attacks have been in constant decline, although both formally and practically the confrontation has not ended.

Attempts to formulate and adhere to partial or full ceasefire agreements have so far been unsuccessful because the PIJ and other organizations stubbornly continue carrying out attacks. During 2005, in view of the disengagement, an internal Palestinian agreement was reached regarding a "lull in the fighting" which was never fully implemented and ended in January 2006. On November 25, 2006, PA chairman Abu Mazen and Israeli Prime Minister Ehud Olmert reached an agreement regarding a ceasefire in the Gaza Strip. The terrorist organizations did not implement that agreement either, and to certain extent terrorism from the Gaza Strip ratcheted up a notch with the suicide bombing attack in Eilat in January 2007.

The terrorist campaign waged against Israel by Hezbollah, which began while the IDF was in Lebanon for the first Lebanon war (1982-1985), continued during the era of the "security zone" (1985-2000). After the IDF left south Lebanon in May 2000 a new stage began: Hezbollah began accelerating the construction of its broad military infrastructure, particularly south Lebanon, kept up a controlled degree of tension along the border by means of sporadic attacks (attacks on IDF posts, abducting soldiers, firing rockets and mortars at Israel, and supported the Palestinian terrorist organizations in the PA with money, weapons and training)

Israel's response was to adopt a policy of restraint intended to contain Hezbollah attacks and made do with treating the problem through the intervention of the international community. Such a policy enabled Israel to focus most of its efforts on Palestinian terrorism, which overshadowed the Hezbollah threat until the second Lebanon war and prevented deterioration along the Israeli-Lebanese border. Hezbollah policy was to continue the attacks while keeping the tension from boiling over. That, along with Israel's policy of restraint generally enabled the settlements along Israel's northern border to live their daily lives in a routine fashion during the six years after the IDF's withdrawal from Lebanon. The price, however, was granting Hezbollah a free hand to construct a broad military infrastructure.

The abduction of two IDF soldiers on July 12, 2006, radically changed the situation which had lasted for six years. Israel abandoned its policy of restraint and, to Hezbollah's surprise, responded forcefully (as Hassan Nasrallah publicly admitted after the war). The abduction, which Hezbollah viewed as "playing by the rules," and expected to produce a limited, localized Israeli response, turned into a fullfledged war between Israel and Hezbollah, leading to the creation of a new situation in south Lebanon and new "rules of engagement."

FACTORS INFLUENCING THE NATURE AND EXTENT OF PALESTINIAN TERRORISM, 2006

Four main factors, influenced the nature and extent of Palestinian terrorism in 2006, which was and is one of the main threats facing the State of Israel.

The effectiveness of the counterterrorism measures taken by the Israeli security forces in Judea and Samaria: During 2006 the Israeli security forces conducted intensive counterterrorism activities which included the detention of wanted terrorists, the exposure of weapons and the killing of terrorist-operatives who resisted detention. That successful activity severely damaged thc terrorist infrastructures, both the leadership and the rank and file. In addition, along with the completion of many sections of the security fence (which has proved its effectiveness), it also led to an additional decline in the number of suicide bombing attacks and forced the terrorist organizations to make do with relatively simple attacks such as shootings and stabbings. At the same time, there was a sharp rise in the number of rockets launched from the Gaza Strip (where the terrorist organizations enjoy unfettered freedom of action) at Israeli population centers in the western Negev "in compensation" for operational difficulties in Judea and Samaria.

Dramatic developments in the internal Palestinian arena, and the most important of which was the Hamas takeover of the Palestinian government after their victory in the Palestinian Legislative Council elections. That resulted in unending power struggles between PA chairman Israel Mazen and Hamas Prime Minister Ismail Haniya, and violent clashes between Israel and Hamas which led to increased anarchy in the Gaza

Strip and the collapse of government institutions. Those events hampered the operational capabilities of the terrorist organizations and sometimes turned attention (especially that of Hamas) to internal Palestinian struggles for power and survival at the expense of terrorist activity against Israel.

Hamas's government commitments were also a restraining factor. Therefore, in our assessment, the cocktail of internal Palestinian developments was an important factor contributing to the decline in volume and change in nature of Palestinian terrorism during 2006. It is particularly worthwhile mentioning Hamas, which kept from focusing on suicide bombing terrorism and left the field open to the PIJ. The Israel's intensive activity in the Gaza Strip, which increased after Israel soldier Gilad Shalit was abducted. That activity included infantry and armored operations in the northern and southern Gaza Strip and targeted killings carried out by the Israeli Air Force. senior terrorist-operatives were killed; arms storehouses and workshops for the manufacture of weapons were attacked; terrorist bases, training camps and terrorist organization offices were attacked; suspects were detained; and tunnels used for smuggling weapons were exposed.

In addition, for the first time since the disengagement, two broad operations were carried out targeting the terrorist infrastructure: Operation Summer Rain during Israel and August, and Operation Autumn Clouds, in October and November. The Israel's activity in the Gaza Strip made it hard for the terrorist organizations to continue the buildup and carry out terrorist attacks. However, it did not lead to the release of Gilad Shalit or a decrease in the amount of rocket fire, but rather spurred the terrorist organizations on to increase their efforts to launch rockets during Israel operations as the only response possible to Israel activity. The second Lebanon war temporarily distracted Israel's attention from the Gaza Strip and focused it on the northern border.

During the war, Hezbollah attempted to activate the Palestinian terrorist organizations it supports to carry out abductions and suicide bombing attacks against Israel to open a second front. Their efforts failed, however, because of the efficacy of the Israeli security forces' counterterrorism activities. After the war the Palestinian terrorist organizations, especially Hamas, made efforts to upgrade their weapons and other military capabilities, primarily standard rockets, such as the Grad (122 mm), and advanced anti-tank weapons (such as Konkurs missiles). That was done to create a balance of deterrence with Israel based on the model Hezbollah created in Lebanon.

IRANIAN AND SYRIAN SUPPORT FOR THE TERRORIST ORGANIZATIONS

Iran and Syria, two states which sponsor terrorism and are subject to increasing pressure from the international community, view the terrorist campaign waged by the Palestinian organizations and Hezbollah as an effective tool to harm and weaken Israel. The support they give the organizations and their terrorist campaign are also effective measures to strengthen the Iranian and Syrian regimes and the Iranian-Syrian axis ("the axis of evil"), to advance and increase the influence of both countries in Lebanon and the Arab-Muslim world and to strengthen their position versus the United States and the international community.

Considering Hezbollah as an important strategic asset, Iran and Syria helped it established an enhanced military infrastructure in Lebanon, turning it from a guerilla terrorist organization into an organization with military ground capabilities similar to those of a sovereign state. The infrastructure included a defensive deployment and offensive options in the form of an enormous (more than 20,000) rocket arsenal, which was prematurely activated during the second Lebanon war. Since the war both Iran and Syria have helped Hezbollah rehabilitate its military capabilities, which had been partially destroyed. Conspicuous was the large-scale smuggling of arms from Syria into Lebanon (especially south Lebanon) in clear and direct contravention of the provisions of Security Council Resolution 1701.

The rise of Hamas to power in the PA and the achievements of Hezbollah in the second Lebanon war strengthened the positions of both organizations Iran and Syria. During the second half of 2006 both countries were conspicuous in their efforts to rehabilitate Hezbollah's military infrastructure in Lebanon, as was Iran's immense involvement in compensating Shi'ite Lebanese residents and in rebuilding Shi'ite areas damaged during the war. Conspicuous as well was the generous financial aid Iran promised Hamas Prime Minister Ismail Haniya ($250 million and aid for development projects) during the latter's December 7-11 visit to Tehran, and the frequent summit meetings held by the heads of the Syrian regime and the Hamas leadership.

In addition to the above, during 2006 Iran and Syria continued their "ordinary" aid to the Palestinian terrorist organizations at the "traditional" levels: direction of the activities of the terrorist organizations in the PA-administered territories continued coming from the terrorist organizations' headquarters in Damascus, especially from the PIJ and Hamas's "external" headquarters (the latter has become a dominant factor in Hamas's internal balance of power); Iran's funding for the activities of the terrorist organizations (especially the PIJ); providing the Palestinian terrorist organizations with weapons to be smuggled into the PA-administered territories; and allowing Palestinian terrorist-operatives to be trained in various military fields in camps in Iran, Syria and Lebanon.

Bibliography

Adams, James. *The Financing of Terror,* New York: Simon & Schuster, 1986.

Alexander, Yonah and Richard Latter, eds. *Terrorism and the Media: Dilemmas for Government, Journalists & the Public,* Washington, DC: Brassey's, 1990.

Andersan, Sean and Stephen Solan. *Historical Dictionary of Terrorism,* 2nd ed. Lanham, MD: Scarecrow, 2002.

Atkins, Stephen E. *Terrorism: A Reference Handbook,* Santa Barbara, CA: 1992.

Bell, J. Bower. *Transnational Terror, Washington,* DC: American Enterprise Institute, 1975.

Burton, Anthony. *Urban Terrorism: Theory, Practice, Response,* London: Cooper, 1975.

Chaliand, Gerald. *Terrorism: From Popular Struggle to Media Spectacle,* Atlantic Highlands, NJ: Saqi, 1987.

Comb, Cindy C. *Terrorism in Twenty-First Century,* 2nd ed. Upper Saddle River, NJ: Prentice Hall, 2002.

Crelinsten, Ronald D. and Denis Szabo. *Hostage- Taking,* Lexington, MA: Lexington Book, 1979.

Crenshaw, Martha. *Terrorism, Legitimacy, and Power,* Middletown, CT: Wesleyan University Press, 1983.

Gay, Kathleen. *Encyclopedia of Political Anarchy,* Santa Barbara, CA: ABC-CLIO, 1999.

George, Alexander, ed. *Western State Terrorism,* New York: Routledge, 1991.

Gurr, Ted Robert. *Handbook of Political Conflict: Theory and Research*, New York: Free Press, 1980.

Harmon, Christopher C. *Terrorism Today*, London: Frank Cass, 2002.

Hoffman, Bruce. *Inside Terrorism*, New York: Columbia University Press, 1998.

Jenkins, Brian. *International Terrorism: The Other World War*, Santa Monica, CA: RAND, 1985.

Kushner, Harvey W. ed. *The Future of Terrorism: Violence in the New Millennium*, Thousand Oaks, CA: Sage, 1998.

Laqueur, Walter. *History of Terrorism*, New York: Transaction Publishers, 2001.

Lesser, Ian O. et al. *Countering the New Terrorism*, Santa Monica, CA: RAND, 1999.

Lewis Bernand. *The Political Language of Islam*, Chicago: University of Chicago Press, 1988.

Miller, Abraham H. *Terrorism and Hostage Negotiations*, Boulder, CO: Westview, 1980.

Moss, Robert. *Urban Guerrilla Warfare*, London: International Institute for Strategic Studies, 1971.

Netanyahu, Benzamin. *The Terrorism Reader*, New York: Meridian, 1986.

O'Neill, Bard E. *Insurgency and Terrorism: Inside Modern Revolutionary Warfare*, Washington, DC: Brassey's, 1990.

Peters, Rudolph. *Jihad in Classical and Modern Islam*, Princeton, NJ: Markus Wiener, 1996.

Picard, Robert G. *Media Portrayals of Terrorism: Functions and Meaning of News Coverage*, Ames: Iowa State University Press, 1993.

Pillar, Paul R. and Michael H. Armacost. *Terrorism and U.S. Foreign Policy, Washington,* DC: Brookings Institution, 2001.

Rashid, Ahmed. Jihad: *The Rise of Militant Islam I Central Asia*, New Haven, CT: Yale University Press, 2002.

Rosie, George. *The Dictionary of International Terrorism*, New York: Paragon House, 1987.

Schamis, Geraldo Jorge. *War and Terrorism in International Affairs*, New Brunswick, NJ: Transaction Publishers, 1980.

Segaller, Stephen. *Invisible Armies: Terrorism in the 1990s*, San Diego, CA: Harcourt Brace Jovanovich, 1987.

Sofaer, Abraham D. and Seymour E. Goodman. *The Transnational Dimension of Cyber Crime and Terrorism*, Stanford, CA: Hoover Institution, 2001.

Sonn, Richard D. *Anarchism*, New York: Twayne, 1992.

Stern, Jessia. *The Ultimate Terrorists*, Cambridge, MA: Harvard University Press, 1999.

Tanter, Raymond. *Rogue Regimes: Terrorism and Proliferation*, New York: St. Maytin's, 1998.

Tucker, Jonathan B. *Toxic Terror: Assessing Terrorist Use of Chemical and Biological Weapons*, Cambridge, MA: MIT Press, 2000.

U.S. Department of State, *Patterns of Global Terrorism*, Washington, DC [Annual].

Venzke, Ben N. *First Responder Chem- Bio Handbook*, Alexandria, VA: Tempest, 1998.

Wardlaw, Grant. *Political Terrorism: Theory, Tactics, and Counter-Measures*, New York: Cambridge University Press, 1989.

White, Jonathan R. *Terrorism: An Introduction*, 3rd ed. Belmont, CA: Wadsworth, 2001.

Whittaker, David J. *The Terrorism Reader*, London and New York: Routledge, 2001.

Zinn, Howard. *Terrorism and War*, New York: Seven Stories, 2002.

Index

U